Peacebuilding and NGOs

Analysing the relationship between civil society and the state, this book lays bare the assumptions that inform peacebuilding practices, and demonstrates through empirical research how such practices have led to new dynamics of conflict.

The drive to establish a sustainable liberal peace largely escapes critical examination. When such attention is paid to peacebuilding practices, scholars tend to concentrate either on the military components of the mission or on the liberal economic reforms. This means that the roles of non-governmental organizations (NGOs) and the impact of attempting to nurture Northern forms of civil society are often overlooked. Focusing on the case of Cambodia, this book seeks to examine the assumptions underlying peacebuilding policies in order to highlight the reliance on a particular, linear reading of European/North American history. The author argues that in fostering a particular form of civil society, such policies have affected patterns of conflict, dictating when and where politics can occur and who is empowered to participate in such practices. Drawing on interviews with NGO representatives and government representatives, this volume will assert that while the expansion of civil society may resolve some sources of conflict, its introduction has also created new dynamics of contestation.

This book will be of much interest to students of peacebuilding, conflict resolution, development studies, Southeast Asian politics and international relations in general.

Ryerson Christie is a Lecturer at the University of Bristol, UK. He has a PhD in Politics from York University, Canada.

Routledge Studies in Peace and Conflict Resolution

Series Editors: Tom Woodhouse and Oliver Ramsbotham

University of Bradford

Peace and Security in the Postmodern World
The OSCE and conflict resolution
Dennis J. D. Sandole

Truth Recovery and Justice after Conflict
Managing violent pasts
Marie Breen Smyth

Peace in International Relations
Oliver P. Richmond

Social Capital and Peace-Building
Creating and resolving conflict with trust and social networks
Edited by Michaelene Cox

Business, Conflict Resolution and Peacebuilding
Contributions from the private sector to address violent conflict
Derek Sweetman

Creativity and Conflict Resolution
Alternative pathways to peace
Tatsushi Arai

Climate Change and Armed Conflict
Hot and cold wars
James R. Lee

Transforming Violent Conflict
Radical disagreement, dialogue and survival
Oliver Ramsbotham

Governing Ethnic Conflict
Consociation, identity and the price of peace
Andrew Finlay

Political Discourse and Conflict Resolution
Debating peace in Northern Ireland
Edited by Katy Hayward and Catherine O'Donnell

Economic Assistance and Conflict Transformation
Peacebuilding in Northern Ireland
Sean Byrne

Liberal Peacebuilding and Global Governance
Beyond the metropolis
David Roberts

A Post-Liberal Peace
Oliver P. Richmond

Peace Research
Theory and practice
Peter Wallensteen

Reconciliation after Terrorism
Strategy, possibility or absurdity?
Judith Renner and Alexander Spencer

Post-War Security Transitions
Participatory peacebuilding after asymmetric conflicts
Edited by Véronique Dudouet, Hans Giessman and Katrin Planta

Rethinking Peacebuilding
The quest for just peace in the Middle East and the Western Balkans
Edited by Karin Aggestam and Annika Björkdahl

Violent Conflict and Peacebuilding
The continuing crisis in Darfur
Johan Brosché and Daniel Rothbart

Peacebuilding and NGOs
State–civil society interactions
Ryerson Christie

Peace Negotiations and Time
Deadline diplomacy in territorial disputes
Marco Pinfari

Peacebuilding and NGOs

State–civil society interactions

Ryerson Christie

Routledge
Taylor & Francis Group
LONDON AND NEW YORK

First published 2013
by Routledge
2 Park Square, Milton Park, Abingdon, Oxon OX14 4RN

Simultaneously published in the USA and Canada
by Routledge
711 Third Avenue, New York, NY 10017

Routledge is an imprint of the Taylor & Francis Group, an informa business

British Library Cataloguing in Publication Data
A catalogue record for this book is available from the British Library

Library of Congress Cataloging-in-Publication Data
Christie, Ryerson.
Peacebuilding and NGOs: state–civil society interactions/Ryerson Christie.
p. cm. – (Routledge studies in peace and conflict resolution)
Includes bibliographical references and index.
1. Peace-building. 2. Non-governmental organizations. I. Title.
JZ5538.C54 2012
306.6'6–dc23 2012010477

ISBN: 978-0-415-69396-7 (hbk)
ISBN: 978-0-203-09653-6 (ebk)

Typeset in Baskerville
by Wearset Ltd, Boldon, Tyne and Wear

Contents

Tables

Acknowledgements

Any text of this nature is a collaboration, and grows out of years of engagement with friends and colleagues. The list of those I would like to thank is extensive. For their support and guidance I would like to first thank David Dewitt and Sandra Whitworth who have been both friends and mentors. For their introduction to Cambodia I must also thank Pierre Lizée and Caroline Hughes. This is a book about peacebuilding and civil society, but it is also centred on Cambodia. I am profoundly grateful for the reception and support I have received from critical, passionate, and driven academics and development workers in the country: unfortunately, as I have strived for anonymity, most of these people will have to receive my thanks in private. However, I must single out Sophea Seng, without whom this book would not have been half as successful. From the University of Bristol and York University (Toronto) many friends and colleagues have shown me how to persevere and who have been of utmost support: Colleen Bell; Lara Coleman; Mark Duffield; Adrian Flint; Torsten Michel; Christina Rowley and Jutta Weldes are just some of those to whom I am very grateful.

I must also thank my family for their unwavering support – Dad, I told you I would finish this. My final thanks are reserved for Sarah, who has been a constant support, who has read far too many drafts of this text (and who probably knows it better than I at this point), and whose love has sustained me.

Abbreviations

ADB	Asian Development Bank
ADHOC	Cambodian Human Rights and Development Association
AHRC	Asian Human Rights Commission
ASEAN	Association of Southeast Asian Nations
CCC	Cooperation Committee for Cambodia
CCHR	Cambodian Centre for Human Rights
CGDK	Coalition Government of Democratic Kampuchea
CDC	Council for the Development of Cambodia
CDRI	Cambodian Development Research Institute
CICP	Cambodian Institute for Cooperation and Peace
CIDA	Canadian International Development Agency
CMAC	Cambodian Mine Action Committee
CPP	Cambodian People's Party
CREP	Construction et Réhabilitation des Écoles Primaires
CSO	Civil Society Organization
CSS	Critical security studies
DAC	Disability Action Committee
DK	Democratic Kampuchea
DPT	Democratic peace theory
FACT	Fisheries Action Coalition Team
FBIS	Foreign Broadcast Information Service
FUNCINPEC	*Front Uni National pour un Cambodge Indépendent, Neutre, Pacifique et Coopératif*
GDCC	Government–Donor Coordination Committee
GDP	Gross domestic product
HDI	Human Development Index
HR NGO	Human rights NGO
HRW	Human Rights Watch
IBRD	International Bank for Reconstruction and Development (aka World Bank)
ICC	International Cooperation Cambodia
ICORC	International Committee for the Reconstruction of Cambodia

ICRC	International Committee of the Red Cross
IMF	International Monetary Fund
INGO	International NGO
IO	International Organization
IR	International relations
JCCP	Japan Center for Conflict Prevention
JFPR	Japan Fund for Poverty Reduction
JIM	Jakarta Informal Meeting
KKK	Khmer Kampuchea Krom
KPNLF	Khmer People's Liberation Front
KPRP	Khmer People's Revolutionary Party
KR	Khmer Rouge
LAC	Legal Aid of Cambodia
LICADHO	Cambodian League for the Promotion and Defense of Human Rights
LNGO	Local NGO
MoEYS	Ministry of Education, Youth and Sports
MOU	Memorandum of understanding
NEC	National Election Commission
NEP	NGO Education Partnership
NGO	Non-governmental organization
ODA	Official Development Assistance
PADEC	Participatory Development Training Center
PDK	Party of Democratic Kampuchea
PPA	Paris Peace Agreements
PRK	People's Republic of Kampuchea
RGC	Royal Government of Cambodia
RUPP	Royal University of Phnom Penh
SIDA	Swedish International Development Agency
SNC	Supreme National Council
SOC	State of Cambodia
SRP	Sam Rainsy Party
UN	United Nations
UNAMIC	United Nations Advance Mission in Cambodia
UNDP	United Nations Development Programme
UNESCO	United Nations Educational, Scientific and Cultural Organization
UNHCR	United Nations High Commissioner for Refugees
UNHRC	United Nations Human Rights Council
UNIFEM	United Nations Development Fund for Women
UNRISD	United Nations Research Institute for Social Development
UNTAC	United Nations Transitional Authority in Cambodia
WB	World Bank
WPM	Women Peace Makers
WTO	World Trade Organization

1 Introduction

Over five days in May 1993, Cambodians lined up at polling booths across the country to cast ballots in an election led by the United Nations (UN) that was designed to put Cambodia on the path to democratization and development, and to begin resolving the sources of conflict within the country. The vote itself is understood to have been a remarkable achievement: there was surprisingly little violence, the Khmer Rouge (KR) did not block participation, 20 parties ran for election, and nearly 90 per cent of the eligible voters cast ballots.[1] This marked the *formal* end of one of the first UN peacebuilding missions: a concept that had entered into popular discourse during the previous year through Boutros-Ghali's *An Agenda for Peace* (1992). However, this was only a momentary return to the 'normal democratic politics' sought by the international community. A struggle for power erupted between the two main political parties immediately after the election, the Cambodian People's Party (CPP), and *Front Uni National pour un Cambodge Indépendent, Neutre, Pacifique et Coopératif* (FUNCINPEC), ending in a power-sharing agreement that largely ignored the election results. This apparent shortcoming of the peacebuilding process resulted in a sustained debate about whether the mission itself was a failure. At the same time, other aspects of the peacebuilding initiative have been lauded, in particular the state's market reforms, the repatriation of refugees, and the dramatic expansion of civil society. This discussion about the relative successes or failures of the mission obscures a broader debate about peacebuilding, and ignores the more profound issues of how peacebuilding has come to dominate the way the North interacts with the South; how it favours particular forms of political organization over others; and how it determines what counts as security for peoples and communities. Crucially, peacebuilding assumes that the introduction of liberalism is the most effective means of addressing the sources of conflict within a given society. This entails plural democratic governance, liberal market reforms, and the formation of a vibrant and independent civil society.

The drive to establish a sustainable liberal peace largely escapes critical examination. When such attention is paid to peacebuilding practices, scholars tend to concentrate either on the military components of the mission or on the liberal economic reforms. This masks the ways in which peacebuilding is a long-term endeavour, diminishes the roles of those organizations and institutions that take over the leadership of peacebuilding after the cessation of the main UN mission and ignores the shift in policy focus of the post-conflict phase of peacebuilding. In particular this has overlooked the roles of non-governmental organizations (NGOs), and the impact of attempting to nurture Northern forms of civil society.

This book opens peacebuilding, including its aims and means of implementation, to critical debate. It seeks to lay bare the assumptions informing peacebuilding policies, and to highlight the reliance on a particular linear reading of European/North American history. This book then argues that peacebuilding policies, in fostering a particular form of civil society, have affected patterns of conflict, dictating when and where politics can occur, and who is empowered to participate in such practices. These dynamics will be explored through an analysis of the relationship between civil society and the Cambodian state. It will then seek, through a process of immanent critique, to determine whether the promotion of civil society has led to a more stable and peaceful state (a central claim of peacebuilding). In identifying when and why the state intervenes in NGO activity, the validity of liberalism's assumptions can be assessed. Building on interviews with both NGO and government representatives, it will assert that while the expansion of civil society may be resolving some sources of conflict, its introduction has created new dynamics of contestation.

The practice of peacebuilding is represented in scholarly and policy literatures as a significant break from the pattern of international intervention that dominated the Cold War. This has involved a partial shift in how conflict in the South is seen as affecting regional and international security, but more importantly it entails a move to address the sources of conflict, rather than just the manifestations of violence. This has been accompanied by an increase in the types of actors involved, with International Organizations (IOs) and NGOs taking on leadership responsibilities in reconstruction efforts. Overarching these changes is a liberal political–economic ethos that shapes both why and how interventions take place.

Though peacebuilding is recognized to be a long-term endeavour, the analysis of peacebuilding has tended to look at the periods of direct UN involvement (defined by the presence of military forces). This is the case with the analysis of peacebuilding in Cambodia, where both critical and more traditional perspectives have focused on the period where the UN ran a formal peace operation and the proximate period after the end of the mission.[2] This has left the post-mission peacebuilding poorly understood, and has obscured how international engagement in the subsequent years are a continuation of the security policies of the North.[3]

The term 'post-mission peacebuilding' is being used here instead of the term 'post-conflict' for two reasons. First, it illustrates the way in which peacebuilding initiatives continue after the cessation of the formal international intervention and how they are entwined with development programmes. Secondly, it reflects a recognition that conflict cannot end; peacebuilding seeks to minimize the sources of conflict and through the introduction of liberal forms of governance to remove violence as a means of resolving disputes. The post-mission phase is dominated not by foreign military force, or an army of UN workers, but by a much broader grouping of international liberal governance actors that constitute the development sector, including: IOs, international donors, state development agencies, and, crucially international international and local NGOs (INGOs and LNGOs). The impact of these agents of peacebuilding exceeds their functional roles in the delivery of various projects and technical expertise. Rather, their very presence promotes particular forms of politics, and the reliance on such groups reflects a commitment to liberal associational civil society. The imposition of civil society reconstruction, informed by liberalism, is assumed to help transform the nature of conflict by removing practices of violence, limiting the abusive powers of the state, and by teaching democratic forms of behaviour. However, when civil society reconstruction is imposed on states in the South, the extent to which this meets the stated goals of peacebuilding are unclear. Studying the first decade of the post-mission phase of peacebuilding permits the analysis of this deepening and widening of liberal governance.

While there are numerous debates taking place within the literatures on peacebuilding, there are nevertheless broad areas of agreement, not the least of which is the validity and moral imperative of peacebuilding itself.[4] There is now a general consensus about how the causes of conflict are best addressed, the core means of which is the establishment of democratic governance and liberal economics. Peacebuilding, then, does not end with a democratic election, though this is often presented as the culmination of the 'formal' process. It also involves the extension of other liberal institutions to the target state.[5] Besides changing the political system, it also works to further entrench market reform to reshape the legal system and, crucially, to reconstruct civil society as a means of achieving a liberal peace (Richmond 2009). It is the last area that is easily measured by the international community, which equates NGOs to civil society, yet which has escaped any substantial critical attention.[6] This is in spite of the influence that such groups wield, the resources they command, and their dramatic growth in size, number and roles in societies in the South.

The term 'NGO' conjures images of young women and men working amongst the poor and downtrodden to selflessly help improve the quality of life of those in the South. It is a difficult thing to consider how such forms of activity might be problematic. Indeed, the impulse to help is not one to be discouraged, but the sector itself – how it has manifested, how it is tied to particular forms of liberal governance, and as will be shown, of depoliticizing life – must be carefully explored. It is imperative that a greater understanding be reached about how these practices of international intervention have become possible, and how they legitimate civil society reconstruction under the rubric of security and development. As will be argued, the expansion of the number of NGOs and their roles in peacebuilding is inseparable from the broader pattern of an expanding liberal norm of governance. Indeed, the centrality of civil society to conflict resolution is laid out in *An Agenda for Peace* (Boutros-Ghali 1992), which explicitly champions the construction of civil society as a keystone of building peace. This is based on scholarly liberal literature which views civil society as a core component of functioning Northern democracies, and as a missing piece in the liberal government puzzle of the South.

In application, this promotion of civil society has been translated into working with INGOs in the reconstruction of societies, and the funding and creation of LNGOs in states such as Cambodia. Richmond (2005b) argues that the reliance on NGOs as a central means of building a bottom-up peace, which he calls the civic peace (2009: 560), is now a core component of the peacebuilding consensus. This has been taken to the point where civil society in the South becomes equated to the NGO sector. As Fisher argues, 'the strength of civil society is roughly related to the sheer number of functioning intermediary organizations between the citizen and the state' (1998: 13). The logic behind this new form of international intervention, which is rooted in liberalism and democratic peace theory, has gone largely unchallenged. This relative lack of critical examination of NGO work results in part from the choice of scholars to focus more on the roles of the more powerful state actors, but also because NGOs (and thus civil society) are assumed to be more ethical in their behaviour (discussed in detail in Chapter 3). Yet the impact of fostering a dramatic growth in LNGOs on communities' wellbeing, empowerment, and quality of life, is unclear.

The need for a critical examination of peacebuilding

This study is not seeking to improve the practices of peacebuilding; rather, the intent is to understand how peacebuilding has served to dictate the nature and limits of politics that can take place within the targeted society, and how it serves to define the very meanings of society, security and politics. This is being undertaken with the intent of illustrating where the inconsistencies of peacebuilding practices are, and thus where there are points at which local communities can assert themselves to shape their own lives. It is motivated by a desire to empower communities to decide for themselves what form politics should take, and to point out the ways in which peacebuilding has served to enable greater local power, or to limit the debates that can take place, to foreclose various options of development and to constrain the operation of politics.

What is meant by 'the political' deviates from the way the concept is used in the liberal sense, where it refers to the jurisdiction of the state (I am drawing on Arendt 1970, 1973; Žižek 1997, 1999; Laclau 1990, 2006; Rancière 2007). In liberal pluralism, which underpins peacebuilding, politics is understood as the contestation between groups to affect decisions by the state (Dahl 1961; Truman 1962; Polsby 1963; Wenman 2003). In such a sense, which is predominately how it is used in policy and academic literature, political issues are those that pertain to the responsibility of the state. There is an expectation that these issues will be struggled over, and that there can be public discussion over these matters. That said, as Truman notes, the ways in which politics is pursued are constrained by norms deeply embedded within various political cultures: 'political competition is understood to take place within certain "rules of the game"' (1962). These are also treated as given, and therefore beyond the scope of political adjudication' (Wenman 2003: 58). Such a proscribed notion of what constitutes the political, of what forms of activity are legitimate for political actors, must be seen as disempowering. It dictates what is open to contestation and which matters are closed off. Simultaneously, the argument that there is a specific space within which politics can be contested, and who is able to participate in such debates, must also be seen as inherently conservative. The sovereign state, which peacebuilding supports, is the container of political action, and dictates the terms of political life (de Larrinaga and Sjolander 1998; Walker 1990).

There is a distinction between the concept of politics from the broader notion of 'the political', where, following de Larrinaga and Sjolander, 'the political is found in the delimitation of an arena that is, in a prior distinction between what is "reasonable" (the legitimate subject of politics) and what is not' (1998: 369). Laclau argues that 'the moment of antagonism where the undecidable nature of the alternatives and their resolution through power relations becomes fully visible constitutes the field of the "political"' (Laclau 1990: 35). Issues are not inherently political, but are made so through practice. The political then stands in opposition to discourses of technicality and security that foreclose debate, privilege particular voices and mask the exercise of power. It is precisely because it unsettles the received knowledge that politics is necessary. It is only in its absence that the possibility for local voices to be heard on how their societies should be shaped disappears. As we will see, peacebuilding – nominally undertaken to empower local communities and provide for their security and development – has approached political reform in a specific liberal way.

In spite of a dearth of analysis of the theory of peacebuilding, there are nonetheless a multitude of articles, studies and books by academics and policy makers on the history of peacebuilding and how it has altered the behaviour of states and the international community.[7] These studies generally assess the impact of various operations on the state, and measure their effectiveness against the markers of democratic governance, declining rates of political violence, and economic growth. As Paris argues, the academic and policy literatures have tended to treat peace operations as 'technical (or non-ideological) exercises in conflict management' (2002: 638). Instead of asking how peacebuilding has been made possible, and what it dictates as reasonable, the vast majority of writing on the subject has sought to determine how such practices can be made more effective.[8] When there is a discussion of theory amongst the proponents of peacebuilding, it predominately centres on how liberalism and civil society are crucial components to the resolution of the causes of conflict. This general lack of theorizing is not politically neutral, and instead serves to reinforce its legitimacy by assuming its very validity. Reconstruction, particularly the post-mission phase, is treated as a technical matter where the goals largely escape serious theoretical reflection. Following from the work of Doty (1996: 127), these connections between reconstruction, liberal democracy and economics, and civil society can then be seen as operating as nodal points in the discourses of peacebuilding, serving to fix the meanings of politics and economics.

As a consequence, positivist approaches are constrained in their ability to understand the issues at stake. The traditional orientations to social science that have been deployed for problem solving (Cox 1986) treat the world as a social reality that the researcher or policy maker is able to make sense of and, through an appropriate application of policy, therefore change in limited ways. More importantly, the mainstream approaches also dictate how the world *should* look: a mirror of Northern liberal states.[9] In searching for causal relations between various phenomena, the social categories and the variables are taken for granted and in turn provide meaning through the very process of problem solving. By making assumptions about the validity of peacebuilding, the crucial discussion about the effects of peacebuilding is subsumed in debates about technique.[10] As Whitworth (2004) points out, this results in claims by the advocates of peacebuilding, such as the UN, that failures are due to insufficient funding or international support for various operations, rather than due to any limitations of the peacebuilding process itself. As a result, peacebuilding as a policy is generally taken for granted in both the academic and policy communities, and assumed to be both feasible and desirable, even if specifics of method and timing are debated. The very possibility that this might not be so is not given any serious consideration. We are not able to ask how peacebuilding may have negatively affected people's lives, how it may make some social groups less safe, or how it may contribute to politics of nationalism.

While traditional social science provides tools with which we can come to terms with specific social relations and problems, it is unable to allow us to see the range of issues at stake. It determines the problems to be addressed, and their means of resolution. In terms of peacebuilding, the central concern is how to build a sustainable liberal democracy. This has the effect of limiting both how the North understands the problems of the

South, but also the sorts of solutions to enduring problems that the South can enact. The range of possible solutions is then curtailed, limited primarily to extrapolations from previous historic examples (as interpreted by the North).

Thus, the peacebuilding project is a universalizing force, presenting a common sense approach to addressing conflict and violence in the South. It operates as a meta-narrative, telling academics and policy makers what to examine, how to approach the subject, all the while serving to cast these inherent political questions as technical issues that foreclose debate. The dominance of the peacebuilding narrative, and its very real material effects on the South, demand a critical examination of its historical roots, of its mobilization into policy, and of its repercussions for peoples in the South. The universalizing impulse of liberalism, while nominally supporting difference, subordinates it to the state and the rational economic individual, and depoliticizes it. Liberalism is incapable of asking these critical questions, as it is constitutive of them in the first place. Therefore, it is essential that an understanding of peacebuilding's intellectual roots be established, uncovering the assumptions upon which it is based. Doing so demonstrates the complexity of peacebuilding, and reveals how its practices must simplify, obscure and mask other representations of politics, identity and security. In short, peacebuilding must be understood as a political, not a technical, process.

This analysis is framed within a critical security studies (CSS) perspective to understand how peacebuilding has come to be a dominant narrative of both analysis and action, and how it is in turn linked to particular forms of global power and societal relations. It then asks at the outset, 'what are the politics of peacebuilding knowledge production'? By demanding a contextual and historical reading of peacebuilding, its connection to, and role in replicating, the liberal global order becomes visible. In short, following in the footsteps of Cox, the politics of the ideas of peacebuilding and civil society can then be laid bare.

To undertake this analysis, this book makes use of the practice of immanent critique to assess the impact of peacebuilding from within its own framework and to explore the extent to which peacebuilding is able to do what it claims to do (this is discussed in detail in Chapter 2). As Browne argues, 'immanent critique is based on an account of the volitional aspects of change and generative processes, typically either of the actions of subjects or the contradictory dynamics of systems' (2008: 17). It is thus premised on the belief that any attempt to universalize is incapable of containing the breadth of diversity of social life. This should result in contradictions in the theories informing practices, and manifest in events that cannot be understood from within the given theoretical framework. By engaging in such an analysis, the contradictions that emerge from within such an approach can be exposed. This in turn points to spaces for resistance, and a reintroduction of politics into the engagement of local communities with the processes of international liberal governance. A critical study of peacebuilding in Cambodia, although historically and culturally specific, will reveal problems inherent with current practices that may work to undermine goals of emancipation for those affected by violence. The policies that were put into action in Cambodia have come to form the basis for the comprehensive peace missions over the last 20 years.

While the subsequent discussions will focus in on Cambodia, the broader dynamics of peacebuilding have remained remarkably stable (with the obvious addition of modern Counter-Insurgency (COIN) operations). As will be shown, focusing on civil society reconstruction is at the heart of modern peacebuilding, which was largely pioneered in Cambodia. This calls for an in-depth analysis of the impact of the UN missions in the country, with a particular attention to the lasting impact of civil society reconstruction. Because Cambodia has served as a proof of concept for modern peacebuilding, the legacy of a focus on liberal civil society reconstruction is essential.

The focus on civil society re/construction

To undertake this critique, this book focuses on the relatively unchallenged assumption that lasting peace and sustainable development are best achieved by strengthening and building civil society associations. The importance of civil society reconstruction to current peacebuilding practices, to construct the civil peace – a peace based on liberal norms and social justice (Richmond 2008: 37) – has been noted by a range of critical scholars including: David Chandler 1999; Duffield 2005, 2009; Heathershaw 2008; and Richmond 2005b, 2008, 2009. A reliance on NGOs for developing states and injecting democratic ideals is, for various historical reasons (discussed in Chapter 4), particularly evident in Cambodia. Curiously, the policy focus on NGOs' role in peacebuilding and development has not been accompanied by a concurrent body of literature that examines their impacts on patterns of conflict in post-conflict states. In particular, there is a remarkable absence of analyses of the effects of the international community's backing of NGOs on the security dynamic within states. As such, it needs to be asked to what extent the promotion of NGOs has led to a more peaceful interaction between governments and communities. How has the reliance on NGOs in peacebuilding arisen and what forms of government and politics does it promote? Has peacebuilding, as it has been pursued in Cambodia, resulted in a less violent form of politics, or has it reduced some forms of violent politics and led to the increased securitization of other issues?

Peacebuilding dictates how development should take place, and the precise spaces within which local communities can participate. In contrast to such practices, which serve as a technique of governance that universalizes from the European experience and bypasses political debate, this text is committed to creating a space for contestations over the nature of development in the South. In short, it is driven by a desire to reinvest the interrelated development and security practices with politics, to reopen the concepts and their goals and methods to public debate. This will be done by illustrating how peacebuilding and civil society reconstruction rests on an ahistoric reading of Northern development, and how its practice relies on the normalization of liberal global governance. On the other hand, in revealing how civil society and the state have come into conflict in Cambodia, it will illustrate how what is assumed to be 'ahistoric' and 'natural' requires profound changes to the societal and political fabric of communities. Exposing these contradictions through immanent critique will illustrate the points at which resistance is possible, and where local voices can engage in conversations about what forms of society they wish to pursue.

This study pushes the frame of CSS, which has focused predominately on traditional state security practices. Peacebuilding should certainly be seen as falling within this rubric. That said, the motivation for peacebuilding is different from much of the traditional security practices of states (though ultimately connected to the broader state-centric international system). It is much more closely aligned with liberalism, and nominally seeks to intervene at sub-state levels, and does so in part due to the normative imperative of improving people's lives in the South; it then requires an expansion of the subject of analysis. Therefore, CSS must abandon its narrow focus on security institutions (the military, policing agencies, the judiciary), to explore the roles of non-military, non-state actors.

Peacebuilding now occupies a privileged position in international relations; it has become accepted not as *one* possible form of international activity, but instead has become paradigmatic. Acquiring a greater appreciation for the complexities and effects of peacebuilding is of the utmost importance, not just for our knowledge of peacebuilding's impact on local peace and security, but because its practice continues to determine when, where and how the North intervenes in the South. From Afghanistan, Haiti and Iraq, through a myriad of other post-conflict peacebuilding environments, the dominant narratives of how we rebuild societies are directly affecting lives. A greater understanding of the politics of peacebuilding will shed light on the nature of global governance, and crucially on the contradictions in liberal peace and how, in advocating an ahistorical reading of civil society and democracy, peacebuilding introduces new dynamics of conflict in the South.

Chapter outline

The next chapter provides the conceptual framework for this study, and commences with an explanation of immanent critique. It examines the literatures on peacebuilding and lays out the assumptions that are made in both the theorization and application of peacebuilding. The way peacebuilding is described and defined in the scholarly and policy literatures is established, and in turn linked to the emergence of a consensus around the desired shape of global politics and economics, followed by the ways that the narratives of peacebuilding operate as 'common sense'. Developing this *genealogy* reveals how its historical trajectory has provided meaning and value to civil society, and how peacebuilding operates today. This has important implications for the target society as it serves to replicate particular forms of politics. As was stated at the outset, the critique of peacebuilding that will be developed focuses on the role of NGOs in peacebuilding, and how their growth has affected the goals of both establishing non-violent forms of conflict resolution in the state, and addressing the causes of conflict. By focusing on the assumptions informing the practice of peacebuilding, we provide a deeper understanding of why NGOs and civil society have become central to bringing peace and development to post-conflict states. Peacebuilding practices rest on a particular reading of European and North American political developments, and treats that context as being consistent across different cultural and historical experiences. Civil society is thus produced as a universal category. According to liberal literatures, civil society simultaneously empowers local communities, and reduces conflict between communities and the state. At the same time, civil society is perceived as acting as a check on the power of the state, and thus being in tension with the government. This represents a paradox at the heart of peacebuilding literature and policy. It is this contradiction embedded in peacebuilding that the method of immanent critique is able both to identify and to understand.

Chapter 3 provides a brief review of the literatures that have been nominally critical of NGOs. The literatures are mapped out, and the main positions are described. As will be shown, these literatures are predominately (if not exclusively) 'friendly' to the NGO sector. The vast majority of the work, while sophisticated and empirically rich, is nevertheless motivated by a desire to improve the quality of work of NGOs, and to ensure that the broad goals of liberal peacebuilding and/or development are achieved. The main exception to this arises from scholars who see NGOs as contributing to neoliberalization.

After developing the genealogies of peacebuilding and civil society, and showing how the pursuit of civil society has concentrated on the promotion of NGOs, Chapter 4 provides the historical context for the peacebuilding mission in Cambodia. The chapter moves from a brief overview of Cambodia's ancient history, which provides a backdrop for subsequent discussions about the struggles over identity formation, and then moves to Cambodia's twentieth-century history. This provides depth to the discussion of the complexity of security and politics in the country. This context is essential to avoid replicating universalized renderings of civil society–state interactions.

Following the historical overview, the study turns to four different issue areas around which the government of Cambodia intervened in the work of NGOs over the decade following the end of the formal UN peacebuilding mission. In each instance the particular dynamics at play around the issue are discussed and the forms of government–NGO interaction are assessed. To understand how the various actors relate to one another, we concentrate on the discourse of the NGO sector. The reasoning for this decision is that the peacebuilding literature asserts that civil society (NGOs) is a positive phenomenon for peace and democratic behaviour, and thus puts the focus on such groups as agents for change. At the same time, surprisingly little is said in work on post-conflict resolution about the relationship between local civil society and the state. For this reason, an examination of the forms of interaction between NGOs and the state is imperative. Rather than centring the analysis on the policies and projects of the NGOs, an exploration of how they perceive the relationship between the civil society sector and the state points to the reasoning for policy decisions. As a result, we will focus on the associations' narratives of the state and its intervention in civil society on the one hand, and on the state's actions and public narratives about NGOs on the other. In each of the case studies these observations and arguments are used to frame a discussion about a pattern of conflict between civil society organizations (CSOs) and the state. Each pattern will then be related to the liberal theories of peacebuilding and civil society to determine whether the conflict can be understood from within a liberal framework, or if it represents a more fundamental contradiction within the theories and practices of peacebuilding.

Pattern 1: conflict around personal politics

The first pattern of interference revolves around the struggle by powerful individuals within the state to secure and expand their particular power bases. As capitalist development has taken hold in Cambodia, some individuals have sought to gain control over sources of income in order to fund and expand their power networks. This has, in some instances, pitted the needs of local communities against those of elites, raising the potential of intimidation and violence of locals. When NGOs have come to intervene in these conflicts they have had to face many of the same forms of intimidation. As powerful individuals have perceived some NGOs as working to undermine their sources of influence, they have on occasion used the state to defend their own interests. This has been manifested through police and military intimidation, and the threat of legal proceedings.

This pattern could be anticipated through a liberal approach to peacebuilding. By focusing on the struggle between individuals' interests in a self-maximizing world, the drive by some people to exploit the system could be expected, as could the subsequent clash between them and particular communities. The obvious solution would then be greater democratization to ensure that individuals' desires could be tempered by broader societal claims and that individuals' ability to access state power could be mitigated. Within this image of politics, civil society plays a central role in adjudicating these claims, and of teaching people how to resolve such disputes in a non-violent fashion. Unfortunately, even a cursory examination of NGOs in Cambodia shows that they seldom emerge from the communities they are seeking to assist, and are seldom internally democratic in nature. Furthermore, it was related during interviews that many NGOs are reluctant to become involved in disputes between individuals and communities for fear of undermining their ability to work on whatever issue they happen to specialize. When groups have chosen to become involved in such activities they are not perceived by the state as an arbitrator, but rather as having chosen a side.

What this does illustrate is that there is an inevitable struggle that takes place when restructuring a society, and that changing the mode of power is exceedingly complicated. Civil society is operating within this milieu and must recognize that it has an active role in this process. By undercutting traditional sources of power, and seeking to empower local communities, NGOs are creating *new* dynamics of conflict. However, these processes do not represent a fundamental contradiction of liberal peacebuilding, but can rather be understood as a part of the process of altering the dynamics of power in the state away from personal power politics towards liberal democracy.

Pattern 2: conflict between NGOs and the bureaucracy

The second pattern of conflict revolves around competing attempts by both the state (including its government and bureaucracy) and the NGO sector to dictate development priorities. This is an unequal relationship where the NGOs, with their financial resources and technical expertise, are often able to determine types, methods and locations of service delivery. During periods of reconstruction, when the state is intent on embracing the development project, IOs, international donors and NGOs are able to operate with significant freedom because of their financial and technical capacity combined with a development environment that prioritizes NGO activity.

This liberty of action, without government oversight, has resulted (at least in some instances) in competition between NGOs to deliver comparable programmes, in the failure to put in place sustainable programmes, and in NGOs paying greater attention to donor interests than local needs. As the state has slowly regained the capacity to provide policy oversight, including the ability and desire to set state priorities, it has begun to confront the NGOs working in the country. The state has sought to bring civil society under control, to dictate development priorities and delivery models and to determine where services are to be provided (all things that are taken for granted in the North). Yet, NGOs often resist such moves, seeking to avoid what they perceive as government control.

If the confrontation in this sector were only around issues of efficiency then one would expect these to be resolved with some ease. After all, the terms of the debate would be largely agreed upon. Underpinning this dynamic of conflict, however, is the struggle to understand the role of the state, where the state is seen as being a necessary force, while still one to be controlled and limited. Within the civil society literature, NGOs are supposed to be more effective in recognizing and representing the needs of local communities. This alone would likely lead to confrontation with the state over policy, yet there is another crucial aspect that traditional peacebuilding literature obscures. Peacebuilding, with its reliance on civil society, establishes and reinforces a narrative that sees the development state as inept in contrast to the efficient and moral NGOs. This makes it exceedingly difficult to foster cooperation between civil society and the state. However, this pattern of conflict will also be shown to be comprehensible from within a liberal framework, which prescribes a minimal state that needs to be monitored by civil society associations.

Pattern 3: conflict around identity

The next form of conflict that has emerged relates to issues of national identity. There is a broad belief (articulated by the New Wars literatures) that identity politics are an increasingly central component of conflicts in the developing world that need to be addressed as a part of any coherent peacebuilding programme. However, the liberal-centric nature of peacebuilding is constructed on assumptions about what should be the dominant expression of identity, and how the state and civil society should deal with it. Within liberal pluralist democracy any expression of identity that is used to make claims on the state other than that of a rational and rule-abiding citizen is seen as inherently problematic. In this respect peacebuilding assumes that religious, ethnic and other forms of collective identity should be subsumed by the needs of individualism. Individuals in turn are then expected to identify with the state collective identity, epitomized in their shared citizenship. While there is a broad recognition that other collective identities exist, and continue to have a hold on communities, liberal pluralist democracy is assumed to hold the means of effectively resolving such conflicts that may arise as a result of communitarianism.

The irony is that the emergence of democratic governance may encourage the mobilization of society along identity lines. Civil society cannot be extracted from this context, embedded as it is within the notion of the modern state, yet most NGO workers do not perceive their work as resulting in politics of identity. In short, the liberal peace presupposes, and seeks to develop, a form of identity politics in its own right. What will be demonstrated is that NGOs are implicated in identity politics in a number of ways. To begin with, their decisions whether to work with particular communities serve either to legitimize, or to invalidate, claims of citizenship and belonging. In seeking to avoid confrontation with the state and ignoring various ethnic and religious minorities, NGOs are ceding the debate about who is 'inside' and 'outside' of the state. NGOs also affect identity politics by advocating and representing particular forms of societal interaction. As with the discussion of the politics of the political, the dynamics of the conflicts over identity cannot be fully contained within a liberal framework. Rather, liberal peacebuilding is partially constitutive of this dynamic of conflict.

Pattern 4: conflict around the meaning of politics

The final form of NGO–state conflict centres on issues of human rights (HR), freedom of the press and legal reform. The competition around these matters is frequently raised in both the academic and policy literature, and is marked as an example of how many post-conflict states have a great deal of distance to travel before they meet Northern standards of HR and good governance. The track record in Cambodia on these issues is one marred by confrontation between NGOs and the state, often by the threat or use of violence. Human rights organizations have been denigrated by the state, and on occasion their workers and offices have faced violent attack. The freedom of the press has been undermined over the past half-decade and legal reforms have been resisted. These measures are most often represented as attempts by the state to limit critique, undermine support for the opposition, and to sustain their hold on power.

The policy orientation of the writing on peacebuilding, combined with its liberal orientation and embeddedness in traditional social science, means that it treats issues of politics as settled. It assumes what the appropriate forms of governance and interpersonal and inter-communal relations should be; the validity of liberal democratic forms of governance is taken for granted. This extends to assumptions about the nature of civil society, and what the division of responsibilities should be between civil society and the state. Disputes between civil society and the state, in part, arise precisely because of the imposition of Northern norms and expectations about the working of politics, and the division of roles between the two sectors. This comes down to a struggle around defining what is and is not *political*, and thus what is in the purview of NGOs and what is not. The public explanation for the government's intervention in NGO work does not contradict liberalism or its understanding of civil society, but rather is embedded within it. Liberalism sets up this confrontation by stating that civil society is apolitical, but then predetermining what is and is not a political issue. This becomes particularly evident when we turn our attention to the role of advocacy. Both the state and NGOs see such activity as problematic, and share the same explanations for why this is the case. Peacebuilding creates a new avenue of dispute, and one for which there is no cultural precedent to rely on for its resolution. This points to an inherent contradiction within the peacebuilding literature that is revealed through immanent critique.

Following the four empirical chapters, this book returns to a discussion of the meanings of civil society and peacebuilding. If the claims of peacebuilding are accurate, then we should expect its application to result in increased cooperation between civil society and the state, decreased tension and, crucially, a change in the nature of the polity so that the growth of civil society harkens a concomitant growth of democratic governance and a reduction of violent conflict. Using the conclusions from each of the forms of government intervention, a broader critique of the theory and practice of peacebuilding is put forward. It will be argued that peacebuilding has been constructed as an ahistorical phenomenon, attempting to replicate a particular form of society that is inherently unreproducible in any facile way. Instead, in seeking to build a Northern form of civil society, new forms of tensions have emerged within Cambodia, and some conflicts between local communities and the state have been intensified.

This book further develops our critical understanding of peacebuilding, and advances the ways in which CSS can be applied. In adopting CSS as a framework for analysis, the study is pushing the approach beyond its narrow focus on state security actors and international organizations, and the narratives and practices that have reproduced their particular visions of international relations and security. The particular critical analysis used here is centred on the associated roles of CSOs to demonstrate how both the state and civil society are implicated in the practice of security, and how their roles affect the safety and dignity of peoples in ways that are unanticipated by the dominant liberal framework. Such issues are more generally treated as domestic concerns, and thus understood as the purview of comparative politics. However, they are at the very heart of modern security practices, and as such, need to be studied in detail as a part of any critique.

2 Critical analysis of peacebuilding

International peacebuilding initiatives directly affect the lives of peoples across the globe in countries such as Mozambique, El Salvador, Somalia, Cambodia, Bosnia, East Timor, Iraq and Afghanistan.[1] In Cambodia the intervention of the international community after the Paris Peace Agreements (PPA) resulted in what was, in 1991, an unprecedented drive to reconfigure the state along a democratic and liberal economic model. Yet for all of the research that has focused on the peacebuilding mission in Cambodia (Boua 1993; UNRISD 1993; Chetty 1993; Akashi 1994; Doyle and Suntharalinam 1994; Farris 1994; Jennar 1994; Um 1994; Brown and Timberman 1998; Chong 2002; Collacott 1994; Lizée 2000; Roberts 2001; and Hughes and Öjendal 2006), there have been relatively few attempts to assess peacebuilding generally from a critical perspective (Richmond 2005a, 2005b; 2008, 2009; Heathershaw 2008; Pouligny 2005; Duffield 2002; Fetherston 2000; Chandler 1999; Campbell 1998a). Any critical analysis of peacebuilding needs to commence with an appreciation of the assumptions built into the concept; in so doing its theoretical roots can be identified, and it can be tied in to broader patterns of liberal global governance. As such, it will be grounded within a particular understanding of history and social relations that is culturally specific, at the same time as they are represented as being grounded in a universalized conception of the nature of the liberal man (Richmond 2005b). This in turn provides the basis for identifying the contradictions inherent in theories of peacebuilding, and the ways in which peacebuilding works to reinforce and produce particular visions of the world.

The case for critical security studies (CSS)

The rise of CSS since the early 1990s has offered radically different understandings of the nature of security discourse and practice. In contrast to theories that start from the position that there is a world we can know and explain, critical theories focus on the production of this knowledge, and its political implications (Cox 1986; Doty 1993; Krause 1998). Crucially, this knowledge is not neutral; it serves the interests of power and re/produces particular social dynamics. Theories are then inherently normative in character, as the very act of theorizing cannot be independent of society. As Zalewski and Enloe argue, 'theory does *not* take place after the fact. Theories, instead, play a large part in constructing and defining what the facts are' (1995: 299). CSS is then committed to exploring the political implications of knowledge production, and to uncovering the ways in which common sense approaches to security are in fact productive and supportive of particular forms of politics. By working at the level of discourse, and its material effects, and taking seriously the argument that social reality is contingent, malleable, and inherently rife with contradictions, we are in a superior position to understand the dynamics at play in a particular social context. If we ignore this and treat the social categories as given, and take the world out there as a 'reality', we will be unable to identify the possibilities for change, or barriers to social transformation. In short, the best that could be hoped for is an improvement of the given system, rather than substantive change.

CSS tends to concentrate on the linkages between security and identity (Ashley 1986; Campbell 1998b; Doty 1996; McSweeney 1998; Razack 2004), demonstrating how security practices are socially productive. Security narratives not only dictate what constitutes security, but also crucially reproduce who is to be secured and from whom, and who can make a claim for security. Obviously peacebuilding is not the only security narrative that is directly engaged in the process of normalizing and legitimizing a state-based international structure. However, as will be shown in greater detail, peacebuilding is an international response to internal civil strife (defined in large part by a lack of government legitimacy). Peacebuilding, in attempting to alter the political dynamics of the target country through complex combinations of top-down and bottom-up measures, seeks to redefine what it is to be a citizen, and how people should relate to one another and the state. In particular these practices are intended both to resolve the sources of conflicts and to alter how conflicts are mediated. The expectation is that the imposition of a liberal peace (Richmond 2009) will achieve these ends. This becomes particularly evident when we examine the civil society literature underpinning the practice of peacebuilding. The associational literature on civil society rests on the notion that the ideal society is constituted by rational individuals who are capable of cooperating for mutual benefit. The 'liberal man' is at the heart of this model, which is a form of identity. In short, the peacebuilding process, as a security narrative, is implicated in identity politics.

The next point on which critical theory deviates from positivism in the social sciences is on the search for immutable and ahistorical truths. Critical approaches share a belief in historical and thus cultural contingency. Clearly political science has long been concerned with history; however, as Campbell argues, positivism pays insufficient attention to the subject. In treating history as a predictable and/or structuring phenomenon, the depth of context and specificity is lost. As Campbell says:

> Focusing on historical constitution suggests the conflict was constituted *in history*, which implies that the hostility has an identifiable point of origin and is transmitted from generation to generation until it reaches the present. History is thus naturalized, and historicity extinguished.
>
> (Campbell 1998a: 84)

Rather than seeing particular events as the natural culmination of historical events, critical theory sees the unfolding of history as being both contingent on choices, and affected by broader patterns of social practices; history understood in this way is thus immanent with the possibility of change. This requires that one pay attention to the way that specific histories are picked up and propagated as relevant. How, for example, has peacebuilding become so widely accepted in the international community as a means of establishing peace and order? How is it connected with the particular world order? How has the historical context in a given case affected and been affected by international peacebuilding?

Peacebuilding is embedded within a broader narrative of world order that seeks to produce the world in a way that is consistent with the North's imagination. This means that a critical discussion of peacebuilding's effects on NGO–state interaction must take into account historical and cultural contexts, in this case looking at the Cambodian experience both in terms of its local context and with respect to the broader patterns of peacebuilding and international liberal governance. If peacebuilding is constituted in history, we need to also pay attention to the ways in which it is constitutive of politics in the South.

The final point on which CSS is differentiated from positivist international relations and security is that it refuses to pretend to take a neutral stance on issues of politics. CSS foregrounds this, and, while there are a range of political positions that can be located within this broad approach, strives to *change* the political domain. The approach used here is embedded within a politics of emancipation that is committed to empowering local voices in the developing world.[2] This critical perspective enables a comprehensive critique of peacebuilding, and focuses attention on the ways that the literature and practice of peacebuilding make particular forms of politics seem commonplace. By challenging these assumptions the possibilities for change are reopened. This is being done by attacking the received wisdom of peacebuilding and identifying the points of contradiction in peacebuilding practice. In opening these spaces for debate, opportunities for local agency can be increased. Rather than seeking to impose solutions and particular forms of governance upon 'them', the intent here is to open up space within narratives of security for the practice of politics where a broad range of people in a given society are able to have a voice in defining their own priorities.[3]

There have been a number of critical examinations of peace-support and peacebuilding operations that have had a direct impact on this study.[4] In one of the earliest critical assessments of international intervention, Campbell's (1998a) *National Deconstruction* focused on the way that identity and territory were linked in the international engagement in Bosnia. Fetherston, applying a Foulcauldian analysis of peace operations, argues that most work on the topic 'lacks ... a self-reflexivity which casts a critical gaze on the assumptions which – mostly – confine both the theory and practice of conflict resolution to the problematic discourse of modernity' (2000: 195). Stamnes (2004), has examined the metatheoretical assumptions that inform our analysis of UN peace operations.[5] Orford (1999), in turn has explored how the narratives, 'intervention stories', rely on particular renderings of the 'other', and on racialized and masculinized heroic narratives, which act together to demand particular forms of intervention. Duffield's work (2005) has sought to highlight the ways in which peace operations have moved from short-term to indefinite and open-ended missions to achieve a limited form of security. He argues that this has occurred at the expense of peoples in the South, where their freedom from the immediate fear of death is seen as sufficient justification for intervention by the North. Finally, there are a number of scholars who have sought to explore both the viability and impact of the pursuit for the liberal peace (Richmond 2008, 2009; Heathershaw 2008; Pouligny 2005). The work of Richmond and Heathershaw has been influential to this study through their drawing of connections between current conceptions of peacebuilding and older narratives of what constitutes peace.

While all of these studies have critically engaged peacebuilding theories and practice, their foci have been on what has enabled the North's interventions in the South. This study, while building on their work, proceeds along a different tack and engages in an immanent critique of peacebuilding.

An immanent critique of peacebuilding

Immanent critique is engaged with the identification, and, politically, the exploitation of contradictions inherent in the social world and theories that attempt to explain them.[6] As Neufeld (2007) asserts, these are 'relational' rather than 'logical' contradictions. He goes on to lay out the premise of immanent critique:

> It begins by drawing out the core assumptions and thought-processes of a particular theoretical approach. It then shows how these assumptions and thought-processes are simultaneously necessary for and undermining of the objectives sought, and how the ensuing crisis can be overcome only by embracing different assumptions and thought-processes.
>
> (Neufeld 2007: 450)

Wyn Jones echoes this (1995: 312), arguing that to perform immanent critique is to relate the practice's justifications with its actual outcomes. At the same time there is substantial debate about whether immanent critique must be associated with a dialectic theory of history. Certainly it emerged from Marxism but, as it is used in this research, it is possible to separate the method (and its underlying logic) from a teleological reading of history.[7] It does, however, demand that it be conducted from within a particular historical context, and that it recognize the contingent nature of the theory to be critiqued. As such, this book is interested in how, in applying metatheoretical assumptions to the discourse and practice of peacebuilding (as with any theory that rests on notions of universality), the inevitable contradictions arise, and how they can be identified. The practice of immanent critique then requires the examination of assumptions informing a given theory, with the intent of locating the nodes at which contradictions become apparent.

Immanent critique of peacebuilding entails analysis of the assumptions informing theories of these forms of intervention, and of the practices that emerge because of them. The range of theoretical underpinnings will then be explored, and the ways in which they are historically embedded will be illustrated. However, immanent critique goes further, asserting that these contradictions can result in observable effects. As Browne (2008) argues, this method links the normative and empirical modes of analysis, and does so by treating the concept/theory to be examined on its own terms.

The limited debate around the validity of peacebuilding, and its impact on the targeted societies, removes entire ranges of questions from consideration. With this in mind we need to break open the most fundamental assumptions. In doing so, it is asked whether peacebuilding has resulted in a more peaceful, stable and democratic society. By turning to a critical approach that is deliberately being used to unsettle assumptions surrounding peacebuilding, room for political discussions of the value of peacebuilding, and the impacts it has on states and societies, can be opened up. This chapter lays out both the dominant understandings of peacebuilding that are currently informing decision-making, and in turn illustrates how these theories are proscribed by a specific liberal logic. In so doing, the way peacebuilding is supposed to operate will be shown to be politically biased, and to contain inherent contradictions arising from a drive to universalize from American and European experiences with political development.

This requires, first of all, an examination of the peacebuilding literature to identify the underlying assumptions. This is done by tracing the emergence of the concept, re/constructing its history, and illustrating how it is linked to particular forms of power and governance. However, the practice of peacebuilding will also be explored, paying attention to the construction of civil society, which is seen as a necessary component of building peace. This chapter then turns to examining the evolution of writing on civil society to illustrate the contradictions inherent in liberal writing on associational behaviour. Five main points will then be made: that peacebuilding as it is currently understood assumes a particular reading of civil society that sees it as separate from politics; that this accommodation between the state and civil society about what constitutes their respective areas of responsibility emerged within the European context; that in operationalizing this notion of civil society, peacebuilding theory equates civil society with the NGO sector; and that NGOs working in the area of civil society are necessarily implicated in states' internal politics. This will shed light on a core contradiction in the practice of peacebuilding: that promoting civil society as a means of alleviating conflict is introducing new dynamics of contestation to society.

Narratives of civil society–state interaction

After identifying potential sources of contradictions in the practice of peacebuilding, in particular focusing on the potential conflicts between NGOs and the state, this study presents four patterns of conflicts that have emerged in peacebuilding. While the theoretical literature is the backdrop of these discussions, at centre stage are the practices, and narratives about, state intervention in NGOs. The methodology for this study was guided by the need to identify moments of state intervention in NGOs, and, crucially, how associations understand their relationship with the state and society. As such, a wide variety of sources have been used, including primary and secondary documents reporting on the relationships between NGOs and the state. News reporting, in particular the English language dailies (*Cambodia Daily* and the *Phnom Penh Post*), was invaluable as it provided regular reports of state interventions in NGO activities, as well as broader reporting on the government's views of the civil society sector. This has been supplemented by primary documents from a broad range of NGOs and IOs, such as the Cambodian Human Rights and Development Association (ADHOC), Human Rights Watch (HRW), Global Witness, NGO Forum, LICADHO, the International Monetary Fund (IMF), the World Bank (WB), and the Asian Development Bank (ADB). While these documentary sources have provided crucial evidence about state interventions in NGO work, this material has not been analysed in isolation, but rather has been used to supplement the primary sources of data for this study.

The stories about NGO–state interaction naturalize and regularize political decisions, and provide legitimacy for various actions. While these can be revealed in part by an examination of popular media and official documents, such forms of discourse are only partial and, as they operate in the public domain, are entwined with the politics of the aid and donor community. With the major exception of the HR sector, most of the NGOs (but certainly not all) produce rather straightforward policy documents that avoid any confrontation with the state, tending to highlight successes and opportunities, rather than stressing environmental and political constraints. With the decision made to focus on the NGOs' understandings of the relationship with the state, the question then was how to access the narratives in a way that would be consistent with the immanent critique.

I have opted to focus on how NGOs' representatives understand and portray the nature of their relationships with the state for two reasons.[8] First, civil society is assumed to be a powerful force for democratization and empowerment. NGOs are understood to be the sources of the liberal civic peace, therefore if their representatives believe that they are in conflict with the state that means there is potentially a failure of the theories of liberal peacebuilding to account for processes of change within the state, so focusing on its narratives is an effective way to proceed with the immanent critique. Second, for practical research reasons it is far easier to gain interviews with representatives of NGOs than the state.

The core of the empirical evidence comes from interpretive interviews with individuals representing NGOs and the Cambodian government. Throughout this primary and secondary research the emphasis has been on identifying the narratives provided by civil society actors (the NGO representatives) and the state about what constitutes state intervention in civil society, what they perceive as the nature of the relationship between the state and civil society, and what may lead to conflict between them. As such, the emphasis has been on uncovering patterns of state intervention in civil society, and tracing the narratives about these patterns (whether they are perceived by various actors or not).

Following Schwartz-Shea and Yanow, this research has relied on interpretive methods, which are responsive to the needs of critical scholarship (2002: 481).[9] These techniques focus on the exploration of the 'ideational' sphere, where what traditional methods treat as rational decisions are placed within historical, cultural and power contexts. However, as Bevir and Rhodes (2003) show, these contexts cannot be simply extrapolated from objective facts, such as whether the NGO is a local or an international group, or whether it works in one issue area or another. They state, instead, that 'practices can only be understood through the beliefs, and actions of individuals located in traditions and in response to dilemmas' (Bevir and Rhodes 2003: 198). The problem then becomes how to access these narratives. The intent of these interviews is to determine whether the narratives of the relationship are consistent with the broader liberal framework of peacebuilding, and if not, then where the discourses and practices deviate from what we would expect from the peacebuilding literatures. To achieve this it was essential to forego highly structured and scripted interviews. In contrast, Rubin and Rubin (1995) advocate an approach to interviews that they argue is not rooted in positivism, but rather starts from the premise that meanings are socially constructed (in contrast to other authors, such as Bevir and Rhodes (2006), and Hay (2002), who argue in favour of interpretivist methods that are nevertheless consistent with traditional social science). Crucially, the ways in which narratives are presented are not politically neutral, and the discourses are themselves contested in the public arena. As Finlayson argues, 'politics is the place or moment where traditions and narratives can no longer be taken for granted, where the 'web of belief' is ruptured because rival traditions and narratives have clashed' (2007: 549). This shapes the way that interviews are conducted, and how they are used. According to Rubin and Rubin:

> Underlying our approach to qualitative interviews are three guiding themes. First, successful qualitative interviewing requires an understanding of culture. Culture affects what is said and how the interview is heard and understood. Second, interviewers are not neutral actors, but participants in an interviewing relationship. Their emotions and cultural understandings have an impact on the interview. Third, the purpose of qualitative interviewing is to hear and understand what the interviewees think and to give them public voice.
>
> (Rubin and Rubin 1995: 19)

In keeping with this understanding of interpretive methods, this study's interviews were structured as a form of a conversation between the interviewer and interviewee, where a discussion could evolve naturally.[10] The over-riding advantage of this approach was that it allowed a far more in-depth exploration of issues than would have been possible in a scripted interview. The process was both flexible and continuous. This technique is also advantageous in the pursuit of the narratives of peacebuilding. Patterson and Monroe explain:

> Narrative methods ... differ from interview methods that seek short answers to relatively specific questions or that closely structure the answers given by the speaker. Some of this unexpected aspect of narrative is what makes it so exciting for the analyst.
>
> (Patterson and Monroe 1998: 326)

The usefulness of this technique was clear early on in the field research, when it became apparent that some topics could not be broached early on in a discussion, but could unfold naturally as a part of a conversation.

In general the people interviewed were quite willing to talk about the work of their organizations, and their sense of the general relationship between NGOs and the various levels of government. On numerous occasions, as the interviews unfolded, the interviewees would begin pushing the discussion along different avenues around the topic of state–NGO interaction. The discussions lasted on average just under one hour, with some being conducted in a compressed schedule where necessary, and others held over several days while travelling and conducting site visits with various groups. Particular attention was paid to how the NGO and state representatives described the interaction between the state and civil society.

In keeping with an interpretivist model, I did not set out with a preconceived definition of 'intervention', and was willing to allow the individuals being interviewed to define the concept, as well as to find examples where government intervention was positive for communities in Cambodia. This also meant that I was interested in the narratives that the various actors used to describe intervention, and the relationship between the state and civil society. Exploring this issue has provided insight into how the various participants perceived the nature of politics, and the limits of acceptable civil society activity within the state. It has also shed light on the mutability of these concepts.

The majority of interviews were conducted in either English or French. The humanitarian rescue industry overwhelmingly operates in these languages, driven by the large INGOs and large donors (both state and non-state). This puts extensive pressure on local organizations to have some English language skills to apply for funding, and to meet the regular reporting requirements that often accompany this money. However, I also relied on Sophea, my research assistant, to act as a translator on numerous occasions. The two of us talked at length about the project, which enabled her to maximize the value of those interviews that were translated between English and Khmer. She was also invaluable in deepening my appreciation, and understanding, of Khmer culture and Cambodian politics. This provided much more depth to the analysis that follows in the subsequent chapters.

Selection of NGOs for interviewing – and classifications

I endeavoured to interview representatives of as many CSOs as possible, usually in their own offices, but on occasion also in less formal environments (such as in coffee shops, restaurants and bars). In addition to the formal interviews, there were numerous informal talks with NGO representatives in a wide variety of social settings. However, these have been used strictly for context and have not been cited within this study. With over 1,500 organizations reportedly operating in Cambodia, it was not possible to interview representatives of them all.[11] As such, decisions had to be made about which NGOs would be approached. To prioritize NGOs for interviews, they were categorized according to: whether they were local or international associations; the issue areas that they addressed; where they ran projects in the state; and what sectors of society they targeted. Following this categorization interviews were pursued with as broad of a range of groups as possible, seeking a reasonable distribution between: groups focusing on rural and urban projects; international and local groups;

groups across the various work sectors; and associations that focused on different sectors of society. A breakdown of the number of groups interviewed by sector is included in Annex A.[12]

In summary, this study makes use of a variety of types of empirical information in order to conduct the immanent critique of peacebuilding. It relies on both a careful textual analysis of academic and policy writing on peacebuilding and civil society reconstruction, as well as on numerous interviews with representatives of NGOs and the state in Cambodia. The interviews, which followed an interpretive methodology, were designed to be open-ended, with the intent of gaining insight into the discourse and practice of state–civil society interaction in Cambodia. Following the interviews, common themes of interference have been identified and are discussed in depth in Chapters 5 to 8. In each instance a particular dynamic of state intervention in NGO work is discussed, and is related to the broader practices of peacebuilding. This then provides the empirical case studies for the final chapter, which discusses the implications of the state–civil society conflict, and what this in turn reveals about contradictions within peacebuilding.

Conceptualizations of peacebuilding

The usual history of peacebuilding tracks the evolution of the concept from traditional peacekeeping, through peacemaking or peace enforcement, to today's peacebuilding exercises.[13] This continuum of peace operations is defined specifically by the type of military action, which serves to stress the security component of peacebuilding, as well as to highlight its connection with policies of intervention in sovereignty. This form of intervention is described as arising after 1988, reflecting the emergence of a liberal consensus after the Cold War that has allowed states to agree upon a form of international action, and of a perceived change in the nature of warfare that made such interventions 'necessary'.[14] Peacebuilding is then written as a new form of intervention which, while retaining a core military component, has a much broader mandate than previous forms of peace operations. While it is a security practice, peacebuilding is clearly comprised of more than military action; UN documents provide a very broad definition of the concept that stresses economic and social development, although the necessity of military force is still present.[15] This linking between development and security practices (made explicit in the New Wars literature led by Kaldor (1999)) has been described by some as a remarkable change in the activities of states (Krause and Jütersonke 2005; Duffield 2005). However, as Krause and Jütersonke note, this division has long been more important in the organization of Western bureaucracies than it is 'in the field' of the developing world.

Any attempt to deal with the notion of peacebuilding is complicated by the breadth of available definitions, which vary according to the scope of activities included, and the centrality of military action. Despite this, there is a common normative goal, notwithstanding the range of prescribed means of achieving it. Cousens' description, for example, is quite broad:

> The defining priority of peacebuilding thus becomes *the construction or strengthening of authoritative and, eventually, legitimate mechanisms to resolve internal conflict without violence.* At its base and at best, peacebuilding should bolster the possibility of vibrant, responsive political life in societies where politics have been supplanted by military contest and violence.
>
> (Cousens 2001: 4)

There is a clear assumption here that a liberal democratic government is the model of legitimacy. Furthermore, the idea of political life refers to a particular axis of interaction between rational individuals and the state, rather than between civil society and the state. In contrast, the UN definition of peacebuilding is narrower:

> Comprehensive efforts to identify and support structures which will tend to consolidate peace and advance a sense of confidence and well-being among people. Through agreements ending civil strife, these may include disarming the previously warring parties and the restoration of order, the custody and possible destruction of weapons, repatriating refugees, advisory and training support for security personnel, monitoring elections, advancing efforts to protect human rights, reforming or strengthening governmental institutions and promoting formal and informal processes of political participation.
>
> (Boutros-Ghali 1992, para. 55)

While obscured, the formal and informal processes clearly refer to those found within liberal democracy.

Griffin takes a more holistic approach, and describes peacebuilding as having 'as its primary goal the healing of human relations within the target community' (1999: 9). As in the previous definitions, the assertion is that the 'normal' forms of interaction between individuals and the state have been broken. Thus, while there is debate over the scope of peacebuilding, there is a broad consensus that it involves more than the cessation of violence or the maintenance of the status quo. This serves to separate it from other interventionist security practices that are focused on the military components, specifically from war-fighting, peacemaking (the difference between peacemaking and war-fighting is sketchy at best), and peacekeeping. This does not mean that the use of force is absent in peacebuilding operations, but rather that the sum total of the exercise extends beyond such limited mandates.

David (1999) advances a comprehensive definition of peacebuilding that serves to distinguish it from other forms of international intervention. It has the advantage of providing a description of the concept that is broad enough to encompass the range of approaches to peacebuilding, yet specific enough to focus attention on those forms of international intervention that have emerged since the late 1980s. His definition defines three separate elements that together constitute peacebuilding (David 1999: 27):

1 The rehabilitation, reconstruction and reconciliation of societies that have suffered the ravages of armed conflict;
2 The creation of the security-related, political and/or socio-economic mechanisms needed to build trust between the parties and prevent the resumption of violence; and
3 An external (foreign) intervention (national, multilateral or UN) to help create conditions conducive to peace.

Peacebuilding, as opposed to peacekeeping and peacemaking, is seen as being engaged in directly resolving the underlying causes of conflict, and therefore engaged with the transformation of society as well as its economics and politics (David 1999; Goodhand and Hulme 1999; Ramsbotham 2000; and Cousens 2001).

As David's definition illustrates, peacebuilding is engaged in more than the stabilization of the state; it is broadly accepted that peacebuilding is aimed at *both* government and society. This reflects the general thrust of peacebuilding practices that are oriented towards the reconfiguration of politics (understood as the interaction between the community and the state, and the state's power), economics and societal relations. Finally, his definition illustrates how peacebuilding is seen as essential to the maintenance of international order, and to sustain the state system. Crucially, the ideal state has become one that is a liberal democracy and integrated into the global market place. In addition to attempting to address the sources of conflict, peacebuilding also strives to change the ways in which a society deals with internal conflict. Essentially this means replacing the use of overt forms of violence with more consociational systems of resolution. *Peacebuilding is then a coordinated effort by external actors to address the sources of conflict through economic, social and political transformation with the goal of introducing liberalism.*

While the above definition provides an effective summary of what is now commonly understood as peacebuilding, it also serves to highlight two other bodies of literature that underpin current thinking on the subject. In particular we find within peacebuilding links to literatures on conflict prevention (Annan 1999; Lund 2002; Carment and Schnabel 2003; and Ackermann 2003), conflict management (Butler 2009; Burton and Dukes 1990), conflict transformation, and conflict resolution (Ramsbotham *et al.* 2005). The fact that peacebuilding can be linked to these bodies of work is important, as they were not developed to deal with intra-state violence; rather their focus has been on how to ameliorate the risks, and in the case of conflict resolution to solve the root causes, of state-to-state conflict (Carment and Schnabel 2003: 11). Emerging during the Cold War, conflict management and conflict transformation pursued limited forms of peace defined in negative terms as the absence of violence. It is with the post-Cold War era of expanding interventionism and a broad consensus on the viability of conflict resolution that *solving* the causes of the interstate conflicts became more accepted. The language of conflict transformation and resolution has been transferred to the attempt to deal with civil conflicts. Whether this is possible in domestic politics is largely unexplored, yet there is an assumption that the causes of domestic conflicts can be resolved, as has been stated, through the imposition of liberalism as the principal means of ensuring peace and stability.

Imbedding peacebuilding in history

In approaching the issue of peacebuilding, one is struck by the manner in which it is so pervasive in the discourse of modern international politics and policy, gaining credence as a category of action that is disconnected, even within a positivist sense, from any coherent theorizing. We are told that the concept is a relatively new one, and that it has emerged as a policy or theory only within the last 15 years.[16] However, peacebuilding has not sprung into the public consciousness without reference to prior historical events. Rather, it is provided meaning and context through readings of Northern history. Describing it as emerging in the post-Cold War era obscures how it is rooted within older narratives of intervention. If peacebuilding is about foreign states imposing the dynamics of peace, then there is a long history of such action.

It is important to ground this particular reading of the history of peacebuilding in an environment defined by the emergence of the sovereign state in a modern sense.[17] The international community revolves around the state, and peacebuilding today is about the imposition of dynamics that will lead to the establishment of sustainable state structures. This, however, demands that we consider how peacebuilding today is not far removed from other projects of imposing social reforms on states and societies, the most obvious process of which was colonization. Colonialism, which came in a vast array of forms, nevertheless shared a common belief in the scientific, moral and political superiority of Europe over the political communities they encountered. There was also a belief that in imposing its will, the European states could reform these societies and to bring them closer to European norms of behaviour. In this way the people of the South could be delivered from forms of barbarism. This *mission civilisatrice* (described in Paris 2002) bears striking similarities to today's approaches to rescuing Southern countries from processes of structural/cultural violence (Paris 2002; Harvey 2003).

The language of reforming societies, of building peace, of establishing patterns of democratic behaviour, is replete with connotations that these societies are incapable of achieving such ends themselves, and that the North is in a position to impose the conditions that will lead to peace and stability. Local societies that are affected by violence are still not seen as being empowered to deal with the situation they find themselves in. It is worth noting that the perception of the conflict affecting these communities is disaggregated from broader patterns of global political economy and international relations (intervention is seen as the solution, *not* the problem). This has even been noted by some cautious advocates of peacebuilding, like David Chandler, who has argued that:

> Today there is little faith in people rebuilding a post-conflict society; emergencies are seen as being 'too complex' for (inevitably) non-Western people to handle. This sentiment lies behind the increasing calls for the international community to take a lead in developing long-term solutions, usually under the rubric of democratization or the construction of civil society.
>
> (David Chandler 1999: 110)

Rather than stressing the ways in which peacebuilding can be an internal process, and is likely most sustainable when it is, the focus of peacebuilding is on how the international community can dictate or build a framework for peace.

While peacebuilding literature is reticent to engage the clear echoes of its colonial past, it does make reference back to the post-Second World War reconstruction of Germany and Japan. The Marshall Plan is held up as an example of how states that have moved through periods of violent behaviour can be structurally conditioned by external actors to reform that behaviour (Harvey 2003). The Marshall Plan had strong economic, structural, and institutional reformative elements that parallel modern peacebuilding.[18] The massive economic reconstruction provided high levels of employment and served to repair many of the ravages of the Second World War. Perhaps more importantly, the imposition of constitutional restrictions on both Germany and Japan are held up as cases where states were actively transformed by changing the terrain of politics within them.[19] Harvey, in critiquing US policies in Iraq, has shown how this logic has informed even the most recent attempts at building peace:

> The [US] neo-conservatives look to the reconstruction of Iraq along the lines pioneered in Japan and Germany after the Second World War.... The necessary social, institutional, and political infrastructures will be put in place under US administration, but gradually give way to a clientelist Iraqi political administration (preferably as weak as the Japanese liberal party).
>
> (Harvey 2003: 197)

This reading of history operates as evidence of the potential for peacebuilding, and of the viability of such practices. Even a brief consideration of these cases reveals the dramatically different conditions facing Germany and Japan and those confronting states that are now being targeted for peacebuilding. Japan and Germany were both industrial countries with broad-based economic sectors. Both states had decisively lost interstate conflicts in which they had clearly been the initiators, and the societies themselves were not internally divided in the way that confronts states that are now targeted for peacebuilding.[20] However, despite these obvious differences in historical context, peacebuilding is still provided legitimacy through such readings. This serves to validate the goals of the North's interventions, and to render the states in the South open to such practices.

While there is a general consensus of the validity of peacebuilding, there is considerable debate about what needs to be reformed and how peace can best be guaranteed. Ramsbotham (2000: 171), drawing on the work of Lederach, sees peacebuilding as an attempt to address the underlying structural, relational and cultural roots of conflict. In contrast to this broad definition, the United Nations has taken a more limited approach; Boutros-Ghali focused on restoring order, and reforming and strengthening government institutions in *An Agenda for Peace* (1992: para. 52), although, importantly, the fostering of a strong civil society is seen as going hand-in-hand with such initiatives. However, many policy makers and academics have asserted that such an approach is far too constrained. Fetherston (2000: 201), for example, has taken issue with Boutros-Ghali, arguing that while such policies may be necessary, they must also be part of a broader transformative project. To address the underlying cause of violent conflict, broader socio-political change is needed and institutional change is neither sufficient, nor able to lead to societal transformation quickly enough. Fetherston's critique, while important, misses the mark in one crucial respect. While the international community has come to focus extensively on institutional reconstruction and has been fixated on the process of elections, their policies are informed largely by a belief in the transformative power of democracy and its accompanying civil society. Even while the theory of transformation is not explicit, we can see a common thread in the literature produced by the UN that civil society, if strengthened and supported, is capable of bringing about an alteration in patterns of violent politics. The range of approaches to peacebuilding shares this goal, though they are often not clear on the logic of how this is possible. Peacebuilding policy and theory are then marching in step with liberal global governance, and are tools in its expansion through the South. As is shown in Chapter 4, this dynamic is evident in the UN's goals for Cambodia, as laid out in the PPA, and implemented through the United Nations Transitional Authority in Cambodia (UNTAC) and subsequent donor plans for the state's reconstruction.

There are numerous debates that take place amongst those studying peacebuilding. While it is impossible to list the full range of disputes, a few main themes need to be highlighted. The first is a division within the field concerning whether security and development problems can be handled separately.[21] Some authors are now distinguishing between peacebuilding, which seeks to rehabilitate the pre-existing state apparatus, and nation-building, which seeks to define, shape and facilitate 'the creation of new processes and organizations, rather than reforming existing structures' (Talentino 2002: 28). This is indicative of the way in which the state is taken as a core narrative of thinking in political science. This debate does not revolve around whether the state system is effective, but rather if the state *as it exists* is the best basis of a sustainable politics, or if new institutions and new political arrangements are needed. At the same time, Duffield has been arguing that there is no inherent tension here as peace and development are increasingly seen as interrelated, and that security and development are inextricably linked.

> Achieving security in the borderlands, and hence international stability, is now seen as lying in activities designed to reduce poverty, satisfy basic needs, strengthen economic self-sufficiency, create representative civil institutions, encourage thrift, promote human rights, gender awareness, and so on: the name of this new security framework is development.
>
> (Duffield 2005: 20)

Duffield's work has been crucial in highlighting the ways in which peacebuilding is tied into broader narratives of action that link security in the South with that of the North, and which then demands interventions to secure both the lives of people in the periphery and life in the developed North.

The second debate in the literature emerges when peacebuilding is considered to have more to do with the rehabilitation of societies than the reinforcement of existing state apparatuses. This then requires a consideration of where the international community should target its intervention, and what policies are best suited to building a lasting peace. While studies of peacebuilding tend to focus on one or the other (Call and Cook 2003b: 242), the practice in the field is generally to work at both ends.[22] 'Peacebuilding approaches now ... have the objective of rebuilding states via both top-down high level and bottom-up grass roots methods' (Richmond 2004b: 141). Obviously the division between these approaches is not hard and fast. Most theorists and policy makers advocate some form of a mix between the two, where the balance is dictated largely by their view of the interaction between civil society and the state. It is clear then that notions of peacebuilding presume that there is such a thing as 'civil society', and that it can be manipulated and altered to affect a more peaceful politics within a state.

This is not to claim that there is a complete absence of attacks on peacebuilding from within the mainstream of political science; realists, including Mandelbaum (1994) and Henry Kissinger, argue that it takes away from states' military capacities and ultimately empowers intervention and increased military conflict.[23] Theorists working from institutionalist or behaviouralist perspectives can also argue against its effectiveness, but usually do so from a proscribed position where the blame is placed on a society. In this way, rather than the validity of peacebuilding being denied, we are instead told that these states are not yet 'ready' for peace, and that they need more time to learn the necessary lessons. Another way that this is articulated is to say that the necessary preconditions do not exist. The assessment is then that the goals of peacebuilding are laudable and appropriate, but that its application has been problematic for some reason. As such, even within many of the critiques of peacebuilding operations, peacebuilding itself is not challenged.[24] In its worst manifestation this can take shape as a form of 'blame the victim', effectively obscuring the complexity of the dynamics at play in these states. In terms of providing a basis for a critique of peacebuilding, turning attention to the recipient state in isolation from the theory of peacebuilding is ultimately supportive of peacebuilding narratives.

Theoretical underpinnings of peacebuilding

What, then, are the theoretical roots of the writing on peacebuilding? These can be located through an examination of the ways in which the academic and policy literatures discuss methods of implementation. The internal logic of their arguments, and the ways in which they presuppose natural (and thus ahistorical and acultural) social dynamics, can then be uncovered. This reveals the theories of social relations embedded in peacebuilding theories and practices. It should not be surprising that a link can be drawn from peacebuilding to two related, yet distinct, bodies of literature. To begin with, peacebuilding is rooted within the democratic and liberal peace theory literature, which provides a justification and reasoning for the imposition of liberal democracy in the South. The second body of literature that it relies upon is the breadth of thinking about liberal civil society. This provides the framework for the means by which democracy can be applied to the state.

The literature on peacebuilding is based on the groundwork laid by democratic peace theorists, which is, in the words of Call and Cook (Call and Cook 2003b: 237), the central *liberal presumption* of peacebuilding. Following in the footsteps of Immanuel Kant and Woodrow Wilson, advocates of peacebuilding have argued that to ensure international peace we must encourage the spread of democracy.[25] Their thesis is that liberal democratic states are unlikely, if ever, to go to war with other democratic states (Russett 1993; Owen 1994). This logic runs through much of the peacebuilding literature, which consistently argues that democratic forms of governance are the most able to ensure the peace and stability of their states, both domestically and internationally. This connection between democratic peace theory (DPT) and peacebuilding is reflected in the work of Call and Barnett (1999: 44–45), who have argued that the main reason that nations are involved in peacebuilding today is that states see a connection between internal instability and regional instability. However, this does not work against the liberal goal of delivering democracy to the South; stabilizating the state system is now seen to depend on the liberalization of the periphery.

These positions see democratic governance leading to the adoption of a democratic culture, defined by a set of attitudes that restrict the potential for violent resolution of conflict, and that are therefore supportive of a culture of peace (Duffield 1997; Clapham 1998; Bellamy 2004; Pugh 2004). The most common articulation is that liberalism entails a sense of individual rights, which are then projected by the individual on the rest of society. Owen defines the benefit of liberal democracy as:

> a state that instantiates liberal ideas, one where liberalism is the dominant ideology and citizens have leverage over war decisions.... Liberals believe that individuals everywhere are fundamentally the same, and are best off pursuing self-preservation and material well-being. Freedom is required for these pursuits, and peace is required for freedom; coercion and violence are counter-productive. Thus all individuals share an interest in peace, and should want war only as an instrument to bring about peace.
>
> (Owen 1994: 89)

In keeping with this is the belief in non-violent methods of conflict resolution. Therefore, a person living in, and encultured, to a democratic system will see other members of society as deserving of, and invested with, equal rights. In addition, they will strive to resolve problems in a peaceful manner. This then ties into interstate peace through an institutional intermediary. The state, dependent on public support, will be unable to justify violence against states that also share the same norms and values. This position is perhaps best represented by Russett (1993), who has made a case that while democracies can be violent, they are generally not so towards other democracies.

The practices of peacebuilding are much more complex than this initial discussion of what constitutes peacebuilding implies. Policy makers and academics have advised and implemented a broad range of policies that have targeted virtually the entire set of actors within the recipient countries. This has led to attempts to clarify the types of peacebuilding practices. Here two particular frameworks stand out, those of Heathershaw (2008) and Richmond (2009), and while they offer slightly different formulations, they share in common an analysis of what level peacebuilding is aimed at, and the logic behind various strategies. Of particular interest here is their joint focus on peacebuilding's new emphasis (in contrast to the older practices of conflict management, transformation and resolution), on what Richmond refers to as the civic peace.

Underlying the notion of peacebuilding is a conception of 'peace' that is remarkably underexplored, a point that has been made by Richmond (2005b; 2009), and Boulding (2000). For example, Doyle and Sambanis' (2006) book on UN peace operations does not make a single mention of what constitutes peace, or what they mean by conflict. They merely state that peace is 'the outcome of a dynamic process, which is shaped partially by the peacekeepers' performance and their peacemaking and peacebuilding efforts and by the parties' relations to those efforts' (27). In contrast to Heathershaw (2008), who sees three forms of liberal peace, Richmond has argued that there are in effect four strands of thought about the liberal peace: the victor's peace; institutional peace; constitutional peace; and civil peace (Richmond 2009: 559).

Richmond gives a description of how peace is conceptualized in international relations, and he demonstrates that there is surprisingly little discussion around the topic, illustrating how there is just one 'ideal liberal form' (Richmond 2008: 8):

> Peace in this framework can be constructed by actors with the necessary knowledge and resources, probably resembling a Kantian 'Perpetual Peace'. This is commonly referred to as the liberal peace, embodied in the UN system and a post-Cold War 'international society'.
>
> (Richmond 2008: 14)

He argues that peacebuilding now represents the convergence of thinking about peace in peace studies, conflict resolution and conflict management approaches:

> These debates offered a sophisticated methodology through which peace could be rationally created through the scientific application of liberal knowledge systems. This widespread acceptance that the liberal peace could be created by the proper actions on the part of international agencies, actors and NGOs following the requisite procedures, required that liberal institutions should be created and that human needs should be provided for civil society actors. An important aspect of the liberal peace is the argument that conflict really be 'resolved' unless the concerns of civil society are met and, furthermore, that there cannot be a liberal peace unless there is a vibrant civil society.
>
> (Richmond 2008: 105)

At the same time, what it means for a state or society to be at peace is left largely unexamined. The main exception to this, and the body of literature that is broadly cited, is derived from the field of peace studies. As such, peace is seen in both its negative (freedom from the immediate threat of violence) and positive (freedom from structural violence) components (Ramsbotham *et al.* 2005; Galtung 1996; Lederach 1997, 2005; Boulding 2000). When we turn to the peacebuilding literature we find that its goals are broader than the limited scope of the negative peace (Call and Cook 2003b: 236). Instead there is the deliberate attempt to transform the local communities to permanently alter behaviour. Within liberal thought there is the presumption that peace can arise from the potential of rational cooperation. After all, 'individuals prefer peace, freedom, rights and prosperity' (Richmond 2008: 23). The transformative element is most closely associated with the civic peace, with NGOs as its vanguard (David Chandler 1999: 111; Mertus and Sajaad 2005; Heathershaw 2008; Richmond 2008).

At the same time, there is a more fundamental issue at stake here. Peacebuilding is meant to transform not just the propensity for violence, but also to resolve the sources of conflict (Patrick 2001: 53). However, the literatures are entirely unclear on what conflict is, and what its place is within society. In a way this is not surprising as it is a fundamental lacunae within literatures on democratic transition and the liberal peace. In short, to what extent is it a natural, and thus unavoidable, aspect of community life? At least in rhetorical terms peacebuilding practice, in particular its civic form, is seeking not only to move the contestation to the realm of politics, but also to *solve* many of the conflicts outright.

Embedded within the rubric of conflict prevention, Talentino (2003: 71) argues that peacebuilding is not only about prevention, but also has a 'resolutive dimension'. This is a point further made by Heathershaw (2008) and Bertram (1995):

> The defining priority of peacebuilding thus becomes the construction or strengthening of authoritative and, eventually, legitimate mechanisms to resolve internal conflict without violence. At its base and at best, peacebuilding should bolster the possibility of vibrant, responsive political life in societies where politics have been supplanted by military contest and violence.
>
> (Cousens 2001: 4)

The connection between democratic peace and peacebuilding through democratization is clearly presented in Boutros-Ghali's *An Agenda for Peace*:

> The social stability needed for productive growth is nurtured by conditions in which people can readily express their will. For this, strong *domestic institutions of participation are essential*.... Democracy at all levels

> is essential to attain peace for a new era of prosperity and justice.... This work provided important legitimacy to this position on democratic peace.
>
> (emphasis added, 1992: para. 82)

This belief in the stability of democratic governments, arising in large part through the ability of individuals through civil society to assert their interests, informs the analysis of current conflict management and international relations (IR) policy makers. To create a peaceful system of states, we are told that we must encourage the development of democracies. And as Boutros-Ghali argues, this requires an active civil society. Democratic participation in associations, clubs and various groups is seen as a necessary precondition to achieving sustainable peace. Mertus and Sajjad argue that 'in the heady democratisation climate, civil society tends to be invoked triumphantly, as a panacea to all that ails a state' (2005: 119). As is illustrated in Chapter 4, this thinking informed the PPA and the implementation of the UN Advance Mission in Cambodia (UNAMIC) and the UN Transitional Authority in Cambodia (UNTAC).

In addition to the liberal democratic logic of peacebuilding, there is also a strong tie with liberal economics where the pursuit of particular market forms are seen as crucial for the development of society. Economic progress (measured by the penetration of the market) is seen as a core component of addressing underlying causes of conflict.[26] Knight, examining the link between peacebuilding and development, argues:

> Those who hold this position focus primarily on social and economic development. ... Thus, it is not surprising that researchers at the World Bank (IBRD) and the International Monetary Fund (IMF) adopt this approach to peacebuilding.
>
> (Knight 2003: 248)

At the level of interstate conflict, the argument for complex interdependence, while compatible with democratic peace theory, has a distinct rationale for the emergence of peace. Whereas some assert that democratic society will lead to more peaceful state behaviour, both internally and externally, the economic argument follows a different logic. Instead of placing confidence in learned associational behaviour this perspective sees liberal economics as resulting in complex institutional ties at all levels of state and society, but sees them as dominated and defined by the business sector. States then become sufficiently entwined to make interstate conflict unlikely at best. The argument is then more structural in nature; rather than seeing democratic behaviour within the state spilling over into international relations, the structuralists see the economy as demanding peaceful interstate behaviour in order to perpetuate the economic system.[27] This logic is also present within the peacebuilding literature, where the adoption of liberal economics is advocated as the means by which to secure a lasting peace within the conflict states. Advanced by the Washington Consensus, and continued in the post-Consensus era, liberal economic reforms have become a cornerstone of peacebuilding.[28]

This is not to say that all the arguments presented for economic development within peacebuilding are structural in nature, as seen in assertions that the alleviation of poverty is crucial to the elimination of sources of conflict (within either a 'greed' or a 'grievance' perspective). As a result, economic transformation is expected to lead to a more stable and more peaceful society, a process that is broadly supported by the breadth of the development spectrum. What differs is the means of development, the form that such economic growth should take, and the degree to which faith is placed in a free-market liberal economic order in state-led industrialization, or in micro-economic projects oriented towards community growth. The obvious limitation of such arguments is that they fail to account for matters of economic distribution, or provide any explanation about how the capitalization of markets can result in a more equitable distribution of wealth when the system starts from one of inequality. What is clear, though, regardless of the position that is adopted, is that economic reform is a part of the peacebuilding practice.

The next set of assumptions in peacebuilding are embedded in the literatures that value European forms of social community, and believe that such patterns of associational behaviour can be imposed or promoted globally. While the state is retained as the main political agent, its role is greatly diminished, and in its stead societal groups, and the private sector, are seen as being the most effective in delivering a wide range of services. In seeking to regulate society it is not the state that is relied upon; such a role for government is seen as problematic with current liberal thought that pursues a minimal state. Instead, the promotion of democratic civic culture is seen as being a function of civil society, a common theme running throughout the application of peacebuilding (Goodhand and Hulme 1999; Griffin 1999; Ross and Rothman 1999; Cousens 2001). At its base, the argument is, as Orjuela asserts, that civil society can 'provide popular support for peace and ... promote dialogue and reconciliation between polarized groups' (2003: 196). Civil society is thus at the very heart of the theories and practices of peacebuilding, and the manner in which peacebuilding is put into action in the field further reinforces the centrality of associational behaviour.

The narratives of civil society have come to define how the international community thinks about social reconstruction. While the international community continues to focus on redeveloping infrastructure within war-torn societies, and to redevelop political institutions, there is also a drive throughout to support the growth of civil society. Civil society is described as a positive democratic force capable of sustaining peaceful politics, and of forming the basis of a successful policy to alter the framework of politics within states. Its expansion within conflict states is anticipated to result in a move away from violence as a means of conflict resolution and towards consociational behaviour. Clearly, as it is at the core of discourses of peacebuilding, we must explore the ways in which civil society is conceptualized and used. This in turn demands an examination of how the narratives of civil society reproduce particular forms of politics, and are linked to particular dynamics of power.

The liberal theories of civil society

While there is an incredibly broad body of academic writing on civil society, with intense debates over its providence, its relationship to the state and its emancipatory potential, this has not limited its use within academic and policy circles. Its importance is espoused in virtually the entire range of literature dealing with peacebuilding and economic development, and its value as a central concept remains unchallenged in the policy community. There is a remarkable consensus about the necessity of promoting a space for independent associational behaviour, whether it emerges from the WB's promotion of social capital, or the liberal or the critical left's advocacy for civil society growth. This brief overview of the various ways the concept is treated contextualizes current approaches to peacebuilding to illustrate how it is confronted by inherent contradictions arising from the universalization of Northern societal developments.

Civil society means many things to many people, and as such is an essentially contested term, consistently open to re/interpretation. There is a surprising range of meanings of civil society, which complicates any attempt to establish one clear link between peacebuilding and civil society literature. As an example, Van Rooy has focused on how the concept has been deployed in the academic and policy communities. In constructing a typology she argues that there are five ways in which civil society is generally conceptualized (Van Rooy 1998):

1 as *value*: where the stress is on *civil* society as *good* society;
2 as a *collective noun*: where NGOs constitute civil society;
3 as a *space*: where the world is divided into organization types;
4 as an *anti-hegemony*: this is the antithesis of Western Liberalism; and
5 as the *anti-state*: civil society is a control on the state.

While her breakdown is interesting in terms of identifying different discourses around civil society, it fails to provide any way to understand when and why they are used in conjunction with one another. Her notion of civil society as a space, for example, is not linked with any particular notion of the state, nor is the idea of civil society as anti-hegemony connected in any meaningful way to civil society as anti-state.

Cohen and Arato's (1995) comprehensive review of the concept traces the term's current usages to the evolution of state sovereignty.[29] It is only through the articulation of a distinct realm of responsibility and privileges for the state and of a separation of political and non-political action that the notion of civil society (distinct from the home and the state) begins to make sense. Cohen and Arato argue that the establishment of the state as a geographically confined political structure, with the right to rule within its borders, results in a division within the state of what activities are permissible. This goes beyond a discussion of sovereignty, which provides the exclusive right to exercise force to the state, and categorizes all forms of social activities into 'political' and 'non-political'. Civil society is ascribed the legitimacy to act only in the latter, but also to critique the power of the state when it begins to pass outside of 'political' issues.

As with much of current thinking in political science, the terminology and accepted meanings of civil society derive from the Enlightenment. In contrast to Rousseau, who saw no clear separation between state and society, or in other words who saw both civil and political society as the state, Montesqieu, Locke and Voltaire set the two in opposition (Seligman 1992: 15–17; and Cohen and Arato 1995: 89). This reifies a division between civic issues and politics, where the latter is the jurisdiction of the state. Political forces are then contested between individuals and the state. However, it is also from their work that we derive the current belief, prevalent in both the academic literature and in the field of policy work, of an evolving contest between civil society and the state. This is at the core of an inherent contradiction in peacebuilding theory. On the one hand, there is a perceived separation between the roles and jurisdiction of the state and civil society. On the other, there is a promotion of civil society as a check on the power of the state. The state is viewed with suspicion and its powers are seen as a potential threat (though necessary as the sovereign use of force) to democratic society (Palmer 2002). In contrast, because civil society is supposed to be constituted from, and to be representative of, society it is seen as being more democratic than the state, and inherently more responsive to people's needs. This is a position largely advocated by the LNGOs and INGOs in Cambodia. There is a constant theme within the various groups' literature that they are best able to represent Cambodians because of their proximity to the people. They argue that by being in daily contact with the people on the ground they are able to articulate their needs better than either the government or larger international organizations such as the WB.[30]

In contrast to Hobbes, Cohen and Arato follow Montesquieu and Locke in arguing that peace arises from civil society rather than from the state. '[B]oth the rhetoric of antiabsolutism (Montesqieu) and opposition to privilege (Voltaire) were united in a single conception of a (civil) society opposed to a state whose components were formally equal, autonomous individuals as the sole repositories of rights' (Cohen and Arato 1995: 89).

As there are two structures, both of which claim to represent the people, there is inevitable struggle between civil society groups and the state over which is best placed to interpret the will of society, and to enact policies that meet its needs. The belief in a tension between state and society is at the heart of current discourses and practices of peacebuilding that seek to limit the roles of the state while simultaneously pursuing an expansion of civil society.

While the writing of Montesqieu, Locke and Voltaire focused on the question of society–state relations with an eye to politics, there was an emerging alternative that had economics as its central concern. The Scottish Enlightenment introduced another aspect to the discourse of civil society. Adam Ferguson, David Hume and Adam Smith came to equate civil society with the organization of economies. This serves to separate politics and economics, and to remove the state as the legitimate forum of economic control. This further disaggregates the contestation over the life world in distinct economic, political, and domestic issues, which also dictates who is allowed to speak on such issues. Carothers traces the modern notion of civil society through both the Scottish and Continental Enlightenment in the eighteenth century:

> [T]heorists, from Thomas Paine to Georg Hegel, developed the notion of civil society as a domain parallel to but separate from the state – a realm where citizens associate according to their own interests and wishes. This new thinking reflected changing economic realities: the rise of private property, market competition, and the bourgeoisie.
>
> (Carothers 1999–2000: 18)

Civil society is thus perceived as being governed by economic logic where rational individuals are able to come together and interact free of interference from the state. While there are crucial differences between Montesqieu and Voltaire, and the Scottish Enlightenment thinkers, they do share common ground. Most importantly they retain the notion that there is an inherent conflict between the state and civil society, that there is a shared normative preference of society over the state, and that there is a need to limit the powers of the state. The sense of a struggle between civil society and the state is grounded in the emergence of both democratic government and capitalism.

Clearly the Enlightenment thinkers were responding to particular historical dynamics when developing their theories of civil society. However, rather than stressing its cultural and historic specificity, there is a drive to trace civil society back through history in order to show its enduring relevance. For example, Van Rooy (1998) in contrast to Carothers, and Cohen and Arato, attempts to link the concept to Roman thinking. This detaches civil society from modern conceptions of the state, and in the process writes civil society as an enduring characteristic of human society. It also serves to make civil society a cross-cultural and universal category. It legitimates the notion that there is an ahistoric separation between the state and civil society, and thus of a division between the political and apolitical.

Modern political thought has seen the emergence of numerous approaches to civil society that need to be explored in greater depth. These current theories of civil society are representative of the way in which the concept has been used in various quarters of the peacebuilding and development communities. Associationalism and social capital are, today, the dominant theoretical articulations of civil society.[31] While they all have distinct understandings of the concept, it will be demonstrated that they share core assumptions. This study concentrates on the first two theorizations (associationalism and social capital) as they dominate both the theoretical and policy literatures on peacebuilding.

The Associational School

Currently, the dominant theory of civil society is what Hyden (1997) has called the Associational School, which focuses on the value of autonomous associations and their assumed capacity to both achieve greater democratic participation and to check the power of government. He stresses the importance of civil society to democracy:

> [a]lthough the argument of this associational approach to civil society accepts that the development of civil society is not sufficient for the consolidation of democracy, its advocates have a generally high expectation of the role that civil society can play in achieving democracy.
>
> (Hyden 1997: 8)

Stepan (1966) and Diamond, two of the leading advocates of this approach, follow in Alexis de Tocqueville's steps in elevating civil society to a normative position superior to the state. In the words of Diamond (1994), civil society is 'the realm of organized social life that is voluntary, self-regulating, (largely) self-supporting, autonomous from the state, and bound by a legal order or a set of shared rules' (Diamond 1994: 5). At the same time that associations fight for their members, deliver services to sections of society, or provide a place for people to meet and interact, they have a broader impact, which is understood as more important than their institutions' narrow foci. Crucially, associations foster public interaction and therefore encourage consociational behaviour. They teach people how to interact peacefully, and how to resolve disputes in non-violent ways. As a consequence, for countries experiencing civil conflict, fostering civil society is seen as essential to the survival of under-developed democracies (Siaroff 1999: 405). However, while civil society is seen as being beneficial for instilling forms of culture that are amenable to democracy, the associational literature also sees it as being in opposition to the state.

The normative valuation of civil society occurs at the expense of the state, which, in keeping with the classical liberal and current neoliberal literature, is viewed as the potential source of repression and violence. Rodan (2001) has argued that the positive connotations ascribed to civil society arise from a belief in liberalism, in particular liberalism as developed by Diamond, who sees the state as coercive and civil society as a remedy to this, and in turn idealizes civil society. The result of this interpretation is, Rodan asserts, a zero-sum game between civil society and the state; any empowering of the state is necessarily perceived as a disempowerment of civil society. It stands then that the reverse must also be true; the state must see the transfer of responsibilities to civil society as an erosion of its own power. For nascent democracies this logic has the potential of setting up a dynamic of conflict.

The question then is why there is little intense conflict between civil society groups and the state in Northern democracies? Certainly tensions can be identified, manifested in enduring disputes about the influence of special interest groups on government, and the responsiveness of the government to such groups' demands. However, such disputes stand out as exceptional moments that serve to demonstrate how little conflict there actually is between these respective sites of social engagement. The contradiction is obscured in the North because of an accommodation that has been reached between civil society and the state about their respective areas of responsibility. This results in a division of issues as either inherently political or social. Clearly this is not a hard division, and is undergoing a constant reappraisal. But in the North this accommodation has developed slowly, and changes to it occur gradually in a way that generally avoids major disruptions with past experience. This stands in contrast to the way in which liberal associational forms of civil society have been rapidly exported to the South.

The associational approach has also attempted to account for cultural and historic variations of civil society. Of particular relevance here is the writing about civil society in Asia, which attempts to locate forms of associational behaviour (Acharya *et al.* 2001; Hedman 2001; Alagappa 2004; O. Roy 2005; Pradhan and Roy 2006). Pye (1999) has tried to show that the concept is not alien to those communities. While he is clear that associational behaviour is often not robust, he is a strong advocate for its role in Asia. In keeping with the associational literature, civil society is thus understood to be separate from the state, as being apolitical, and yet as acting as a check on the state's power. This sense of the technical and moral superiority of civil society over the state is intensified in reference to the development state, which is viewed as more repressive than Northern bureaucratic governments. Pye states that: '[t]he creation of a civil society is critical for the effective performance of democracy' (1999: 764). He proceeds to argue that democracy in Southeast Asia is more likely to be secure in those states where civil society is strongest, pointing to Thailand and the Philippines as having the most vibrant associations (782). Once it becomes ahistorical in this way, it can be imagined as pre-existing in some nascent way in all societies.

We can see a strong connection between peacebuilding literature and the associational approach to civil society. Both have a clear preference for democratic forms of governance, both have a confidence in the ability to develop a democratic political culture through institutional reform, and both advocate the encouragement of the growth of civil associations. This associational approach to civil society closely matches the manner in which civil society is used within the literature on peacebuilding, and within the NGO community. Hyden argues: ‘many non-governmental organizations, whose development agenda in recent years has come to incorporate democratization goals, also operate on this assumption’ (Hyden 1997: 8). Proponents of peacebuilding have come to see, whether out of necessity or theoretical commitment, the NGO sector as a necessary partner in reconstruction and development. The advocacy by the proponents of peacebuilding of a vibrant civil society is often linked with the notion that the promotion of peace and development must be preceded by the spread of NGOs and other forms of community organizations.

Civil society literature is not merely descriptive, but is also productive of particular forms of politics. This literature rests on the notion of an inherent distinction between those issues that are properly the purview of the state, and those that belong to civil society. The former, then, are political, while the latter fall outside of this category and thus are not open to the same types of contestation.

Civil society as space

This separation between the roles of the state and civil society is particularly evident in the work that approaches civil society as space. While distinct from the associational literature that centres on organizations, it nevertheless shares the same normative commitments, and provides support to the same policies. Besides illustrating the complexities of trying to fix civil society with a specific meaning, describing it in spatial terms shows the division between the roles of the state and society. According to Lehning, ‘civil society, or ‘civic space’, occupies the middle ground between government and the private sector. It is the *space* we occupy when we are engaged neither in government activities nor in commerce’ (emphasis added, Lehning 1998: 223). Imagining civil society as a geographic space requires that specific forms of social activity are attributed to different locales. This serves to differentiate between the state, the home, the realm of economic activity and civil society. In effect, this defines civil society less as a series of issues and institutions, and more as a conceptual terrain where activities, defined as neither political nor domestic, can take place.

As with the associational school, civil society as space provides the opportunity for people to learn consociational behaviour, and to interact in a peaceful way. As Lehning argues (1998: 241), it is the site where people are able to solve their problems jointly. Thus it resembles the associational approach in its normative support of the concept, and shares a common logic about why civil society is beneficial. It also represents the potential space of democratisation, where alternatives to the state's politics and policies can be offered. This literature, while not as prevalent as the associational stream, nevertheless serves to highlight how civil society is conceived of as being separate from the state, and to show that the types of activities that take place in both are understood as being distinct.

Contradictions emerging from divisions between civil society and the state

The concept of civil society operates in the same way as other meta-narratives in defining the world around us, determining the limits of the possible. By actively shaping communities, and encouraging the establishment of vibrant associations, there is a push to make the state–societal relations of Cambodia, East Timor and Bosnia resemble the United States, Canada and the United Kingdom. It is imperative that the types of actions the discourse of civil society makes possible (and as such also impossible) are spelled out. The implications of the connection between civil society and peacebuilding need to be laid bare.

Starting with the term itself we can begin to see the strong normative content of 'civil society'. To begin with, 'society' connotes a community with shared experiences and expectations. The literature does not refer to a multitude of civil *societies* but refers instead to 'it' as a singular entity. Therefore, while civil society is held up as a means of encouraging plurality and of supporting diversity, it is at its end a means of 'resolving' difference. This is evident in the associational literature, which argues that one of the roles of civil society is to teach individuals to 'get along', and to learn to moderate their particular demands within society. This ignores the operation of power in determining who dictates the public good, and which particular interests are deemed to be best for the state as a whole. Civil society, conceived of in these ways, is a space where individuals, rather than communities or larger groups,interact.

The other aspect of this term derives from a reading of the 'civil' in civil society. This word is imbued with meaning, and shapes the way the concept, and those groups and activities included within it, are perceived. To be civil is to be well behaved, polite and respectful, which stands in opposition to anarchy and chaos. Furthermore, the notion of civil or civility is cast in opposition to ideas of anarchy and barbarism. At the same time, if we understand ourselves to be civilized, it is as a binary opposite to the wild and dangerous 'other' that resides beyond our borders. In this way, to deliver civil society can be understood as a continuation of older patterns of delivering civilization. In the very language that is used, civil society is set up as something both desirable and something to be both defended and promoted, regardless of whether or not the concept itself is ultimately hollow and baseless. These assumptions can be seen informing the scholarly and policy literatures on peacebuilding that advocate the construction of civil society as a means of eliminating the use of physical violence to resolve disputes, to promote the acceptance of modern standards of property rights, and to instil a respect for individuals' rights. Our understanding of civil is therefore linked to our understanding of civilized and civilization, terms that are, within current discourse, irrevocably connected to a value for progress. We also must consider the historic and cultural context of what is a proper functioning civil society. The experiences of North America and Europe are treated as universals that other societies should eventually achieve.

The narratives of civil society do not just argue that individuals within society must learn to cooperate, but also entail prescriptions of how government should relate to civil society, and what roles each should play. This has the effect of disciplining, of defining what is and what is not acceptable as civil society. To this point we have dwelt on a series of approaches that have largely shared a positive orientation towards the value of civil society. Peacebuilding, in fostering an environment in which civil society can flourish, is seen as a means of lifting the target society out of their condition of poverty and violence. This replicates the discourse of certain societies and states as being incapable of helping themselves. The solution, the adoption of a European model of political organization, is taken for granted. Clearly then civil society as a concept does not signify an existing and independent entity. The evasive character of civil society, the incredible range of its meanings, reveals how the narratives of civil society do not capture a reality, but rather reproduce and sustain a particular vision of societal–state interaction. In doing so, civil society provides and sustains particular forms of politics. As such, it is a discourse that serves to reproduce particular dynamics of a separation between state and society, and within the associational use of the concept, to limit the role of the state. Rather than seeing civil society as an objective 'thing' that needs to be defined and categorized, we must view it as a narrative practice that simultaneously limits and facilitates 'political action'.

While civil society is a contested discourse, there is a general consensus of its value as a social category and its importance to the resolution of conflict. At the same time, there is broad recognition that while civil society is in total a positive social force, not all groups contained within it are *necessarily* peaceful or promote forms of politics that are inclusive and democratic. As MacLean states, 'however conceptualized, the realm of voluntary association that has been designated as civil society is currently an arena of major social and political dispute and transformation' (1998: 37). As a base narrative underpinning peacebuilding, civil society must be seen as a bulwark against violent politics, and in turn assumed to have a transformative power on state politics. A vibrant and effective civil society is expected to be able to alter patterns of violent conflict and to replace them with a peaceful form of politics that is democratic in nature.

The problem-solving aspect of social science, particularly as it is employed around peacebuilding, necessarily confronts the dilemma of how to establish policy on the basis of a commitment to civil society.[32] There is a requirement in setting peacebuilding agendas to explain how civil society can be fostered, constructed and supported. The lack of any coherent 'thing' that can be identified and measured has resulted in the search and use of stand-ins: identifiers that signify the existence of civil society. The predominance of the associational school, with its strong liberal roots, has meant that NGO activity is now treated as a measurement of civil society (David Chandler 1999; Abiew and Keating 1999a; Goodhand 2002; and Orjuela 2003). This has been noted by David Chandler in his examinations of peacebuilding in Bosnia: 'the main focus of civil society-building has often been local non-governmental organizations (NGOs) as a sphere for articulating needs independently of vested political interests and involving grassroots community "voices"' (David Chandler 1999: 110). This position is advocated by Kaldor (2000), who argues that international/global (that is, trans-boundary) civil society can be equated to the independent NGOs that operate across national boundaries. Fisher has similarly stated that 'what is undeniable is that NGOs, because of their rapid proliferation, are the vanguard of civil society in most of the Third World' (Fisher 1998: 12). The argument is that for any given Southern state civil society can be effectively represented by the totality of local and international associations. This is the case even when most definitions of civil society are far more inclusive, encompassing church groups, unions, business associations, and sports and recreation clubs, to name just a few.[33]

As will be explored in more depth in the next chapter, if civil society is supposed to be the space of social learning for society, then the inclusion of NGOs of any type is perhaps problematic. NGOs are seldom democratic in their internal structure, either organized along bureaucratic and hierarchical lines, or based principally on a strong charismatic figure. This is in contrast to the democratic behaviour they are supposed to foster. Furthermore, neither INGOs, nor many LNGOs, may be representative of the local communities they are supposed to be speaking for. Thus the focus on NGOs as a measurement of civil society is likely to be inconsistent with the goals of civil society reconstruction.

Even the assumption that NGOs are inherently separate from the state is problematic, as the relationship between civil society and the state is complex. Civil society, and organizations that exist within it, are seldom completely separate from the state. The complicated nature of the interaction between the state and NGOs is particularly evident in Cambodia. During its period of communist rule under the Vietnamese, the state was centrally involved in a range of associations throughout the state. As Cambodia moved from a communist system to a democratic form of governance, the relationship between the government and these associations had to be reconfigured. As NGOs in post-conflict states often work in areas that overlap with government mandates (such as health care), there can be considerable interaction between the government and NGOs. Finally, as the salary structures within NGOs are often significantly greater than those offered by government, there is a substantial pull for bureaucrats and political leaders to pursue work within NGOs. All of these dynamics serve to blur the line, as imaginary as it is, between civil society and the state. In fact, NGOs can be supported overtly, and at times co-opted, by the state.[34] Support can range from moral, to financial subsidization, to administrative assistance. The role NGOs play in interest articulation, the substantial organizational structure they can have, the reach into society and the perceived distance from the state, are all motivations for the state and political parties to utilize the NGOs for their own political goals. NGOs provide communities of interest that are ready to be mobilized by political actors. These associations are then potential sources for the destabilization of transition democracies because they can reinforce identity politics. These are all dynamics that can be studied from within a liberal perspective. However, the question itself is unlikely to be raised in the first place, because the supposed answer is already contained within the theories.

As NGOs are expected to perform a key role in producing social capital or developing civil society, we must examine the nature of the relationship that develops between NGOs and the state. If the revitalization of civil society leads to an improved security condition for people in a post-conflict state, then we should expect to see a peaceful politics emerge between NGOs (civil society) and the state. Yet, as has been illustrated, the literature on civil society sees it as being in opposition to the state, which implies the emergence of new dynamics of conflict as civil society is strengthened. This paradox needs to be explored in greater depth. If NGOs are the vanguard of civil society, which provides the basis for long-term democratic peace, then the relationship that develops between NGOs and the state in societies undergoing peacebuilding societies must be studied.

The narrative constructions of civil society as one of the cornerstones of democracy and an essential component of the resolution of conflict has meant that it is seldom linked to the outbreak of violence; on the contrary it is generally written as being the victim or target of repression.[35] The studies that have offered critiques of the effects of civil society on the safety of peoples and the pacification of dispute resolution have tended to focus on historical examples when 'civil society' has been implicated in various atrocities. We can turn to Rwanda to see the manner in which civil society has been linked to some of the most reprehensible examples of violence over the past 20 years (Storey 1997).[36] But in these instances, the concept of civil society itself is not critiqued. The point that is made is that particular manifestations of civil society are not only problematic, but also exceptional.

Intriguingly, some studies of civil society have been willing to recognize that it can in fact be a source of conflict. If we accept a definition of civil society that is inclusive of the full range of organizations and associations, we must include groups that may not be forces for stability, peace and democratic behaviour, a point recognized in much of the literature on civil society in the developing world. Knight, for example, has stated that: 'not all elements in civil society are benign or progressive. Some of them represent the criminal underbelly of society and others represent reactionary and exclusionary movements' (Knight 2003: 256). These observations are made regularly by liberal advocates of civil society, and are inevitably noted in most studies of the role of civil society in states emerging from conflict. Studies of American associational life have identified the existence of the Ku Klux Klan, and neo-Nazi movements, and analyses of Europe have observed similar characteristics. Van Rooy has argued: 'civil society organizations can sabotage democracy by promoting factionalism, ethnicism and excessive self-interest' (1998: 29). These statements, while showing an awareness of the multifaceted nature of the civil society they describe, also quickly dismiss these types of groups in one of two ways. In the first instance there is a simple case of ignoring their activities, dismissing their overall relevance to the democratic societies in which they are embedded, and in the second there is an attempt to link the study of civil society with a more clearly normative definition so that such groups can be ignored. But once again the focus is on how the society that has given rise to civil society is somehow to blame. It is unfortunate that studies which pay lip service to this potential problem do not fully develop these thoughts, and leave them as footnotes to studies that laud the role of civil society. Within Cambodia, as we will see later in this book, civil society is constituted by a range of associations that span the spectrum from HR organizations through to organizations that espouse a variety of racist ideologies against a host of minorities. The emergence of civil society within developing states cannot be treated seriously without including such groups within the purview of our analysis. Cambodian civil society contains organizations that work towards peace and democracy and others that have vitriolic positions on minority rights, some even do both. It would be misleading to assert that the NGO sector in Cambodia is universally advocating for an open democratic society. Certainly my experiences in dealing with NGOs in the country revealed that the vast majority of groups are staffed by caring and motivated people, with a seemingly genuine drive to help Cambodia, but this does not mean that their work is to be universally praised, or that the effects of their work should not be interrogated.

One of the insights of the 'discursive' turn in political science has been the observation that the language of social science is not neutral. There is no division between the academic and policy realm; the two are constantly informing each other in a perpetual dance of rearticulating the 'world out there'. While the language of civil society may contain internal contradictions, to the extent that it does have cultural and historic linkages, it nevertheless is reshaping the world around us. The concept of civil society has been picked up and used as a means of understanding and changing politics. Its use has reproduced the liberal world order, which sees a separation of the state, the family and the market. At the same time, the expansion of civil society is seen as a bulwark against repressive states, and to form the basis of a democratic sensibility amongst the citizenry.

Conclusions

Discourses in political science, development literature and the policy realm are neither value-neutral, nor independent of the social world they are trying to explain and affect. This is particularly true when it comes to narratives of peacebuilding and civil society. As has been shown, the various approaches, while differing in their treatment of core concepts, nevertheless all reproduce a number of social-political concepts. There is a complex series of processes of both political practice and representation that have led the public and policy communities to accept peacebuilding as a valid endeavour.

Peacebuilding remains under-theorized and yet has acquired a surprisingly broad base of support. As a narrative of political action it has become accepted as a legitimate practice. In this respect its power as a discourse is not dependent on its depth of theory. Peacebuilding is reliant on notions of civil society that are based on liberalism and make sense to the Northern public because it reflects the social environment in which this public finds itself. This 'common sense' base of the theory serves to make it that much more difficult to assail, as it is presented as a narrative grounded in the purported experiences of modern society. The pervasiveness of the discourse of peacebuilding has made critique of its validity exceedingly difficult, forcing a debate about techniques and application rather than permitting a discussion of the concept itself. In doing so, the policy alternatives available to provide assistance to communities suffering from protracted violence are curtailed. Attempting to address problems of civil strife, the solution promoted by peacebuilding is to re/construct the state, and to put in place dynamics that will enable the development of characteristics supportive of democratic political structures. Therefore peacebuilding relies on the state and is captive to a contradiction inherent in modern conceptions of state politics.

Peacebuilding literature does not challenge, and in fact supports, the conventional notion of security where the state is the best guarantor of maintaining stability, but the paradox is that the state is also seen as a source of repression and undemocratic behaviour necessitating a strengthening of civil society. In contrast to such security narratives, CSS demands that the categories of the agents and subjects of security be explored. The expression of this position with respect to peacebuilding has shown how it serves to normalize and depoliticize the process of imposing a particular political order on a given society. This is certainly the case with peacebuilding in Cambodia, where the post-UNTAC years have been marked by the broad-based consensus on a liberal democratic development model.

Through the process of immanent critique, where the concept of peacebuilding is treated on its own terms, and thus judged according to what it claims to do, the inherent limitations of the framework can be exposed. As this chapter has illustrated, peacebuilding practice relies on particular understandings of NGOs acting as a vanguard for civil society, resulting in a liberal civic peace that is extrapolated from an ahistorical reading of Northern political development. This in turn has provided the justification for the promotion of NGOs, which have become *the* dominant expression of faith in the capacity of civil society not just to transform the means of addressing conflict (by rendering violence illegitimate), but crucially to resolve many of the endemic sources of conflict. While this has been shown to be rife with internal contradictions, the analysis of the impact of peacebuilding must then move into an examination of the empirical. It is only through the exploration of how the promotion of civil society (NGOs) has contributed to the resolution of the sources of conflict that we can complete this immanent critique.

3 Critiques of NGOs in peacebuilding

Given the dramatic rise of peacebuilding over the past 15 years, accompanied by the increase in the number and roles of NGOs, it should not come as a surprise that there has been an associated growth in academic attention paid to the subject. To this point the focus has been on the development of literatures on peacebuilding, demonstrating the ways in which both the academic and policy literatures have drawn on liberal thought. In particular it was illustrated how this has led to civil society promotion as a core tool in addressing the causes of conflict. As peacebuilding has incorporated humanitarianism, as well as development narratives and practices, there has been a commensurate increase in the importance of NGOs. While the ways in which NGOs have come to act as the vanguard of civil society and have received broad support from across the political spectrum was explored in the last chapter, there is a growing critical literature that is challenging the efficacy and value of NGO-centric policies. It would be a gross simplification to assert that NGOs in peacebuilding have received little academic or policy scrutiny. In fact, as this chapter demonstrates, there have been numerous critiques levelled against NGOs' roles in peacebuilding and development.

That said, the majority of the literature that critically examines NGOs' roles and impacts on Southern states does not seek to discard NGOs (let alone civil society). Most of the analysis should be seen as providing 'friendly critique', striving to make the sector more effective in both development and democratization. This is not to say that this body of literature has ignored potential problems emerging from the modern practice of civil society-centric reconstruction and rehabilitation. Rather, that by paying close attention to the problems that have emerged, numerous authors and policy makers have striven to correct and improve policies surrounding peacebuilding. There is a secondary body of literature, which challenges the viability of NGOs, in particular the international organizations that are at the heart of the modern rescue industry. However, this work has generally sought to privilege local civil society. In this way, it will be argued that the critiques do not fundamentally undermine the assumptions informing liberal civil society-centric peacebuilding.

A word or two is necessary to indicate what this chapter does not cover. With the expansion of thought on counter-insurgency operations, there has been growing concern within both academic and policy circles regarding the use of NGOs to combat resistance to Western missions in Iraq and Afghanistan. This has sparked a considerable debate about the militarization of aid. On the one side are the Counter-Insurgency (COIN) advocates (Kilcullen 2009, 2010) that see NGOs as crucial for a battle for the hearts and minds of local populations. This echoes, though problematically, the assertions made within the NGO sector that their work is largely progressive, benefiting local communities, and thus popular and legitimate. On the other hand, there are criticisms that the incorporation of NGOs into COIN erodes the established norms of aid delivery on the basis of need. These arguments are constructed around the assumption that local populations and insurgents will come to see the work of NGOs as a core component of broader interventionism, and jeopardize the presumed neutrality of aid.

Interestingly, these debates over the role of NGOs in winning hearts and minds largely ignore the ways in which there is a shared logic legitimizing the interventions that make it possible – and indeed necessary – to involve simultaneous military and development components. Both sides of the debate now tend to share a belief in the importance of civil society in combating insecurity, and of NGOs as playing a role in instilling democratic practice. While obviously important, and involving ethical and practical issues that will shape peace operations in the years to come, the precise debates surrounding the militarization of aid are beyond the purview of this book.

This chapter concentrates on the critiques levelled against NGOs, not the broader missions that have enabled their presence in particular spaces. While there is a growing literature that seeks to critique the roles of NGOs in peacebuilding, given the extent of the roles of NGOs in addressing peace and development, this body of work is still quite small. As Mercer pointed out in 2002, there were very few critical reviews of the role of NGOs in democratization, and much of the work that addressed the topic tended to share core assumptions about NGOs' inherent benevolence. In fact, it is necessary to turn to the development studies literature to find sustained critical explorations of the roles and impacts of NGOs. This field has focused on the shortcomings of NGOs, highlighting instances when they have failed to live up to the emancipatory and/or liberalizing potential promised by civil society. This line of critique is important, as it demonstrates continued support for the principle that a vibrant civil society is a crucial component of a sustainable democracy.

One of the themes that emerge in the literature is a simultaneous support of civil society reconstruction with a critique of the NGO-centric model that has emerged since 1990. These studies tend to lay out the ways in which a vibrant local civil society is necessary to conflict resolution and transformation. However, there is concern with the ways in which NGOs are taken as indicators of civil society, which extends to the ways in which NGO growth may not usher in a strengthening of civil society. Indeed, some of this literature contends that the support of NGOs by the international community may actually be at the expense of broader forms of civil society. This reflects the general consensus on the value of civil society, and is illustrative of how pervasive the civil society-centric approaches to peacebuilding have become.

A unifying theme of this strand of criticism is that civil society incorporates a far larger range of human endeavour than formal associations. Instead this literature highlights how writing on civil society theory explicitly identifies an incredible range of forms of group behaviour. Carothers, who has written extensively on theories of civil society, writes:

> NGOs are outweighed by more traditional parts of civil society. Religious organizations, labour unions, and other groups often have a genuine base in the population and secure domestic sources of funding, features that advocacy groups usually lack, especially the scores of new NGOs in democratizing countries.
>
> (Carothers 1999–2000: 20)

As a result of these observations, some academics have warned against the overt focus on NGOs. Stubbs, for one, has called for caution in the assumptions informing donor support for such associations. The focus on NGOs has emerged as a result of this policy work, but their presumed ability to foster the growth of local civil society is questioned. Stubbs argues that much more direct attention needs to be paid to the ways in which NGOs impact on civil society growth, rather than the current focus on service delivery. This is a position that is echoed by Marchetti and Tocci (2009: 204) who have expressed concern that favouring NGOs has come at the expense of broader forms of associational behaviour. NGOs, within such studies, are either unrepresentative of local civil society, or as representing only a particular section of society. By concentrating on development and relief agencies, the extensive range of associational behaviour is ignored.

Interestingly, there is little interest expressed within these works in abandoning an NGO-centric approach to civil society reconstruction. Despite the expressed caveats about the capacity of NGOs to foster vibrant civil society, these studies have continued to support the international funding of NGOs. Instead the argumentation has entailed a cautionary note about the democratic potential that can be realized through NGO expansion, while reaffirming that NGOs are important development players. This literature also reaffirms the importance of civil society.

Echoing the concerns that NGOs may not be representative of civil society, there is a second strand of analysis that has explored the relevance of European-centric conceptions of civil society formulations. This literature has sought to develop contextual understandings of the growth and expressions of civil society. Not surprisingly, the work has tended to concentrate along geographic lines. The material is generally bound by a consideration of whether local and regional contexts have shaped both the emergence of CSOs, and their relationships with both local communities and the state. There are, for example, distinct literatures looking at East and Southeast Asia (Hedman 2001; N. Thayer 1991; C. Thayer 2009; Knapman 2006); Sub-Saharan Africa (Barnes 2006; Bratton 2003; Heurlin 2010); and Latin America (Nonan-Ferell 2004); and finally an extensive body of literature focusing on the Balkans (Fischer 2006; David Chandler 1999; J. Hall 1995). To varying degrees these have sought to examine the assumption of universalism. While the precise expressions of civil society are often seen as distinct, shaped by particular historical and cultural contexts, this has not led to a challenge of the meaning of civil society. Studies of NGOs in the developing world that attempt to account for local or regional context are nevertheless rooted within a universalist conception of civil society. Where countries are seen as lacking Western forms of independent associational life, there is a clear sense permeating most of this literature that these countries need to be placed on a trajectory where civil society can flourish. Despite calls for more local context in the analysis of NGOs, and of sensitivity to this context in setting policy towards peacebuilding, the more sustained critiques of NGOs in peacebuilding and development have looked at the common behaviour across the NGO sector, focusing on the particular associational form of civil society (NGOs) cross-cutting cultural spaces.

Much of the critical attention that has been paid to NGOs in post-conflict societies has more to do with the efficacy and roles of NGOs in development than in peacebuilding per se. However, the various strands of critique are of direct relevance to the capacity of NGOs as a component of civil society to address and resolve sources of conflict. Those that have provided general critiques of NGOs, speaking to a wide range of issues that have prevented these associations from achieving democratic and development goals, include: M. Anderson 1999; Barber and Bowie 2008; MacLean 1998; Hulme and Edwards 1997; and Mercer 2002. All of these scholars have highlighted the growing complexities of the operating environment of humanitarian and development NGOs, as well as the ways in which NGOs themselves have become increasingly diverse. These critiques include concerns that NGOs are facilitating neoliberalism, that their democratic culture is limited, and that they are not responsive to local needs.

Critiques of NGOs as forces of neoliberalism

The most vocal critical position is informed by attention to the impact of neoliberalism. The essential argument is that NGOs, through their delivery of services, have reinforced economic and social neoliberalism in post-conflict zones (Rieff 1999; Brannan 2003; O'Brien 1998; I. Roy 2008; Marchetti and Tocci 2009; Wallace 2004). There is a shared concern amongst these scholars about the ways in which neoliberalism has rolled back the capacity of the state to provide for the welfare of citizens: the erosion of protections for local industry and the commensurate downward pressure on wages, the privatization of land and the ability of corporations to reorient economies away from meeting local needs, and of the privileging of individualism over community building. While the precise nature of the critiques of neoliberalism depends on the particular theoretical commitments of scholars and activists, there is a shared conviction that neoliberalism is eroding the quality of life of peoples and the legitimacy of states. In short, neoliberalism may be contributing to insecurity in post-conflict states in both the short and long term, rather than addressing poverty, perceived as a source of insecurity. NGOs, crucial to modern conflict transformation and resolution, are thus implicated in this dynamic.

The focus on NGOs in this context is complicated. To begin with, NGO workers seldom express support of economic *or* social neoliberalization. As Hulme (2008) argues, while development workers have been concerned with neoliberal impacts, and are driven by a desire to improve the lives of the poor, they have focused efforts on helping the South, rather than combatting the neoliberal orthodoxy (or its softer poverty-reduction expressions). In fact in over 100 interviews with NGO representatives in Cambodia, not a single individual indicated a support for neoliberal dynamics (though there was support for the value of free markets). Indeed the exact opposite is common, with development and humanitarian relief workers seeing their work as off-setting or alleviating the impact of neoliberalism. The critiques of NGOs are respectful of the intentions of NGO workers, and tend to focus much more directly on how the rescue industry is unintentionally supporting neoliberalization. However, scholars have pointed out that their actions in effect reinforce neoliberal reforms, and facilitate the diminishment of the state.

The main thrust of this argumentation is that NGOs, through the provision of services to the global South, are stepping in to the sphere previously occupied by the state. This is particularly evident in the social welfare sector, including a wide range of activities ranging from health care, education and the provision of care to children. This is not to say that the role of NGOs is greater in this respect than the market and international organizations in forcing a rollback of the state (Hulme and Edwards 1997: 9). The emphasis must still be placed on the conditions imposed by donors, the IMF, and on the diplomatic community's privileging of liberal market and democratic reforms as core components of negotiated peace settlements. Intriguingly, this resonates with the expressed support of NGOs in post-conflict states as serving to limit the powers of abusive and coercive states. In this light, Nonan-Ferrell (2004) has highlighted how civil society (in particular NGOs) aids in restricting the powers of the state. This is a point echoed by Barnes in her examination of the interaction of NGOs and governments in Western Africa, where she argues that some African leaders are concerned 'that NGOs become stronger at the expense of state institutions' (Barnes 2006: 89). Filling in for the state, and providing social services that had previously been seen as the remit of the government, serves to lessen the immediate impact of the diminishment of the state. In other words, in the neoliberal moment, NGOs are acting to preserve some forms of social care for society. Yet by providing these services, the sector may be facilitating the process by eliminating a point of short-term dissent to the structural changes in the state. The result of this is that NGOs, in stepping into the gap left by the state, are providing cover to the neoliberalization of the South.

There is a second dynamic observed by scholars that further entrenches neoliberalism. NGOs themselves are increasingly turning to market solutions to poverty and the diminishment of the state. The advocacy of micro-credit is emblematic of this faith in the capitalist market to raise communities out of abject poverty (Hulme and Edwards 1997: 11). While Hulme and Edwards assert that NGOs' representatives are quite capable of deciding for themselves whether to pursue market-oriented or community-oriented programmes, the donor preference for micro-credit tilts the consideration in favour of market solutions. As Duffield (2001, 2007) has shown, this has not led to a consistent rise in the quality of living in the South, and may instead have the contrary effect of entrenching a bare life.

As with the previous general critiques, most of these scholars have not sought to challenge the validity of civil society. Indeed, NGOs are seen as failing in their tasks of assisting local communities. NGOs, within this frame of analysis, are unfortunately implicated in the neoliberal economic practices from which they need to extract themselves.

NGOs and the distortion of local economies

Arising from the observation of NGOs operating in post-conflict zones, the next set of critiques are concerned with the ways in which the sudden influx of NGOs can negatively impact upon local economies. International humanitarian workers are often well paid, and command wages well beyond those of impoverished local communities. The work done by professional development workers can be physically and emotionally demanding. In order to retain professional staff, INGOs need competitive wage packets to ensure that employees are willing to continue to work in the global South, rather than pursue work in their Northern homes. However, the impact of this is that INGO workers' wages are far beyond the dreams of most local populations. In addition to INGO workers, post-conflict zones are increasingly defined by the presence of donor agencies, Northern embassy and international organization representatives and independent contractors. In the mid-1990s Cambodia, for example, was awash with the ubiquitous white hi-lux truck adorned with the emblems of NGOs and donors. This is a dynamic currently seen in South Sudan and Afghanistan. The influx of the Western employees, with ample financial resources at hand, has directly impacted on local communities. In a number of countries this has had the effect of establishing a parallel economy for the rescue industry workers, alongside the local economy.

The spending power of INGO workers can divert goods and services into the rescue sector, enabling the workers to live in choice accommodation and obtain access to the highest quality of goods and services. This can serve to remove valuable resources from the reach of the broader society. As Pouligny explains, the influx of substantial amounts of development dollars into economically depressed environments can completely alter the functioning of the local economy. The result is that local peoples can find that the presence of the rescue industry actually makes it more difficult to access real estate, and that food and water can be in short supply. In the long term this can result in the peculiar situation where NGO work is amongst the most sought-after form of employment. Pouligny (2005: 501) has gone further and illustrated how this situation can actually prohibit the growth of local civil society, as resources are taken away from locals and competent individuals are drawn to the international humanitarian sector. These economic effects, though deleterious for the post-conflict states, particularly the urban core, may be tolerable if the NGO sector is able to live up to its promise of contributing to a democratic culture.

Democratization/accountability

At the heart of the promotion of civil society as an agent of peacebuilding is a hope that the sector will be able to foster democratic change. NGOs, particularly LNGOs, as the vanguard of civil society, are seen as crucial agents of democratization (Clarke 1998a; Silliman and Noble 1998; Fisher 1998, Bebbington *et al.* 1993, Lambrou 1997). From *An Agenda for Peace* (Boutros-Ghali 1992) onwards, there has been a presumption in favour of democratization and civil society reconstruction as a means of redressing violence. In his words, 'a richly pluralistic civil society, generating a wide range of interests, is held to mitigate polarities of political conflict and develop a democratic culture of tolerance, moderation and compromise' (David Chandler 1999: 110). The hopes that have been attached to NGOs have not been clearly realized, and there is now a concern that NGOs might not be ideal advocates for democratization, a point echoed by Frangonikolopoulos: 'NGOs owe it to the international public to be accountable and transparent themselves. Yet, few NGOs have democratic systems of governance and accountability' (2005: 62). Indeed Mercer's review of academic and empirical literature on the topic has led her to argue that 'given the current climate of economic and political neoliberalism within which NGOs are necessarily embedded, their role in democratization is far more complex than the liberal democratic model would suggest' (Mercer 2002: 6). Rather than being an inherent force for democratization, the breadth of the sector, and the wide variation in type and focus, often result in countervailing effects on the development of a democratic culture. There are numerous critics who assert that NGOs may serve to undermine democratic action.

The most sustained critique in this regard is that NGOs, despite claims to be responsible downwards, may often be accountable to entirely different communities. Some authors are quite explicit in this regard, asserting that NGOs are rarely representative of local communities (Mercer 2002; Parks 2008). Parks notes, following Hulme and Edwards, how development agencies are increasingly accountable to donors (Parks 2008: 217). The demands of results-based management, and of impositions of external financial accounting instigated to ensure Western monies are being spent properly, has entrenched this process of upwards responsibility. At the same time, some NGOs have been noted as actually rejecting local views and opinions. David Chandler argues that in Bosnia, NGO representatives were remarkably dismissive of local capacities, seeing Bosnian peoples as uneducated and inherently undemocratic. Chandler goes further in his argumentation, asserting that the dismissal of local capacity, and their perceived inability to practice democratic politics (as NGO representatives have argued), creates barriers for democratization (David Chandler 1999: 122).

The next set of critiques emerge, in part, around the assertion that NGOs, as democratic spaces, should be able to reflect and act upon local needs and wants (Bebbington 1997). Here there are two threads of argumentation, both of which at their heart pertain to the question of representation. First, there is a common refrain that NGOs do not often respond to local needs and wants; instead, their activities more often follow the interests of donors, or the personal interests of their own leadership. In order to survive, NGOs need to find funding for their projects. This has often resulted in organizations becoming driven by the pursuit of financing, rather than being primarily 'need driven' (Frangonikolopoulos 2005: 57). This is particularly acute for smaller LNGOs, which are unable to diversify funding. As Parks has identified, there is a structural problem in the long-term sustainability of NGO work that emerges as a direct result of this reliance on donor money, particularly when donors are increasingly reluctant to provide long-term core funding. As such, NGOs can lose project funding, and then need potentially to refocus their work so as to remain solvent. '[T]here is growing evidence that the shifting priorities of international donor funding undermine the credibility and effectiveness of the very advocacy NGOs that they are trying to strengthen' (Parks 2008: 214). While local communities are highly unlikely to turn down any projects that might benefit them, projects that do not reflect locally identified priorities are not likely to provide people with a sense that NGOs are governed in a manner that respects local opinion. In other words, NGO activities of this sort are not about to reinforce democratic behaviour, a point made by Atack:

> Northern-based development NGOs can bypass existing local organizations when either setting up their own projects or selecting partner agencies, for example. This sort of problem is particularly acute where NGOs take on the functions of local government, without any mechanisms of accountability or appeal for the local population.
>
> (Atack 1999: 859)

Zaum argues, 'even if NGOs involved in civil wars and peacebuilding are formally independent from governments, this independence has been increasingly undermined by their dependence on donor funding' (Zaum 2009: 28). As Edwards illustrates, this in the first instance pushes NGOs to focus on broad themes in order to respond to changing funding priorities. There is 'a tendency to concentrate on general issues (systems and ideology) rather than on detailed policy lobbying tied to specific circumstances. Consequently themes for advocacy then tend to be determined by the international debate – even fashion – instead of by the work of the NGO and its local counterparts' (Edwards 1993: 168). However, critiques of this nature tend to focus on how this interferes with the effectiveness of NGOs, instead of exploring the impact of such structural limitiations on their ability to instil democratic values.

Second, NGOs' activities in a particular issue area can be rapidly dropped as funding cycles end and new priorities emerge. In the health sector this is particularly acute as endemic health issues, such as Leprosy or Dengue fever, receive scant attention as the global community has concentrated its attention on HIV/AIDS and malaria. This is not to denigrate such work of obvious social importance, but to highlight that other important issues, some of which may be of more immediate concern, are underserviced. Directly related to this line of analysis is that in addition to not responding to local needs and wants, the responsibility of NGOs is towards their donors, rather than the target population. Critics of this upwards accountability (Parks 2008; Hulme and Edwards 1997; Buiter 2005; J. Ferguson 1994; Frangonikolopoulos 2005) all argue that this undermines democratic accountability and indeed embeds notions that development issues are beyond local remit.

The final point that needs to be raised here regards the capacity of NGOs to empower local communities. If the value of democracy derives in part from its ability to give a voice to the subaltern, then we should find a number of NGOs reflecting the needs of these sectors of society. Drawing on an analysis of India, Indrajit Roy (2008) examines the assumptions that good governance relies on a robust civil society. It is then argued that while service delivery to the poor might be increased by effective civil society, it does not inherently increase the available political space for the poor. Roy draws on Theda Skocpol's work to frame this study. The broad argument then is, as David Chandler (1999: 114) points out, that CSOs are rarely representative of local needs, and that NGOs in particular are much more representative of the middle class.

The next set of critiques emerges as a direct result of liberal assumptions about the democratizing potential of civil society. If NGOs, as a representative component of civil society, are expected to help inculcate a democratic culture, there is an expectation that behaviour within the sector should reflect the forms of decision-making and conflict resolution consistent with liberal governance. If local communities are to learn about democracy through participation in NGOs, then the workings of such groups should be consistent with democratic norms. Unfortunately, even a cursory examination of the operations of most NGOs operating in peacebuilding environments does not exhibit such forms of internal governance.

The internal decision-making of NGOs, whether one focuses on local or international organizations, is seldom democratic, let alone consensual. As Gordenker and Weiss point out: 'NGOs themselves are not necessarily democratic, which raises the question of who represents what to whom.... NGOs do not function the way representative governments do' (Gordenker and Weiss 1995b: 553). Groups are often hierarchical and imbued with a bureaucratic managerial structure; given the size of the large INGOs, it is hard to imagine any other possible form of organization. This has important implications for the argument that NGOs can act as exhibitions of democratic behaviour. The difficulty of using NGOs as exemplars of democratic accountability is further complicated by the ways in which the leadership of larger organizations is seldom co-located with the project-delivery components. Yet, the decision-making within large NGOs is often, though not exclusively, driven by the leadership in head offices. This means that NGOs often demonstrate top-down leadership, in which elites are removed from local communities.

This is exacerbated at the local level where NGOs are often driven by charismatic leadership. While it is not surprising that NGOs grow up around individuals with exceptional drive and determination, this does erode the capacity for such groups to act as a model of liberal democratic behaviour. The irony is that the forms of governance exemplified by NGOs are often remarkably similar to the forms of state decision-making that civil society is held up as acting against. The charismatic leadership, the top-down decision making, the removal of elites from local communities, all run counter to the idealized democratic behaviour that the peacebuilding literature expects civil society to promote.

These extensive criticisms relate to both the presumed capacity of NGOs to take a leadership role in meeting the global South's development needs, and of the sector's ability to promote democratization through the support of a democratic culture. The bulk of the criticisms that have been levelled against the sector relate to failures of NGOs to achieve these goals. However, these criticisms need to be understood as being embedded within a general support of civil society. After all, the focus is on NGO failure, not on the broader conceptualizations of associational life. In terms of peacebuilding, these critiques, while serious, relate more to the application of policy, than to the underlying logic of the liberal peace.

NGOs and the state

The final area of critique of the roles of NGOs in peacebuilding addresses the ways in which NGOs and state interact in post-conflict states (Marchetti and Tocci 2009; Chazan 1992; J. Ferguson 1994). NGOs are expected to transform methods of conflict resolution, and to help address the sources of conflict. The next line of enquiry has sought to identify moments when the work of NGOs has had the opposite effect. Arising from the observation that states are often suspicious, if not outright antagonistic, towards NGOs (and broader civil society), this group of scholars point out that the rise of development and humanitarian NGOs can create new conflicts.

This contestation emerges as a result of two complementary processes. First, NGOs are moving into areas of policy and service delivery previously occupied by the state. Governments are then concerned with both the loss of authority over policy, and of the potential erosion of legitimacy as non-state actors take over service delivery. The second dynamic arises as a result of the watchdog function of some components of civil society. NGOs working in areas such as human rights, the promotion of democracy, and environmental protection, are often engaged in challenging the actions of states, and/or state elites. This is illustrated by Edwards *et al.*:

> Relationships between governments and NGOs have often been characterized by antagonism, yet there are sound reasons for NGOs to enter into a creative dialogue with the institutions which determine official development policy and deliver basic development services. The State remains the ultimate arbiter and determinant of the wider political changes on which development depends, and controls the economic and political frameworks within which people and their organisations have to operate.
>
> (Edwards *et al.* 1992: 78)

While Edwards *et al.* argue that there is a space, indeed a requirement, for cooperation, governments can perceive the increased power of NGOs as a challenge to their authority. As Downie and Kingsbury have argued, '[w]ithout a full understanding of the role of civil society, some government members regarded civil society, especially *non*-governmental organizations, as *anti*-government [italics in original] and therefore as opposition' (Downie and Kingsbury, 2001: 57). This process has also been observed by Barnes, who in reference to West Africa argues: '[s]ome governments see NGOs as competitors for resources, as well as competing for 'voice' and credibility within their own society and with international actors' (Barnes 2006: 89).

This struggle between states and NGOs is linked back to a number of the former critiques that have mentioned. The hollowing out of the state can lead to issues of legitimacy for Southern states. Being seen to be delivering services, and of setting priorities can be crucial to building support within the population. This is obviously all the more important in post-conflict states, which, by definition, suffer from a lack of legitimacy. Conflicts can also emerge when NGOs support local communities, or publicly advocate for policies that run counter to the state's policy initiatives. Johnson and Forsyth (2002), in a study of forestry conservation in Thailand, demonstrated how NGOs come into conflict with the state over both environmental protection and community empowerment when they opt to become involved in advocacy for local people.

NGOs and politics

While the roles of NGOs in peacebuilding have been examined by numerous scholars, and there is a burgeoning body of literature that seeks to understand the circumstances in which NGOs' activities might be counter-productive to the goals of conflict resolution, there has been little attention paid to their impact on politics. Here the term 'politics' is being used in its dominant expression as the struggle for power. Most of the literature on NGOs in peacebuilding makes a virtue of their non-political nature. It is seen as crucial to enabling their work, enabling them to work regardless of the political context. As Zaum, for example, argues it is when they become politicized through their linking to donor state agendas and modern Counter-Insurgency (COIN) operations that their work becomes problematic and more difficult. 'The dependency on donors for funds and access in civil wars has undermined not only the independence of NGOs, but also the non-political nature of their work' (Zaum 2009: 29). This literature must be distinguished from the broader body of academic and policy literature, which sees NGOs as making positive contributions to the democratic politics of states.

Where there has been some attention given to the issue of the political role of NGOs, it has tended to focus on the ways in which civil society can lead to the political development of communities. Mercer explains, 'the NGO literature reproduces the liberal maxim that democracy within capitalist society requires a vibrant and autonomous civil society and an effective state capable of balancing the demands of different interest groups'

(Mercer 2002: 7). However, in application this has not translated into argumentation that NGOs in post-conflict states should be 'political'. Instead it has been interpreted as a need for NGOs in the global South to empower local communities, but to leave communities to engage in politics on their own.

Authors working within this frame tend to start from the assumption that NGOs can embed democratic behaviour and consociationalism. Ulvila and Hossain (2002), for example, have drawn on fieldwork to make arguments about the ways in which NGOs have, and can, promote democratic political participation. Yet as has been demonstrated, there is a general critique of the capacity of NGOs to instil democratic culture on the basis of their internal organization or local accountability.

This conceptualization of a political role of civil society has clear roots within both liberal thought on civil society, as well as within the Gramscian-inspired approaches. In both instances the attention has been on the ways in which civil society can transform (or at least reinforce) political norms and/or culture. For example, Downie and Kingsbury (2001) have taken issue with the assumption that increasing the size of civil society, particularly through the promotion of NGOs, should result in a changing political culture. In fact, they argue that there is little evidence that civil society expansion has led to a simultaneous growth in political activity. As with many of the critical examinations of NGO activity, they are not inherently rejecting this form of conflict transformation and resolution. Instead they place at least a good part of the blame for the failure of political transformation of post-conflict states on to Southern states.

Of the various authors that have sought to explore the political impact of the expansion of the NGO sector, I associate most closely with the work of Pouligny, and her concerns about the ways in which peace policies may have misplaced efforts in assuming a democratic political transformative role of civil society:

> The second limit of the 'civil society' concept, as it is commonly used, is that it conveys the idea of a clear dichotomy between what is supposed to be and what is not supposed to be political. Obviously, even in Western contexts, this distinction is far from being so clear-cut, but it tends to be considered in an even more rigid way in places where 'civil society' is presented as an alternative to dysfunctional or even 'failed' state.
>
> (Pouligny 2005: 500)

Similarly, but from a more Marxist orientation, Indrajit Roy critiques what he sees as the 'false dichotomy between the social and the political (drawing on Jenkins 2002), which comes about from traditional liberal understandings of civil society, and from the growing literature on good governance (I. Roy 2008: 679).

At the margins there are a few scholars (Pouligny, Carlyle Thayer, Jenkins, Indrajit Roy) who have sought to challenge the apolitical nature of NGO action. Carlyle Thayer sees within civil society the potential of mobilizing populations, and confronting issues of politics head-on. This is a direct challenge to the ways in which liberal associationalism has perpetuated a belief that NGOs should avoid any perception of being 'political'. Thayer advances the idea of 'political civil society' as a correction to the ways in which the activity of associational life in Vietnam is not captured by traditional liberal conceptions. In this respect he is returning to the literature on civil society in Eastern Europe in the 1970s and 1980s. 'The study of political civil society groups has been largely marginalized by mainstream academics who privilege the role of so-called developmental non-governmental organizations (NGOs) and community-based organizations (CBOs)' (C. Thayer 2009: 2). These arguments have formed the basis of a debate on how civil society, and in particular NGOs, can effectively encourage local disadvantaged communities to engage in politics. In so doing these authors reject the notion that this is most effectively done through a focus on teaching communities about democratic politics, or concentrating on capacity building. Instead it is pointed out that the absence of NGOs from this sphere can be explained by the fact that they were oriented towards development, rather than politics, a lack of donor interest, or worry about the running of their programmes (Ulvila and Hossain 2002: 153). In contrast, there is an implicit assertion that some development organizations need to take a more forceful position on issues, and move into the realm of politics.

Conclusions

There has been substantial attention paid to NGOs' actions in post-conflict states. They have come under scrutiny because of their perceived limitations and failures in achieving the promises of liberal civil society on the one hand, and of their shortcomings in the development sector. These critiques, for the most part, have not sought to challenge the underlying assumptions supporting NGO-centric policies. Most of the literature is informed by a desire to improve the operation of the sector. While much of the scholarship and policy work done on this topic has been framed within the context of development and democratization, the relevance of this material to peacebuilding is clear.

NGOs have been seen as core components in building peace, and as being central to the alleviation of sources of conflict, yet the critiques all demand a degree of caution around the assumed benefits of pursuing peace and development through policies that favour NGOs. NGOs, while clearly important players in peacebuilding and development, have not proven able to resolve the full spectrum of issues surrounding instability and underdevelopment. In large part the problems confronting states emerging from protracted insecurity and underdevelopment are simply too complex and too entrenched to respond to the efforts of NGOs in the medium term. We are now at least two decades into the era of the NGO, and underdevelopment and civil conflict remain as intractable today as they were in the late 1990s. All the various arguments that have been briefly presented within this chapter attempt to come to terms with this gap between expectation and observed effect. In fact many of the scholars have identified dynamics that may result in at least some NGOs having the exact opposite impact of what would be predicted from the liberal associational and peacebuilding literatures. Rather than resulting in the alleviation of sources of conflict, NGOs can complicate local politics, exacerbate some forms of conflict and introduce new areas of contestation.

In much of this body of criticism there is a concern with the capacity of NGOs to achieve the ends expected of a vibrant civil society. NGOs may not be representative of civil society, nor do they necessarily act in ways that are likely to achieve the presumed benefits of providing for a vibrant civil society. Indeed, in some instances NGOs may actually erode local forms of civil society as resources are moved into formal associational forms that echo Northern development agencies.

Despite the range of critiques of the operation of NGOs in peacebuilding environments, the vast majority of this literature must be conceived of as 'friendly'. The criticisms are not generally aimed at undercutting NGO activities, but instead reflect disenchantment in their practical capacities. This has emerged as a result of a commitment to civil society, and specifically NGOs, as a key actor in peacebuilding. The problem-solving form of this literature is evident in the work of all of these authors. Barber and Bowie (2008), for example, provide a number of the common critiques of NGOs (which draw heavily on M. Anderson's observations), but then provide a series of solutions to these issues. This drive is also evident in the work of Hulme and Edwards, and permeates the regular Manchester Conferences that they have organized on the themes of NGOs and development.

The subsequent chapters explore the dynamics of conflict between the post-conflict state and NGOs in greater detail. The effectiveness of organizations in achieving their various policy aims will not be examined in any detail; rather, the next chapters focus more narrowly on the subjects of debate and contestation. Attention is focused on the perceived areas of contestation between the state and NGOs, with the aim to demonstrate when the tensions between civil society and the state can be understood through liberalism, and crucially, when liberal norms are unable to account for the dynamics of conflict.

4 A brief history of Cambodia and peacebuilding

In order to understand the dynamics of interaction between civil society actors and the Cambodian state, it is essential to provide some context into Cambodian history and politics. Examining the relationships that have developed between government and NGO representatives enables the analysis in subsequent chapters, which look at specific areas of state intervention. The present chapter also demonstrates the complexities of societies that are subject to peacebuilding and argues that these show the limitations of the application of policies derived from the universalization of Northern norms of political organization. Peacebuilding is intended to transform the patterns of politics within a state through the re/imposition of the characteristics of 'normal' politics, including democratic governance, liberal markets and the creation of civil society. Peacebuilding practices, however, are not applied on a *tabula rasa*; rather, the peoples that occupy the country have histories of their own, with particular social dynamics. To understand the ways in which Cambodia has experienced peacebuilding it is not only necessary to look at the peacebuilding policies implemented by the United Nations, and subsequently by the donor community, but we also need an understanding of the history of democracy and civil society within the country.

It is a complicated task to decide where to commence in providing historical context to Cambodia's encounters with peacebuilding. It is not sufficient to begin with the PPA, which set the framework for the UN mission, as these cannot be understood outside of the context of the preceding Cold War politics. There is a compelling case to start the narrative with the KR overthrow of the Lon Nol regime. Certainly a number of histories of Cambodia start with that moment. But as with the PPA, this would obscure how the KR was embedded within broader processes, both within local culture and international politics. In providing a brief historical overview, this chapter sketches out the ways in which ancient Cambodian history is portrayed, with the modest goal of illustrating how the current portrayals of Cambodia's past serve particular interests and reproduce modern state politics.

This chapter will provide context for the subsequent discussions about the dynamics of peacebuilding's influence on state–civil society interaction. This will demonstrate that the emergence of civil society in Cambodia must be contextualized with its past experiences of associational behaviour, and show how the liberal model currently being promoted within the state has no clear precedence. In terms of the specific discussion of peacebuilding, the roots of the conflict are briefly explored to illustrate the complexity of the conflict, as well as to discuss the impact of violence on the associational life of the state. The chapter then traces the modern events that resulted in an international peacebuilding effort in Cambodia. The processes leading to the deployment of UNAMIC and UNTAC will be described, and then linked to the post-UNTAC era of peacebuilding. This will illustrate how the peacebuilding process was informed by a particular logic (liberalism) and show that it placed an emphasis on civil society reconstruction that, in policy terms, translated into a promotion of NGOs. Finally, the chapter assesses the relative successes of peacebuilding in Cambodia according to its own goals. As such, the extent to which the international engagement with Cambodia has been able to transform the nature of conflict resolution away from violence, the success of poverty reduction, the imposition of democratic governance, and the promotion of civil society will be examined.

Imagining a past and present Cambodia

Interpretations of Cambodia's links to the Khmer empire continue to inform modern Cambodian politics (discussed in greater detail in Chapter 7). A detailed understanding of this period is not possible here, nor of Cambodia's experiences with the ebb and flow of its neighbouring Thai and Vietnamese societies. An appreciation of Cambodia's more recent history, as it relates to this study, starts with the era of European colonization. It was the French who imposed Northern notions of the state on Cambodia during their rule between 1863 and 1953. Bit, drawing on the work of David P. Chandler (1983), argues:

> Before the arrival of the French in 1863, Cambodia was not defined in the minds of the Cambodians by borders drawn on a map. The concept of nationhood was embodied in a cultural version of political geography. Cambodia was where Cambodian was spoken in the villages and where the village leaders received their official authority from a Cambodian King.
>
> (Bit 1991: 10)

The idea of a Cambodian state that is related to a particular (Khmer) people is further developed by Lizée, who shows that:

> [the] nationalist project was literally imported to Cambodia by the French as they attempted to emulate the Western model of the state: if this model called for the nation as a counterpart to the development

> of state institutions, then it had to find its parallel in Cambodia as incipient state institutions were being established there.
>
> (Lizée 2000: 33)

The era of French colonial rule affected much of the social fabric of Cambodian society. Bit argues it destroyed the 'traditional system of reciprocity in which personal patrons could serve as a form of social insurance to ameliorate the risks associated with a subsistence survival' (Bit 1991: 29).[1] In addition to the way in which Cambodian political culture and organization were torn asunder by the French, Kamm (1998: 26–27) argues that the colonial government also had a damaging effect on the administrative capacity of the country. Because of the colonizer's preference for the Vietnamese in French Indo-China, based largely on a patronizing racism, the Cambodians were provided few opportunities to work in the colonial bureaucracy.[2] Additionally, Cambodia and Laos received considerably less investment by the French than Vietnam. There was only limited investment in physical infrastructure, few opportunities for formal French education and, crucially, less exposure to European forms of societal organization. Notably, this extended to a lack of development of Northern forms of civil society. While many colonies in Southeast Asia were introduced to European styles of civil associations, this was never the case in Laos and Cambodia. For example, there was no equivalent to the Young Men's Buddhist Associations (modelled after the Young Men's Christian Association (YMCA)), which became important sites of socialization and politicization in British Southeast Asia and Thailand. While there was an introduction of Northern state structures under the French, there was no concurrent introduction of associations that would form the basis of 'normal' liberal forms of associational behaviour. This does not mean that there was an absence of associational behaviour, rather that the primary source of such activity remained the village and the Sangha, organized geographically around Wats.[3] Therefore, even though European forms of statehood and nationalism were being introduced in Cambodia, it was not accompanied by an adoption of related forms of state-societal divisions, or of the development of an independent civil society.

In 1940 the Franco-Siamese war broke out, resulting in the Thai seizure of Cambodian and Laotian territory, which Thailand had ceded in the early 1900s to the French. While the French defeated the Thai naval forces, the Japanese brought the French to the negotiation table, resulting in Thailand reclaiming some 65,000 square kilometres, including Battambang and Siem Reap. This loss of land also led to a breakdown of the relations between the colonial administration and the monarchy, complicating the secession in 1941 following King Monivong's death in April of that year. The French selected Norodom Sihanouk as the heir, hoping to select a 'more malleable and less independent minded' monarch (David P.

Chandler 1996: 167), a position that would prove ironic as Sihanouk played a key role in shaping Cambodian politics for the next 60 years.

When the Japanese disarmed French forces on 9 March 1945 throughout Indochina, and removed French colonial administrative officers from their positions, the monarchy was able to reclaim a modicum of independence. This is described by David P. Chandler:

> On March 13, in response to a formal Japanese request, King Sihanouk declared that Cambodia was independent and changed its name in French from 'Cambodge' to 'Kampuchea,' the Khmer pronunciation of the word. Sihanouk's decree invalidated Franco-Cambodian agreements, declared Cambodia's independence, and pledged Cambodia's cooperation with the Japanese.
>
> (Chandler 1996: 170)

Sihanouk seized the moment, and used the emergent nationalism to help legitimize his rule. In particular the government took steps to 'Khmerize' the state, putting in place the Buddhist lunar calendar, and using Khmer rather than French in the workings of government.

Following the Second World War, the French re-engaged in Cambodia, though with substantially less influence than they enjoyed in the pre-war era. Of the changes that were introduced in the years following the War, the introduction of the popular vote is particularly important. Three political parties were born at this time, the *Krom Pracheathipodei* (Democratic Party), the *Kanaq Sereipheap* (Liberal Party) and the Progressive Democrats (who quickly faded into obscurity). The Democratic Party, which favoured independence and democratic politics, gained the backing of the intellectual elite and the *Mahanikay* sect of the Sangha.[4] In contrast, the Liberal Party, preferring a gradual move to independence, was representative of the interests of the wealthy elite, the landowners and the Cham and Sino-Cambodian populations. The parties found further strength through the patronage system as the elites were able to rally support from their traditional clientele.

Following this initially positive start to democracy, there was a polarization of politics with the emergence of a right-wing anti-communist movement that was connected with King Sihanouk, and a growing left-wing resistance to the French presence in the country. The latter resulted in the formation of the Cambodian Communist party, the Khmer People's Revolutionary Party (KPRP) in 1951. The Democratic Party, which occupied the political middle ground, lost legitimacy as neither the French nor the monarchy were willing to work with it. Meanwhile the communists were cooperating with the Viet Minh, conducting guerrilla operations against French troops within Cambodia. It is important, though, not to overestimate the impact of this period of democracy on the country's population. David P. Chandler points out that for most Cambodians, the effect of independence would have been hard to notice. The central government remained uninterested: in his words 'indifferent' to the people (1996: 187).

King Sihanouk, working with the French, took power from the National Assembly in June 1952. Using foreign French troops Sihanouk surrounded the National Assembly, threw out the Democratic Party and subsequently appointed himself Prime Minister. When the Assembly refused to ratify his budget in January 1953, Sihanouk used the event to dissolve the Assembly. Over the next year Sihanouk then entered into negotiations with France for independence, winning control over all aspects of Cambodia's governance, except international trade, in October 1953. In March 1955 Sihanouk abdicated his throne, founded the *Sangkum Reastr Niyum* (People's Socialist Community) party, and ran for Prime Minister in a national election. The election, though the last to be popularly contested until 1993, was hardly 'free and fair'. The state used its coercive powers to limit the effectiveness of the opposition parties, including shutting newspapers that supported opposition parties, imprisoning newspaper editors, and harassing and in some instances killing candidates and party workers (in many ways this was to be echoed in the elections following the exit of UNTAC). The end result was that Sangkum won all the seats and over 75 per cent of the popular votes. This ushered in the era of Sihanouk's direct rule through the *Sangkum Reastr Niyum*, from 1953 until 1970. In 1962, Sihanouk formally dissolved the monarchy, an institution that had been present in Cambodia for over 1,000 years. That year also saw new Assembly elections in Cambodia and the outbreak of war in South Vietnam. Sihanouk attempted to use the Vietnamese conflict to Cambodia's benefit, playing the Americans and Soviets against one another. David P. Chandler (1996: 193) argues that Sihanouk's manoeuvring managed to save Cambodia from direct conflict between 1961 and 1970, in large part due to his declarations of neutrality. However, the ongoing war in Vietnam undermined Cambodia's economy, increased poverty and gradually destabilized the country.

There were some limited attempts during Sihanouk's indirect rule to introduce nascent forms of civil society outside of the Sangha and village structure.[5] Bit illustrates:

> Prince Sihanouk organized associations of special categories, such as youth, women, men and school children as an innovation in Cambodian society. The association served the political party's goals and were supervised closely by cadres but also provided a frame of reference for its members beyond the family and work experiences.
>
> (Bit 1991: 49)

Because of the close association of organizations with the political party, and with government, their independence was limited, and cannot be taken as a precedent for liberal forms of association. This state control of associational life would be replicated later under the People's Republic of Cambodia (PRK). This illustrates the ruling elite's awareness of the ways in which such associations can serve to socialize individuals and communities, and can be core sites for the legitimation of the political order. It also points to the ways in which there was no natural division between the areas of control of the state, and that of civil society. As a result these groups, and associational life more broadly, cannot be described as 'apolitical'.

The 1966 Assembly elections represent the end of Sihanouk's dominance over Cambodia's political development as General Lon Nol became the new Prime Minister and Sihanouk began to transfer the reins of power. The royalist government came to a formal end when the multiple pressures of the Vietnam War brought down Sihanouk's government in 1970 (Kiernan 1996: 18).[6] On 17 March 1970 Sisowath Sirik Matak led a coup that Lon Nol was forced to back by securing a National Assembly vote to depose Sihanouk. While the coup was welcomed amongst the educated elite in Phnom Penh and the Cambodian military, it shocked the countryside where Sihanouk remained popular (David P. Chandler 1996: 204). It also signalled the end of the country's neutrality in regional politics, as the new Lon Nol government shifted allegiance towards the US. This provided further impetus to the Cambodian communist guerrillas and contributed to the eventual victory of the KR (Brown and Zasloff 1998).

Cambodia, facing a guerrilla war on its own territory, was becoming increasingly entangled in the Vietnam War. Cambodia's communist movement, the KR, had been engaged in a protracted civil war with the Cambodian military and was initially beaten back into Cambodia's uplands. However, the American government had begun its secret war in Laos and Cambodia in the early 1970s. Numerous authors have placed the lion's share of the blame for the rise to power of the KR directly on the US bombing campaign (Mysliwiec 1988; Roberts 2001). During the early 1970s, predominately in early 1973, Americans dropped nearly 555,000 tons of bombs on Cambodia in an attempt to prevent the shipment of personnel and equipment from North to South Vietnam, and to disrupt Communist sanctuaries inside Cambodia (Deac 1997). This exceeded the amount of munitions dropped by the Allied forces during the entirety of the Second World War in Europe, equalling some 150 Hiroshimas. The resulting devastation caused massive loss of life, led to internal displacement, drastically reduced crop yields and pushed the country deeper into poverty. This combination of the policies of the Lon Nol regime and the American military strategy in the region created an environment where the millennialism of the KR was increasingly embraced by the rural population. Whether the KR was a peasant revolution, as Vickery (1984) asserts, or an elite-led peasant army as Peou (2000) argues, it was clearly a popular movement that derived its strength from the rural poor.[7] The movement picked up considerable support in the early 1970s and began to push back the Cambodian military. On 17 April 1975 the KR walked into Phnom

Penh, signalling the beginning of the new state, and the start of a drive to redesign Cambodian society.

It is easy now to forget that the KR did enjoy considerable popular support, and that their arrival in Phnom Penh, as with much of the country, was welcomed. This was not to last. By the time Vietnam invaded in December 1979 nearly half a million Vietnamese had fled Cambodia, the physical infrastructure of the country had been destroyed, and perhaps upwards of one million Cambodians had died from a combination of famine, disease and political violence. The *Angkar* (organization), as the KR referred to itself, was styled as a form of communist movement following in the steps of Stalin.[8] The leadership envisioned a forced transformation of society and undertook dramatic and horrible measures to achieve it. In trying to do so the Angkar initiated policies for 'Year Zero' for the country, which it renamed Democratic Kampuchea (DK). The choice of terminology is itself indicative of the movement, representing a complete break with the recent past, and an attempt to re-imagine society. The KR sought to level society and to remake everyone in the image of the ideal peasant worker. This was combined with an economic plan that focused, at least at the outset, on the production of rice. Contrary to common assertions that the KR wanted to establish a strict agricultural society, it is now clear that the aim was to use the export of rice to provide the means for later industrialization in a form that would be controlled by the KR. The leadership had a utopian vision of the future of the country that required a complete restructuring of the state's economy and society.[9]

We cannot ignore the issue of Cambodian society and identity in any analysis of the KR. The Angkar was preoccupied with this issue, striving to achieve some idealized image of a presumed past 'Khmerness'. In seeking to remake Khmer identity they set out to break down all perceived impediments to this process and tried to eradicate sources of cultural 'pollution'. This included education, which was deemed to promote foreign values. Religion was similarly attacked, and its practice was banned as a competing ideology. Monks were defrocked and sent into the rice fields alongside the rest of Cambodians, and many of the Wats, predominately in the rural areas, were sacked and burned, while others were turned into storage sites (Vickery 1984: 179).

It is the evacuation of urban centres, which created around one million new peasants, that has been the most discussed aspect of the KR's drive to create its new society. These people became, in the lexicon of the Angkar, 'New Cambodians', and as such were not seen as equals by much of the rural Khmer, but were invested with the *potential* to become a part of the new Kampuchea. The exodus itself was not a simple matter; groups of people were moved throughout the country, with communities, villages and families split up and moved to entirely different parts of the country. The moves to eliminate the non-Khmer and non-worker influences were systematically applied with results that continue to affect Cambodia today.

In May 1975 Pol Pot and Nuon Chea, who in conjunction with Ieng Sary formed the core leadership of the KR, stated their intention to expel anyone of Vietnamese background (Kiernan 1996: 107).[10] All schools were closed and Cambodians that were perceived as educated (wearing glasses was often sufficient to draw the attention of the KR) were re-educated, if not executed.

Perhaps the most damaging aspect of the KR legacy for the long-term democratization of the state was the attempt to unravel the family. The KR turned to collectivization in 1977, with the goal of eliminating vestiges of private ownership, and to control and manage the Cambodian population more effectively. As a part of this process, children were taken away from their parents and moved into communal child-rearing arrangements. At the same time, the children, seen as being unpolluted by bourgeois ideals, were often encouraged to be distrustful of their parents and siblings. Bit has described the purpose underlying these moves. 'The intent behind these policies was to negate the distinctiveness of the original family and recreate the Cambodian family as a collective political entity, with political authorities now in the role of parental figures' (Bit 1991: 47). From the standpoint of critical scholarship that highlights the connection between identity and security in modern state politics, such policies make a perverse sense. The notion that everyone within a geographically delineated political system, the modern state, should share a common identity is a modern phenomenon, one that is not connected to a prior form of Cambodian politics.

These policies have had far-reaching implications for Cambodian society. As one of the first INGO representatives in Cambodia after the expulsion of the KR from Phnom Penh in 1980, Mysliwiec was well placed to report on the effects of the policies enacted in DK:

> One Khmer told an aid official that one of the more serious effects of the Khmer Rouge regime was the destruction of the traditional relationships within the family, especially between children and parents. Children who had been separated from their parents and taught to report on them, today no longer have the traditional respect for them.... A Khmer man told an NGO representative that it is hard to overcome the fears inherited from the Khmer Rouge regime.
>
> (Mysliwiec 1988: 11)

Numerous authors have noted the impact of the KR on undermining the trust between Cambodians. In fact the trend is to blame much of the country's current woes, especially the centrality of violence in the resolution of conflict, on the KR leadership. While being cautious about placing all of the blame for the country's problems in recent years on the KR, Downie and Kingsbury (2001: 50) note how the KR has had lasting effects on some aspects of social life:

> While it is sometimes easy to blame the Khmer Rouge for many of Cambodia's shortcomings, three aspects of contemporary social and administrative behaviour can be attributed to experiences during that period: reluctance to trust, to plan, and to make decisions. During the Khmer Rouge period, through experience, people realized they could not trust friends, neighbours, siblings, or even their own children. This lack of trust has remained, and has hampered the development of civil society, and can be seen in the lack of co-operation and co-ordination between associations and NGOs.

These observations have important ramifications for current drives to instil a Western liberal form of civil society. The foundations of social structure were torn asunder, and social organizations were replaced with one political entity, the Angkar. In the words of one Cambodian:

> They attacked the individualist idea successively, in material terms, in terms of thought, and in terms of feelings. Materially, we had to denounce those who had more than the people. In terms of thought, each of us had to keep an eye on everyone else, to disclose any attitude that didn't conform to the line of the party. Everything was interpreted: words, gestures, attitudes.
>
> (Ong Thong Hoeung, cited in David P. Chandler 1991: 284)

The way in which the Angkar came to maintain control, through intimidation, violence, and the undermining of trust amongst people, has hampered attempts to re-instil characteristics associated with liberal forms of civil society. Downie and Kingsbury relate how some current problems in conflict resolution are legacies of the social upheaval wrought by the KR:

> Cambodian society was polarized from top to bottom, cutting across political, economic, social, religious, ethnic and familial lines, and the effects of this are impacting on the development of civil society. The concept of neutrality has been difficult for Cambodians to accept, as politically or militarily, everyone was regarded as partisan, either 'with us, or against us'.
>
> (Downie and Kingsbury 2001: 51)

Cambodia experienced a systematic erosion of trust, peaceful social interaction and non-violent forms of conflict resolution during the KR era. This is precisely what civil society is supposed to be able to re/introduce during peacebuilding, and it is the theoretical underpinning behind the move to build an LNGO sector. Civil society, as an associational space, is presented as a means of imbuing a community with trust, cooperation and responsibility. The difficulty is that the literature on civil society has little to say about situations where nearly all forms of social trust have been systematically torn apart. As will be shown, both within the remainder of this chapter, and in the subsequent case studies of state–NGO interaction, there has been a fundamental struggle in Cambodia to define the scope of civil society and the state; a struggle that challenges the liberal conceptualization of civil society.

Post-Khmer Rouge

It was not internal unrest that brought an end to KR domination; rather the regime's military expeditions across the Vietnamese border resulted in Hanoi's invasion of Cambodia and its ousting of the KR.[11] Vietnam crossed the frontier in force on 25 December 1978, and was able to quickly push the KR westward, and within two weeks the Vietnamese captured Phnom Penh, on 7 January 1979.[12] The Vietnamese put in place a Communist government under Cambodian leadership, and appointed Heng Samrin, who had fled the KR to Vietnam, as President of the new People's Republic of Kampuchea (PRK).

The invasion (or liberation), brought an end to the KR experiment and provided a window through which the world could see the extent of the horrors of the KR period.[13] The droughts that had hit Southeast Asia in the mid-1970s had exacerbated the impact of the KR leadership's plans to restructure the state, and doomed the attempts to refocus the economy around rice production. Between the execution of Cambodians, and the deaths caused by famine and disease in the rice fields, society was devastated and unable to provide for its own basic needs.[14]

Cambodia was in the midst of a complex humanitarian emergency. The Vietnamese state and the government installed in Phnom Penh were initially supportive of the international response to the Cambodian famine and internal displacement:

> Vietnam's role in staving off further socio-economic decline in the immediate aftermath was important. Despite much anti-PRK/Vietnamese propaganda, Vietnamese officials were ready to co-operate with aid deliveries that were made available, according to early missions from Oxfam organised by Jim Howard.
>
> (Roberts 2001: 50)

During this period the aid agencies delivering assistance were faced with problems providing humanitarian assistance to rural areas that the government did not control. 'While the aid helped the Heng Samrin regime to set up government offices and carry out some rehabilitation programmes in the 1980s, it did nothing to address the underlying causes of conflict or to build durable state institutions' (Chong 2002: 197). The INGOs and the UN response in 1979 and 1980 focused on children and food relief. Chong cites how the International Committee of the Red Cross (ICRC) and UNICEF fought hard with the Heng Samrin government for permission to feed people throughout the state, not just in government-controlled areas (ibid.). However, international assistance from Western governments, international organizations, and INGOs was short-lived (Cambodia did continue to receive assistance from the Soviet Union and Vietnam).[15] The international humanitarian assistance that flowed into the country was limited to emergency relief, and work on broader development issues was neither feasible (given the centrality of dealing with the aftermath of the KR and the food emergency), nor allowed by either the Samrin government, or the international community.

After the initial humanitarian relief, the realities of Cold War politics set in. Cambodia, backed as it was by both Vietnam and the Soviet Union, was isolated by the West. In one of the crueller ironies of the twentieth century, the American government chose to recognize the KR government rather than accept the communist party installed by Vietnam. The result was that the de-facto government in Phnom Penh was not recognized by the United Nations; the seat was occupied by a KR representative, and the North took measures to cut off any assistance to the new government. Nor was the global South, led by the non-aligned movement, willing to legitimate the Vietnamese-backed regime as they refused to countenance external interventions into states' internal affairs. This meant that the West continued to support the KR and Royalist factions rather than legitimizing the PRK.

It is possible that the Vietnamese military and the army of the PRK might have been able to limit the impact of the KR and the other rebel groups that had taken up arms against the perceived occupation by Vietnam. However, the Thai and American governments began supporting the rebel forces. Roberts (2001: 8) argues that the US chose to use the opportunity to seek to undermine Vietnam's post-1975 communist regime. This gave the various factions the excuse to sustain a guerrilla war against the PRK throughout the 1980s. There were three main guerrilla groups: Prince Sihanouk's party (FUNCINPEC), Son Sann's Khmer People's Liberation Front (KPNLF), and the Party of Democratic Kampuchea (PDK) which was the heir of the KR.[16] During a meeting in Kuala Lumpur, Malaysia, in June 1982 the three factions agreed to establish the Coalition Government of Democratic Kampuchea (CGDK), to provide a common voice; Prince Sihanouk became the president, Son Sann the premier, and Khieu Samphan the Vice-President in charge of foreign affairs. They were bound together in an uneasy alliance, but continued to fight the Phnom Penh government through the next decade.

The second way in which the West worked to isolate Cambodia was through limiting assistance to the government. This was translated into the severance of virtually all official aid to Cambodia. Western states and the UN suspended all direct and indirect funding to the Cambodian state. This had an immediate impact on INGOs that relied on government and

UN support, leading most organizations to withdraw from the country; few organizations were willing to work in Cambodia and risk losing funding from state sponsors (Mysliwiec 1988). Chantou Boua illustrates how it was only those large groups with stable sources of funding that were willing to remain in the country. 'A dozen or so international NGOs responded to their needs. One of them was the AFSC [American Friends Service Committee],... (o)thers from America included Church World Service, Oxfam America, and the Mennonite Central Committee (MCC)' (Boua 1993: 275). With these exceptions Cambodia was denied Western development aid during the Vietnamese occupation.

The organizations that did work in Cambodia during this period were restricted in their movements and activities by the PRK (Chong 2002). NGOs were limited to working as advisors to government, and to providing various forms of scientific expertise. Though, as Curtis (1994: 37) has noted, they were able to assist the Heng Samrin regime to set up government offices and carry out some rehabilitation programmes in the 1980s, they were not accorded sufficient freedom to pursue their own development programmes. The INGOs did lobby the West to loosen their regulations on engagement with the PRK, and to recognize the de facto government, but were unable to compete with the strategic interests of either the non-aligned movement or the West (Boua 1993; Mysliewiec 1988). Owing to the limited nature of the INGO presence in Cambodia over this period, and the constrained nature of the work that they were allowed to engage in, it is reasonable to assert that the country had little exposure to NGO activity and Western liberal notions of civil society. The era of the PRK (1979–1989) was marked by a less violent central government, and a limited return to 'normal' patterns of life in much of central and eastern Cambodia: 'the government came to control roughly 80 per cent of the country' (Peou 2000).

In terms of civil society, the government saw a return to historic sites of socialization, such as the family and the Sangha.[17] Under the auspices of the central party a number of professional associations were also formed. However, these groups, including clubs, professional associations such as the Teachers' Association, and workers groups, were not independent of the state, and were closely entwined with the Party. This then represents a continuation of patterns of civil society–state interaction from the pre-KR governments. The liberal model of associational behaviour was not promoted by the Heng Samrin regime. Bit (1991) argues that Cambodia never developed independent institutions, outside of the Sangha, to deal with political or economic issues. When organization was needed, it was specific to a stimulus and did not endure after the particular issue or threat was addressed (Bit 1991: 11).

The peace process

While the Vietnamese forces were able to oust the KR from the main urban centres and from much of the country's lowlands, it was unable to gain control of the entire state, and the PRK's reach was tenuous beyond the western edge of the Tonle Sap. Cambodia thus descended into a protracted civil conflict as the Soviet and Vietnamese-backed government fought against the Western-backed rebel groups. The CGDK controlled roughly 20 per cent of the countryside, while the State of Cambodia (SOC) was able to exert its authority in the remaining 80 per cent. This does not translate into a complete absence of attempts to resolve the conflict through diplomacy. Brown and Zasloff (1998) argue that the first phase of talks, from 1979 to 1988, was dominated by the actors looking for opportunities to engage in negotiations. These were severely restrained by the structural dynamics of the Cold War, as well as by difficulties in determining who should talk with whom. According to Roberts (2001), the dynamics of the peace process were driven more by external concerns arising from the Cold War than by issues internal to Cambodia. In particular, Vietnam's role impeded a settlement, as both Beijing and Washington were unwilling to make any concessions, while on the other side Moscow was actively supporting Cambodia. There were sporadic attempts throughout the 1980s to break the impasse over how to end Cambodia's civil war. During the Kuala Lumpur meetings in June 1982, Sihanouk made a call for the UN's involvement to resolve the conflict, and called for a UN-supervised general election as a means of ending the violence. However, both the Kuala Lumpur meetings and Sihanouk's recommendations were roundly rejected by Vietnam as a 'gross, barbarous and unacceptable interference in the PRK's internal affairs' (UN GA A/RES/37/6, 28 October 1982).

Despite the inability of the international community to reach any consensus on how to deal with Cambodia, there were occasional efforts to redress the Cambodian conflict in the early- to mid-1980s. They were generally one-sided and were unable to break the walls that were erected between the various positions. It was not until the international environment changed in the late 1980s that serious negotiations became possible. According to David P. Chandler, the most significant change to the negotiating environment came about as a result of Vietnam's slow withdrawal of troops. '(T)he 1980s witnessed a gradual decline of Vietnamese military and political influence on the one hand (particularly after 1987) and a corresponding increase in the autonomy of the Cambodian government on the other' (David P. Chandler 1996: 228). At the same time as the withdrawal, there was a rapprochement in the works between the Soviet Union and the West. Gorbachev's July 1986 Vladivostock speech harkened a revised stance on East Asia, indicating that the Soviet Union would refocus its attention on internal matters. This helped to ease tensions with both

China and the United States at the same time as the ongoing normalization of relations between China and the United States.[18] Brown and Zasloff (1998) argue that the most significant change was Hun Sen's announcement that Vietnamese forces would leave Cambodia by September 1989. This opened space for the first informal talks between the main Cambodian factions, which took place in Bogor, Indonesia, 25–28 July 1988. There was also a series of personal meetings between Hun Sen and Sihanouk during this period. These were followed up by a new round of informal meetings: the first Jakarta Informal Meeting (JIM I) included the four Cambodian factions. From the first proposals that were circulated at this meeting there was a sense that there would have to be some form of interim government, and that the peace process would culminate in a nationally elected democratic government. While JIM I did not end in an agreement, there was significant movement on a core set of issues. The result was that the stage was set for a second round of talks. Despite some initial reservations over the usefulness of another round of informal talks, JIM II, was held on 19–21 February 1989. This paved the way for subsequent formal meetings in Paris, and demonstrated a willingness to negotiate by the various parties.

After a series of on-off meetings, the international community brought the leaders of the different factions together in Paris. The PRK had changed its name to the State of Cambodia (SOC) on 30 April 1989. These talks developed a framework within which the long-running civil war and Cambodia's international isolation might be ended. The process culminated in month-long talks that took place from 30 July to 30 August 1989 in Paris.[19] The four main Cambodian groups were present, led throughout by their respective leaders, Son Sann, Prince Norodom Sihanouk, Khieu Samphan and Hun Sen. There were also representatives from the permanent members of the UN Security Council and the Association of Southeast Asian Nations (ASEAN) as well as Laos, Vietnam, Australia, Japan, India, Canada, Zimbabwe, and the meetings were also regularly attended by the UN Secretary General, Javier Pérez de Cuéllar.[20] The agreements that were reached laid the groundwork for both UNAMIC and UNTAC.

The United Nations missions and setting the terms of peacebuilding

The Secretary General recommended in 1991 (S/23097 and Add.1) that an advance team of civilian and military officials be established to enter Cambodia rapidly in order to enforce the ceasefire reached in Paris. The UN advance mission UNAMIC, authorized subsequently in RES 717 (1991), involved an initial force of 268 military and civilian personnel, the first component of which arrived on the ground on 31 October 1991. With the release of the Secretary General's report (S/23218) on 14 November

1991, UNAMIC was declared to be operational.[21] From autumn of 1991 until early spring 1992, the United Nations continued to develop its plans for UNTAC, culminating in 19 February 1992 with the release of the Secretary General's Report (S/23613) which provided details of the mission's aims and means. Later that same month further details were provided, with the Secretary General's Report (S/23613/Add.1) of 26 February laying out a cost of US$1.2 billion, and recommended Yasushi Akashi to head UNTAC as the Secretary General's Special Representative for Cambodia. Two days later, on 28 February 1992, UN Resolution 745 (1992) approved this plan, directing that elections be held in May 1993, limiting the mission to 18 months. The mission itself was formally established on 15 March 1992, and absorbed UNAMIC.

Though UNTAC has been widely described as a peacebuilding mission, a greater examination of its goals and underlying logic is necessary. The intent behind UNTAC can be ascertained through a close reading of the UN documents, and of the public statements by UN representatives (Acharya *et al.* 1991). Running throughout the documents is an expressed desire not just to end the fighting, but also to redress the enduring sources of the civil conflict. Security Council resolution 668 is prefaced with the statement that it is: '*convinced* of the need to find an early, just and lasting peaceful solution of the Cambodian conflict' (S/RES/668 1990). In short, UNTAC needs to be seen as having sought to transform the nature of politics from one where violence was an acceptable means of resolving conflict to a more peaceful and less violent polity.

The PPA, which constituted the framework of the UNTAC mission and the ongoing peacebuilding after the formal exit of the UN, was informed throughout by a faith in the transformative power of liberal democratic governance and economics. The various parties were not motivated merely by a desire to end/suspend hostilities, but rather by the desire to alter the nature of politics and to address the underlying causes of the conflict. That the international community could impose peace on societies is assured in these types of actions. This faith is demonstrated within UN documents:

> [P]eace can be effectively imposed either by the international community or by foreign states. Attempts are currently being made to do this in Bosnia, Cambodia and Somalia. Such solutions are likely to require the long-term maintenance of peace-keeping forces, and the political independence of the occupied territory will be severely restrained.
>
> (UNRISD September 1993: 8)

When the agreement was reached on 23 October 1991, the result was an unprecedented package of UN-led reforms. The cost was set at US$1.2 billion, but the budget may have exceeded two billion (Acharya 1994: 229), and at the peak of the mission in November 1992, over 20,000 foreigners were working for the UN in the country, of whom 15,738 were in military uniform. In agreeing to take on this responsibility, the UN was moving into uncharted territory. The change in the international dynamic that allowed the development of a comprehensive peace plan to be put together also enabled the UN to consider a radical departure from its past styles of peacekeeping. For the first time the environment was such that an explicit attempt at the construction of a democracy could be undertaken. The centrality of the liberal ethos to the PPA, and thus to UNTAC, is described by Doyle and Suntharalinam:

> [O]ne of the Paris accord's most striking features was that the international community and the Cambodian factions agreed to a system of liberal democracy as the basis for its constitution. The Agreements specified all the elements necessary for a constitutional democracy: periodic and genuine elections; freedom of assembly and association including that for political parties; due process and equality before the law; and an independent judiciary.
>
> (Doyle and Suntharalinam 1994: 122)

It is clear from a reading of the UN documents, and from the public statements of UN representatives, that the cornerstone of this peace initiative would be the implementation of a democratic election. 'In the broadest sense the UN mission was to create conditions that would foster the growth of a democratic nation and society in Cambodia' (Farris 1994: 42). Building on Douglas Pike's 1989 survey of Cambodia, and drawing on Akashi's (1994: 213) statements, Lizée (2000) argues that the role of UNTAC was to put in place a democratic system of governance. He also shows how the assumption that democratic governance is the most effective means of achieving public safety leads to the desire to impose democratic institutions. Thus, UNTAC, and by default peacebuilding, should be understood as a decidedly liberal enterprise, seeking to alter the societal, political, and economic order in a way that mirrored the consensus in liberal global governance that was emerging in the North.

The approach that UNTAC adopted reflects the notion that conflict resolution requires broad-based reform of the underlying causes of conflict, and that democratic governance is the ideal method to provide for the peaceful resolution of political disputes. Faith in liberalism as a means to address the conflict was clear in the negotiations, planning and implementation of UNTAC. Akashi recognized this, arguing that 'the Paris Agreements were essentially based on the concepts of Western democracy' (Akashi 1994: 213). UNTAC's role within this was not only to hold elections, but also to minimize the use of violence in the lead-up to the democratic moment, and to begin providing the groundwork for the economic and civil development of the state. This programme for redeveloping the country involved seven separate components:

1. Human rights. A small office was established to monitor HR and to provide HR education.
2. Civil administration. UNTAC was given the mandate to manage directly five areas of governance in order to provide a neutral political environment for the lead-up to the elections: defence, public security, finance, information and foreign affairs.
3. Elections. The UN organized and conducted Cambodia's first popularly contested national elections.
4. Military. To ensure a free and fair election, the UN military force was to supervise the withdrawal of Vietnamese forces, oversee the cantonment and dismantling of the four parties' military forces, and to assist in the de-mining of the country.
5. Police. The UN would provide training and support to policing in Cambodia.
6. Refugee repatriation. The UN, led by staff from the office of the United Nations High Commissioner for Refugees (UNHCR), was to repatriate 365,000 refugees from the camps inside Thailand.
7. Rehabilitation.

The underlying faith in liberalism can be seen running throughout these various components, in particular in the imposition of human rights (where individual rights were advanced), and reforms to the civil administration and policing (where the drive was to separate the workings of these branches of government from the control of political parties).

What is notably absent from this list of activities is the formation of civil society. However, upon closer examination it becomes clear that civil society was expected to play a central role in peacebuilding. As was shown in Chapter 2, the existence of an independent civil society, with areas of interest clearly delineated from the state, is understood as an essential component to an effective liberal democracy. This is in addition to the ways in which NGOs are seen as important partners in development projects. In fact the logic of peacebuilding, based on the transformative power of democratic elections, and of a renewed civil society, is clearly evident throughout the PPA, as well as in the policy decisions that were made in UNTAC's implementation.

UNTAC and the promotion of NGOs

UNTAC did seek to foster the growth of civil society in Cambodia, focusing on supporting the expansion of the NGO sector. Prior to the deployment of UNAMIC there were only a handful of INGOs operating in the country, and no recorded local CSOs (if the liberal definition of associations as independent from the government is used). Over the course of the mission the growth of this sector was dramatic: after 18 months there were nearly 100 groups (both local and international) operating at the time of the UN-supervised general election. This was not a coincidence, but rather reflected a concerted effort by UNTAC to foster NGO growth (particularly within the HR and democratic governance sectors) as well as a more diffuse orientation towards fostering civil society.

The active campaigns to support the growth of LNGOs by UNTAC have been noted as a particular success (Jennar 1994; Hughes 2001; Downie and Kingsbury 2001). The PPA, in authorizing UNTAC to carry out HR awareness and civic education, and to organize a national election, recognized the importance of local capacity to monitor human rights in facilitating a move to democracy, and took steps to foster such expertise directly. In observing the growth of the HR sector, Hughes notes that: 'UNTAC's Human Rights Component was the first international agency to support and fund Cambodian non-governmental organizations as a means to prompt political reform, from 1991–1993' (2001b: 47). This support came in terms of direct contracts between the UN and domestic NGOs to work on human rights. The UN also provided these groups with materials, training, basic office costs and put in place a library for the various groups to make use of in their work (Boutros-Ghali and UN 1995: 50). As a result, by 1994 four HR groups had been established and were active in monitoring, advocating for and protecting human rights (Jennar 1994: 147). The expansion of this sector becomes more impressive when looked at over the following decade. Downie and Kingsbury state:

> Local NGOs began to emerge during the UNTAC period, numbered 100 in early 1996, and grew to more than 400 by mid-2000. This growth constituted a major step in the development of civil society, and hence political development.
>
> (Downie and Kingsbury 2001: 59)

This dramatic growth of NGOs operating in Cambodia is directly related to the policies put in place by the UN mission, and indirectly to the underlying logic of the liberal peacebuilding project.

The second manner in which UNTAC contributed to the growth of the number of NGOs was through its creation of a general environment where civil society could take hold. While the UN did not have a specific mandate to form NGOs, in providing for the freedom of assembly and communication UNTAC should be seen, from a liberal perspective, as enabling the development of a 'normal' civil society. Certainly, in the course of interviews with NGO representatives who had worked in Cambodia in the early 1990s, a general consensus emerged amongst interviewees that the UN had played a crucial part in facilitating their growth. However, some scholars have asserted that this expansion of civil society did not result directly from UNTAC policies, but is attributable instead to the international organizations and the international donors that entered the state after 1991. Moser-Puangsuwan asserts that the growth of local NGO activity in

Cambodia came about 'due to the intense international presence of many aid groups and media which flowed into Cambodia at the same time as UNTAC' (1995: 116). He further argues that in fact UNTAC did not work well with NGOs. However, his critiques misrepresent the role and purpose of UNTAC. We cannot treat it separately from the logic that underpins its mandate, and here the centrality of the liberal democratic model must be foregrounded. In short, UNTAC was a particular force that fit within a broader narrative of peacebuilding and liberal governance, a narrative that makes the facilitation of NGOs not only possible, but also necessary.

During the UNTAC era peacebuilding policies directly encouraged the expansion and entrenchment of civil society by supporting election monitoring and HR groups, and indirectly by working with INGOs in development projects, and putting in place legal reforms that enabled civil society to continue to grow. This was further strengthened by Northern aid dollars (much of which were funnelled through INGOs and LNGOs).

The 1993 elections

UNTAC was premised in large part on the transformative power of the democratic election. As such it is reasonable that the success or failure of UNTAC be judged in part by the success or failure of the elections. The problem of course is how does one assess this? Rather than arguing that the outcome of the election be adjudicated according to whether it met some democratic ideal, it should be assessed according to the extent to which it serves the broader goals of peacebuilding. From this perspective the success of the election process should be gauged according to whether it helped to transform Cambodian politics away from accepting violence as a means of addressing conflict. The numbers are impressive. There is consensus that at least 90 per cent of all eligible voters were registered, of which 85 per cent cast ballots.[22] The UN itself was predictably exuberant about its accomplishments. As Akashi stated: '(b)y UNTAC calculations, over 15,000 political meetings and assemblies were held, in which close to one million people participated, with little or no hindrance by the Phnom Penh regime or anybody else' (Akashi 1994: 206). The election day was remarkably peaceful; the fears of violence perpetrated by the KR were not realized. As one Cambodian observer, Um, argued in a summary of Cambodia's elections:

> Despite their threats and apparent capability, the Khmer Rouge did not unleash their destructive potential, partly reflecting recognition of their inability to stop the process, but fitting also into their overall strategy of doing just enough to affirm their opposition to a process in which they would be gravely disadvantaged and simultaneously to stress their continued viability as a force to be reckoned with.
>
> (Um 1994: 75)

The election results were surprising. Despite a system that appeared to favour the ruling CPP, Ranaridh's FUNCINPEC won the majority of seats, securing 45.47 per cent of the vote versus the CPP's 38.23 per cent, and was constitutionally able to form the government.[23] However, this did not happen. Following intense negotiations between FUNCINPEC and the CPP, a power-sharing arrangement was announced on 16 June 1993 that effectively ignored the election results.[24] Thus at the end of UNTAC's mission, there was a democratic election with broad popular participation, which resulted in the formation of a coalition that did not reflect the popular vote, but which did accommodate the power structure on the ground. The CPP, with its domination of the bureaucracy, was brought in as an equal partner in the governing of the state (in principle), and FUNCINPEC was able to co-rule. That this happened without resort to political violence has not been adequately noted in the critiques. From a standpoint where success is measured in terms of its creation of a system where violence was eschewed, the outcome of the vote should not be interpreted as a failure, even if it cannot be called an unqualified success.

Assessments of UNTAC

For many commentators, the actual deployment did not live up to the stated goals of the Peace Agreements. There is a wealth of criticisms of UNTAC that predominately focus on the extent to which UNTAC met its goals, and the degree to which liberal democracy has taken hold in the country. This is not to say that the criticisms are unwarranted: such studies help improve the way that peacebuilding is conducted, and point to poor decisions that may have been made in the implementation of the mission.

The most serious criticisms have been levelled at the failure of the UN on the military front. The main argument is that UNTAC was unable or unwilling to enforce the cantonment of the various factions' military forces; this has focused almost exclusively on the KR, which refused to abide by the PPA. The result of UNTAC's decisions not to confront the KR with military force effectively partitioned the country into two spheres: one in the control of the KR (effectively off-limits to UN personnel, as well as INGOs and LNGOs); and the other being under the influence of the Supreme National Council (SNC). While the decision of UNTAC not to use military force may have emboldened the KR leadership, the long-term consequences of this choice are not as apparent. Nor is it obvious whether a different choice by Akashi on the issue of the cantonment of the KR forces would have resulted in a better outcome. Armed conflict would not have been demonstrably supportive of the peace process. If the goal of peacebuilding is to transform the field of politics, reliance on armed force to bring about political negotiation should only be undertaken in the direst circumstances.

The second area of criticism is the perceived failure of UNTAC to reform Cambodian bureaucracy. Under the communist system put in place in 1979 there was no separation of Party and state bureaucracy. The state functioned as a part of the Party, and senior personnel in all of the ministries were members. The interim SNC, which was intended to assist in running the state until a government was formed, was never able to effectively supervise the CPP-dominated bureaucracy. In particular, UNTAC was unable to bring key ministries under its control, resulting in accusations of political impotence and arbitrariness on the part of UNTAC by opposition forces. Furthermore, because it dominated the machinery of governance, the CPP was able to use the government to its advantage during the election campaign, an assessment that many NGO workers claim continues to apply today, more than a decade later.[25] The value of the SNC was also undermined by political manoeuvring between FUNCINPEC and the CPP, a point described by Lizée (2000: 11):

> Political alliances were concluded between the partisans of then Prince Sihanouk, one of the main opposition groups, and prominent figures in the Phnom Penh government. These rendered the Cambodian Supreme National Council (SNC), the body set up by the Paris Agreement to become the guarantor of a 'neutral political environment' in Cambodia, meaningless.

The UN itself pointed to this area of failure:

> The inability of UNTAC to secure peace, and its limited achievements in the field of rehabilitation and development, are also closely tied up with the refusal of the Khmer Rouge to participate in the peace process and the failure of the different factions which make up the Supreme National Council (SNC) to work for compromise and national reconciliation.
>
> (UNRISD September 1993: 20)

It is unclear to what extent the UN could have rectified this problem. The SNC was ineffective in many regards, but it is uncertain what would have been a reasonable alternative.

The final criticism is that the outcome of the initial peacebuilding process, the election, was a failure, as the parties rejected the voter mandate in favour of a coalition government. As the political factions effectively threw out the election results in determining who would govern, there is some basis for this attack. Yet as was stated earlier, if peacebuilding is about the transformation of forms of conflict resolution away from the use of violence, then this political transition needs to be seen as a limited success. The holding of democratic elections, followed by negotiations between the parties, has become a recurring theme in Cambodia.

Continuation of peacebuilding post-UNTAC

The academic and policy communities have generally focused on the UNTAC era in their examinations of peacebuilding. Though this was the start of the international community's attempt to rebuild Cambodian society, peacebuilding did not end with the departure of the UN forces in 1993.[26] Clearly the attempt to alter the forms of conflict resolution within the state away from the use of violence is an ongoing process. The political alliance that had been made between the CPP and FUNCINPEC in 1993 began to unravel shortly after the agreement was made. There were underlying tensions between the two parties that were not resolved through the mid-1990s. Roberts argues that the coup can be traced back to the failure of the power sharing:

> the CPP had effectively refused to grant positions of authority to Ranariddh's followers at the grass roots level. Consequently, Ranariddh could not reward many of his supporters with posts at this level and they became dispirited.... The second problem is directly linked to this. Ranariddh was losing both power and face.
>
> (Roberts 2003: 251)

This is an argument that partially echoes Lizée's (1997) work, which highlights the growing tensions between the two parties as contributing to the violence in 1997. Öjendal and Antalov have described the ongoing political tensions amongst the two dominant political parties, the CPP and FUNCINPEC:

> Cambodia has had political trouble since at least 1995, with the two co-prime ministers hardly talking to each other. Public policy and development programmes were frozen, since the two coalition parties would not communicate. This is a difficult situation in any country: in Cambodia it was approaching chaos.
>
> (Öjendal and Antlov 1998: 531)

In fact, even while there was a power-sharing agreement in the mid-1990s, politics in Cambodia continued to be marked by violence in the years following the 1993 elections. While the election did bring three of the main parties into the government, it did not end the struggle with the KR, factions of which did not abide by the election results and resumed their armed struggle in the North and West of the country, albeit without the external support that had enabled the three political factions to carry an armed conflict with the PRK throughout the 1980s. In this respect the continued violence, though greatly diminished, indicates that the UN mission was only a partial success with respect to its capacity to resolve the sources of conflict.

While the fighting between the Cambodian government and the KR prohibited the development of the North West of the country, the most damaging impact the KR had in the post-War era was in its dissolution. When Ieng Sary set about to seize control of the KR leadership in August 1996, he exacerbated the power struggle between the CPP and FUNCINPEC as both parties sought to secure the backing of the remainders of the KR party and its military.

The two main parties, which had been cooperating only nominally, began to undertake negotiations with Ieng Sary to try to bring his faction of the KR onside. The potential power imbalance that this represented undermined the limited cooperation that had taken place. Events came to a head between 5 and 6 July 1997 with 48 hours of violence, during which Hun Sen seized control of the capital, resulting in Ranariddh's exile (Möller 1998: 1097). While there is a debate over whether the events that took place represented a coup, a nascent civil war, or the ambiguously labelled 'events of 1997', it is clear that the use of violence was still perceived as a legitimate tool of politics.

Troops loyal to the CPP were deployed around Phnom Penh, and there were a series of arrests of senior FUNCINPEC members.[27] The impact of this was far-reaching, and arguably the decisions of the international community to punish the state for the 'coup' were far more damaging than the violence itself. The US government suspended bilateral aid to the country, and did not resume direct assistance to the Cambodian government until 2001. This further strengthened the hand of civil society in Cambodia as development money was moved from direct state assistance to NGOs. It resulted in an increased fiscal capability on the part of NGOs, allowing them to extend their work, both in terms of geographic coverage and issue areas. This enabled NGOs to largely dictate the terms of development of the state, further eroding the government's capacity to determine how development dollars would be spent.

The subsequent national parliamentary elections on 26 July 1998, 27 July 2003, and 27 July 2008, and the commune council elections on 3 February 2002, and 1 April 2007, have been described by some as an unprecedented success.[28] The 1998 election was hailed by Stephen Solarz, a US congressman, as the 'miracle on the Mekong' (Downie 2000). Others, while observing that each election was generally more peaceful the last, note also that they were nevertheless short of being 'free and fair' (Downie 2000; interview, election-monitoring NGO representative, Phnom Penh, 3 September 2005).[29] In particular, the agency responsible for organizing the election in 1998, the National Election Commission (NEC), was seen to be a mouthpiece for the CPP, and was largely composed of CPP officials and supporters (noted by International Crisis Group 1998; National Democratic Institute 1998). At the same time, the initial pattern of undertaking negotiations between the parties following the elections (Möller 1998), has given way as the CPP has consolidated power at the state and commune level.

In examining the way that the opposition parties used the elections, Hughes (2002a) argues that the election may have in fact been deleterious for the average Cambodian, and was certainly so for ethnic minorities. She points out how both FUNCINPEC and the Sam Rainsy Party (SRP) relied heavily on ethno-nationalist rhetoric to garner support.[30] The result is that this fed into the already xenophobic narratives of Cambodian identity. What is found then is that peacebuilding, in demanding an opening up of the democratic process, is not operating in an environment that is free of previous meanings; it must be seen as being embedded in previous politics, and as potentially reinforcing previous security practices. That the NGO sector was unable to ameliorate this process should tell us that it is problematic to assume that the growth of the NGO sector in Cambodia should herald in the groundwork for a liberal democracy.

NGOs and post-UNTAC peacebuilding

As has been argued, UNTAC provided both direct and indirect support for the emergence of civil society within Cambodia. However, the truly remarkable increase in the number of NGOs in the country followed this initial stage, occurring over the next decade of peacebuilding.

The numbers of NGOs active in the country over the past six years is more difficult to measure as the Consultative Group Meetings no longer report on NGO numbers. However, while there has likely been a reduction in the overall number of NGOs over the past few years, the sector is still robust, with over 228 LNGOs registered with the Cooperation Committee for Cambodia (CCC), which represents a small portion of the NGOs operating in the country (registration entails costs and commitments to particular guidelines) (CCC 2011). The way in which NGOs have become a main tool of development, as was laid out in Chapter 2, has been well-documented elsewhere, and the dynamics particular to Cambodia have been discussed by Downie and Kingsbury (2001), Hughes (2002b), and Kao and CICP (1999a, 1999b). What these authors point out is that the growth in the number of NGOs operating in Cambodia resulted from a number of policies that had as their primary or secondary goal the

Table 4.1 Number of NGOs operating in Cambodia[31]

Year	*Number of Cambodian NGOs*	*Number of INGOs*	*Total*
1992	12	56	68
1994	95	85	180
1996	231	120	351
1998	249	153	409
2000	360	172	532
2001	384	185	569
2002	407	200	607
2005	790	339	1,129

Table 4.2 ODA pledges and disbursements, 1992–2005[32] (in millions of US$)

	1992	*1994–1998*	*1999–2003*	*2004*	*2005 preliminary*	*Total 1992–2005*
Pledges	1,000	2,284.2	2,255.2	...	504.2	6,043.6d
Disbursements	572.1	2,205.9	2,408.8	555.4	524.9	6,267
Disbursements as a percentage of pledges	57.2	77.6	80.9	...	95.2	76.9

creation of a Cambodian civil society. Perhaps the most important influence on the growth of the NGO sector was the increase in development funding after 1991. The money flowed into an environment where the government was seen as being incapable of delivering a broad range of development projects, seemingly necessitating the funding of NGO programmes. From 1999 to 2003, 8.8 per cent of disbursements were direct from NGOs. We see then an significant monetary capacity of the NGO sector in the country, providing them with considerable power.

Simultaneously, there was a movement towards grassroots, or bottom-up, development projects, which NGOs were perceived as being better placed to design and implement. The notion that civil society is more responsive to local level needs has informed this dynamic, though the majority of NGO headquarters, where decisions about programming are made, are located in Phnom Penh. This then resulted in considerable amounts of direct aid being funnelled through local and international and NGOs. In turn this funding provided the financial capacity for a large number of organizations to form and deliver projects.

The next issue that must be addressed is that the promotion of civil society is, in itself, now seen as a development goal, rather than a tool. Hughes has stated:

> (c)ivil society analysis has featured prominently in the prescriptions of international activists working in Cambodia, and has been adapted by Cambodian reformers as a framework for action. It was central to the conceptions of political change and, in particular, human rights protection[.]
>
> (Hughes 2001b: 47)

For this reason today LNGOs are being sought out as development partners, and are included in a variety of development projects. International donors, such as the Canadian International Development Agency (CIDA), the Swedish International Development Agency (SIDA), and USAID, have all sought 'local partners', which has fostered the growth of the NGO sector. In addition, INGOs have also endeavoured to 'localize' projects, seeking LNGO partners for their development work.

Besides the promotion of civil society as a goal of development, the growth of the NGO sector in Cambodia is also seen as a core component of alleviating the poverty of Cambodians. Wages for people working in NGOs are considerably higher than the national average, providing the possibility for a substantial increase in a person's quality of life. The manner in which NGOs have become a crucial part of the economy was made clear on a number of occasions when young Cambodians expressed their desires to eventually get jobs with an NGO in the country. I was often asked by my *moto-dop* (scooter) drivers for references to apply for jobs at various organizations. When I asked them about this, they all related how these organizations pay more than the government and are seen by many as offering better career opportunities. This has in fact been the subject of some debate as the entire aid sector has resulted in a skewing of the local economy, where NGO workers contribute to a second economy out of the reach of average Cambodians. This negative impact has been noted by the United Nations Research Institute for Social Development (UNRISD), which stated: '[i]t is apparent, however, that the sudden influx of international agencies and aid has contributed to serious social and economic problems' (UNRISD 1993: 20). It should be pointed out, however, that in the NGO sector there is an effective division between the international employees and consultants, and the majority of Cambodians employed with either international or local NGOs. Though the Cambodians are paid more than the general population, their wages do not approach what is provided to foreigners.[33]

The expansion of the NGO sector has been further supported by a final dynamic that is at play in development policy. In Chapter 2 it was discussed how peacebuilding narratives serve to describe Southern governments as corrupt and inept. This pattern has certainly been followed in Cambodia, where the government is often represented in precisely these terms. This has served to encourage the growth of the NGO sector by pushing international donors to work through local civil society, rather than the state. This process was intensified when governments chose to suspend direct support of the Cambodian state following the violence in 1997.

The end result of all of these processes coming together in Cambodia has been a dramatic growth in the numbers of NGOs, which has been generally lauded in the academic and policy communities. This support of civil society not only continued after the end of the formal UN mission, but it has actually increased. Furthermore, as with the earlier UN mission, the promotion of civil society has, in policy terms, continued to focus on the creation of NGOs rather than broader forms of associations. In part this is a result of the funding for civil society creation flowing through development agencies that wish to see various projects implemented in Cambodia, which lends itself to a support of LNGOs.

The extent of economic growth

The logic of peacebuilding is not limited to the importance of democratic governance, but also advocates the liberalization of markets, and integration into the world economy, as core components of conflict resolution. This aspect of peacebuilding took on greater relevance in the years following the cessation of the formal UN mission, and as such is often not treated as a part of the peacebuilding mission. Yet the logic is consistent with peacebuilding, and it is advocated by the large international donors, including states and international institutions such as the WB and the IMF. This linkage between economic reform and peacebuilding is explicit in the work of the International Committee for the Reconstruction of Cambodia (ICORC), a consortium of international donors and NGOs that seeks to coordinate the development activities of the state.[34] In observing their work, Um illustrates how, following the end of the formal UN mission, the ICORC made the decision during its meeting in Tokyo, March 1994, to shift its attention to economic matters, reflecting a change from '"recovery" to "long-term reconstruction"' (1995: 79). The economic reforms that the ICORC advocates are firmly within the neoliberal economic framework, and have sought to further bind Cambodia into the broader patterns of liberal global governance.

The condition of the economy in the early 1990s was dire, with the state producing little for export, foreign revenues often arising from illegal sales of natural resources, an agricultural sector that was unable to meet the country's basic food needs and spiralling inflation in Phnom Penh driven by the foreign currency and high wages of international development workers. Not surprisingly, economic growth in Cambodia was initially slow, hampered by both internal and external factors. However, the Cambodian government has made concerted efforts to boost the economy and to try to integrate into regional markets.[35] Cambodia is pursuing liberalization as a means of improving the quality of life within the state. As such, the state has undertaken numerous market reforms, opening the economy up to external investment and competition. The government pursued membership of the World Trade Organization (WTO), gaining entry on 13 October 2004 (though it is unclear whether the state has made all of the necessary changes to meet WTO demands in terms of legal transparency).[36] Fiscal reforms were also made, including floating the Cambodian currency, the Riel, and directing the National Bank of Cambodia to focus on inflation control through restrictions to the money supply.

The results of this process have been mixed, though observers do argue that Cambodia can see economic progress, and is making the necessary policy choices (the value of liberal markets goes unquestioned in this literature) to improve the economic situation. The economic indices have been positive since 1994. Peou has illustrated the strides the economy is taking:

> Economic growth was negligible in 1997. The government's early target was a growth rate of around 7.5% (others estimated it would be around 7%); before the coup, the official forecast was down to 6.5%; and by October the Finance Ministry admitted that growth was negative in the second half of 1997 and would be flat for the whole year.
>
> (Peou 1998a: 72)

Since 1997 the country has made remarkable strides in some economic sectors. From 2002 onwards Cambodia has consistently recorded some of the highest economic growth in Asia. In particular, the state has effectively nurtured a garment industry and a tourism trade. Relying on cheap labour and a stable working environment (unions are tightly controlled), the garment industry, non-existent in 1993, is now the seventh largest – in export terms – in the world. The sector increased at an annual rate of 40 per cent between 1995 and 2006, from representing 1.3 per cent of the gross domestic product (GDP) in 1995, to 15.9 per cent in 2006 (CDRI 2008: 41). This accounts for 82 per cent of all exports by value ('Cambodia's garment industry has evolved', *Business Wire*, 9 May 2008). Tourism, driven by interest in the Angkor Wat temple complexes, has also boomed; Cambodia's Tourism Minister, Sam Prona, expected three million foreign tourists in 2008. In 2007 the country welcomed over two million tourists, earning US$1.4 billion (the numbers have remained over two million in 2008 and 2009).[37] Rice production, which 85 per cent of the Cambodian population relies upon for direct and indirect jobs, rose from 2,500 metric tons in 1990 to 6,264 tons in 2006.[38] At the same time yield per hectare has increased to 2.4 tons from yields in the 1960s of 1.6 tons.[39] This all points to an improving economy, which is supported by the growth of GDP.

As impressive as these economic statistics are, they must be interpreted alongside an examination of the human development indicators used by the United Nations and other development agencies. What is found is that while there has been improvement in a number of areas, there are also some points of concern. On the positive side, the state has managed to increase the average income, reduce child mortality rates and raise the average life expectancy. However, Cambodia remains near the bottom of all development indicators amongst East and Southeast Asian states. In 2011 the United Nations Development Programme (UNDP) rated Cambodia's Human Development Index (HDI) at 0.523, placing it one hundred and thirty-ninth in the world, slightly behind Myanmar, and just outside of

Table 4.3 Cambodian GDP growth

	1990	*1995*	*2000*	*2002*	*2003*	*2004*	*2005*	*2006*
GDP annual change (%)	1.2	6.5	8.4	6.9	8.5	10.0	13.5	10.8

their measurement of 'least developed countries', which have an HDI of 0.518.[40] This rating moved to 0.598 in the 2007/2008 UNDP report, though the country moved down one rank to one hundred and thirty-first.[41] The benefits of economic growth have not been equally distributed, with the gains coming to urban areas and accruing principally to the top echelons of society. In a country that is overwhelmingly rural, this is worrisome. The WB's own statistics show a drop in overall poverty rates in the country from 47 per cent in 1993/1994 to 35 per cent in 2004. However, it also states that this decline in poverty has been focused on the urban centres, leaving the 70 per cent of the population that lives in the countryside behind. In terms of the rise in inequality, the countryside represents 86 per cent of the increase.[42] Benefits from the liberalization of markets, and the impressive growth rates that Cambodia has experienced, have not been evenly distributed, resulting in an increasing gap between the rich and poor.

In economic terms, peacebuilding has been a mixed success, assessed using its own systems of measurement. The economy has expanded in some sectors, which has translated into improved quality of life for some portions of society. The economic growth, combined with development money, has brought investment into infrastructure, improving roads, sanitation, access to potable water, and a more reliable power grid. Improved rice production has meant that the state is now self-reliant on this staple, and has begun generating revenue for rural Cambodia through rice exports.

Conclusions

The process of immanent critique entails an assessment of theories and practices according to their own principles. This chapter has briefly explored the history leading up to the deployment of the UN mission in 1991, and then examined both the mission itself, and the subsequent reconstruction in the years following the exit of the UN in 1993. Peacebuilding is supposed to address the causes of conflict and to transform the manner in which conflicts are resolved when they emerge. Peacebuilding, as a component of liberal global governance, undertakes to achieve these ends through political, economic and social reforms. In political terms, peacebuilding entails the introduction of democratic governance. The UN was able to hold an election in May 1993 with an exceptionally high percentage of people casting ballots. At the same time, the results were taken more as a guide to how the state would be governed, as the parties subsequently negotiated how to share power. This is a pattern that continued in 1998 and 2003, but as a consequence of increasing electoral support for the CPP. The 26 July 2008 election saw Hun Sen secure 58.11 per cent of the vote and win 72 of 123 seats.[43] The use of violence to resolve conflicts has diminished, though not entirely disappeared. The rule of law has improved gradually, but the system remains opaque and elites are able to manipulate the system effectively for their own benefit. As such, peacebuilding can be seen to have been a partial success, though clearly the imposition of a liberal democratic institutional framework has not translated into a liberal democratic political structure.

In terms of economic change, peacebuilding has brought the country along the path of economic liberalization. The country has been opened to the global market, and has endeavoured to take advantage of its labour costs, resources, and tourism potential for economic growth. The numbers point to great strides being taken, with the country joining the WTO in 2006, posting the highest GDP growth rates in Southeast and East Asia over the past decade, and dramatically increasing its levels of tourism. However, these numbers only tell a part of the story, as poverty reduction has been less successful. Cambodia remains one of the poorest states in the region, as economic growth has advantaged the Cambodian urban elite, while rural communities remain mired in poverty. Thus, as a form of addressing sources of conflict, economic liberalization has also been only a partial success (if assessed simply as the alleviation of poverty).

Finally, in terms of its ability to alter social relations, and instil cultures of peace, peacebuilding has focused on civil society reconstruction, which in policy terms has meant the support of NGOs. The direct, and indirect, support of this sector has led to a remarkable explosion in the number of NGOs in the country. However, the reading of Cambodia's history of associational behaviour illustrates that liberal assumptions about the working of civil society cannot be generalized to Cambodia. The country had little, if any, experience with an associational space separate from both the family and the state. The extent to which this sector has then been able to foster peace by reducing the sources of conflict, and changing the ways in which conflicts are resolved, must then be examined in greater depth. As the following chapters demonstrate, the growth of civil society has led to new dynamics of conflict.

5 State intervention in NGOs for personal gain

According to peacebuilding theory, the introduction of democratic forms of governance, liberal economics and civil society, defined by Paris (2004) as the liberalization of the target states, should lay the groundwork for a sustainable peace within the targeted country. The expectation is that civil society associations should be able to help articulate community interests, teach people how to interact peacefully, and even while civil society is supposed to be apolitical it is also expected to act as a check on abuses by the state and the empowerment of local communities (David Chandler 1999: 111). The promotion of civil society is believed to contribute to the reduction of conflict within and between communities. In exploring one of the areas of tension between some NGOs and the state, this chapter seeks to understand whether the conflict is a result of the introduction of civil society to Cambodia or whether its expansion has ameliorated or resolved the underlying causes of conflict. In this way, peacebuilding is being held accountable to its own internal norms, a core component of immanent critique (Pearson and Salter 1999: 486).

This chapter focuses on a particular dynamic of conflict between NGOs and the state relating to resource extraction. While the issue area is traced to the economic policies of peacebuilding, and will be shown to be consistent with the broader push for liberalization, this is not the focus of the chapter. Rather attention will be paid to how civil society groups have interacted with the state over resource extraction issues, and when conflict has occurred, whether this is consistent with the expectations of liberal associational understandings of civil society. To address this issue, three main sectors of resource exploitation (fisheries, land titling and forestry) that have experienced state interference in NGO work will be examined. Sex work is also included in this section since some of the difficulties of addressing issues in this sector arise from the wealth generated by powerful individuals. In each instance the ways in which NGOs have been involved in conflict with the state will be described and related to the associational conceptualization of civil society. After these empirical examples the chapter turns to a discussion of the commonalities across the sectors and how these can be understood from within the liberal framework. This then forms the basis of the immanent critique of peacebuilding, as the dynamics of the conflict are related to the broader liberal associational theories of civil society.

Conflicts over resource extraction

During interviews with representatives of NGOs in Cambodia, there was broad agreement that the most difficult sectors for groups to work in were resource-based, where the needs of communities were pitted against the interests of Cambodian elites. This was widely described as the most violent area of NGO work; organizations that were involved in resource issues reported that their members had to deal with direct and indirect violence, that there could be significant pressure from the state to limit their groups' activities and that communities that worked with NGOs were pushed by the state to stop working with civil society actors. This form of conflict between civil society groups and the state points to the role of personal power politics in Cambodia, and highlights how the power of individuals and the powers of the state are not separated. This does not mean that the government has a coherent policy to intervene in the works of NGOs operating in the resource sector; rather that some individuals have been able to use the state's infrastructure for their personal gain. However, in a country where the separation between personal power and politics is narrow at best, we must treat this as a form of state intervention in the work of NGOs.

The fallacy of a separation between state and individual power

The upper echelons of Cambodian society are able to manipulate the political and economic system to their benefit, influencing the implementation of rules and regulations, the enforcement – or non-enforcement – of rules and laws (including whether court cases are heard or not), as well as directly affecting the outcome of such cases. A network of NGOs noted in 2002 that:

> Impunity in one section of the society – politicians and officials, their families and their friends, the military and the rich – means that Cambodia is a country with two laws – one for the rich and powerful and one for the poor. Political interference with the judiciary, together with the ability to buy justice and practice of permitting a privileged section of society to be above the law, mean that rights of property and contract cannot be guaranteed in Cambodia.
>
> (NGO Economic, Social and Cultural Rights Monitoring Committee 2002: 7)

The capacity of individuals to use the state for their benefit extends beyond administrative and legal measures, and includes the capacity to call upon elements of the military and police for their own aggrandizement. As a result, the separation between individual and state power becomes blurred. This in itself does not challenge the liberal associational literature, but rather reinforces one of its core arguments that civil society has an important role to play in protecting communities and individuals from state abuses. It is therefore reasonable to treat the issue of personal pursuit of interests as state policy when it is the state's powers that are being mobilized. However, it should be said that just as the state can be mobilized by powerful individuals, as local civil society emerges from the same society, then it is reasonable to assume that some NGOs can be used in similar ways.

It is important to point out coopting the state for personal advantage is not officially condoned by the central government in Phnom Penh. Indeed, the government has taken a vocal stance against such patterns of abuse. Yet despite the official position on the matter, the country continues to face endemic corruption.[1] In discussing corruption in Cambodia, the policy literature from NGOs has noted how conflicts involving personal interests continue to be an enduring problem, and allegations are made regularly of biased legal decisions, of government corruption and of the interests of the powerful superseding those of poor communities. Within peacebuilding literature, such activities are deemed problematic and liable to hold back development. For the sake of this project, the state's high levels of corruption are indicative of the ways in which some elites presume the state should be working on their behalf.

Interviews with representatives of NGOs that either worked directly on these issues, or those working with communities engaged in struggles around access to resources, demonstrated a consistent proclivity towards direct intervention by the state into their groups' activities. At the same time, there are variations of the pattern across the different forms of resources, with each of the sectors – forestry, fisheries, land titles and sex work – having its own unique characteristics.[2] These in turn have affected the manner in which the conflicts have been resolved, and the nature of the relationship between NGOs and the state. According to the representative of an umbrella group for HR NGOs:

> We have succeeded best when there are less concerns with the interests of high ranking officials. When we try to advocate for the poor we run up against personal interests. However, when there is less personal interest we get a good response from government.[3]

This points to a perception by NGO workers that programmes that are likely to disrupt the power base of Cambodia's elites are liable to result in state intervention in their activities. This pattern is particularly apparent when NGOs seek to engage directly in resource-based disputes between communities and individuals.

Conflicts over access to fisheries

The first area to be discussed is the fisheries sector, which has experienced some of the worst examples of violence being used by individuals against communities and NGOs. The country has two important fisheries: a fresh-water inland and a salt-water fishery. Of these two, the inland fishery is by far the more important to the country. To understand why, one needs to understand something of the country's geography. Cambodia's unique hydrology has defined the state's economy and has made it possible for the Khmer civilization to flourish. The wet-rice agricultural rhythm is defined by the monsoons and the ebb and flow of the Tonle Sap (Great Lake), which fills during the wet season, expanding over 30 per cent in size, and then drains, in an annual cycle. This reveals rich soil ideal for agriculture on the banks of the tributary rivers and lake, and crucially replenishes the nutrients in the water to support a large fishery. The economic importance of the lake has been described by the ADB:

> The Tonle Sap is the largest freshwater lake in Southeast Asia and defines Cambodia's national identity. It provides 40–70% of the total protein intake of Cambodia. Currently, about 15% of Cambodia's populations depend directly on the lake for their livelihood and many more draw indirect benefits.
>
> (ADB 2005: 12)

For the communities living alongside the country's many waterways, fishing also provides a core source of capital. For these reasons, the continued access to fisheries is considered to be crucial to the ongoing vitality of many of Cambodia's small rural communities, and they have proven willing to risk confrontation with powerful individuals to protect this access.[4]

The value of both the inland and coastal fisheries has not gone unnoticed by the state, which has sought to regulate the sector. In 1987 the Cambodian government put in place a Fisheries Law, which effectively limited small-scale fishing (NGO Economic, Social and Cultural Rights Monitoring Committee 2002: 4). In the early 1990s, the government moved to provide some oversight of the fisheries in order to regulate the industry further and develop a source of state revenue through the sale of fishery lots.[5] The Cambodian government appears to have had the country's interests in mind when the fishery policies were established. NGOs have reported that their causes were heard by the Ministry of Fisheries office in Phnom Penh, though as one NGO working specifically with the fisheries sector argued, the Fisheries Department had no resources to patrol or enforce regulations.[6] In seeking to redress the grievances of local communities, the state government made 56 per cent of the fishing lots available to community fisheries in October 2000 (ADB 2005: 12), yet in the provinces where the policies were to be enforced, local leadership often failed to support the central government's policies. Instead, some powerful individuals were able to use the state apparatus to further their own self-interest, resulting in some communities experiencing significant pressure from the state to relinquish their claims to fishing lots. In the village of Kanleng Phe in Kampong Chhnang Province, villagers were told they could not fish any of the waters surrounding their community as they had been assigned to a fishing lot. When they tried to fish, the lot owner hired local police to enforce his 'rights', destroyed village irrigation dikes, arrested people and forced them to work without payment in his lot.[7] There were also attempts to use the legal system to force communities off fishing lots; in one instance a community was forced to pay 40 million Riel (US$50,000) to a lot owner.

The manner in which the system was run provided opportunities for individual interests to supersede those of communities. A coalition of NGOs, the Fisheries Action Coalition Team (FACT), was established to address these issues. They reported that:

> conflicts arise when there is competition for the same resource. For example, although the lot system sets aside fisheries for use by family-scale fishers, lot operators (often with the backing of armed guards or the military) prevent villagers from accessing the resource. Another major factor involved in the conflicts has been the military, which are reported to sell or lease fishing lots to people in exchange for protection.
>
> (Levinson 2002: 2)

With the ability to manipulate the registration system, powerful individuals were able to secure access to fishery lots. The ability of the Cambodian elites to use the state to meet their personal aims was not limited to taking advantage of the legal system. Individuals who seized fisheries were often able to hire local military and police personnel to enforce their claim on particular fish lots.[8] There are also allegations that the people engaged directly in usurping local fishing rights are from the military themselves, including assertions that military chiefs have been involved occasionally.[9] Other published accounts of disputes over fisheries have reported the use of military and police personnel to intimidate and persecute communities that have attempted to regain access to fishing grounds.[10] While government assets are used in support of personal goals, the presence of the military and police provide both a quasi-legitimacy to the individuals' claims, and effectively disempowers the communities. When the police are called upon by a community to respond to what they perceive as the illegal acquisition of their fishing grounds, if individual police officers are in the pay of the offender, it is unlikely that the community's cause will be pursued. In fact, the communities have often been targeted by the state security apparatus. This has resulted in a number of communities being pushed off their traditional fisheries. 'The conflict between fishing lots and local people has been happening everywhere in Battambang where the fishing lots exist' (NGO Forum: Fishing Conflict in Battambang: 5). This process has had severe impacts on the lives of those who traditionally relied on the fisheries as a primary source for sustaining their livelihood. When these communities attempted to access traditional fishing grounds they were often chased off, harassed, and sometimes threatened by people representing the new commercial interests. In the words of the Asian Development Bank, '[f]isheries on the Tonle Sap are characterized by high levels of conflict, emerging from competition between different interest groups, to extract the maximum from the resources of the lake' (ADB 2005: 12). These conflicts, which often turned violent, came to the attention of many NGOs working in the communities.[11]

A number of NGOs, both international and local, became involved in this struggle between traditional fishing communities and the interests of some Cambodian elites. There were a number of dynamics by which the groups came to engage the fisheries issues. The first were the environmental groups that had been engaged with this sector from the outset. These groups, generally conservation-oriented, were involved because of the perceived threat of the industrial scale of fishing that the new companies were introducing.[12] The second grouping were organizations, generally in Phnom Penh, that were approached by community representatives who were seeking assistance in making their claims in courts and to the government. Finally there were LNGOs, such as Leucaena, in Battambang, that were either already working in the communities, or were formed by some village members to work on this issue (though the latter form of formal organization is exceedingly rare). Threatened communities have sought recourse through numerous channels, including direct community action, the attempt to use the legal system, and by turning to NGOs for assistance. This would seem to be a near text-book case of the development of civil society, as communities sought out associations to assist in the protection of their rights. However, the organizations that were approached were rarely local (in terms of emerging from their particular community), and were predominately well-established groups and often international rather than local organizations.

The literature on civil society reconstruction in post-conflict societies leads to the expectation that NGOs will work to defend community interests. In Cambodia this has not always been the case. Initially, most NGOs paid little attention to the issues of fisheries and the emerging conflicts between communities and individuals. It was not until communities began to take direct action to address their concerns that the NGO community began to take notice of the issue.[13] NGOs were thus effectively followers in this sector. However, when groups did begin to work on the issue they were often called upon to mediate between the government and communities, a position bound to create some tension. Crucially, the role of mediator is not one that can be performed if one is clearly representative of one particular group, calling into question the validity of the assumption that NGOs inherently represent the local communities. As is discussed in detail in Chapter 7, this also unsettles assumptions about the apolitical role of NGOs. One INGO worker, involved in instructing LNGOs on advocacy, said that this role of mediation between communities and the state continues to be a problem, with groups fearing the repercussions that might come from the government.[14] It was argued by this individual that, as a result, numerous Cambodian NGOs have stepped away from these issues.

The relationship between NGOs and the government around the fisheries was problematic at first, with regular confrontations between the two. Groups have claimed that when they pressed the government to resolve community claims that they were in turn pressured by local law enforcement agencies. The state intervention into NGO activity in the fisheries included direct pressure on communities not to work with the associations, threats of physical violence against NGO workers, threats of arrest or detainment of NGO workers, and the threat of lawsuits against the organizations and their employees. One group related that the lot owners have accused them, and the community they were assisting, of stealing fish.[15]

The prevalence of violence within this sector led a number of NGOs to form a working group under the auspices of the NGO Forum to address the unique problems posed by this sector. A belief exists within the NGO community that there is strength in numbers, and that the state is less likely to interfere in NGO work if there are a large number of organizations working on an issue, the logic being that it is much more difficult to silence a network than a single organization. The working group began to pressure the government in Phnom Penh to tackle the communities' needs. This relationship has improved slowly over time, with several NGO workers stating that a watershed in the government's position on fisheries occurred in August 2003, with the enactment of legislation that addressed many of the worst abuses of fishing concessions, and ensured that communities had access to sufficient fishing lots to cover their own food security needs.[16] This is not to say that all of the issues have been resolved, but there is now a system in place to attend to communities' concerns, and the government is more receptive to their needs. Communities have regained access to many of their fisheries, and NGOs are reporting that they are now working on these issues and experiencing greater cooperation from the local and state levels of government.

Conflict over land titles

As with the fisheries sector, NGOs have argued that there is an enduring difficulty in addressing land title issues. An NGO Forum Report in 2006 listed 1,551 cases of land disputes between 1991 and 2004 which affected nearly 160,300 families, and its 2010 report on land issues indicated that disputes have 'increased dramatically since 2006 (NGO Forum 2011: 1)'.[17] According to one HR organization, the most difficult problems to resolve are land title disputes when high-ranking government or military personnel are involved.[18] The dynamics here are similar to the conflicts over fisheries, with some NGOs representing community interests in opposition to the elite, who are seeking to exert control over parcels of land. These conflicts often proceed to court where communities have little ability to represent their cases effectively.[19] Even the state level of government has recognized that there are problems in this area:

> The government, donors, and nongovernmental organizations note that land disputes and land theft have become escalating problems. They cite Cambodia's weak legal framework for property rights and corruption at all levels of government as facilitating land theft. Cambodia's 1992 land law is vague concerning the criteria for private land ownership and the process for registering a land claim, according to donors. In addition, donor-funded studies on Cambodia's land management note that government officials at the national, provincial, and local levels often accept unofficial payments in return for approving land title applications, whether the individual making the application lives on the land or not.
>
> (United States General Accounting Office (GAO-02–569) 2002: 8)

As with the fisheries sector, there is a range of NGOs concerned with this issue area. There are those that are engaged in community development and are embedded within the affected communities, those that are focused on land dispute issues, and those involved in human rights and legal representation. Interestingly there are very few groups that specialize in land dispute resolution. This is illustrative of the sensitivity of the sector. Despite a clear need for such expertise, no group has emerged to work solely within this subject area. Rather, groups such as Legal Aid of Cambodia (LAC), and HR groups such as ADHOC and LICADHO have acquired expertise to deal with these issues. The NGOs that have been most directly involved in such disputes are those providing legal assistance to individuals and communities.

The group Outreach reported that in the course of their fieldwork they found people who have encountered problems with government workers stealing land.[20] Representatives from communities have sought out Outreach to raise awareness of the problems, and get assistance in resolving their cases. This particular group's approach is to provide administrative support to the communities to ensure they are able to prepare and submit the necessary paperwork to address the matter through the state's legal channels. Outreach has not encountered any government interference from this strategy. However, while the government does not fight the NGO, they simply do not follow up on various requests for permission to run specific programmes. Because of Outreach's location in Phnom Penh, and its relatively high profile, it is seemingly less prone to attempts at state interference. Furthermore, their involvement in the issues of land titles tends to be legal advice and representation. As such, they interve more commonly between the defendants and the legal system, and less often directly with the bureaucracy; seldom is it directly with the individual/s accused of seizing land.

In contrast, an LNGO representative involved in providing local assistance to communities related that s/he had received phone threats while pursuing cases against individuals connected with the military.[21] As with the fisheries disputes, it is found that some of the groups most able to represent the communities are those that are the most withdrawn from the community itself, and those that are the least representative (in demographics) of the local community.

The main exceptions to this rule are the de-mining groups that have been directly engaged in freeing up land for settlement and economic exploitation.[22] For this reason their activities have led them to be more directly involved between the interests of communities and individuals.[23] Several groups have had to adopt policies aimed at limiting the impact of individuals grabbing land that is meant to benefit communities. One group related that there have been difficulties in the past with high-ranking officials seizing recently de-mined land for their personal use.[24] As a result this group now clears a small swath of ground and then lets the community begin to use it before they clear further parcels.

As with issues emerging around fisheries, land titling is seen as a difficult matter to resolve, and NGOs have been seemingly reticent to become directly involved in the matter, opting to provide legal support to communities, and to press the issue at the central government level. NGOs, both local and international, are much less likely to intervene at the local level on behalf of communities.

Conflict over forestry issues

The next area of conflict between NGOs and the state concerns the forestry industry.[25] As with fisheries, the resolution of forestry issues is complicated by the deep-rooted personal interests of individuals involved in the harvesting of timber, by community claims to traditional access, and by increasing population pressure leading to the clearing of forests for farming.[26] This section focuses on the conflicts between the government and the NGO sector around timber products.[27] There are few resource areas as financially lucrative as the exploitation of the country's timber products. The forestry industry runs the gamut from the industrial scale clear-cutting of logs for export, through the clearing of land by the poor to make way for farming, to the cutting of timber for use as fuel. In most instances these practices run counter to the maintenance of forests, and in most instances are, on paper, opposed by the Government, which has publicly stated its opposition to illegal logging.[28] Referring to the use of forestry resources, Hun Sen has stated that 'any development project affecting and damaging the community's customs, culture and livelihood would not be allowed to materialize'.[29] This also pits the interests of small communities, which rely on the forests for timber for construction, for firewood and for non-timber forest products, against more powerful economic interests that stand to reap significant economic rewards from logging.[30] There are therefore disputes at both the local level between communities and local invested interests in commercial logging, and conflicts at the national level among communities that choose to take their protests to Phnom Penh to pressure the government, and between NGOs and the government. In both instances the conflict between NGOs and the government is defined by the interests of the powerful elites within the sector.[31]

As with other sectors of resource extraction, elites with interests in the forestry sector have been able to use the instruments of the state for personal gain. According to the Cambodian NGO, Women Peace Makers:

> for people living in areas of old-growth forest, one likely source of violence is from logging concessions. Like fishing lots, logging concessions employ paramilitary units (but are much better armed, often with as many as 70 or more armed guards) to protect their concessions and to prevent local communities from interfering in their logging operations.
>
> (WPM 2002: 29)

This has meant that military and police resources have been used against the communities that have pressed their rights. It is important to note that this does not mean that the state has officially supported the rights of industrial farming over community access. Under the guidance of the WB, the government of Cambodia has imposed a law on the export of logs and on the harvesting of timber for export.[32] The WB sought to ensure that the government was able to manage the forestry sector effectively, to ensure a sustainable industry and to reap the appropriate revenues from taxation. The WB and international community thus backed a total ban on logging and on the export of timber. The IMF went so far as to suspend structural adjustment funds over the illegal export of logs in 1996. In 2002, the government instructed all the logging concessions to halt their work until state logging management policies were approved. This was pushed by the NGO umbrella group, NGO Forum, Oxfam UK and some other smaller organizations.

As with the fisheries and land title issues, the forestry sector is prone to both the threat and use of violence when local communities are pitted against local elites and economic interests.[33] NGOs in Cambodia have reported numerous incidents where communities have been intimidated and individuals hurt, arrested or killed. In keeping with the previous areas of conflict, the separation between the interests of individuals and the state are blurred, with the powers of the state being deployed for personal benefit. 'Elements within the ranks of the Cambodian and Thai armies are … known to be directly and indirectly taking huge chunks out of the forest cover.'[34] NGOs that become involved in these disputes have been subject to the same forms of attack by the state.[35] Consider the following case. When villagers wanted transparent public meetings in Phnom Penh about access to forests, the Department of Forestry called in police to break up the protests. An NGO, Global Witness, was accused of instigating the protests, which was the public basis for the organization being kicked out of the country.[36] The Department of Forestry then went to the villagers to find out what NGOs were involved in organizing the protests. Most of the NGOs involved had police show up at their doors.

Interestingly, as with the fisheries and land rights issues, it was related that NGOs are reluctant to engage with the issue of access to forestry on behalf of communities.[37] Rather than being proactive in addressing the communities' concerns, NGOs have (generally) been remarkably reactive, waiting until after an issue has become serious before becoming involved.[38] In the words of one NGO worker familiar with the sector, NGOs in Cambodia have been extremely reticent to become involved in advocating on behalf of communities, choosing instead to focus their limited influence on national-level issues.[39]

Unlike the previous resource sectors, the story of the conflict between NGOs and the state around forestry also has important state and international dimensions. Affecting change in logging practices has the potential to alter the funds available to powerful individuals throughout the state. As a result, the conflict over forestry has an important state-level dynamic. This is amplified by the restrictions put on the logging industry by the WB, which linked its loans with the imposition of new regulatory regimes covering the sustainable exploitation of Cambodia's timber.

In Phnom Penh the dispute over forestry policies can be examined through the case of the NGO Global Witness. The events that unfolded around this group stands out amongst all the state's interventions in NGOs because of the publicity surrounding the case. The situation is unique in post-UNTAC development as it is the only instance of an entire organization, as opposed to individuals linked to NGOs, being told to quit Cambodia.[40] The Government of Cambodia, in seeking to meet its obligations under the IMF and the WB, hired Global Witness to act as an industry watchdog and contracted the group to write a series of reports on the status of Cambodian forestry. It was also to monitor the success of the implementation of a ban on the export of logs. Effectively, Global Witness became a victim of its own success. In meeting its mandate, as the representatives of Global Witness saw it, the group released a series of reports that attacked the government's enforcement of forestry protection measures, one of which – issued in 2002 – laid out in clear terms how the government was not enforcing the ban and spelled out the extent of the ongoing deforestation (Global Witness 2002).[41] Global Witness also provided input to a US Subcommittee on Foreign Operations Report (GAO-02–569) that was critical of the government's performance on logging:

> Reports that the technical advisors and Global Witness prepared indicate that the Forestry Crimes Monitoring Unit has not met its goals toward developing the government's ability to detect and track illegal logging.... They also assert that the Department of Forestry and Wildlife does not effectively pursue reports of illegal logging by commercial logging companies.
>
> (United States General Accounting Office (GAO-02–569) 2002: 24)

The Cambodian government, which has been remarkably open to NGOs in general, took direct public action against this group in 2005 in a manner that ran counter to all of its previous actions towards the INGO sector. On 18 July 2005 a staff member of Global Witness was denied entry to Cambodia, the group was forced to close its Cambodian offices on 13 October 2005, and at the end of the month the Ministry of Foreign Affairs stated that the organization was no longer welcome in the state.[42] Whether out of fear of losing international donor money, or out of a respect for the work that NGOs do, the government has been slow to interfere in the work of INGOs (LNGOs, while generally enjoying freedom of action, are more prone to state intervention). As such, the Global Witness affair points to the sensitivity of the resource sector.

Many NGOs have been critical of the Cambodian government and its implementation of various programmes. From human rights and economics, through to environmental protection and democratic reform, NGOs have produced a litany of criticisms of government action or inaction. By far, the vast majority of these do not result in such dramatic responses by the Cambodian government. However, the government viewed Global Witness as having stepped well over its mandate in its attack on the government's forestry record, and of embarrassing the state. The group has had to defend its reports constantly, and has been threatened with closure and expulsion on a number of occasions. In April 2003 Global Witness apparently supported a public protest relating to community disputes over forestry practices, which the government argues turned violent.

Subsequently Global Witness issued accusations that the state had attacked protestors (which the government denies). In response Global Witness was forced to suspend operations and leave the country on 22 April 2003. The US government protested the move, and declared: 'the United States deplores the actions taken by the Royal Government of Cambodia to terminate the work of Global Witness, a non-governmental organization that monitors environmental degradation worldwide, as an independent forest monitor.'[43] That the Cambodian government would take these actions in such a highly public case is further indication that something had transpired that the government felt strongly enough about to risk angering the donor community.

Here is a case of an NGO publicly embarrassing the government, of critiquing its ability to function and control a resource sector. The Global Witness issue is not reducible solely to the fact that it was engaged in public criticism, though as will be shown this also affects state–NGO relations in other sectors. However, the government has endured public rebukes of its HR record, for example, and has not publicly expelled the respective associations. The difference in this instance is that timber extraction is a significant source of revenue for elites within the state. The forestry sector is marked by tensions arising from the extensive revenues flowing to individuals from illegal forestry, and from international donors' demands for forestry reform. The actions of Global Witness, and the subsequent government response, must then be understood as directly affecting the revenues of both the state and powerful individuals.

Conflicts over addressing Cambodia's sex trade

The issue of the Cambodian sex trade will be discussed further in Chapter 7 dealing with identity politics, but is introduced here as its dynamics are affected by a clash between NGOs seeking to halt or diminish prostitution, and individuals who profit from this sector. In a similar way to other dynamics of resource exploitation, the struggles over the sex trade in Cambodia are defined by a struggle between communities, NGOs and the interests of powerful members of Cambodian society that directly benefit from the exploitation of the 55,000 women and girls estimated to be working in the sex trade.[44] In discussing the sex trade with NGO representatives working within this sector, it was often related that groups found it frustrating to deal with issues of the trade of women when the people involved were rich and powerful. It was related by one NGO working with HR and the sex trade that any case that emerged that involved members of political political parties were the most difficult to resolve, and that it was not unusual for clients to want to stop prosecution.[45] There was a common theme across the interviews that when crimes involved these government officials it was very difficult, if not impossible, to arrest or prosecute these individuals, in comparison to the rest of Cambodian society.[46]

As with the other sectors discussed in this chapter, the government has publicly expressed a position that is generally in lock-step with most NGOs working with sex workers. The government argues that it is seeking to both reduce the prevalence of the sex trade, and at the same time to promote safe sex amongst its practitioners.[47] In one instance representatives of an NGO working in the sector said that the government was relatively supportive of both women's rights and efforts to eliminate the trade of women.[48] However, the same group noted that if the matter involved Cambodian elites it was not possible to deal with the issue.

This reaction could be understood in a number of ways: there may be a different code of ethics for the powerful in comparison to the rest of society; that the government and police do not in fact take these matters seriously; or that the rights of women fall in a subordinate position to the powerful in society. As with other sectors, NGOs attempting to address issues and conflicts around the sex trade are in a position of having to deal with a culture of impunity for the elite, and are often unable to push the needs of the women and children they are trying to represent. Similarly, NGOs are not representative of this portion of society: they are working on behalf of prostitutes, but I found only one example (which is not to say it does not happen more often) of these groups employing women they had 'rescued' from the sex trade.

Civil society organizations and conflict over resource issues

The initial assessment of conflicts between NGOs and the Cambodian state over resource issues was that there was something unique to the sector that was problematic, involving limited resources and inherent competition over access, which sowed the seeds of discontent and eventual conflict between opposing interests. Rather than pointing to a fundamental contradiction within the theories and practices of peacebuilding in general, and of the nature of civil society in particular, this form of contestation is largely consistent with liberal understandings of struggles over finite resources, and the role of the state in balancing and resolving competing claims about access. Clearly, the move to a market economy as a part of the peacebuilding process (though this had begun prior to UNTAC) has exacerbated such disputes. Shifting to a market-based economy presents many incentives for elites to expand their base of power. Moves to privatize land ownership, and to commercialize sectors such as fisheries, in a setting where the rule of law and a respect for human rights are not deeply ingrained, provide the groundwork for conflict. However, as this research is aimed at identifying when the state and NGOs come into conflict, the focus is on how NGOs have affected this dynamic. From the peacebuilding and civil society literature we would expect to see CSOs being formed by local communities, and existing groups to step into the debates to represent the needs of the grassroots against the worst abuses by the state and those individuals able to use the state to their advantage.

What has been found instead is that NGOs have been slow to respond to these matters, and groups representing community interests have been predominately reactive, rather than proacative, in relation to events on the ground. As such, civil society, defined narrowly (but in keeping with the ways in which it is used in practice) neither sets the agenda, nor provides a site for the community's articulation of discontent. Furthermore, while some of the ways in which NGOs come into conflict with the government over economic exploitation have been discussed here, groups more commonly choose policies that favour cooperation with the state, and work on capacity building and national policy.

Liberalism advocates democratic governance and the expansion of civil society as a means of addressing competing demands in a peaceful manner. The tension in the writing about civil society is that the sector is supposed to be both a means of promoting democratic culture as well as a force of resistance against abuses of state power. In this respect, state–NGO conflict around resource exploitation where the interests of elites are put at risk is in keeping with liberal thought, and this pattern of conflict does not represent an inherent contradiction within a liberal theory of peacebuilding.

This would seem to lend itself to an analysis that examines issues of interests, whether class interests or power politics. But upon deeper examination the limitations of such approaches become stark. To begin with, such a position blithely turns its back on Cambodian history and makes no attempt (with the exception of Marxist-inspired studies) to account for differing forms of societal relations or the possibility that the subject matter that is being fought over may have a value that is historically contingent. The introduction of market economics, a core component of peacebuilding, has changed this dynamic and has altered the balance of relations between powerful individuals and the community.

That said, on the issue of state–NGO interaction, the economic system is not itself sufficient to understand the dynamics of conflict. With a few notable exceptions, such as with Global Witness, NGOs generally did not publicly struggle with the government on resource management issues. In the words of one NGO working on forestry issues, there was far more to be gained by cooperating with the bureaucracy than always being critical. There are a great number of groups that are engaged in advising, providing technical expertise and doing programme delivery in resource-based sectors across the country in collaboration with the government. In each of the areas discussed in this chapter, there are more NGOs working effectively alongside the government than are in conflict with the state. Of the groups that were interviewed that work on resource-based issues, most reported strong working relationships with the government in general and the Ministry of Environment in particular.[49] Of note, though, is that these groups saw their mandate as working with the government, and of improving the state's ability to manage resources, even if they were critical of the enforcement of policy. Consider the Wildlife Conservation Society (WCS), which in 2003 had 120 staff members working on nine projects. Their aim was to effect management of resources through the government. They worked closely with government and employed several department workers (who continued to receive government pay) in the NGO. While their work often directly addresses forestry-related issues, they stated that they had not had problems with the government.

At risk of tautology, those groups whose mandate it is to directly influence government policy have sought a cooperative relationship with the government. Such NGOs therefore avoid direct confrontation with state elites. There are benefits for associations that use such tactics: if they achieve 'buy-in' from the central government they are in a much stronger position to handle local elite interests. As a direct result of striving to nurture a cooperative relationship, such NGOs have proven reluctant to pursue projects that would put them at odds with the government. Indeed relationships with the government departments overseeing the resource sectors, whether they be fisheries, land titles or forestry, demonstrate a desire to make positive changes to the benefit of the affected communities. If the source of conflict around resource issues is not at the state level, it is necessary to return to a consideration of the dynamics of politics at the community level where the conflicts are, for the most part, occurring.

The nature of conflict over resource exploitation is predominately one of community interests being pitted against individual interests. To understand this requires an appreciation of the cultural dynamics of the region and the nature of personal power. Without delving deeply into the issue, it is important to note the enduring importance of patron–client relations to societal relations in Cambodia. Lizée (2000) describes how the cultural legacy of the patron–client relationships has resulted in individuals seeking to secure their own positions in society by trying to secure as much wealth (the means of supporting their clients) as possible. Within a newly capitalizing economy the nascent free market provides new means for the elites to pursue greater power and influence. Clearly this was part of the issue; the changing societal dynamics can be traced to the evolving economics of the country. The move to a market-based economy, and the development programme of Cambodia, are changing the very nature of societal relations. The network of support that provides the basis of personal power increasingly requires that the powerful have the capital to support their networks. This has meant that the individuals in patronage positions have had to find ways to take advantage of opportunities to make money in the increasingly capitalist economic system. Because of the close link between an individual's power and the state, influential individuals have been able to call on the assistance of members of the military, police, and legal system. The search for additional sources of revenue is therefore not only important to sustain their own quality of life, but is also crucial to ensure they are able to continue to support their own subordinates. Attempts by communities to regain control of their resources can then be seen as a real threat to the continued viability of each of these individuals' ability to meet obligations to clients and to maintain their status.

This form of conflict should not be essentialized. Struggles over access to resources need not be prone to violence, nor is there necessarily a conflict between the needs of communities versus individuals. Why particular resources have become subjects of dispute is historically contingent upon the movement towards market-based capitalism, on the enduring patterns of patron–client relationships, and the emerging notion of civil society. They also depend on the international market for the product and the ability of elites to achieve profit by its exploitation. As such there are two primary areas of conflict between NGOs and the state within the resource sector:

1 conflict around community versus individual interests; and
2 conflict around the legitimacy of NGOs doing advocacy.

This has in turn revealed some of the difficulties in the assumptions of civil society literature, particularly as it pertains to NGO activity in developing states. NGOs are seldom constituted by communities, but more often are outside organizations that try to speak on behalf of sections of society. The notion then, that they will put the needs of a community above the needs and expectations of the NGO, is far from a given. Indeed, numerous studies (discussed in Chapter 3) have shown how NGOs are more beholden to their donors than to local communities (Edwards and Hulme 1996; Fowler 2000a; Kilby 2005).

It is within the area of advocacy that a gap emerges between the expectations of the civil society literature and the way associations are behaving in Cambodia. NGOs are often not the leaders when it comes to advocacy on behalf of communities. NGOs are afraid of the repercussions that are likely to come from the government – especially in the area of land rights. As a result, a large number of Cambodian NGOs have stepped away from these issues. In fact, during some interviews NGO representatives argued that in seeking to avoid confrontation with the state their organizations could hamper the activities of community groups.

Despite the overall improvements to the resource sectors in Cambodia since 2000, it continues to be a sensitive area for NGOs. One NGO worker argued that violence continues to surround this issue. The Government can make it difficult for an NGO to work at the local level, and permission to work could be withdrawn. There is also the risk of imprisonment and of court cases being launched. These concerns are more acute for the local organizations that do not have the same protections as the international or large Cambodian NGOs, and which are more vulnerable to government intervention.

NGO–state interaction in the resource sector has been marked as much by cooperation as by conflict and violence. Yet, conflicts over resource issues were consistently noted as being the most difficult to resolve and the most prone to violence. This all demonstrates that the notion that NGOs will inherently represent the needs of communities is problematic. Clearly NGOs can do so, but this is not automatic, and with the INGOs that pursue long-term cooperation with the government, doing so can actually be detrimental to their broader goals. Groups that are seeking to contribute to the technical capacity of government ministries should be expected to be loath to represent community needs against those embedded interests of powerful members of society. Surprisingly, many NGOs that are involved in community development have also shown a reticence to engage in these types of issues. Most groups involved in development programmes deliver services in far less controversial areas such as microfinance, the construction of local infrastructure and community planning. These groups then do not become engaged in advocacy on the more sensitive issues of the control of resources.

However, to understand why the state can intervene in NGO work in the resource sector we have to recognize that the liberal pluralist image of a separation between individuals and the state with an intermediate civil society is of limited applicability to countries emerging from periods of civil strife. Personal power and state power are not readily extricated and the process of development through market capitalization can simultaneously increase the need of powerful individuals to extend their control over areas that were previously held by communities, as well as providing the legal frameworks for them to do so.

For civil society literature to provide an understanding of politics in developing states, we need to have a working state against which civil society can be contrasted. In the absence of a clear division between individual and state power the meaning of civil society becomes unclear. NGOs operating in post-conflict peacebuilding step into this morass and must often negotiate the complexities of a polity where powerful individuals are able to manipulate the political system for their own needs. In Cambodia (where there is a functioning government), as you move away from the centre of state power individuals can hold a greater sway over local politics. Their basis of power shifts as the economic and political landscape changes. Conflicts over access to resources between communities and individuals can then be prone to violence as the vested interests are able to deploy the powers of the state at the local level to protect their power base and economic wellbeing.

A preponderance of INGOs and LNGOs has emerged in Phnom Penh and the other large urban centres, with relatively few sprouting up in rural Cambodia. For this reason, the claim that NGOs are embedded in local civil society is a stretch at best. However, the civil society literature recognizes this point, and argues that NGOs are able to better respond to local needs because of their proximity to the communities within which they work. They may claim to speak on behalf of the community, but are not 'of it'. When it comes to the resource-based conflicts, NGOs have been relatively slow to address the issues, with many associations outright avoiding these matters altogether. If the NGO is trying to keep a professional working relationship with the central government, such a situation can be perceived as threatening to the work they hope to do in the country. As such, the NGO community reported that groups were reluctant to step into resource-based conflicts or to engage in advocacy work on behalf of villages. In the words of one NGO worker, some issues, such as those around access to natural resources, are far more controversial than others. There is simply too much money being made for NGOs to resolve these problems quickly.

Despite the ways in which NGOs have often been unable to negotiate effectively between powerful individuals and local communities, this is not an inherent contradiction in the liberal framework of peacebuilding or civil society. Civil society is expected to act as a check on the unfettered power of the state, and it is supposed to provide a space for communities to articulate and communicate interests. As has been shown, these dynamics can be understood from within a liberal framework, and the appearance of conflict in this sector does not represent a failure of liberal assumptions. Indeed, the exact opposite could be argued: that the presence of such forms of contestation demonstrate the unfinished nature of peacebuilding, and that conflict, in this respect, is to be expected in the course of changing (for the better) Cambodian political culture.

6 Bureaucratic intervention in NGO activities

> The government under the leadership of the Prime Minister regards NGOs as the partners of development with government.
>
> Interview, His Excellency Ek Sam Ol, Deputy Chairman of the Legislative Committee, 1 September 2004

In planning and implementing development programmes, NGOs regularly address issues that are within the purview of state bureaucracies. The relationship that unfolds between them is not always productive, and can be marked by competition for donor resources, project priorities and methods of service delivery. In Cambodia, this has sometimes resulted in the state seeking to control the work of NGOs, which may run counter to the goals of fostering an independent civil society. As peacebuilding relies heavily on NGOs, this raises important questions for peacebuilding theory and practice. Why do NGOs and bureaucracies come into conflict, and how should we understand such competition? Can such conflicts be understood within the framework of both the academic and policy literatures on peacebuilding and the associational literature on civil society upon which they draw? The images we have of development projects in the South invariably include INGOs providing food aid to the starving, of drilling wells, and of motivated Northerners working amongst the dishevelled masses to help communities rebuild their lives. It should be no surprise that these narratives are accurate in some respects, but misleading in many others.

INGOs do rely heavily on workers from the North, who are, in my experience, incredibly motivated and highly capable. But this is only a part of the picture. At the same time that NGOs are seen as compassionate and efficient in their work, the Southern government is generally portrayed as the binary opposite. Instead of being understood as a part of the solution to the country's development, the Southern state is described as obstructionist and as the source of insecurity, corruption and ineptitude. These representations of post-conflict governments affect development policies and shape the relationships between the NGO sector and the state. This chapter focuses on the tensions that such portraits of development put in place, and explores how the narratives and practices of peacebuilding, with their focus on civil society reconstruction, contribute to these tensions. In particular, this chapter looks at the dynamics of cooperation, competition and conflict in Cambodia between NGOs and the bureaucracy over the delivery of services to the public.

While the state and the NGO community are engaged in the development of the country, they both assert that they ought to be able to dictate development priorities and how they should be met. However, due to the historic processes particular to Cambodia (described in Chapter 4), and to broader liberal patterns of development policy and global governance, NGOs have acquired considerable power to pursue their own development agendas. As the state has gradually regained technical, managerial and financial capabilities, it has sought to reassert some control over the country's development agenda. It is argued that this has resulted in struggles over who should legitimately dictate development policy within the state, leading to moves by the state to regulate NGO behaviour.

Up to this point the argument, following the neoliberal logic of a minimal state, has been that the less state intervention in NGO work the better. Yet, some forms of state intervention in NGO work may be beneficial. The following discussion of state attempts to set policy agendas illustrates the ways in which some forms of government intervention in the work of NGOs have been favourable. However, the drive to provide oversight and control of the policy environment can conflict with the goals of NGOs and international donors, which Riddell and Robinson (1995) assert is predominately focused on poverty reduction. While such goals are clearly laudable, to argue that such policies can be pursued free of any other considerations obscures local conditions and ignores the debates that governments must engage in. The Southern states' freedom to set development priorities is limited, given their dependence on aid money and NGOs. They are thus largely beholden to the interests, initiatives and policies of the donors and NGOs operating within their state: Cambodia is no exception.

The limitation of the state's capacity to set development priorities is reinforced by the new creed in development studies which, particularly evident in the 1990s, has favoured bottom-up development and poverty reduction programmes. These programmes have not only been understood as important for the economic progress of the state, but are seen to play a core role in liberal peacebuilding. Addressing the underlying economic malaise, seen as both causing conflict, and holding back the broader resolution of civic conflict, thus becomes a key element of the liberal peace (Aggestam 2003; Richmond 2009). Stiles illustrates how this has resulted in the promotion of NGOs as core participants in development:

> Since the mid-1980s, development experts have turned their attention from such conventional notions as structural adjustment and basic

> needs toward a new approach that emphasizes participatory, small-scale, community-based development involving nongovernmental organizations (NGOs) and grassroots associations. A good descriptor of this approach would be the 'civil society empowerment' model. It attempts to reverse a long-standing policy of placing the recipient government at the centre of the development process[.]
>
> (Stiles 1998: 199)

This has meant a move to community-centred development where NGOs are seen as the core actors (Feldman 1997). The centrality of NGOs to peacebuilding is exacerbated by the way in which much of the aid community tends to denigrate the state and its bureaucracies. NGOs involved in local-level development projects seemingly ignore the government where possible, often avoiding close cooperation with government's ministries in setting policy priorities and agendas, and in implementing projects. This was clearly expressed during interviews with employees of LNGOs and INGOs. With few exceptions, these individuals saw their organizations as possessing greater technical expertise, of being less corrupt and of being more responsive to local needs than the government.[1]

To understand the general orientation towards the government on the part of NGOs, international donors and academics, consider the following statements by representatives of NGOs. In the first two there is a clear belief that NGOs are more effective in policy design and implementation than the state:

> In Cambodia there isn't a lot of cooperation between NGOs and government; government doesn't do much.
>
> (Interview, health LNGO representative, Phnom Penh, 13 August 2004)

> [T]he government was very flexible with NGOs, [because] in many cases the NGOs can do a better job than the government. They have a greater presence in communes and villages.
>
> (Interview, Cambodian NGO representative, Phnom Penh, 28 October 2003)

The second quote echoes the associational literature in asserting that NGOs are closer to society, and thus better placed to understand and respond to local needs. This is then taken further by another NGO worker, who argued that the state is not only removed from local interests, but also that it undermines the implementation of development policies:

> There is not a sense that government/bureaucracy works for the public. Corruption is everywhere and works at every level.
>
> (Interview, HR LNGO representative, Phnom Penh, 17 December 2003a)

This corruption in turn is seen as not only limiting the capacity of the state, but is also understood to impact on the effective delivery of NGO projects:

> We are a NGO and we work for the benefit of the people, but we can have problems when the ministries are most interested in gaining money. Also often have to deal with many different ministries for the same project. For example work on roads requires us to work with the Ministries of Transportation, Land Management and Finance.
>
> (Interview, research LNGO representative, Phnom Penh, 11 August 2004)

These quotes illustrate a clear divide between the way that CSOs (particularly those that are international or led by Northerners) and the government are perceived by development workers and academics.[2] While the effectiveness of government is criticized, CSOs are seen as being essential to implementing development programmes in the South. The WB, for example, has argued that NGOs are crucial in:

> addressing the problems of developing societies and the needs of their poorest members in a manner not matched by government officials. NGOs have learned how to work with grassroots organisations and how to put together projects with minimal financial and external technical assistance, thus helping poor people to help themselves.
>
> (WB 1989, cited in Pulpampu 2003: 137)

These views do not merely represent reality 'out there', but also serve to shape the perceptions of both NGOs and states in the South. By informing development policies, such narratives may serve to undermine state capacity further, re/producing the ineffectual Southern state. Furthermore, the view of Southern bureaucracies, and the preference for civil society associations, operates within a broader discourse that helps organize thinking about development policies.

Within the new framework of community-led development, described by Munck (1999) as constituting the 'holy trinity' of gendered, sustainable and bottom-up development, CSOs are given preference as they are seen as being more responsive to local development needs than the state. This belief, common amongst the NGO community, is found throughout their documentation, and was a regular refrain of the NGO workers that were interviewed. The groups' proximity to the communities is supposed to provide insight into local development needs. In turn, NGOs are expected to be able to develop and deliver more effective programming. In contrast, the state is portrayed as removed from the local level, of often being geographically distant (located as it is in Phnom Penh) from rural villages, and of not being willing or able to determine local needs.[3]

This position receives intellectual buttressing from academic literatures on civil society, which are explicit about how governments are more distant from communities than CSOs (which as was argued in Chapter 2 are equated in policy terms to NGOs). The state is then seen as being distant, coercive and limited in capacity. This then makes working through NGOs preferable, a point made clear by Makoba, who argues:

> NGOs are seen by their proponents as a catalyst for societal change because they are responsive to the needs and problems of their clients, usually the poor, women and children.
>
> (Makoba 2002: 59)

The logic behind this argument is consistent with the liberal civil society literature, which sees associational behaviour as arising from communities, and thus responding to the communities' needs (Hojman 1993; Clarke 1998b; Fisher 1998; Silliman and Noble 1998; Garrison 2000). The behaviour of NGOs is then understood in the same way, as being more connected with grassroots than government, and as such, better situated to know the needs of local communities. However, in Cambodia NGOs rarely emerge from the local communities, and do not practice democratic forms of self-governance. Crucially, groups that have a central office (usually situated in Phnom Penh) and one or more project delivery sites do not set policy at the local level. Rather, the policy direction of the organization is led from the organization's core, leaving the project offices much less room to accommodate local needs. This means that the argument that NGOs are likely to be more responsive to community's interests than the government is based in large part on ungrounded assumptions that do not bear out in practice. Some scholars, including Bell and O'Rourke (2007) and David Chandler (1999), have argued that in fact NGOs' claims to represent local communities effectively is in contradiction to their lack of electoral accountability.

The second way in which NGOs have come to be the favoured instruments of development relates to a belief in their technical superiority. This process is described by Abiew and Keating:

> Donor governments and international institutions have increasingly channelled resources through NGOs and delegated tasks to them because they are perceived as more reliable than some recipient government agencies and better able to deliver aid where needed without having to go through official recognition of rebel groups implied by direct government involvement.
>
> (Abiew and Keating 1999b: 101)

NGOs are viewed as being far more likely to have a professional cadre of workers, more often than not with Northern-educated managers. Many of the representatives of NGOs with whom I spoke had received either specific training in project management and development, or had obtained their knowledge through years of involvement in the development community. Indeed, much of the current LNGO leadership in Cambodia gained experience in project design, implementation and management working with INGOs in the refugee camps inside the Thai border.

As with the positive light within which NGOs are examined, the negative conception of the bureaucracy in the developing world is informed by the same narratives of civil society, development and peacebuilding. The ways in which we come to understand these affects peacebuilding policies and in turn affects the relationships between NGOs and the state. There is an important cautionary note to be sounded about the manner in which the discourses of ineptitude and corruption operate. The language has strong echoes of colonial-era views of non-European states being corrupt and their administrators largely inept. This is not to say that policies in Cambodia that enable or tolerate corruption are acceptable, rather what needs to be asked is what has led to such a situation and how can it be changed.[4]

The third narrative of NGO superiority over the bureaucracy has to do with their characterization as being democratic and representative, the exact opposite of the language used to describe Southern governments such as Cambodia. Countries' entire systems of governance and public management are dismissed as unable to effectively address the development needs of their populations. NGOs are thus not only capable of delivering projects and supervising development strategies, but become the preferred bodies through which to ensure that effective programming is implemented (though this particular narrative applies much more to international than local groups). Local organizations are often described by the INGOs and Westerners working for LNGOs as having the same characteristics as the bureaucracy, and of being nothing more than blatant attempts to raise funds for personal gain.

The fourth and final way in which civil society groups are described as more effective than the state is through the narratives of social capital. Related to the preference for bottom-up development, these arguments see development programmes aimed at the broadest strata of society as improving the over-all capacity of communities in such things as management and technical skills (Portes 1998; Narayan 1999). These are roles that NGOs are expected to excel at by engaging local communities, involving local volunteers, helping educate locals on how NGOs function, and in providing specific technical skills. NGOs are thus seen as being able to increase social capital. Abom (2004), for example, focuses on NGOs' support of community and grassroots organizations, and sees this as an essential part of social-capital construction.[5] When it comes to development practices, the social capital arguments tend to concentrate on NGOs to the exclusion of the state. Yet the broader social capital literature, such as that of Putnam (1995a), was initially interested in the connection between social capital and state capacity. This is a relationship that is often pushed aside in the discourses of social capital and international development. For example, Abom's discussion contains no reference to the relationship between NGOs and government, nor does one find any explanation of how building social capital in a particular community translates into a broader capacity for either local development or democratic governance, let alone how social-capital construction at the local level will trickle up. To take this further, if associations are a place of learning, then the negative conception of the state that some international development organizations have should be expected to erode support of government at the local level. This would run in direct opposition to the claims made in the social capital literature. Some studies, such as Buckland's (1998: 239), have found that NGO intervention tends to increase networks between NGO practitioners, but have a minimal impact on the strengthening of social capital in the community. Goodhand and Lewer (1999: 84), in a study of NGOs in Sri Lanka, argue that in fact social capital has been undermined rather than enhanced. But even these studies hold to the view that the CSOs are more capable of delivering services than the government.

The promotion of NGOs' roles in development

With this brief account of the intellectual reinforcement of NGOs' roles in development, the present chapter can turn to the ways in which NGOs have been promoted in practice. First, NGOs have been advanced through the current prioritization of bottom-up development schemes. Hughes, who has studied both Cambodian development and politics, has shown how civil society has figured into the development discourse of the country:

> Civil society analysis has featured prominently in the prescriptions of international activists working in Cambodia, and has been adapted by Cambodian reformers as a framework for action. It was central to the conceptions of political change and, in particular, human rights protection promoted by the United Nations Transitional Authority in Cambodia.
>
> (Hughes 2001b: 47)

These are in contrast to previous development models that relied on various forms of state-led modernization; grassroots models of development stand in opposition to 'state socialist' and 'trickle-down' alternatives, which are seen as incapable of addressing the needs of the poor adequately, and of not providing a voice for the disenfranchized (Makoba, 2002: 60). As NGOs are regarded as the institutions that are closest to the 'bottom', and that are most responsive to local needs, they are then the favoured development partners. International donors have thus turned to NGOs to manage their programmes and deliver projects to communities.

In one of the few cautionary notes about this framework, Goodhand argues:

> one should not assume that bottom up peace-building approaches will automatically have a cumulative effect. Agencies have tended to avoid working with the authorities at the national level and efforts in all sectors have remained highly localised, not to say fragmented. Moreover, such community-based approaches tend to overestimate the capacity of 'civil society' to have an influence on an unaccountable leadership, which came to power with the gun rather than through consent.
>
> (Goodhand 2002: 849)

However, the argument is not that the concept of civil society is itself problematic, or that NGOs may not be a natural solution to development programmes. Rather, that the state itself is the problem and civil society cannot be expected to influence it.

This discourse of ineptitude and irresponsibility has played out in the aid packages of major Northern donors, and has been observed across the developing world. 'Donor agencies increasingly funnel development assistance through NGOs and other non-state institutions because states in Sub-Saharan Africa are considered both inefficient and corrupt' (Makoba 2002: 58). Clearly the donor and NGO community is basing its arguments about developing states on observations of past and current practices. As a result, the justification for the focus on non-state aid providers is quite compelling. States that have experienced protracted civil conflict may be in a situation where the government has lost much of its ability to govern, and to deliver the programmes that are expected of it. As discussed in the previous chapter, powerful individuals have been able to use the state for their own aggrandizement; this is also common in the Cambodian bureaucracy.[6] Such practices are not surprising when government workers are paid meagre wages and require additional income to support their families.[7] However, such 'corrupt' practices are portrayed as eroding the state's capacity. This extends particularly to foreign-funded development projects, where there is a concern that money will be siphoned off, resulting in less efficient projects. As a consequence, the international community has turned to NGOs for the implementation of both short- and long-term development programmes. This resulted, in the words of Curtis (1998: 72), in an 'aid market' in Cambodia during the 1990s. Numerous commentators have remarked on how this led to far more money flowing into the state for development than the government and existing NGO sector was able to manage effectively. This contributed to a reconfigured patron–client structure within the country (Curtis 1998; Lizée 2000; Roberts 2001; Hughes 2003; Öjendal and Sedara 2006). Indeed, the Council for the Development of Cambodia (CDC) argues that nearly 20 per cent of aid programmes (in terms of the value of the projects in US$)

are delivered through NGOs, numbers supported by a 2010 Cambodian government report on aid delivery.[8] This increasing role of NGOs, in particular international organizations, has been noted by the UN:

> International NGOs are playing an increasingly prominent role.... Huge amounts of money pass through these organizations, and their influence on international thinking and policy-making is likely to grow. They already channel more money into the South than the World Bank.
>
> (UNRISD September 1993: 11–12)

The financial clout of the NGOs then translates into a freedom of action, as the Cambodian state is reticent to risk investment in the country.

The international community brings with it significant capital (especially for cash-strapped states), and extensive technical expertise in the likes of medical professionals, engineers and project managers. Because these funds often come either linked to particular issue areas, or are funnelled through NGOs, the recipient government can find itself in a position where it is unable to control the public policy agenda within its own borders. Certainly the government is often consulted by the large international donors about its perceived needs and identified priorities, which provides the bureaucracy input into policy making. This process was formalized through the Government–Donor Coordination Committee (GDCC), which held its first formal meeting on 2 December 2004 (nearly a decade after the formal end of the UN mission). But this is distinct from saying the state is the arbiter of decisions. After all, the government is not the only group consulted; donors are under no obligation to follow the state's recommendations, and many smaller NGOs that are funded independently of the large state donors do not participate in this process.[9] When it comes to funding NGOs, the government can be excluded completely; international donors can then effectively set the local development priorities. Duffield describes this as part of the growth of 'therapeutic governance' that has been defined in part by a dramatic expansion of the roles of the aid community. He argues that 'over the past 25 years, donor governments, UN agencies, regional bodies, NGOs, commercial companies, and so on, have gained new forms of economic, social and political influence in relation to the internal affairs of contested states within zones of insecurity' (2005: 18). In addition to consulting the state, the large international donors also consult directly with the civil society sector (NGOs) to help identify needs. Umbrella groups, such as the NGO Forum, are then able to exert direct influence on the donors to set funding and project priorities. This reverses the traditional Western model of public policy where the state plays a crucial role in making decisions about what activities are in the public good. Because the government of Cambodia relies so heavily on foreign funding, it is hard pressed to pursue agendas that contradict donor priorities.

Replicating neoliberalism through NGOs

This reduction of the state's capacity does not run counter to the theoretical base of peacebuilding practice, rather it can be seen as consistent with current patterns of global governance that privilege market-based solutions and concurrently look to minimize the role of the state. The ways in which NGO activity in the South serves to replicate neoliberalism have been discussed by a number of academics (Hulme and Edwards 1997; Dicklich 1998; David Chandler 1999; Zaidi 1999; G. Harris 1999; Kilby 2005; I. Roy 2002). The common argument amongst these scholars is that NGOs, by delivering services to the populations of developing states, are then eroding the role of the state.[10] For example, Dicklich's (1998: 6) study of Uganda illustrates how NGOs have increasingly taken over service delivery while governments have moved away from it. Hulme and Edwards (1997: 9) take this further, and argue that many NGOs have played a role, though smaller than that of the market, communities and the state, of rolling back the state. They worry that NGOs are increasingly market-driven, and as such are coming to advocate market solutions. That said, they also see NGOs as still being able to decide whether to pursue market-oriented or community-oriented programmes (ibid.: 11). In one of the stronger criticisms of NGOs' roles in propagating neoliberalism, David Chandler argues:

> donors (and many international NGOs) now characterize their interest in supporting local NGOs as an investment in a strong, pluralist, socially integrated civil society. And yet what has been happening in Bosnia is something entirely different: in funding NGOs, donors have essentially sought – and found – cheap service delivery.
>
> (Chandler 1999: 111)

NGO involvement in service delivery then diminishes the role of the state in such activities, and may lead to the privatization of social services. However, in Cambodia there is little evidence of businesses moving in to deliver social services for financial gain. A detailed study of this particular dynamic is necessary before making any conclusive arguments about the marketization of social programmes.

Clearly though, NGO involvement in the range of social programmes is promoted as they are expected to be more efficient than the government, which is the same logic underpinning the privatization of social services.[11] Referring to the health sector in Cambodia, Kristina Mitchell, working for the Canadian Cooperation Office, noted that the competition between NGOs to deliver services to communities has not necessarily resulted in efficiencies, and has in some instances fostered the duplication of services between NGOs and the government.[12] As a consequence, there has been roll-back of state capacity during the peacebuilding era, and NGOs have been an important part of this dynamic.

The formal UN peacebuilding mission, UNTAC, also directly contributed to the diminishment of the state's capacity, a point that international donors have noted (NGO Statement for the Donors' Review Meeting, 25 February 1993: 1). Besides funnelling development dollars through NGOs, the international development community has diminished the state capacity through its hiring practices and high rates of pay. This led to both rampant inflation in Phnom Penh and made it difficult for government workers to survive on the salaries they were provided. In 2000, the Asian Development Bank (ADB) argued that: 'low public sector salaries are perhaps the most fundamental structural problem in Cambodia with direct implications for the extent of public sector accountability and transparency as well as the ultimate success of ongoing public sector reforms' (ADB 2000: 47). A somewhat ironic statement as the ADB promotes the neoliberal orthodoxy of limiting state expenditures, lowering taxes and privatizing service delivery. NGOs, however, were also major contributors to this dynamic; a fact recognized by the UN, which argues that 'the sudden influx of international agencies and aid has contributed to serious social and economic problems' (UNRISD 1993: 20). The wages that the INGOs are able to afford, their takeover of the service industry, and the flow of international development funding through the NGO sector all undermine the government's capacity to govern by poaching many of the trained professionals in the state, and pursuing the delivery of services at the expense of the state.

The NGO sector has become a preferred place of work, with positions seemingly much more sought after than those within the government. My own translator in Cambodia, Sophea, asked for assistance to help find employment with NGOs. She also held a part-time job teaching English to young Khmer, where she observed that most of her students hoped to find work with an NGO. This is not to say that these dynamics were intentionally pursued by the NGO sector, indeed the opposite is true, but the end result has been noted by NGOs, academics and government policy makers. Here the functioning of the medical sector is indicative of the broader environment in which the government has found itself. It was related by a number of government and NGO workers that the government's ability to deliver medical services has actually eroded from pre-1991 levels. McCargo (2005: 102) argues that because pharmacists, doctors and nurses are no longer paid a living wage they often work privately or seek bribes for their services, a point also made by Hughes about teachers and judges (2003: 50–52). Many professionals no longer work full-time for the state medical system, even though they are technically being paid to do so.

This system is justified on the basis that it is supposed to provide for the development needs of the global South. NGOs are seen as being more capable, more representative and more accountable than the governments and their bureaucracies in developing states. This may, in many instances, be true, but is not *necessarily* the case. Furthermore, relying on NGOs for the development of the state has not nurtured a government that will be capable of taking on increasing responsibilities for the provision of services. From this, a potential for conflict is put in place, where the state and NGO sector disagree over priorities and means of service delivery. This is occurring within a context where the government is seeking to establish its legitimacy, and needs to be seen to be delivering the services expected of the state. However, as Puplampu and Tettey point out in a discussion of NGO–state relations in Africa around agricultural development, '[b]y providing the necessary services and resources for their target groups, NGOs highlight the failings of the state and weaken its legitimacy' (2000: 257). To establish and maintain its legitimacy, the government needs to meet society's minimum expectations, and providing social services to its citizenry is a core component of such an endeavour. The ways in which this process might be exacerbated with the emergence of greater local governance from the empowerment of commune councils have been noted by Öjendal and Sedara (2006). The dilemma for the Southern state is how to exert control over development policies, particularly as it slowly regains financial and technical capacity. Within a context where NGOs have become used to operating with a great deal of freedom, the state's attempts to dictate development policy can be perceived as inappropriate intervention.

History of NGO–state interaction in Cambodia

To this point the emphasis has been on how the language and practices of development and peacebuilding have served to reinforce the roles of NGOs and civil society, while simultaneously contributing to the erosion of the state's capacity. However, it is necessary to provide some historical context to illustrate that not all of the erosion of the state's capacity can be traced to the peacebuilding process. In many regards, the description of the Cambodian government as being incapable of delivering services throughout Cambodia was accurate. The situation that Cambodia found itself in during the early 1980s after the defeat of the KR, and again in the early 1990s, was one where the government was limited in its ability to reach the country's remote provinces due to damaged infrastructure, and a relatively small corps of professional bureaucrats. Much of the intelligentsia and bureaucracy had either fled or died during the KR era. Following the Vietnamese ousting of the KR from central and eastern Cambodia, the new regime faced an uphill battle putting in place an effective bureaucracy. At first it had to rely heavily on Vietnamese and Soviet expertise, and only slowly was able to reconstruct a domestic bureaucratic capacity (Vickery 1984; Hughes 2003: 20–30). At the same time, the depiction of an inept Cambodian bureaucracy from 1991 onwards is also problematic for a number of reasons.

The first is that there was a functioning, though politically biased, bureaucracy in place prior to UNTAC's arrival. The Soviet bloc provided substantial training to Cambodian elites during the 1980s and the Vietnamese government had further supported the establishment of a functioning bureaucracy (Hughes 2003: 39–41).[13] In fact, the state had commenced transforming its economy to a market-based system prior to the arrival of the UN in 1991. The story of how NGOs and the government ministries relate does not begin with the arrival of the UN in 1991. In fact, the SOC had a history of working with INGOs, though this was limited as a result of the West's isolation of the state throughout the 1980s:

> Vietnam's role in staving off further socio-economic decline in the immediate aftermath was important. Despite much anti-PRK/Vietnamese propaganda, Vietnamese officials were ready to co-operate with aid deliveries that were made available, according to early missions from Oxfam organised by Jim Howard.
>
> (Roberts 2001: 50)

The groups that did opt to work in the country throughout the 1980s were tightly controlled by the government and had limited ability to deliver projects, focusing instead on technical advice to the state. The government and the NGOs that were present in the country through this era therefore developed a close working relationship (Mysliwiec 1988), and the state demonstrated a limited ability to manage NGO activities. The groups that did remain in the state were able to develop a stable relationship with the regime. A representative of Oxfam UK stated that 'because we have a long history here in Cambodia we have built up trust with the government'.[14] The government of the time was appreciative of the groups that continued to engage the state despite the West's isolationist policy. These groups have reported a continuing strong working relationship with the current Cambodian government.

The NGOs, as they were working in relative isolation from the West, also ended up forging close working relationships with one another. This facilitated the development of the NGO Forum, an umbrella organization with the mandate to provide a location for NGOs to share their experiences, coordinate their work, and to develop a common voice on select issues. This would, in the late 1990s, provide the basis for a coherent voice of opposition to some government policies, a means of organizing cooperation in some sectors with various ministries, and in others of sheltering those who would critique government practices in areas such as HR abuses and the conduct of elections.

The government's cooperation with NGOs has depended on the personal ties between NGO and government workers, the sector of activity, the type of work done and the size of the organization. In part this can be attributed to the personalized nature of the modern Cambodian state, which remains highly clientalist in character (Lizée 2000; Peou 2000; Roberts 2001; Hughes 2003). The further that one moves from the political centre of the state outwards into the rural periphery, the greater the influence of local political elites is likely to be. As such, it is important to nurture a close relationship between an NGO and the local expression of the state to ensure the capacity to deliver projects (the way this has resulted in various forms of rent-seeking was decried at a meeting of the Consultative Group of international donors in May 2000 (noted by Hughes 2003: 53).

In a separate line of argumentation that complements rather than contradicts the prior point, Peter Swift, who has worked with numerous NGOs in Cambodia, stressed the importance of the size of the organization in affecting relations with the bureaucracy.[15] The government is dependent on the money and services offered by NGOs, but at the same time can be quite resistant to working with small projects because there is nothing in it for the government (local, provincial or state). While Swift did not make reference to the ways in which individuals stand to benefit from large projects, this is easily extrapolated and was echoed in numerous personal conversations with NGO representatives.

The importance of the NGO sector to the Cambodian bureaucracy must be examined within the broader context of the importance of aid to the country. Official development assistance (ODA) increased at an annual rate of 22 per cent from 1992 to 1996 (it fell by 26 per cent as a result of the coup in 1997), but began to increase again in 1998 (and was projected to increase in 2010). This resulted in an average increase of 9.10 per cent in the annual ODA budget (RGC 2000: 1). In 2003, Hughes (2003: 53) noted that international aid accounted for nearly half of the state's budget. While in 2006, 76.9 per cent of development assistance was implemented by the government, such funding normally comes with attached guidelines on its use. This effectively ties the hands of the government in determining development priorities. The government decried this in 2000 as representing a form of 'donorship', which they wanted to reform to provide for greater local (meaning Cambodian state) control of development dollars (RGC 2000). The importance of the NGO sector becomes more evident when considering that in the same year it was responsible for the implementation of 19 per cent of development programmes.[16] This is *in addition* to the US$113.2 million disbursed by NGOs in 2006 (which includes donor funds delivered through NGOs). Chanboreth and Hach (2008), in a report on aid effectiveness, place a much higher value on NGO activities by including all sources of funding for monies disbursed by NGOs (this includes state and IO funding that is moved through NGOs). They put this number at US$461 million in 1998, increasing to US$823 million in 2006. In the last year of available data, NGOs provided US$103.3 million of their own funds (which excludes money flowing through NGOs), accounting for just over 10 per cent of all Aid disbursements in 2009 (RGC 2010: ii).

The INGOs, staffed by a professional cadre, were able to quickly set up and deliver programmes throughout the country. The rapid growth of

NGOs in Cambodia seems to have reached its nadir, though this is based on the observations of individuals working within the sector rather than on hard empirical data. I was told on numerous occasions that Cambodia is currently undergoing a consolidation of organizations, with those remaining tending to be larger and more capable of managing projects.[17] According to one local NGO representative, many of the current LNGOs are likely to disappear, which s/he then directly linked to a reduction of civil society.[18]

This consolidation also highlights another aspect of the responsiveness of NGOs to local community requirements. NGOs that rely on donor funding for project design and implementation are necessarily responsive to the funding priorities of various agencies. Groups that work outside such areas are less likely to be able to secure the finances to continue to operate. This dynamic was regularly identified by NGO representatives as leading to a concentration of NGO activity in narrow areas, with other areas of work being missed. For example, one representative noted how organizations have focused programmes on HIV/AIDS, while other pressing health issues, including malaria, leprosy and mental health, have received much less attention.[19] This was then attributed to the donor policies. Certainly the case of the US funding seems to support these observations. American backing for Cambodian NGOs was being increasingly managed through the East–West Foundation, as opposed to USAID, which has a narrow mandate. In particular, it was argued by NGO representatives that this cut the capacity of groups with a focus on gender issues, which had previously relied heavily on USAID money. The role of the donor community in agenda setting, and of NGOs to these financial incentives, calls into question the extent to which NGOs are in fact reflective of local needs. In this way they can be understood to be just as vulnerable to external pressures as the state. The argument then, that civil society groups are more likely to recognize and advance local development needs than the government, is difficult to sustain in light of their vulnerability to donors' priorities.

Patterns of conflict between NGOs and the Cambodian bureaucracy

In examining the relationship between NGOs and the Cambodian bureaucracy it was observed that there are three general forms of NGO activity, each displaying a distinct form of interaction with the government. The first grouping comprises those organizations that work directly with government ministries and departments. These organizations, predominately INGOs, tend to focus on providing technical advice and capacity building. Such forms of NGO activity were particularly evident in the forestry sector, where groups including Save Cambodia's Wildlife (an LNGO), the World Wildlife Fund, and the Lutheran World Service, provide technical assistance to the Ministry of Forestry on the transformation of laws around forestry management, as well as how to develop and implement sustainable forestry practices. This NGO activity was not restricted to the forestry sector; from one issue area to another, organizations were found to be directly engaging with government ministries, seeking to educate government workers in order to improve their technical and managerial capacities. In general, NGO representatives involved in such programmes reported positive working relationships with the government. The second grouping of NGOs includes those that do not focus their work on the government, opting instead to implement projects at the community level. Such NGO activity is more in keeping with the popular portrayal of humanitarian and development NGO work where programmes are designed to assist local peoples and respond to their needs. As with the first grouping, such forms of activity were found in all issue areas. The final type of NGO work is that of INGOs, and some LNGOs, which work on building the capacity of local NGOs (this is a relatively small percentage of the NGO activity in the country). Organizations rarely limit their work to one form of activity, and depending on their size may undertake programming that targets all three levels. Furthermore, groups can shift their focus year after year according to the donor funds available and changing priorities within the organization.[20] The matter that then arises is how groups that engage in these different types of activities relate to the state.

It was expected that programmes that concentrated on providing capacity building to LNGOs would have little engagement with the government. Indeed, there were no instances found where such organizations actively consulted with the government on their programmes. In terms of NGOs that do capacity building for the government, there was obviously extensive collaboration in all stages of project delivery, from the conceptualization of the various programmes, through their design, implementation and feedback after the programme was completed. However, the dynamics of groups that do service delivery in communities was more varied. In the course of interviews with NGOs there were very few (and those were restricted to the health and education sectors) that stated that their organizations worked closely with the government in either designing or delivering their projects. Even in those sectors, interaction with the government was usually constrained to asking permission to operate and to acquire the necessary documents and/or letters to enter a given community. In retrospect this is not surprising given the way in which the liberal literature on peacebuilding and civil society understand CSOs as being better placed to determine local needs. While this derives from arguments that such groups emerge from local communities, the majority of NGOs in Cambodia are not rooted in the communities that they wish to assist. When they are, the participants are rarely representative of the population they are seeking to help.[21] Rather, the NGO leadership in general has more education and a much higher standard of living than the average household in Cambodia. This requires a questioning of the extent to which NGOs are actually better able to understand local and state-wide needs.

Overall the government of Cambodia has been remarkably supportive of the NGO sector. While NGOs recognize this, the way in which they understand this cooperation is embedded within the belief that civil society is more efficient than the state. The representative of an NGO involved with government capacity building said that the state has been flexible with NGOs because it recognizes that in many cases 'the NGOs can do a better job than the government. They have a greater presence in communes and villages.'[22] This individual perceives the acquiescence of the state as being due to recognition that NGOs are more capable than the state, a position publicly replicated by the government. According to Prime Minister Hun Sen, 'to tackle the remaining tasks we do need the continuing support and good cooperation of international development partners, NGOs, and civil society at large including generous individuals' (Hun Sen, Cambodia New Vision, 29 June 2004). The government has recognized the importance of NGOs to the state's future development, and is publicly supportive of the sector.[23] They laud the various groups' achievements and often try to garner a portion of public attention to larger programmes by sending government and party representatives to the public NGO events (Kao and CICP 1999a: 37). However, this is not the entire story. Trust in the work of NGOs appears to generally diminish the further one moves from the political core, both in terms of geographic location, and level of government. This is exacerbated by the political affiliation of the local representatives, with the CPP being less likely to cooperate than other parties.

Over the past half-decade the government has built up its capacity in some sectors, such as education, health, and forestry, and has begun to seek some policy control over these areas, a point that was acknowledged by several NGO representatives who argued that the state's technical and managerial ability has increased. One individual related that his/her organization had moved away from capacity building and had refocused their efforts on local NGO capacity because the government has become stronger and more capable.[24] At the same time, a representative of an NGO research group with long-standing relations with the Cambodian government argued that part of the issue for the government was that they too were experiencing a drop-off in funding and that NGOs had become more influential in state policy. This is occurring as the government has begun to show increased desire to regulate the broader NGO environment through: increased monitoring of NGO work and new government reporting requirements; the pursuit of legislation to govern the NGO sector; and financial regulations to ensure greater transparency in the funding of NGOs. These measures demonstrate that the state is not satisfied with the status quo, and believes that NGOs' activities require increased regulation.

The following discussion explores three specific examples of how the government is trying to gain greater influence over social policy within the country, and how this in turn translates into attempts to govern NGO activities.

Legal measures to regulate civil society

The first form of state intervention that needs to be explored is current efforts to pass legislation to regulate the activities of NGOs. In seeking to enact a law governing NGOs, Cambodia is following the example of numerous Southern states that have already undertaken such measures.[25] The Council of Ministers in Cambodia established requirements in December 1999 for INGOs to sign a memorandum of understanding (MOU) with the Foreign Ministry before implementing projects.[26] This is intended to provide the government with an understanding of which international groups are operating in the country, as well as to develop a picture of the range of activities ongoing within the state. Additionally, the Ministry of Interior currently requires NGOs to submit quarterly reports and has stated that it will penalize organizations that are late in their submissions, though what this means in practical terms is unclear.[27] LNGOs, in contrast, currently face a much looser regulatory regime and are relatively free to act. This has been seen by some international organizations, such as the ADB, as being untenable, and requiring greater state regulation:

> The Government's approach to NGOs is generally liberal but there is currently no law that specifically regulates NGOs, a subject of heated debate. Cambodian NGOs have a generally weak financial position and are highly dependent on foreign sources of funding. Some appear to be under the strong influence of political parties, whereas others abuse their NGO status for profit-seeking purposes.
>
> (ADB July 2000: 49)

This position illustrates a desire to keep NGOs firmly within a liberal understanding of civil society, separate from both active engagement with politics and from profit making. While some IOs nominally support such forms of regulation, the NGOs themselves are much more resistant. In 1996, 24 LNGOs signed a letter expressing concerns of an earlier version of a draft NGO Law. They asserted that two Articles in the Law (25 and 27) would effectively declare war on LNGOs, and HR NGOs in particular. This concern has continued, with the Asian Human Rights Commission (AHRC) lobbying against recent incarnations of the draft law, asserting that:

> [it] would highly restrict the rights and activities of NGOs in the country. The decision to do this has come at a time when leading

political figures have openly criticised the role of NGOs in Cambodia and accused them of speaking too freely.

(AHRC 2006)

However, since 1996, some local legal experts have argued that the law would be benign and is designed to ensure that NGOs would not run a profit (a standard regulation in developed countries).[28] Though the NGO bill was put in abeyance by Prime Minister Hun Sen in 1999, the issue re-emerged in early 2001, and again in 2003, and 2006.[29] The 2003 and 2006 drafts contained many of the same measures that were of concern to NGOs as previous versions.[30] The fourth draft Law on Associations and NGOs (LANGO), has come under criticism from major HR organizations, including HRW, and Cambodian groups such as LICADHO, who have expressed concern about the ways in which it will enable the Government to shut down organizations that might be critical of the state (HRW 23 December 2011).

Bunleng Men, who is working on projects relating to good governance in Cambodia, observed that this proposed law represents a desire, increasing since 2000, on the part of the government to control the activities of NGOs.[31] This law has been pushed sporadically over the past decade, but appears to have returned to the attention of the government over the past few years.[32] His Excellency Ek Sam Ol, Deputy Chairman of the Legislative Committee, expressed the government's position this way: 'to get a smooth transfer of responsibility we need to have a good relationship with NGOs. We need a law to enforce this and help it'.[33] This statement illustrates a concern that NGOs do not necessarily operate in ways that are seen as beneficial to the state, and that the legal system is the most appropriate means of resolving potential conflicts between the state and NGOs. The NGO sector, while not opposed in principle to regulation, has lobbied against various drafts to avoid what they see as undue forms of control and financial exploitation of their activities through taxation.[34] Some organizations, such as Star Kampuchea, are concerned that the law will unduly restrict their work, and have actively lobbied for a series of revisions, while other groups are worried that the law will be directly used to control the work of NGOs.[35] There is a broad concern then that the NGO law will limit the freedom of civil society, and extend state control over NGOs.

Rather than seeing such measures by the state as opposed to liberalism, these forms of regulative measures should be seen as being consistent with the broader peacebuilding project of transforming the nature of conflict within the state. Furthermore, legislation to govern civil society is not unique to the South; across European and North American states charitable organizations are heavily regulated and must demonstrate their compliance with proper accounting procedures and show that their activities coincide with accepted charitable practices. However, the intriguing question is why the Cambodian government has not yet passed the NGO law, despite repeated moves to do so. Clearly the pursuit of this legislation should be understood as a concern by the government over the influence of NGOs. Prime Minister Hun Sen stated in a radio broadcast in 2008 that 'Cambodia has been heaven for NGOs for too long.... The NGOs are out of control ... they insult the government just to ensure their financial survival (*Asia Times*, 14 November 2008)'.[36] In some respects, the criticism of the 'free for all' enjoyed by NGOs has also been made by some international donors and NGOs operating in the state.[37] One NGO worker said that NGOs need to ask themselves, 'When are we getting in the way of state initiatives?', indicating that NGOs may be hindering the state's ability to deliver programmes.[38] Representatives of the Canadian government working for CIDA also took this position. Chris Turner, the Cambodian project manager of the Canada Fund, stated that there was a potential problem when NGOs conducted work that ignored the government's needs.[39] Hulme and Edwards (1997: 13) argue that this dynamic plays out in states throughout the South as governments are driven to regulate the activities of NGOs in large part out of concern about how NGO activities can weaken state legitimacy. This dependence on international donor funding and NGO support for the continued development of the state is understood to be the reason why the draft law has yet to be passed. The government is in a bind, where it sees its legitimacy being undermined by NGOs delivering the types of projects the public expects of it, and in doing so, highlighting the state's lack of capacity. At the same time, the state depends on the NGO sector and does not want to unduly risk their continued investments in the country.

The two following cases illustrate the ways in which the state has sought to dictate policies for programme delivery by NGOs. While the government's approach has been similar in the two issue areas, the results have been different. In the case of health, the Cambodian government is exerting increasing levels of control over CSOs, while in education the government has been much slower in achieving influence over policy.

State management of the health sector NGOs through MEDiCAM

In examining the relationships between the government and NGOs in Cambodia, it became apparent that the health sector is the subject of more robust regulative mechanisms, and paradoxically greater state–NGO cooperation, than other sectors.[40] The extent to which this is due to a desire to cooperate by the various parties is unclear. The capacity of the Ministry of Health, and the health sector in general (including hospitals and education facilities), has expanded over the past decade.[41] One Northern NGO worker, who has spent time working in government ministries facilitating work between NGOs and the government, said that while some ministries, such as the Ministry of Social Affairs, have very little capacity to manage their portfolios, whereas the Ministry of Health was steadily increasing its ability to set national policy and deliver various medical programmes.[42] Another LNGO representative argued that the Ministry of Health was well organized and had good internal leadership.[43] The state's growing capacity in health management was noted by organizations working with the Royal University of Phnom Penh (RUPP) medical programmes. Their representatives asserted that while NGOs initially set the agendas at the medical training facilities, they now respond to needs identified by the Faculty, and programmes such as dentistry education that were run by NGOs have been taken over by the Faculty. However, the Ministry of Health does not yet have the capability to run all of its programmes, and as a result continues to rely on donor funding and NGO project delivery.[44]

In specialized areas of health services, such as assistance for peoples with disabilities, the Ministry does not have the means to run comprehensive programmes, so it continues to work closely with NGOs.[45] Additionally, there is a continuing process of health sector NGOs taking over the management of some district level health services.[46] Thus, the health sector is marked by increasing state capacity, and by relatively close cooperation between many NGOs and Ministry of Health officials. Much of this can be traced to the evolution of a particular organization that has come to serve as a means of limited state regulation: MEDiCAM.

The creation, in 1989, of MEDiCAM, an umbrella group representing NGOs working in health, and its continued evolution has provided a means by which the government is able is exert control. This forces NGOs to abide by government priorities, and encourages NGOs working in the sector to participate in this process; today MEDiCAM has over 50 INGO and 37 LNGO full members.[47] Its stated mission is:

> MEDiCAM is the primary networking agency for the country's health-related NGOs. It seeks to link all health sector stakeholders by representing the voice of its NGO members, facilitating policy, advocacy, building capacity of MEDiCAM's members and health partners, and sharing relevant quality information.[48]

The group received official recognition by the SOC in 1991, and began representing NGOs working on health issues. The interaction between

Table 6.1 NGO disbursements in the health sector, 1998–2002

	1998	*1999*	*2000*	*2001*	*2002*
Value of disbursements (millions, US$)	31.391	27.832	27.553	27.385	33.100

Data source: CDC database: www.cdc-crdb.gov.kh/cdc/ngo_statistics.htm.

MEDiCAM and the government has become quite formalized, with the umbrella group being invited to the majority of meetings touching on health. According to MEDiCAM, 'this has provided a golden opportunity for NGOs to actively contribute to both the policymaking and the implementation of the Health Sector Reform, engaged in by the government since 1996'.[49] But this relationship has also increased the ability of the government to direct NGO activity in the health sector. This has been brought about in large part by the support of a number of international donors, which now require NGOs be approved by the MEDiCAM board, which includes a government representative, prior to being granted funding. The Canadian Government, for example, insists that groups that receive funding belong to MEDiCAM, and that projects are vetted by the government.[50] To achieve this approval, organizations must demonstrate that their work meets a government priority, as laid out in its Health Sector Strategic Plan (Ministry of Health 2008), that the goals are obtainable, and the programme is sustainable.

Chris Turner, stated that there is a problem when NGOs do work and ignore the government's needs.[51] Pierre Lacerte went further and argued that without being forced to cooperate most NGOs would opt not to work with the government.[52] This is the case in the education sector where, without the influence of donors, there has not been the same cooperation between NGOs and the state, and the state has not been able to dictate the policy agenda. While the NGOs have been willing to work within the framework, the process has been largely donor driven.

A case of limited government influence EDUCAM

The education sector is an area where one might expect to find significant cooperation between NGOs and the state. After all, the delivery of education is both a government priority and is one where the state – through public education – delivers the majority of services. Indeed, one finds that on an NGO-by-NGO basis there is close cooperation between the Ministry and NGOs.[53] That said, the attempt to introduce a programme similar to MEDiCAM has been rejected by both the Ministry of Education, Youth and Sports (MoEYS), and NGOs.[54] Intriguingly, the Ministry saw such a large-scale programme as potentially eroding ministerial control over education. This shows the extent to which the bureaucracy is concerned about the influence that NGOs have, and that it is worried about losing authority over policy and service delivery to these groups. Indeed, NGOs disburse a significant amount of monies in this sector.

In addition, the NGOs also fear a loss of control and being subject to a Ministry that has been unable to meet its own strategic planning goals, replicating narratives of the state as lacking capacity, and of the NGOs as being better placed to ascertain development priorities.

Table 6.2 NGO disbursements in education, 1998–2002

	1998	*1999*	*2000*	*2001*	*2002*
Total NGO disbursements (millions, US$)	8.162	9.032	8.770	8.479	14.067

Data source: CDC database: www.cdc-crdb.gov.kh/cdc/ngo_statistics.htm).[55]

An education sector working group was established in 1991 that included both Ministry and NGO representatives. This group, EDUCAM, has a steering committee with both NGO and Ministry officials, and holds regular meetings and invites outside speakers on a range of topics addressing education in Cambodia. However, according to NGO employees working in the education sector, EDUCAM has been of limited use and there is little to no government participation. In contrast, the Department of Education sees EDUCAM as being overly critical of the government and of not being particularly constructive. The result is that EDUCAM meetings are often held without any government representation.[56]

The other organization that is in place to facilitate cooperation between NGOs and the Ministry is the NGO Education Partnership (NEP). This group also has both NGO and government members, and is fairly representative of the range of state and non-state actors involved in the education sector. The goal of the NEP is to develop a mechanism to promote dialogue among its own members and MoEYS, in order to improve the quality of education in Cambodia.[57] The NEP now has a small office with three full-time staff and has 65 member NGOs. There have been periodic attempts to move the NEP to adopt some of the aspects of MEDiCAM, specifically government control over the recognition and funding of groups working on NGOs. NGOs have resisted this move, and are worried that it would lead to groups being constrained by the government. They are also sceptical that such a model would result in positive change in Cambodian education, and feel that such activity would erode the quality of the projects being delivered. They point to a System Wide Action Plan (SWAP), which the education NGOs had advocated in 2000. In the words of one NGO worker: 'we all went along with it. The government however was unable to deliver in the end. There have been no reforms to date of the education management'.[58] Because of a perception that the government was unable to reform its management of education, this NGO opted to release an alternative strategic plan in 2003. This initiative is an example of how NGOs are attempting to directly influence the MoEYS policy direction. While the government expressed its support for this initiative, it was never effectively implemented.

Sieng Sorvathana, a representative of the MoEYS Gender Secretariat, argued that the relationships between NGOs and the department were defined by money.[59] The NGOs had the ability, because of their funding from international donors, to implement projects, often without the support or approval of the Ministry of Education. She further argued that the Department does in fact rely on the experience of NGO workers and that the government appreciates their capacity-building initiatives. This was echoed by the Ratanakiri Provincial Director of Education, who said the province relies on the technical capacity of NGOs.[60] This reliance on NGO technical support was still evident in 2010 during my fieldwork in Banlung. However, Sieng Sorvathana argued that what defines the relationship between the government and a specific NGO is whether they share the same goals, and that if they differed there was bound to be a poor relationship. When the two cooperate, hold regular meetings and share problems, they are able to work together to resolve whatever issues may arise. This indicates that what in large part determines the relationship between the state and the NGO is the extent to which the NGO is willing to support the Ministry's policy initiatives.

Unlike the medical sector, which has seen a great deal of cooperation, both sides in education have been reluctant to take any steps that might erode their influence. The government would clearly prefer to have greater oversight on NGOs working on education, and to ensure that the programmes that are put in place meet with its own priorities. In contrast, NGOs see the Ministry as having not yet demonstrated the capacity to manage the broad spectrum of educational needs in the country. However, as the Ministry continues to develop its technical expertise and to acquire the necessary resources to manage the state's education system, the trend of seeking a modicum of control over NGOs is likely to increase.

Conclusion

The peacebuilding process has put in place dynamics that have led to limited forms of conflict between civil society actors (NGOs) and the state over setting development goals and priorities. While the state has focused on measures that are likely to bring about stability (Slocomb 2006) and facilitate rent-seeking, the international community (and in particular INGO and LNGOs) have privileged wide-ranging reforms (Lizée 2000; Roberts 2001; Hughes 2003). By both advancing neoliberal reforms that have reduced the size of the state, and simultaneously promoting bottom-up development and funnelling development dollars through NGOs, the state's capacity to deliver services was curtailed in the first decade of post-conflict peacebuilding. As a consequence, NGOs have acquired considerable freedom of action, and are generally able to run programmes without significant bureaucratic interference. The government relies on the NGO sector for the delivery of various development programmes, a situation that while reportedly resented by some government officials, is also recognized by the political elite as currently necessary. Additionally, the state bureaucracy also draws on NGOs for technical expertise, for funding, and the delivery of projects. In some sectors, such as resource management, this has resulted in a nominally cooperative working environment between the bureaucracy and some NGOs.

Outside of the health sector, many NGO workers reported that the bureaucrats were suspicious of the influence and intentions of NGOs, which extended to NGO representatives that were involved in capacity building within the bureaucracy. At the same time, NGO workers regularly expressed a lack of trust in the ability of the government to adequately meet the needs of its populations. The mutual distrust reinforces dynamics wherein representatives of NGOs and various levels of government may be unwilling to work together, and NGOs are reluctant to take direction from the Cambodian state. Because of the financial clout of the large INGOs, the international donor support of LNGOs, and the relative shortage of state capacity, this has created an environment where NGOs have been able to set their own priorities and implement programmes of their own choosing.

This chapter has described a gradually changing environment where the state is regaining financial and technical capacity, and is beginning to reassert itself in some policy areas. The Cambodian government has, as a result, begun to push for increasing influence over the development priorities of NGOs, and with the backing of some international donors, has been able to implement some means to set the policy agenda for the delivery of health services across the country. Within the education sector, though the MoEYS has been increasing its capacity and has begun driving for greater control over the activities of NGOs, civil society groups have proven reluctant to enter into a situation where they would be under even indirect control or supervision by the state.

This form of conflict between the state and NGOs over development priorities – how they should be designed, and who should implement them – must be considered within a wider context. This struggle between NGOs and the state is embedded within broader discourses of the nature of civil society and the Southern state, as well as the neoliberal promotion of free markets and a small state. NGOs, the representatives of civil society, are seen as being more capable and democratic than the government. Additionally, because supporting civil society is in itself a goal of peacebuilding, international donors have come to rely heavily on NGOs. This has resulted in a situation where NGOs have gained an increased capacity in Cambodia vis-à-vis the state, where the support for the organizations has validated the initial belief in their agency, and where the state is portrayed as corrupt and inept. This has very real implications for Cambodia's development. It makes it difficult for the state to exert policy control, and to set its own development agendas. Furthermore, as the state gradually regains the ability to manage programmes, it is on a path that puts it at odds with some NGOs. The increase in government capacity does not have to manifest in problematic ways, indeed the functioning of MEDiCAM is an excellent example of how the state and NGOs can cooperate. In contrast, the modest successes of EDUCAM point to the enduring tension between NGOs and the state, and illustrate how resolving the mistrust can be exceedingly difficult. Finally, the on-off movement towards an NGO law is evidence of the government's attempt to bring this sector under control, and to regulate its behaviour. This is a dynamic readily accepted in the West, where charitable groups are tightly regulated, but when it comes to the South there is trepidation of state control. Once again, it is faith in the viability and appropriateness of an independent civil society, and one that is more representative and effective than the Southern State, that continues to inform this debate.

Many of the assumptions of NGOs as being able to articulate local community demands effectively and democratically are problematic. NGOs are generally not representative of the communities they work in, are not organized in a democratic fashion, and can be charismatically led. In fact, the priorities of NGOs are often not set according to local need, but more often reflect donor interests, which in some instances are established without any reference to the local context in Cambodia. This should not, however, be taken as a broad critique of the associational literature on civil society. It does, however, point to a need for more local input into NGO activities, and a requirement for donors to set priorities based largely on local requirements rather than foreign domestic considerations.

The conflicts that have emerged between the state and NGOs over policy priorities can be understood from within the liberal framework, and as such do not *necessarily* represent a potential logical contradiction within peacebuilding theory and practice. They do highlight the dilemma faced by developing states where they need, within a neoliberal framework, to find a balance between fiscal responsibility to foster sustainable economic growth, and a degree of service delivery to the population that meets some minimal demands. The NGOs, within this context, are able to step in where the state is lacking and deliver projects. Peacebuilding has put in place the dynamics for conflict between the state and NGOs; however this does not in itself necessarily represent a contradiction within its theory and practice. Indeed, the tension over development priorities is not in itself a criticism of the peacebuilding process. Nor, as the state regains capacity, is its drive to assert itself in policy settings. The state has been opting for legal measures, such as the NGO law, as a means of resolving conflict, a point that appears to validate the liberal peacebuilding model. Thus while peacebuilding has put in place the dynamics for conflict between NGOs and the state, these do not signify a limitation of the application of liberalism to the resolution of conflict in Cambodia. As with the prior chapter, these forms of conflict can be predicted within a liberal framework, and attempts to foster civil society can simultaneously be seen as the means of resolving such crises.

7 Intervention on identity issues

[W]e are all Khmer because we all eat fish from the Tonle Sap.
(Conference participant talking about who should be able to vote in Cambodia)

On 29 January 2003, Phnom Penh experienced city-wide riots that culminated in the destruction of numerous Thai businesses and the storming of Thailand's embassy. The trigger for this event was an assertion that Suwanan Kongying, a Thai soap opera star, said that Angkor Wat was in fact Thai.[1] Though the riot itself was clearly being manipulated by political factions in Cambodia, the issue still resonated with the general populous, who saw this as an attempt to rob Cambodia of its cultural traditions and history. The riots highlight how interpretations of the country's ancient past have become a core component of modern Khmer nationalism and nation-building, with the major political parties vying to promote images of what constitutes Cambodia, and what it means to be Cambodian. Building on insights of CSS, this chapter explores the ways in which struggles over state identities are affecting the relationship between NGOs and the state. Although these literatures have tended to look at cross-border dynamics, recognizing the interaction between security and identity practice demands an examination of the role of identity in peacebuilding. In turn this chapter pays particular attention to the ways in which identity is a security issue in Cambodia, and how this has led to state intervention in some types of NGO activity.

While the subject matter of conflict over identity has been flagged by the critical security studies literature (Ashley 1987; Shapiro and Der Derian 1989; Walker 1993; Campbell 1998b; Neumann 1999), this study has sought to examine more narrowly how it affects the Cambodian state's interactions with NGOs. The core question is whether there is a pattern of state intervention in NGOs' activities that is understood by either government or NGO representatives as relating to identity. Following Hekman (2000), this chapter looks at instances when the government has intervened in the work of NGOs in part for reasons of promoting or repressing particular articulations of how groups (including gender, race and religion) should relate to the state, and whether these communities are able to make claims for a collective voice vis-à-vis the state or other groups within society. While the breadth of scholarly literatures on state identity construction recognizes the roles of political parties, religious bodies and other arbiters of culture, the role of NGOs in the process of identity construction is generally obscured or ignored. Yet as we shall see, the state's sensitivity to issues of identity impact on its relationship with NGOs, and NGOs are, by virtue of promoting civil society, involved in the process of re/forming Cambodian identity.

This chapter proceeds by providing a brief overview of the emergence of Cambodian national identity to illustrate how it is embedded within broader historical processes of state building. It will lay out the dominant narrative of 'Cambodian national identity', and demonstrate how this has relied on both an ahistorical reading of the country's ancient past, and a racialized rendering of who is and is not Khmer. The chapter then turns to an analysis of how particular aspects of identity (youth, gender, race and religion) have affected state–NGO interaction. In each instance the reaction of the state to NGOs working in the given areas are described, and the extent to which the government has or has not intervened in civil society activity is discussed. After the empirical cases are presented their implications for liberal conceptions of peacebuilding and civil society will be addressed. The liberal framework, which has informed peacebuilding theory and practice, is unable to account for these dynamics of conflict over identity formation. Rather, it will be shown that a critical analysis that draws on a Foucauldian understanding of identity and power offers a more compelling understanding of this issue.

Cambodian identity – what is 'inside' and 'outside'

Despite the common sense manner in which we understand a nation such as Cambodia to exist and to have an ancient and traceable pedigree, the emergence of Cambodian nationalism is a relatively recent phenomenon. David P. Chandler (1996: 163–164) argues that Cambodian nationalism developed in the late 1930s from three main sources, the Lycée Sisowath, the Institut Bouddhique and the newspaper *Nagara Vatta*, and was largely restricted to the intellectual and religious elite. His work carefully lays out how the modern state deliberately set out to establish a link to the nadir of the Angkorean Empire under the King, Jayavarman VII (ibid.: 165). The Khmer people are then constructed as the heirs of the Angkor civilization. As Chandler argues:

> Without any socialist or internationalist component in Cambodian nationalism, one could proclaim Cambodia's *intrinsic* greatness, referring repeatedly to Angkor and making racist slurs against the Vietnamese.

> This was the route that Sihanouk chose to follow in the later 1960s, and it was also followed by Lon Nol and at several points by the Pol Pot regime.
>
> (ibid.: 182)

Chandler is careful in his writing to illustrate how this particular narrative of Cambodia erases the existence of many other linguistic communities within the geographic space of what is now Cambodia, and simultaneously determines who can make claims to be authentically Cambodian. The enduring presence of people speaking Vietnamese, as well as the Cham and the many highland societies, is effectively obscured in this way.

The ethno-nationalism that was advanced from the early 1930s onwards took on a much more racialized tone under Lon Nol who espoused a particular mis/reading of Cambodia's past that favoured ethnic Khmer identity. While the evidence is that it was a mingling of Khmer and Mon groups that led to the introduction of Indianized culture to Cambodia, Lon Nol promoted a different chauvinist vision. According to Kamm, Lon Nol:

> formulated ... a vast theory of what he called the 'Khmer-Mon civilization,' reversing the order of what historians and archaeologists classify as the 'Mon-Khmer civilization,' a term that follows the chronological sequence of the entrance of the Mon and Khmer people onto the stage of recorded history.... But to Lon Nol it was the Khmer part of the equation that represented the highest in Buddhist culture, and before long he had derived from it a philosophy that he entitled 'Neo-Khmerism'.
>
> (Kamm 1998: 102-103)

Thus from its outset, modern Cambodian nationalism has been imbued with a strong anti-Vietnamese and anti-Thai character.

The second point that emerges from this history relates to the issue of identity and security in Cambodia. While the horrors that occurred during the lead-up and subsequent rule of the KR were widely felt, a number of communities bore a disproportionate cost. To understand this, it is essential to recognize the importance of identity constructions during the KR era. The first point that needs to be made is that the KR did not completely break with all previous narratives of Cambodian identity. While the KR leadership articulated a new Marxist-inspired vision of the 'people', it did so in ways that echoed the discourses of identity that preceded them. While they worked to dismantle many of the structures of social life and to alter notions of identity and belonging, they did not present the new forms of identity as being disconnected with previous experience. Pol Pot and others within the KR were apparently motivated by notions of identity that relied on reading the ancient past as an integral part of what constitutes the modern Khmer. The boundaries of what constituted an ideal

'Khmer' can be mapped through a reading of what was excluded. In their fervour for a pure Cambodia, the KR began to attack ethnic minorities within the country (David P. Chandler 1991; Kiernan 1996; Clarke 2001: 420). People of Vietnamese, Cham and – to a lesser extent – Chinese heritage were specifically targeted by the Angkar. The Vietnamese were expelled from the state, while the Cham bore a particularly heavy human cost, which has become one basis for allegations of genocide. This illustrates how ethnic nationalism has come to determine who can claim protection from the state, and who is rendered a threat to the society. Despite this history, the PPA make no mention of this dynamic of violence, choosing to focus on the ideological divides between the main Khmer political factions. As is discussed after the subsequent empirical cases, this is not because peacebuilding is blind to the matter of identity politics, but rather because it assumes a particular answer to the 'problem' of identity.

The current articulation of Cambodian identity rests on the pillars of language, ethnicity, religion and monarchy. As they are at the heart of narratives of what it is to be 'Cambodian', interviewees were asked to comment specifically on how they saw youth, gender, race and religion as affecting the relationships between NGOs and the state. When organizations' activities potentially affect the narratives of who is, and is not, Cambodian, the state becomes more likely to intervene in their activities. This chapter examines the engagement of the Cambodian youth by both the political institutions of the state and by NGOs. This sector of society is seen as having an unsettled sense of identity, and of being able to be formed and moulded by various political actors. It is then understood by both the state and civil society actors as a necessary target to alter future political culture.

State intervention in youth-run NGOs

In the course of interviews with NGOs, the clearest pattern of state intervention in NGOs involved associations run by Cambodian youth.[2] This was not overly surprising, as there is a common refrain within peacebuilding policy literature of the importance of altering the behaviour of young men and women. As the young are commonly portrayed as being more malleable, and as developing, rather than possessing, fully-formed attitudes and beliefs, then targeting the youth becomes a necessary component of changing patterns of violence.[3] The reasoning is also consistent with the associational literature, which views civil society as having the potential to transform the behaviour of people, and ideally to instil democratic political culture. There is powerful historical precedence for targeting Cambodian youth to shape political culture. Under the KR they were identified as the future of the state and were deliberately separated from their parents to ensure that they could be properly educated into the new society; the children were seen by the leadership as having the potential to be remoulded into 'new people'. The physical and emotional separation of children from parents, the extensive political education and the methods of indoctrination were intended to alter the youths' sense of self and community, effectively to change their identities.[4] The current generation of young men and women have no direct memory of the KR era, and little recollection of the pre-UNTAC political dynamics. Their formative years are in the post-United Nations epoch, and their demands are often related to issues of economic development, rights and nationalism. Student groups have also shown a willingness to be politically engaged, pursuing agendas that support the range of Cambodia's political spectrum.[5] This represents an important opportunity for the government and the agents of peacebuilding to affect change by altering the ways that the youth interact, and how they perceive themselves interacting with their community. In short, the potential is there to help reshape the identity of Cambodia. This is a process, however, that the NGO community has been surprisingly unwilling to engage with.

Interviews with INGOs and donors revealed two main arguments for why youth-run organizations seldom receive direct funding from Northern donors. Firstly, such groups are not seen as being 'professional' or competent. This is expressed in a number of ways. An interview with an INGO worker who conducts capacity building for LNGOs related that the youth and student groups are very nascent organizations, and are essentially just 'budget seeking': as such they have very little ability to represent student needs.[6] The donors argued that youth groups lacked the expertise to deliver projects, where expertise is defined as either holding some diploma or university degree or having gained significant experience in working for another NGO. In addition, this lack of experienced staff also made it more difficult for these groups to complete the relevant application forms effectively and thus secure financing. When I spoke with representatives of youth groups, I was asked why their organizations were unable to secure the support of donors, and whether I could help them in this regard.[7] Representatives of these organizations were well aware of the difficulties they faced and yet were also committed to continuing their projects.[8]

The second reason that youth organizations are avoided by the donor community is that they are seen as being overly political (meaning that they are both affiliated with political parties and are involved in electoral campaigns). One Northern NGO worker, who had extensive experience in working with NGOs and international donors in Cambodia, argued that student organizations were very political and often party-aligned.[9] Putting aside how this is problematic for its perpetuation of a liberal notion of what is and is not 'political' (this is discussed at length in the next chapter) it raises two questions. First, to what extent does this politicization follow from a neglect of this sector by the international donors? Second, if the groups are being politicized should they not be supported and encouraged to adopt norms of behaviour, such as democratic decision making and respect for human rights and the rule of law, which are seen as being at the core of effective peacebuilding?

The intent here is not to leave the impression that the youth of Cambodia are ignored by the NGO and donor community. Yet when youth are engaged, it is predominately through an INGO or LNGO that is run by adults. In fact, young Cambodians are relied on extensively to provide a volunteer workforce that can be mobilized in support of various public awareness initiatives, and are often recruited to fill jobs within LNGOs and INGOs. On 11 October 2003, I attended and participated in an anti-small-arms march that had been organized by OXFAM GB. The march in Phnom Penh was led by adults, but the marchers themselves were almost exclusively youth.[10] While such approaches may allow for a more effective delivery of programmes, it is unlikely to serve the interests of encouraging associational behaviour and altering the sense of community and belonging.[11] Additionally, youth are the target of numerous projects, from anti-smoking and safe-sex to environmental awareness campaigns, all which intend to change societal behaviour. This is a common theme in projects in Cambodia; the youth are seen as both a target for NGO activity, and as a volunteer labour pool. They are not, however, provided the opportunities by international donors to lead their own projects.

Youth groups that do operate in Cambodia do not have the same freedom of action that other NGOs enjoy, and have been subjected to significantly greater political intervention. In contrast to the way that donors have ignored this sector of Cambodian society, political parties have paid close attention, seeking to shape the political affiliations of Cambodian youth. A number of LNGO representatives asserted that many student-run NGOs essentially act as youth wings of the various parties, and are often established by the parties.[12] The parties invest heavily in student groups and provide funding to some LNGOs that target the country's youth.[13] The student groups represent both a politicized movement that political parties can tap into, and a formative population that needs to be shaped into the next generation of Cambodians. Furthermore, in a similar fashion to the international donors and INGOs, parties have seen student organizations as a resource to be used to mobilize, or demobilize, the broader public by either spreading a positive message about party positions, or in the case of the Pagoda Boys, to intimidate the public.[14] One NGO representative, when asked about youth organizations stated: 'I feel sorry for the youth because they have been manipulated by the politicians'.[15] He then argued that student-run NGOs are quite vulnerable and come under considerable pressure by political parties. In particular, groups working with university students come under significant scrutiny and are restricted where they can operate. The state-run universities are particularly politicized, and only groups that are tied to the CPP are permitted to operate on the campuses.[16] One NGO worker who was working at the RUPP stated that the CPP has 'absolute political control of the University', and that 'this is a CPP University – all of the public institutions are'.[17] This provides yet more evidence of the concern of the country's political elite for the importance of winning the 'hearts and minds' of the next generation of voters.

This socialization is inherently connected to the politics of identity, as it seeks to define how individuals and communities interact. As will be argued, the willingness of the state to engage directly with youth-run NGOs is consistent with the broader pattern of intervention in organizations it perceives as being engaged in re/defining how communities relate to the government and broader society.

State–NGO interaction and gender

Drawing on gender studies and CSS literatures, I expected to find considerable pressure by the state on NGOs focusing their work on gender and/or women's rights. These bodies of literatures have demonstrated the ways in which national identities are gendered, which could be anticipated to translate to a concern by the state in NGO activities that might undermine the broader hetero-centric state narratives of Cambodian identity. However, in contrast to other areas of identity construction, there has been little direct conflict between the state and NGOs around issues of gender and women's rights. This is in spite of the ways in which gender roles have been affected by peacebuilding.

Interestingly, while much of the academic literatures on peacebuilding in Cambodia have tended to ignore most issues of identity politics, the policy literature has paid a great deal of attention to gender.[18] This is most clearly demonstrated by the ways in which international donors have pushed gender mainstreaming as a core component of development programmes which, as a consequence, has led to most LNGOs and INGOs implementing related programmes. Certainly during conversations with NGO representatives, gender was discussed in a rather sophisticated way, understood as comprising socially constructed roles, and as affecting men and women differently. In policy terms, this translates into programmes that seek to educate communities about gender and/or programmes to empower women. On this basis civil society should be seen as striving to alter the gender roles within the state. However, peacebuilding's ability to alter gendered practices within Cambodian society, and its ability to improve the lives of women, is mixed. Though there are numerous projects to improve women's quality of life, and to empower women within society, peacebuilding has also re/produced images of women as sources of free (and thus non-valued) labour, and as sexual objects for men.

As Whitworth (2004) illustrates, UNTAC's military component was directly implicated in the growth of prostitution in the country and the dramatic spread of HIV/AIDS. One NGO, International Defense for

Children (DNI), argues that the number of prostitutes in Phnom Penh increased from 6,000 to 20,000 between 1991 and 1992 – with a venereal disease infection rate of 80 per cent.[19] According to the Human Rights Task Force on Cambodia, while the numbers of prostitutes in Cambodia fell slightly after the exit of the military troops, so did the age of the workers.[20] Though this aspect of peacebuilding has been well recognized amongst NGO representatives in Cambodia, many of the same individuals have asserted that the non-military components of the mission have promoted gender awareness.

In discussing the advances made on gender issues, some NGO representatives have argued that the government of Cambodia has become more open to discussions of women's rights, and is willing to listen to NGOs' concerns about gender (though somewhat less likely to act on any concerns that might be raised).[21] The main evidence that was cited to support this assertion was the formation of the Ministry of Women's and Veteran's Affairs. This Ministry, headed in 2003 by Muo Sok Huor, a member of FUNCINPEC, is argued to be progressive in its politics, advocating equal rights and opportunities for women. It has also been proactive in consulting with NGOs on issues affecting women, such as its draft domestic violence law.[22] The Minister has said that the rights of women in Cambodia have benefited from a strong NGO movement that has lobbied the government and introduced participatory development practices, which have provided a greater voice to women.[23] This has been supported by Prime Minister Hun Sen, who has called for increased roles for women in society, and argued that women are the backbone of the country's economic and social development.[24]

Outside of this particular Ministry there has not been significant movement by the state on women's rights. According to one NGO representative, there is a clash between international standards and local cultural norms, with some powerful men arguing that drives for women's rights are external impositions on Cambodian culture, and that the realities of domestic violence are overplayed.[25] This is in spite of the ways in which violence against women can go unpunished. In 1999, the NGO Forum critiqued what it described as the 'impunity of those who murder women', citing 13 cases in the previous year where 'clearly identified suspects go free despite the presence of witnesses'.[26] Some NGO representatives working in this area pointed out that the core issue is not the government's impeding of legislation, so much as the broader Cambodian culture, as represented by the phrase: 'men are gold, women are a white piece of cloth':

> When this white piece of cloth is stained, it's stained forever, which means society expects us to hold a certain position, to have a certain status only. But once you move beyond that, you cannot reenter society. And men will always be gold.[27]

This reinforces a culture wherein women need to be protected, rather than empowered. As a result, the government has not been willing to adopt legal frameworks that would entrench the rights of women. This is precisely what civil society is expected to be able to change, albeit slowly, through its engagement with communities. Furthermore, the government is described as 'not being opposed' to the activities of women's organizations. This does not mean that it is proactive or working in support of the NGOs' goals, quite the opposite. Groups that seek to focus their work on either women or 'women's issues' thus appear to operate in a state of benign neglect.

Although the government has been slow to react to the demands for legislated protection of women's rights, on other issues that directly pertain to women the state has been more responsive. For example, on the issue of the trafficking of women the government has been willing to work with NGOs.[28] The state has worked with civil society associations to identify and prosecute foreigners pursuing sex with children, and has cooperated with NGOs in 'rescuing' women from brothels.[29] Even with this apparent government action, human trafficking remains a serious problem in Cambodia. Furthermore, the degree to which the sex trade is addressed depends, as was discussed in Chapter 5, on who is involved in terms of the age and ethnicity of the sex workers, and the wealth and power of individuals running brothels. Some NGO representations noted that working on issues pertaining to the sex trade can be difficult when it involves either Vietnamese sex workers or high-level government officials.[30] The ways in which the issue of ethnicity affects policies around sex work are evident in the state's different policies on sex workers. Khmer women are treated as being trafficked, and government initiatives have tended to seek to return women to the home communities. In contrast, Vietnamese women in near identical circumstances have had to face the threat of arrest for 'illegal immigration'.[31] Despite taking action on the trafficking of women and children, the state has not been willing to address other concerns around the sex trade, and has avoided working with NGOs on programmes that can be seen as empowering sex workers (with the exception of educating women about the use of condoms). While the state is amenable to LNGOs and INGOs that seek to work with Cambodian prostitutes, they have not allowed a local women's prostitutes' union to register as an NGO.[32] While greater research is required to delve into narratives of race and gender in Cambodia, particularly as it plays out around issues of prostitution, the state's position appears to be consistent with practices that write the state's role as one of 'protecting' Cambodian women. However, more focused research is required on whether this represents a significant alteration of gender practices within Cambodia, or whether it is a re/articulation of previous narratives of the role of women and men.

While the government has been willing to take action on some issues surrounding women's rights, and the NGO community has been deliberate in the attempt to include gender considerations in programming, there has been surprisingly little cooperative action on women's issues.[33] I was surprised to find a relative lack of cooperative action on women's issues.[34] When asked during interviews which organizations worked predominately on women's rights, one donor stated that there was only one significant group working in this area: Gender and Development (GAD).[35] Yet nearly every organization talked about gender in their policy publications, and claimed to promote equality in their programmes.[36] There are also many organizations that have programmes that provide services and programmes that specifically target women. These range from micro-credit for women, small enterprise skill training and the protection of sex workers to health and environment awareness programmes. However, direct engagement of the issue of women's rights, and groups that talk about 'gender' in contrast to 'women', have been surprisingly absent. In addition, while most groups will recognize issues of gender, they are also quite willing to take advantage of volunteer labour – which is constituted predominately of women. Rather than empowering women, such activities can also be seen as perpetuating notions that the work of women is not as valuable as that of men.[37]

In general, the rights of women are nominally supported by the government, but tangible examples of the state's defence of women's rights are hard to find. The state can be proactive in women's rights when the women being discussed are Khmer, as opposed to Vietnamese. NGOs reported a good working relationship with the state on issues such as the sex trading of Khmer women. On other issues, these organizations appear to be able to operate without fear of government intervention. This then describes an environment wherein the state is neither particularly defensive of any particular articulation of gender roles, nor effectively supportive of increased women's rights. This of course belies the extent to which gender is a core component of state identity, and how the roles of men and women are both ascribed meaning within the broader national identity. So long as struggles for equity for men and women are not taken seriously by the state, and do not undermine broader state identity narratives, then it should not be surprising that there is little basis for conflict between NGOs and the state on the issue of gender.

State intervention in NGOs over issues of religion

In contrast to the matter of gender, the state and its constituent political parties explicitly place religion at the core of what it is to be Cambodian. Theravadan Buddhism currently occupies a privileged position in the state, and is closely connected to the monarchy (Vickery 1984: 10–12; I. Harris 2005). That the KR moved to systematically eliminate this aspect of Cambodian life illustrates how it is understood to be a main component of traditional Cambodian identity, and that it was seen as connected with the exercise of power within the state. Buddhist narratives continue to be integral to debates about the nature of society and how its constituent members should interact, and to struggles for power by political parties. Hughes demonstrates how this extends to debates over the nature of human rights:

> The language of 'rights and freedoms' is linked by militants to a language of Khmer nationalism, and by mystics to the teachings of the Buddha. In both cases, the more familiar frames of reference predominate, and sometimes prevail.
>
> (Hughes 2001b: 60)

The use of Buddhist discourse has been a dominant strategy by Cambodian political parties to justify their respective platforms.

It is not just the political actors that use religious narratives: local civil society and social movements also make extensive use of such discourse. From the *dhammayietra* (annual peace marches led by monks), to LNGOs such as Buddhism for Democracy, local religious tradition has been an important component of civil society organization in Cambodia.[38] In fact, using Buddhist concepts, relying on *bhikkhus* (monks), and hosting events in Wats are seen ways of protecting an organization or movement from government interference. In contrast, the government has demonstrated that it is concerned with the impact of other religious movements within Cambodia, although this has not often translated into state intervention in the affairs of religious groups.

The country's constitution provides a remarkably open environment for the practice of religion, allowing individuals to choose which faith to follow. Because Buddhism is so widely adhered to within the state, with nearly 95 per cent recognized as being Buddhist, it is not regularly portrayed as being threatened. In general, the state has allowed non-Buddhist religious groups, and NGOs with connections to various faiths, to operate with a minimum of government interference. However, the government pays attention to the spread of non-Buddhist religions, and has, on a few occasions, intervened in the work of religious organizations. There are also signs that the state is considering greater monitoring and control over the broad spectrum of religious groups (including churches and NGOs with religious connections).

The SOC recognizes two types of religious organizations, differentiated by their primary role. On the one side are groups engaged in 'mission work' (proselytizing), who are expected to register with the Ministry of Cults and Religion. On the other side are those organizations with a religious mandate that are engaged in service work, performing development activities: these 'service oriented' groups register as any other NGO with the Ministry of Interior. While the organizations may see their mandate as arising from various religious traditions, and the workers may be quite devoted to a particular form of faith, these organizations are not supposed to proselytize actively. The difficulty is that the line between service work and mission work is easily blurred, sometimes subtly and sometimes blatantly.

One Cambodian NGO worker, who expressed a Buddhist inspiration for his work, argued that groups undertaking mission work are not appreciated by Cambodians, but that they are tolerated because they do bring funds to very poor sectors of Cambodia.[39] He also argued that such groups were not seen as being too dangerous as they were not taken seriously by Cambodians.[40] This demonstrates that the 'threat' of religious groups is judged according to whether they may undermine the position of Buddhism within society. This extends to some government workers who expressed suspicion about the intent of NGOs that are engaged in service delivery, but which have a religious grounding.[41] Indeed, the UN has expressed a concern that some NGOs use the delivery of services to propagate particular religious traditions.[42] Sieng Sorvathana argued that 'most religious groups use their programmes to try to promote their religion'.[43] Such statements clearly illustrate that the government is concerned with the issue of religion in NGO work. This was reportedly reflected at a conference hosted by the Cambodian Development Research Institute (CDRI), from 12–14 May 2003, for the Governors of Cambodia. According to one observer, the Governors viewed non-Buddhist religious NGOs with suspicion, as they were seen as being motivated by a drive to convert Cambodians.[44]

The government's attention to matters of religion is perhaps most aptly demonstrated by the Ministry of Cults and Religion. The Undersecretary of State in the Ministry of Cults and Religion, His Excellency Kin Thoan, stated that the government is more concerned with some religions than others, in particular Christianity (which he was worried might erode the Buddhist faith) and Islam. To highlight the government's apprehension about the influence of Christian and Islamic groups, he related that in 2003 there were 43 pagodas in Phnom Penh, 288 Christian churches and 47 mosques.[45] He then argued that his Ministry had become particularly concerned with Islam, stemming from a lack of knowledge about what is transpiring in the mosques, and that involvement of INGOs and religious organizations with the Muslim population is less transparent. The Minister argued that Islamic groups should have to receive permission to deliver programmes in Cambodia, a restriction that he did not advocate for Christian organizations.

State concerns about Islamic civil society organizations

Cambodia has a small but significant Muslim minority divided between the Khmer and Cham populations, with the Cham being predominately Muslim. While some NGOs receive Western donor funds to work specifically with the Islamic community, most organizations that specifically target Muslims in Cambodia either receive funding from, or are based in, Saudi Arabia, Indonesia and Malaysia.[46] This is a closed community, and despite extensive efforts to arrange interviews with the non-Western funded groups I was unable to secure such an opportunity. Additionally, these organizations do not generally interact with NGOs that advocate Christian, Buddhist or secular world-views, and according to the CCC no such organizations participate in any of their NGO networks. That the government expresses a greater disquiet about Muslim groups, when there is no evidence that they are proselytizing (while several Christian groups are doing so actively), must be understood against the backdrop of the broader war against terror. Cambodia has been drawn into this as a result of public comments by Hambali, who has been accused of orchestrating the Bali bombings, that he had spent time in Cambodia.[47] And in May 2003 Cambodia arrested and deported 11 Thai nationals who were allegedly involved with Jemaah Islamiyah, an Islamic terrorist network. One of these men was the director of Umm al-Qura, an NGO running Islamic schools for the Cham.[48] These events, combined with American pressure on Cambodia to combat 'radical Islamism', have served to make the practice of Islam a security matter.

The government's concern with NGOs working with the Islamic population has been reinforced by worries that such associations are operating beyond the influence and control of the state. One NGO representative related that there was an Islamic group that wanted to deliver a health sector project in an Islamic school in 1997.[49] The government, however, turned this project down, which he saw as significant given how desperate the Ministry of Health is for money. The only explanation the representative could offer for this was that the project was led by, and targeted, an Islamic community.

State involvement with Christian NGOs

The history of Christianity in Cambodia is relatively short, with Catholicism only being introduced in the mid-1800s during the era of French colonial rule. As the development industry has entered the country in force, there has been a rapid growth in missionary activities. Today there are a large number of groups, including INGOs and LNGOs that either draw their mandate from religious teachings, or engage in religious work. While many organizations, such as Caritas Cambodia and the Mennonite Community Council (MCC), draw a hard line between the mission work and service delivery, some associations straddle the line uneasily. One organization, which claims to be strictly service-oriented, holds weekly bible meetings that its Khmer staff are 'welcome to attend'.[50] An employer's 'invitation' to such events must be considered in relation to the power dynamics between the Khmer workers and the INGO management; as a result these meetings have a coercive element, even if it is not intended as such. There are also allegations (though unconfirmed) that some mission groups provide rice or other forms of assistance as enticements to listen to Christian gospel. All of this, in a country with extreme levels of poverty, also raises serious questions of power relations. However, the NGO representatives of these groups all said that they do not discriminate against people who do not attend these activities, and assured me that they employed Buddhists. Despite this, Christian-based groups reported little in the way of government interference. If they encounter obstruction from the government, the perception is that it is due to the personal politics of individuals, or the subject matter that they are working on. This implies then that the religion of the NGO workers is not the *core* concern of the government.

The state begins to pay much more attention to issues of religion when development organizations work with minority groups. Religious groups operating in Mondulkiri and Ratanakiri have come under significantly more state attention than groups in other parts of the country. In one instance a large INGO, open about their Christian motivation, which conducts a range of programmes throughout the state, ran into difficulties with a project it delivers to various highland minority groups. In contrast, the organization has been able to deliver similar programming in other parts of the country without facing the same government scrutiny.[51] This indicates that while there is a concern about NGOs spreading Christianity, it is more acute when it pertains to indigenous populations.

State–NGO interaction and ethnicity/race

The third area of state identity revolves around the issue of race. As Hughes points out, the notion of race has been incorporated into Cambodian discourse. 'The Khmer term for race (*puuc*) … emphasizes the notion of a group united by common kinship or blood' (Hughes 2002c: 548). The major political parties have all espoused a connection between race and citizenship, arguing that Cambodia is the country of Khmer, defined as a racial group as opposed to a language. Of course language is a core component of Khmerness. The state has been pursuing a project since at least the early 1970s to make the state's geographic boundaries and nationality coincide. While the borders themselves are now largely fixed, this has been undertaken by redefining the nationality of the various minority groups throughout the state as either being 'Khmer', and thus 'inside' the community, or to ascribe them as being 'outside' and not being able to make full claims for rights as citizens.

The NGO community in Cambodia has been aware of the issue of minority rights, yet for the most part few groups focus their work on the various ethnic communities within the state. This marks Cambodia as being separate from much of Southeast Asia where:

> [a]s a result of political liberalisation, non-governmental organizations concerned with ethnic minorities and indigenous peoples have proliferated ... and are now implementing development projects with government and donors and lobbying for further policy reform.
>
> (Clarke 2001: 429)

A representative of one INGO that provides training and assistance to LNGOs, when asked about whether his organization worked with groups targeting or run by minorities, declared that it had not. Not because his group overlooks these groups, but because they 'simply don't really exist'.[52] This was echoed by a representative of another institution that provided research to NGOs, who stated that there were very few groups that specifically target ethnic segments of society.[53] The exception to this rule is the Khmer Kampuchea Krom (KKK) community. The individual then speculated that this was because the Khmer have had more opportunities to advance NGOs, and have acquired greater organizational capacity.[54] These comments illustrate both a sense that general Cambodian society is represented by the Khmer, and that somehow the ethnic minorities lie outside of the norm. When organizations do focus on minority communities, it is often to deal with sources of problems to broader society, rather than to specifically assist the particular community. The following overview of how NGOs and the state interact around various ethnic groups further illustrates this point.

The lack of NGO engagement with the Cambodian Vietnamese population

A *New York Times* article, discussing the impact of the 1997 coup on the Vietnamese in Cambodia, interviewed a 56-year-old man, Ngo Van Xeng, asking him where his home was in Vietnam. In response he shouted, 'I don't know! We were all born here. Our home is here. My father and their mothers – we are all from Cambodia!'[55] This outpouring shows the problematic nature of linking ethnicity and territory, and shows the extent to which there has been an interweaving of cultures throughout Southeast Asia. Yet the Vietnamese population in Cambodia has been routinely targeted for violence by both the state and opposition parties. The narratives of a threatening Vietnamese force have been present at least as long as the territorial state project in Cambodia. David P. Chandler relates how one poem, intended for wide dissemination in 1869, constructs a particularly frightening image of the Vietnamese. The poem about the period of Vietnamese domination of Cambodia 'sees the many-faceted Vietnamese *mission civilisatrice* in terms of torture, corruption and corvée and as a corrosive assault on Cambodian values' (David P. Chandler 1996: 68). Since the start of the peacebuilding mission in Cambodia in 1991, there have been numerous examples of Vietnamese communities being attacked.

These attacks, while usually verbal, have also manifested in anti-Vietnamese protests riots, and physical assaults on Vietnamese people and their property. Furthermore, anti-Vietnamese rhetoric has been used to rally support by various political parties and has been used to undermine the base of political opponents.[56] Even the CPP – which has close links with the Vietnamese government – has been willing to tolerate and use anti-Vietnamese discourse.

There is no issue area as telling of the importance of identity to the government's perceptions of NGOs, and of NGOs' views of the state, as the Vietnamese. The numbers themselves relate a part of the story. Of all of the NGOs in Cambodia, I found none that focused their work on Vietnamese communities.[57] The size of the population is substantial, though due to the politics of identity the numbers themselves are hotly contested. The government of Cambodia argues that there are only around 109,512 in the state, while others place the numbers around 500,000.[58] Despite the substantial size of the community, a Vietnamese translator who has grown up in Cambodia, and works with NGOs and the press in Cambodia could not identify a single NGO that worked directly with the Vietnamese. She said that the Vietnamese are afraid of the government and afraid of the Khmer, and that as such they would be wary of working with any state-supported NGOs. She also thought that any group that did try to begin to work specifically with the Vietnamese would be shut down by the government. The groups she could identify that had some programmes that engaged the Vietnamese, all entailed work with sex workers.[59] Even in terms of community development, which is considered to be beneficial by the state, not a single group could be named that undertook such activities specifically for Vietnamese Cambodians. This is in spite of the fact that the Vietnamese may account for up to 10 per cent of the state's population. As an example, one 32-page grant proposal to the Japan Fund for Poverty Reduction (JFPR) targeting the floating communities on the Tonle Sap and Tonle Bassac contains only a single mention of the issue of ethnicity, despite the fact that it has directly affected how the state authorities have dealt with the floating communities, many of which speak Vietnamese. While the proposal lists ethnicity as one issue facing the fishing communities, it is placed alongside poverty, indebtedness, lack of education, and gender discrimination (ADB 2005: 14). This reflects either a lack of awareness of the centrality of ethnicity to state–community relations, or a deliberate attempt to underplay the issue. Most Cambodian NGOs are not interested in working with the Vietnamese, but in the words of one INGO representative, even if they were they would most likely stay away.[60] He also stressed that this was a very delicate matter, even though the government was nominally in support of Vietnam. In either case this is indicative of the way that NGOs in Cambodia avoid the politically sensitive issue of the status of Vietnamese Cambodians.

Though there are NGO programmes that reach out to the Vietnamese in Cambodia, the organizations do not define their projects as focusing on this particular ethnic group, but rather do so in much more vague geographic or subject-matter terms. For example, rather than stating that a group works with Vietnamese sex workers, the project would be labelled as seeking to help sex workers within a particular commune. Describing programmes in geographic or issue specific terms is seen as avoiding the politics of race and belonging. Some HR organizations, while having undertaken some cases that involve Vietnamese people, have not publicized such activities. When such programmemes have come to the attention of state authorities, they are at risk of being shut down. This was noted in an overview of Cambodian human rights by Vijghen, 'LICADHO was forced after police and government pressure to suspend a project aimed to assist Vietnamese victims of slave labour' (2001: 9). At the same time, the dominant theme of groups working with the Vietnamese was in terms of either voting rights or prostitution. The former speaks to the ongoing struggle over Cambodian citizenship and identity, and the second to the inherent fear of the Vietnamese 'polluting' Cambodian society.

Such strategies by NGOs are not neutral in terms of identity construction; rather they serve to reproduce the notion that the Vietnamese are not a natural part of the Cambodian state. Cambodian LNGOs often replicate the discourse of the Vietnamese as distinct and separate from Cambodian society, and as representing a threat to it. One Cambodian LNGO worker said that the Vietnamese are not like the Cham: they live in boats and are not interested in Khmer activities.[61] Even a number of Cambodian HR groups expressed negative views of the Vietnamese. In one instance, a HR group representative, working with sex workers, stated it was difficult dealing with Vietnamese women because, unlike Khmer women, they enjoyed their work and wanted to remain in the brothels.[62] The Vietnamese women were thus presented as hyper-sexualized and morally corrupt. This is in keeping with the Khmer discourse about the relationship between Cambodia and Vietnam, where the Vietnamese are seen as threatening to overrun the Khmer, and to eradicate their culture.

This theme of a threat to Cambodian society and culture was laid out most coherently by Say Va, the Deputy Director of the Khmer Literature and Culture Association (ICLCA). In talking about the effects of the neighbouring states on Khmer culture he said that both Thai and Vietnamese cultures were eroding the traditions in Cambodia. While he expressed concern over the effects of Thailand, he reserved the majority of his comments for the impact of the Vietnamese. 'Now we are having HIV problems and glue sniffing and gangs, these are because of Vietnamese culture'.[63] This is in keeping with Rodney Hall's writing on identity where he argues that we must 'note ... how the representation of the Other implies an opposing representation of the [Cambodian] self' (R. Hall 2001: 104). My own translator and Khmer language instructor, an otherwise thoughtful, reflective and compassionate individual, was quite willing to share her negative views towards the Vietnamese. It was, she explained to me, a fact that the Vietnamese were slowly taking all the jobs in Phnom Penh.

The state and the major political parties are struggling to define the Cambodian nation, and the presence of Vietnamese within the state represents a potential threat to the way the state identity has been constructed around Khmer identity. The very idea of the nation being under siege from its neighbours is at the heart of how the state's history is described. This discourse of a Khmer identity being threatened by the Vietnamese has created an environment where NGOs are either reticent to engage the Cambodian–Vietnamese population publicly, or have their own perceptions of the community shaped by the common narratives. Rather than challenging the government's views on the matter, and openly working with the communities, NGOs have opted for more selective interaction with Vietnamese peoples, seeking to obscure their engagement with them, and avoiding public pronouncements of such activities.

State non-engagement with NGOs representing the Khmer Kampuchea Krom (KKK)

The case of the KKK further illustrates how the construction of Cambodian identity is replete with internal contradictions. The KKK speak Khmer, and understand themselves to be ethnically Khmer. They practise the same form of Buddhism, and ascribe to a common history. The difference is that this population comes from the Mekong delta inside what is now Vietnam. This poses serious difficulties for the Cambodian government, and makes any recognition of KKK claims of abuse within Vietnam, or of calls for the return of KKK to Cambodia, politically unpalatable. The difficulty for the KKK population does not end at this point. Despite this sense of a historic and ethnic connection with the Khmer peoples, the KKK feel that they are discriminated against by the broader Cambodian–Khmer society and the government. They feel it is difficult for their community members to find jobs, to get support from the government and to register to vote.

However, unlike dealing with the Vietnamese, NGOs are able to work openly with the KKK community, and make the fact that they target this ethnic group specifically a part of their core mandates. Such groups are able to register with the Ministry of Interior, which signals that the government at least accepts the validity of such organizations. To address the obstacles that are in place for the KKK a number of INGOs and LNGOs have been working with this population. Some groups, such as the KKK Human Rights Association, work to promote the rights of the KKK peoples. There are other groups that provide a variety of services such as job-skills training, environmental awareness, and medical assistance. Additionally the broader NGO sector in Cambodia has shown a willingness to work with this community. During interviews with this community I was not told of any instances where the government has sought to stop or limit the work of the organizations, though this does not translate into active support. Indeed, it was related that the government was generally unhelpful and nonresponsive to LNGOs working with the KKK.

The nature of the relationship between the government and NGOs focusing on the KKK community indicates that identity politics do affect state interaction with civil society. The difference in the treatment of groups working with the KKK and the Vietnamese must be interpreted in terms of how the two communities are perceived as relating to the narratives of national Khmer identity. Insofar as the KKK self-identify as 'Khmer' and share common cultural myths, the government is able to accept or at least tolerate CSO engagement with this sector of society, though this does not translate into support for the community's controversial demands for the return of portions of the Mekong Delta to Cambodia.

National identity and the Cham

In contrast to the narratives of identity used by the KKK, the Cham population within Cambodia is not subject to obvious exclusion or discrimination in the current political atmosphere. Here the term Cham refers specifically to ethnicity rather than religion. There is an intriguing divergence opening up in Cambodia's identity narratives where the Cham are seen as Cambodian, while Islam is seen as potentially dangerous, which complicates the perceptions of the community, as it is predominately Muslim. The narratives pertaining to the Cham population is at odds with the arguments made about either the KKK or the Vietnamese. On a number of occasions it was related during interviews that the Cham were Khmer, that they had lived in Cambodia for a long time and that thus they were expected to have all the same rights and responsibilities as other Khmer.[64] His Excellency Chea Sophorn, Secretary of State for the Council of Ministers, argued that the Cham were actually Khmer Islam, and that they felt completely Khmer.[65] One group went so far as to say that Cham were like Cambodians. 'We don't think they are "Cham" or "Khmer"'.[66] The issue of their religion was rarely raised, and in those instances when it was mentioned the worry was not the Cham, but rather the outside influence of Islamic organizations on them. This has not always been the case. The recent history of the attacks on the Cham by the KR indicates how flexible the narratives of community belonging are. Mysliwiec noted that: 'during the Pol Pot period national minorities were persecuted; the Cham suffered especially. The Islamic Cham population fell by 100,000 during this time' (1998: 12–13). In contrast, the Cham are not often portrayed now as representing a threat to Cambodia.

As the Cham are predominately Muslim I had little success (for the reasons described earlier) in securing interviews with NGOs focusing on these communities.[67] The one group that was interviewed received American funding to promote international human rights norms with an obvious mandate to combat Islamic terrorism. The Islamic donors and NGOs that are active in the Muslim communities do not participate in the various NGO coalitions such as the CCC. As was stated earlier, the Cambodian state is concerned with this dynamic, and seems to fear that foreign Islamic influence will somehow undermine the 'Cambodian-ness' of the Cham. This threat, as it is perceived, is sufficient to warrant the attention and action of the state.[68]

State attention to NGOs working with highland peoples

The complexity of the state's identity politics becomes particularly evident when examining state–NGO relations around Cambodia's highland peoples. Due to the historic geographic isolation of these groups, they have sustained languages, religious practices, social customs and agricultural systems that differ substantially from those of peoples in the lowlands. For example, their modes of agriculture do not revolve around wet rice, but instead rely on various forms of farming that have been adapted to their environment, with some of the groups continuing to practice swidden agriculture and to follow semi-nomadic patterns of life. The archeological evidence points to a long history of interaction between the Khmer of the lowlands and the various highland groups; though, as Higham relates, the nature of the relationship was often not one of mutual respect. He illustrates this point by referring to the writings of the Chinese diplomat, Zhou Daguan, who visited what is now Cambodia in 1296, which talk about how the Khmer empire took slaves from the forested highlands (Higham 2001: 135). This contrasts with current practices in Khmer political discourse of referring to these peoples as 'our highland brothers and sisters'. The relationship between the Khmer and the highland peoples began to change dramatically in the 1970s with the central state seeking to extend its control over the country's territorial periphery, and its drive to incorporate the peoples living in these zones into the broader Khmer nation. This led to increased contact between the remote communities and the central government, and to attempts to reconcile their modern nation-building exercise with these peoples. This meant, in part, an attempt to rectify the internal divisions that contradicted the myth of territorialized national identity.

With Lon Nol, the Cambodian state began a process of trying to assimilate the highland societies into the narrative of a broader Khmer nation. The way in which these people were referred to changed, with the term *Khmer Loeu* being used by Lon Nol to indicate how these people were part of Cambodia. Today the highland groups are widely considered by Khmer to be 'brothers and sisters', and to be a part of a wider Khmer peoples (though there is still systematic discrimination against them). Their Cambodian-ness is reproduced through public discourse where the political elite refers to the peoples as 'Khmer', and in public spaces such as the

Cambodian Cultural Centre in Siem Reap, where the various highland peoples are shown alongside Khmer, and thus are represented as Khmer, and not a separate and distinct people.

This process was made most stark when a Khmer translator brought me a photograph of some highland peoples. She wanted to show that the highland peoples were in fact more 'authentic' Khmer. She pointed out the curly hair, the ruddy complexions and the facial characteristics as being what used to characterize all Khmer. The reason for the difference in their appearance today, as she saw it, is because the Khmer themselves have slowly taken on physical traits from the neighbouring Thai and Vietnamese. In this way the highland peoples are ascribed meaning as somehow more pure, being in closer connection with the Cambodian land, and less corrupted by the outside influences of adjacent societies, even if they are simultaneously seen as less sophisticated. Such understandings of these peoples may provide a justification for allowing the various communities to develop at their own pace, and to minimize the impact of the outside world on their villages; however it also supports and justifies programmes to develop and incorporate them back into the greater Khmer community. Such arguments can also be found in the work of some Cambodian writers:

> Until present days the *Khmer Leu* have not been able to get out of their traditional tribal lifestyle. Comparing the tribal *Khmer Leu* and the *Middle Khmer*, we notice that the latter group has a much higher development rate.
>
> (Moniroth 1995: 36)

It is not their geographic isolation from the lowlands, or the lack of local infrastructure, that is seen as hampering their development, but rather something inherent to their culture.[69] The drive to integrate these peoples into the Khmer nation is more pressing when one considers the fear of Vietnamese encroachment on Cambodia, and the ways in which the various ethnic groups straddle the border between the two states.

Underlying much of the politics around the highland communities is the ongoing attempt to define the boundary between Cambodia and Vietnam, a process that has encompassed the highland peoples who live in zones that do not coincide with the state boundaries. The border itself is contested, with allegations by the Cambodian press and opposition parties that Vietnam is slowly extending its frontier into Cambodian territory.[70] The highland peoples are being forced into categories of citizenship that do not agree with their familial linkages which often straddle the border. The drive to incorporate communities into one state or another, and to define portions of one community as Cambodian, and others as Vietnamese, is politically charged and directly affects relations between the two governments. This has been highlighted over the past five years as refugee claimants from various minority groups within Vietnam have crossed into Cambodia to seek asylum.[71] At the behest of the Vietnamese government, Cambodia forcibly deported at least 89 individuals from highland communities from the provinces Mondulkiri and Ratanakiri in early May 2001.[72] In July 2004, Prime Minister Hun Sen went so far as to threaten to use the Cambodian military to push out Montagnards (a term first used by the French colonial regime to refer to the collection of highland peoples) who were using Cambodia as a haven from which they could fight for independence from Vietnam.[73]

One of the few examples in Cambodia's peacebuilding history of the government directly interfering in the work of a UN agency occurred around this issue, as the state demanded that refugee camps in Ratanakiri and Mondulkiri be shut, and after people were evacuated from the sites, the physical infrastructure was destroyed. The government remains acutely sensitive to politics amongst the various highland groups, and has paid close attention to refugees from Vietnam. This is in stark contrast to the remarkably open environment for other refugees in Cambodia; the state is one of the few states in Southeast Asia to have signed on to the international refugee conventions, and it has a relatively transparent adjudication system, but this process has not been applied equally in the case of the Montagnards.

NGOs that have come to work with the highland groups find themselves implicated in the identity politics of the region. Unlike in other parts of the country, groups in the provinces of Mondulkiri and Ratanakiri are aware of the issue of identity and were, during my interviews, reflective of their role in the regions' identity politics. Representatives of NGOs working in the health, education and development sectors all reported that they were under significant scrutiny by the government at provincial and state levels. In the words of one NGO worker in Ratanakiri, 'there has been a lot of suspicion by the government of NGO work here'.[74] The NGOs' representatives perceive the government's approach to civil society groups as being supportive if their organizations were present to spend money, but at the same time they feel that the government fears that groups may be empowering local people. As a result, the provincial government took the unprecedented move of requiring NGOs in the province to request permission to leave the province.[75] They specifically targeted one locally based NGO, Non-Timber Forest Products (NTFP), ordering two of its staff to stay in a house near a police outpost.[76] While the concern over empowerment has been identified by NGOs throughout Cambodia, the difference in this case is that it comes linked to a fear of a potential drive for a separation from the state by the various ethnic communities. This fear has manifested in bans on reporters covering the Montagnard issue, and in one instance in July 2004, the detention of two journalists.[77]

From 2001 until early 2004 two waves of peoples crossed into Cambodia from Vietnam claiming refugee status, leading to conflicts between the government of Cambodia and NGOs both in Phnom Penh and in the highlands. The UN, various HR organizations and the press were accused of helping and smuggling the Montagnards into Phnom Penh.[78] At the height of the two crises there were 900 refugees in Phnom Penh in April 2002, and two years later, in April 2004, there was another peak of 300 people undergoing the UNHCR screening process in Phnom Penh, alongside an estimated 54–90 asylum seekers in Ratanakiri and Mondulkiri.[79] Allegations of the government forcibly returning refugees to Vietnam were made by the press and various HR monitors, including the UN human rights envoy, Peter Leuprecht.[80] During the first refugee period (2001–2002), the United Nations established camps for the refugee claimants in the provinces. These camps experienced numerous incidents of intimidation by soldiers and police, and allegations that Vietnamese soldiers arrived to force the Montagnards back across the border. When the last group of refugees finally left the UN camp in Mondulkiri, government officials burned down the facilities within one hour of the last refugee leaving the site, in what has been interpreted as an attempt by the government to prevent another UN camp being established.[81]

During the second influx of Montagnard refugees in late 2003 and early 2004, the government of Cambodia sought to restrict outside involvement in the situation and took steps to limit access by NGOs, the press and the UN to the refugees in the provinces of Ratanakiri and Mondulkiri. In Phnom Penh the police began to pay particular attention to the offices of the Jesuits, who were providing legal and procedural support to claimants.[82] In terms of NGOs operating in Ratanakiri, the provincial governor wanted all groups to apply formally to work with minority groups; several groups such as CARE and Health Unlimited told the government that they would not write for permission.

Christian groups, including both mission and service-oriented organizations, are being scrutinized by the government in the wake of the refugee crisis. The state's concern with Christian organizations is more apparent in some districts, in particular where the Jarai peoples are resident (the refugee claimants were predominately Jarai), and there is a vocal US-based Montagnard separatist movement that is centred on this ethnic group. The case of the Seventh-day Adventist church is instructive. The church went to Ratanakiri in 2000, but was forced out of the province within a year due to the government's strategy of passive resistance against the group. The non-cooperation made it almost impossible for the group to operate in province, and communities recognized from the government's stance that they should not deal with the church's representatives. It should be stressed, however, that other religious groups did not see a significant impact on their organizations during the 2003/04 influx of Montagnard refugees.

The other dynamic affecting the state–NGO interaction around highland communities is the ongoing economic transition in the remote provinces of Cambodia:

> The indigenous people in the highlands are subject to pressure and sometimes violence to sell their communal land. HR NGOs are in the forefront to assist these people. Fortunately, the draft land law to provide communal land ownership to indigenous minorities that receives a strong support from the Prime Minister and the King might correct this situation.
>
> (Vijghen 2001: 9)

This has not translated in all cases into interference by the state, but NGOs are nevertheless aware of the government's concerns around minorities. In part, the extent to which the groups are subject to state interventionism depends on the outlook of the provincial government, in particular the views of the Governor. In Ratanakiri, the Governor, His Excellency Kep Chuktema, showed significant interest in the workings of NGOs, which contrasts with the Governor of Mondulkiri who was, according to NGOs working in the province, less worried about NGOs working with the highland groups.[83] NGO representatives reported that they had excellent relations with the Governor of Ratanakiri in the late 1990s; they argued that he was concerned with the land rights of highland groups.[84] However, since he left to take up the post of Governor of Phnom Penh, the new Governor has focused on bringing in more commercial farming to the province, which has resulted in some tension between NGOs working on land rights and resource management, and the state.

Certainly, some forms of state intervention in NGO work with minority groups fit the first framework of state intervention for personal gain. After one organization released a study around resource concessions and how they were benefiting individuals at the expense of highland communities, the head of the organization was threatened with expulsion from the province.[85] According to this individual, it was only through the tacit support of the governor and other NGOs (such as CARERE) that he was able to stay on in the province. Although personal aggrandizement is an important component of state intervention into NGOs working with highland communities, the struggle to incorporate these communities into the Cambodian nation also affects state actions.

Unlike the land rights, which are tied up with personal interests, the issue of the education of highland peoples cannot be explained in this way. It is only by looking specifically at the issue of identity politics, and struggles over territorialization, that we can begin to understand the dynamics of state–NGO interaction around the literacy programmes.

State interventions in highland peoples literacy programmes

In order to meet the United Nations Educational, Scientific and Cultural Organization (UNESCO) goals for literacy, the Cambodian government has undertaken a process of delivering non-formal education programmes to the various minority groups in Mondulkiri and Ratanakiri.[86] A core component of this process is increasing the literacy rates of regional peoples, which required the development of orthographies (systems of writing) for the different language groups.[87] Lacking the domestic expertise in linguistics, the government has turned to NGOs to develop scripts for various languages, and to provide basic education services to the highland peoples. In Ratanakiri alone, the Education Ministry reports that it has worked with the following groups on a variety of education projects: Non-Timber Forest Products (NTFP); International Cooperation Cambodia (ICC); UNICEF; UNESCO; Participatory Development Training Center (PADEC); CARE International; Construction et Réhabilitation des Écoles Primaires (CREP); and the Japan Center for Conflict Prevention (JCCP). In terms of the development of literacy programmes, both the ICC and CARE have been involved in orthographic development for different languages.[88] In contrast to other education programmes, which were discussed in Chapter 6, education programmes administered to the highland peoples have been closely supervised and regulated by the Ministry of Education offices in Phnom Penh, and by the provincial education offices and provincial Governors.

The government has been explicit in demanding that the orthography utilize the Khmer system of writing in order to facilitate the bridging from local languages to Khmer. The development of scripts has been scrutinized, and on a number of occasions particular orthographic symbols have had to be adjusted to bring them into closer alignment with the current Khmer script. In some instances, where there has been a previously developed script in use, which was the case with the Vietnamese-based writing system that had been developed for the Phnong people, the government refused to allow this to be used, demanding instead that a Khmer script be developed.[89] Most of the difficulties in developing a writing system have occurred in Ratanakiri, a province that has a greater proportion of Jarai (a group that is feared by the provincial government to be pursuing independence from Vietnam). In contrast, NGOs working in Mondulkiri reported fewer problems (and less government interference) in their literacy programmes.

In addition to the development of scripts, a few groups have been working on non-formal education programmes designed to provide a rudimentary understanding of a range of issues including hygiene, nutrition and basic medicine.[90] Some programmes have sought to deliver non-formal education to peoples in their own languages, and using their own myths as context for various lessons. These have also come under the scrutiny of the state, which stands out because similar programmes, delivered to Khmer speakers throughout the country, have not received similar state attention. At public meetings the Governor of Mondulkiri, His Excellency Koi Kunhua, stated that such programmes were an enormous waste of money.[91] According to NGO representatives in Sen Monorem, Mondulkiri, such statements by a prominent politician set up a poor working environment between local bureaucrats and the NGOs, amounting to a form of intervention in NGO affairs. Tellingly, the Governor also told NGOs involved in the non-formal education programmes that such activities would inevitably result in a desire for independence, revealing an understanding of a link between education, identity and state security. This belief in a connection between education and a drive for separatism is not supported by any empirical evidence, and rests more on the fear of empowerment of the highland peoples. In contrast, the Provincial Director of Education in Ratanakiri, discussing education projects for Phnong communities, argued that most people identified themselves first as being Phnong, and then as Cambodian. He argued that a member of the community would say, 'I am Phnong that happens to have been born in Cambodia'. While this challenges the narrative of the Phnong as Khmer Loeu, it also illustrates that various highland communities may not have goals for independence. Regardless, there was a sense throughout interviews on education programmes in the highlands that the government did not see such actions as politically neutral, but as affecting the communities' interactions with the state and their demands for power.

The non-formal education programmes have gained increased acceptance amongst the provincial governments, in large part because they have been promoted by the NGOs as a bridging system into Khmer. While the instruction material relies heavily on indigenous myths and tales to get across various education points, the intent is to slowly move into Khmer material. This supports the narrative of the peoples being Khmer, and the desire to prevent the emergence of any separatist movement. In Ratanakiri the provincial government was initially opposed to this form of schooling, and publicly denounced the opening of the first school. However, since then the provincial director of education has become a supporter. Though the provincial governments in Ratanakiri and Mondulkiri have come to support the various language and education programmes, their initial concerns are telling of the extent to which struggles over defining who is and is not 'Cambodian' continues. Teaching the various groups Khmer is not portrayed as inherently problematic: rather, it is the development of writing systems for their own languages, and the non-formal education programmes in the various indigenous languages that is deemed dangerous. The notion that various ethnic groups might have their own language, separate from the dominant Khmer, is seen as a threat to territorial unity and drives to integrate the communities into broader Cambodian society.

This close connection between the Khmer language and Cambodian identity is not a new phenomenon, and has important historical antecedents in prior regimes. The linkage between the Khmer language and national identity was made explicit during the era of the KR, when the leadership reworked the language to remove any foreign words (David P.

Chandler 1996: 208). This echoes the current government policy of ensuring that the script used for the highland groups is rigorous in applying the Khmer orthographic system. This then both separates the Cambodian highland communities from those living within Vietnam or Laos, marking them as Khmer, and contributes towards their gradual immersion into broader Khmer society:

> We want all the children to learn Khmer, but here we use bilingual education because we have difficulties with teachers. When they use bilingual education we can get them in school, and it is a bridge we can use to get them to learn Khmer. In the future, because we start with local language, we can teach more Khmer.
>
> (Interview, Provincial Director of Education, Banlung, 25 August 2004)

Khmer identity, defined in large part by the language, requires an attempt to integrate all supposedly 'Khmer' peoples into the same linguistic group.

Civil society organizations are a core participant in this process. On the one hand their initiatives, under the control of the state, serve to reproduce the state identity narrative, while on the other their provision of such programmes may also serve to empower communities to engage more effectively with the various levels of Cambodian government to push for local demands. Civil society groups, which are working with the highland communities (but have not emerged from them), are thus entwined with the state's identity politics. The government perceives their work as affecting the way communities interact with broader Cambodian society, and as such, pay close attention to their activities.

Of identities, politics and security

These various cases demonstrate a pattern of state intervention in NGOs to contest what constitutes a national identity. The Cambodian state has come in to conflict with NGOs when their presence in, or their programmes with, contested communities potentially alters the relation between the communities and the state. Underpinning this is a belief by the government that civil society actors can affect the ways in which communities self-identify, and how they in turn engage with the government. The promotion of particular universalist forms of human rights, and advocacy on behalf of individual or community rights vis-à-vis the government, inherently alters notions of community. The advocacy of civil society is based on a claim of the nature of the interaction of people, as well as how people and the state should interact. Unfortunately, few groups are self-reflective about this aspect of their work. The exceptions are those organizations that have identity practices at the centre of the mandates, particularly those involved with advocating for minority communities (such as the KKK), and those focused on gender awareness (as opposed to groups that incorporate gender into their programming). In fact groups conducting mission work were much more self-aware, and conscious of their roles in altering the worldviews of the populations. How people are to interact with one another, and how they are to relate to political structures, is in effect a question of identity.

NGOs are therefore inherently implicated in the construction of identity in two ways. First, such organizations are actively involved in promoting particular forms of politics and identity. This entails the breadth of NGO activity, both deliberative and unintentional, that alters the state's attempt to propagate a particular hegemonic national identity. Second, by their very existence, and in advocating a role for civil society, groups are altering the political domain. By operating merely as civil society, NGOs are effectively shaping the discourse of how and where people should interrelate, and how they should understand themselves as relating to society. The NGOs are well aware of sensitivity over matters of national identity, and it has been illustrated in this chapter how organizations often avoid working with groups whose presence in the country is a point of public debate.

The broad commitment to Northern/international norms of human rights and individualism does not mean that organizations eschew racialized articulations of identity. Indeed, the employees of LNGOs in Cambodia often fell into such discourses in describing non-Khmer communities (particularly the Vietnamese). As the discussion of the Vietnamese in Cambodia illustrated, racialized notions of identity can be promoted by groups that otherwise struggle for liberal norms of human rights. This has had the effect of reinforcing the state's identity narratives. Opting to not work with the Vietnamese population may serve to strenghten public perceptions that this community is not Cambodian. In this respect NGOs need to be aware of their potential impact on minority groups. The absence of NGOs working with the Vietnamese population in Cambodia illustrates that discourses of belonging within a state affect whose needs and concerns are promoted and recognized. Even though NGOs purport to, and largely do, advance the interests of communities over those of the elite, they have not done so in all instances. This is consistent with Hoogensen and Rottem's (2004) arguments about the links between identity and security, and how a person's (or a community's) identity affects their capacity to make security claims. 'Security claims cannot be heard from identities that have been enveloped and hidden by the dominant discourse…' (Hoogensen and Rottem 2004: 165). Despite the ways in which Khmer identity has relied on 'non-Vietnameseness' (David P. Chandler 1996: 69), there have also been points of dissent on this construction of Cambodian identity.

During a conference held in Phnom Penh on the 2003 election, the issue of Vietnamese voters came up. One representative of a small LNGO stated that distinguishing the Vietnamese from the rest of the electorate was problematic; instead he provided an alternative construction of Cambodian identity based on territory: 'we are all Khmer because we all eat fish from the Tonle Sap'. His point was that Khmer nationality should be seen as being conveyed by lifestyle and where one lives, not on language or religion. This aptly demonstrates that Khmer identity, while presented as fixed and largely ahistoric, is in fact a concept that is open to transformation. This potential for change is liberating as it opens up the possibility for constructions of state identities that are inclusive and that embrace the breadth of Cambodian society.

Determinations of who is and is not Cambodian, and what the markers are of Cambodian-ness, are in constant tension and undergoing continual re-articulation. This is a process that peacebuilding is engaged with, but which has received little attention. While much of what it is to be Cambodian is narrated as settled, the inconsistencies, the politics of it, become apparent in the struggles over descriptions of the limits of the nation. In this way we can understand why the state has intervened, or NGOs have expected the state to intervene, in the debates over religion, over linguistic/education programmes and over which communities NGOs should work with. However, this also plays out over attempts by NGOs to articulate individualism over communitarian identities, and to assert a space for civil society that is separate from the state. As peacebuilding is inherently engaged in the promotion of civil society, and in supporting NGOs, then it is by default a process of identity re/construction.

Peacebuilding, in encouraging the growth of civil society in Cambodia, has contributed to this new dimension of conflict over identities. The question that must then be addressed is whether the liberal framework provides a basis for understanding this dynamic of state–civil society conflict. To answer this it is first necessary to ask how identity is conceptualized within literatures on peacebuilding. As Dunne has shown, the concept of identity has often been central to analyses of political science, with a lineage can be traced back to ancient Greece:

> [T]he question 'what are we' and its corollary 'how do we differ from *them*' is at least 25 centuries old. Ancient Greece developed its identity by contact with, and in contrast to, its neighbours in the 'near' East. Everyone who was not Greek was a 'barbarian'.
>
> (Dunne 1997: 310)

Questions of belonging, citizenship and nationalism have been explored at length in the canons of political science. However, these issues have often been taken as things to be explained, or as a variable that can be used to explain other social action. As peacebuilding emerges from liberalism, and in turn propagates this form of politics, it is appropriate to ask what liberalism says on the matter. Liberalism does engage with the question of identity, and how to deal with a diversity of ethnicities and cultures has been at the heart of much of liberal thought. In short, liberalism proposes solutions to these enduring problems.

Liberalism privileges the rational self-maximizing individual as the ideal primary identity. It simultaneously denigrates, in much the same manner, communitarianism, religious affiliation, and other senses of belonging that interfere with the basics of a society of individuals. The literature on gender and identity has long examined this issue and has shown the multitude of ways in which this form of society is replete with gendered meaning. These narratives serve to reproduce social roles, to marginalize systems of knowledge that are not embedded in the accepted male-dominated discourse (Pateman 1988; Okin 1989). As a result, the form of identity promoted in peacebuilding is implicated in propagating and normalizing particular dynamics of power that favours some segments of society over others while silencing dissent through claims of being universal.

The role of civil society must be considered within this context. Liberal associational literature on civil society is not merely reflective of the nature of civil society, but by naturalizing a particular understanding of it serves to re/produce how people are expected to interact, and what issues are off-limits to civil society due to a divide between the public and private (this last point is discussed in the next chapter). Though liberalism as a theory may not claim to do all of this, the terminology and its purported epistemelogical substance cannot be separated from how it is used – how it is transformed into material practice. In this respect liberalism, with its focus on the rational man, is a powerful discourse about identity and defines what are, and are not, acceptable forms of community.

While liberalism tends to ignore the relevance of questions of identity (including race, gender and religion) in shaping political claims, it does talk about the formation of national identity (Smits 2003: 347). In practical terms, much of this debate over how liberalism can accommodate communitarianism has focused on the issue of multiculturalism. In fact, liberalism has long struggled with the question of how to handle a range of preferences, and of group belonging, within the liberal democratic polity. This complexity of accommodating differing moral and political values was noted by John Rawls (1973) in *Political Liberalism*, his follow-up work to *A Theory of Justice*, wherein he came to advocate 'political liberalism', rather than 'comprehensive liberalism'. He argued that the liberal state does not need to be homogenizing, and that it can incorporate a breadth of cultures. Today this position has been most forcefully advanced within liberalism by the proponents of multiculturalism, such as Kymlicka, who has argued that to defend individuals' rights, it must be recognized that they live within shared social contexts (Kymlicka 1989: 2). This then highlights the common refrain within liberalism, and crucially within the derivative scholarly and policy peacebuilding literatures, that identity politics is a problem to be resolved, particularly when the identities themselves are ethnic or religious.[92]

The solution then, within peacebuilding, is to put in place democratic government, to introduce constitutional reforms and to foster a local civil society to enable communities to interact peacefully and to instil consociational culture. However, what this chapter has described is a situation wherein these precise policies have resulted in conflicts over identity, rather than resolving them. This is contradictory to expectations of liberal peacebuilding and reveals a fundamental tension within peacebuilding and indeed within the broader logic of associational civil society.

The identity-making process is open-ended and ongoing, and is subject to the actions of both NGOs and the state (clearly the range of voices in Cambodia's identity politics is extensive, but the focus here has been on the state and NGOs). This does not mean that NGOs and the state share a common narrative of identity (indeed, there are points of both congruence and dispute even within the NGO community). As such, in some circumstances these points of divergence on what the identity of Cambodia and Cambodians *should* be, can lead to friction between the CSOs and the government. The issues that lead to conflict, or crucially that NGOs deliberately avoid – such as the development needs of Vietnamese Cambodians – provides insight into how the narratives of identity are constructed in the state, and how particular forms of identity have become linked to state legitimacy. In turn, these narratives affect the safety and dignity of various communities, determining who is to be included in Cambodian society.

Clearly national identities in Cambodia, as with anywhere, are not stable, nor are they primordial – though they are presented as such. The dominant identities are embedded within *interpretations* of the past, interpretations that serve modern interests, and reinforce particular distributions of power within the state. The establishment of national identities is related to the modern territorial state, even while the drive to harmonize state territory and identity (territorialization) is at odds with the ways in which such entities incorporate a multitude of peoples with shifting and overlapping identities. As Campbell has described, the logic of the modern state, which peacebuilding defends, places demands on society/elites to realize a continuity of state power, geographic continuity and identity. While the geographic boundaries of the state are usually recognized (though often contested), the boundaries of the identity of the community are not clear, and need to be established and re/produced. In so doing, some forms of identity, and thus some self-identifying religious and ethnic communities, must be marginalized.[93] In short, this inability of the hegemony of the nation state to capture and propagate a single narrative of who 'belongs' in the state, and how they should relate, results in the continual claims and counter-claims of identity politics. This constant struggle between the modern ideal promoted in peacebuilding, and the postmodern 'reality', is described by Walker:

> [C]ontemporary struggles for particular identities occur in the context of reiterated claims about the forging of a common identity, of a sense of connection in some shared enterprise of production, distribution and exchange, perhaps, or of modernity as a universalising cultural condition, even of rights attributed to humanity as such.
>
> (Walker 1993: 161)

As Walker illustrates, there are contradictory pulls towards universalist identities of liberal individualism, of state-wide identities and of more localized forms of affiliation. This is a process that is not only participated in by citizens and the state, but must crucially also be struggled over by CSOs. As such, while there is a generally recognized role of the state in promoting identities, this is also a process within which all NGOs are inherently implicated.

Because identities are social constructs, they can never be fully constituted and will be inherently rife with internal contradictions. For this reason identities require constant re/articulation. This is not to argue that identity formation is always a conscious process, in fact such situations would be rare exceptions. Rather, it is done time and again by the multitude of agents through their daily actions. McSweeney argues that we must not adopt a position that sees identity as something that must be defended. 'Identity, unlike the state, has no empirical referent other than the process of constructing it' (McSweeney 1998: 137). Therefore, there is no independent thing that can be referred to as constituting a naturalized identity. We cannot then make claims of what is the Cambodian identity. In keeping with McSweeney, it is only the process of identity formation can be followed. This allows us to see in whose benefit particular identities operate, and helps us understand the dynamics of power that favour particular discourses over others. What we can do is talk about what we are told a particular identity is, how people are to see themselves and how they are to relate to one another. Thus while the state is driven to promote a common national identity, because such master narratives are impossible, the state's policies must inevitably exacerbate tensions between social groupings. This is a process that is obscured or ignored by making the state the centre of analysis, and largely subsumed by discussions of civil society.

This portion of the immanent critique has shown how the liberal logic of peacebuilding is unable to account for the dynamics of conflict that have emerged between CSOs and the state in Cambodia around identity issues. Rather than being a force to resolve the underlying causes of conflict within society, peacebuilding practice, through its promotion of civil society (in particular by NGOs), has created new dimensions of conflict while reproducing particular narratives of who is 'inside and outside' of the state. Liberalism, while appreciating that conflicts over identity are an enduring issue in modern politics, purports a particular solution (which it is incapable of seeing) that merely seeks to replace some forms of identity with another hegemonic form as represented by the rational self-maximizing individual. This points to an inherent limitation of peace-building. These contradictions cannot be understood from within the liberal paradigm, which occludes any examination of the issue. As is shown in Chapter 9, these matters only come into focus through critical readings that centre issues of identity and politics.

8 The non-politics around the meaning of politics

> Democracy within nations requires respect for human rights and fundamental freedoms, as set forth in the Charter. It requires as well a deeper understanding and respect for the rights of minorities and respect for the needs of the more vulnerable groups of society, especially women and children. This is not only a political matter. The social stability needed for productive growth is nurtured by conditions in which people can readily express their will. For this, strong domestic institutions of participation are essential.
>
> (Boutros-Ghali 1992 (*An Agenda For Peace*), para 82)

Peacebuilding practice, in advocating for an expansion of civil society, is proceeding on the basis that associational behaviour will be able to instil democratic culture while seeking to limit the power of the state. This second component of civil society is directly related to the role of many NGOs that strive to reduce and prevent states' abuse of power. In seeking to understand when civil society and the state come into conflict, it is crucial to focus on those NGOs running programmes that are aimed at restricting the reach of the state. The story that is normally told about the struggle between NGOs and the Southern state is that CSOs run into difficulties when they try to promote the natural rights of peoples and empower locals over the government. Such a view, while perhaps descriptively accurate, takes for granted the universality of HR norms, and aligns with a particular liberal vision of rights that emerges from Northern traditions. This is not to say that introduction of individual rights, democratic governance and freedom of the press should be opposed. Rather the point is to understand the forms of conflict that emerge in post-conflict states between governments and NGOs. This recognition of a dynamic of conflict between NGOs and the state needs to be explored in greater detail in order to appreciate whether this form of contestation is consistent with liberal peacebuilding. However, it does necessitate that we see this as an inherently *political* process that requires shifts in the way in which politics is practised in a society. NGOs, as they represent particular positions on the nature of society and politics, are implicated in the debate. In terms of the pursuit of democratic governance, civil society associations have tended to concentrate on the empowerment of locals vis-à-vis the state; a policy choice that is embedded within broader narratives of states as inherently repressive, especially in the developing world, with local rights and interests taking precedence over other concerns. While the merits of such a position should be discussed, such a conversation has not taken place. Instead, the matter is treated within the policy and academic community as settled, as being beyond politics.

This chapter explores the dynamics of interaction between NGOs and the state that arises from conflicting interpretations of what is and is not political. To do so it focuses on conflicts between NGOs and the state over the issues of human rights, freedom of the press and advocacy. It will be demonstrated that these conflicts cannot be fully understood from a liberal perspective, and that in fact the discursive practices of the state in seeking to limit the roles of NGOs are largely consistent with liberal associational literature. Peacebuilding has then introduced this new dynamic of conflict. This, as with the struggles over identity, points to the limits of the peacebuilding framework and of contradictions within its treatment of civil society. This chapter proceeds by examining the three issues areas of HR, foreign policy and advocacy. In each section the ways these conflicts have manifested are described, followed by an account of how liberalism may account for such processes. However, such accounts rely on a liberal and ahistorical rendering of civil society, and of the issues being contested as being beyond the scope of politics. This means, following the way the term 'politics' is used in most policy and academic circles, that it relates neither to competition for state power nor to public contestation of issues of public import. In this way NGOs' activities around these issues are not political, as the NGOs are neither vying for state power nor advocating positions on which there is a legitimate public debate (the universal liberal position is assumed to be valid and beyond contestation).

This dynamic cannot be understood as simply a struggle over power, with the state striving to continue practices of domination and intimidation on the political stage, and civil society seeking to empower local communities, and to instil and reinforce democratic culture. Instead, the public statements of Cambodia's leadership, and the observations of NGOs, point to another important aspect that is often obscured or missed. The manner in which a liberal conception of rights has become universalized, and is accepted as such in an unproblematic way, glosses over how arriving at any particular agreement on rights is a political process. The outcome itself is not, and should not, be preordained, and the various parties need to debate openly not just the methods of democratization and how to increase the size of civil society, but also their meanings for particular societies. It requires a profound re-imagining of the relationship between peoples in a community, and a reconstruction of the meaning of politics. To understand state–NGO struggles around HR, press freedoms and advocacy, we must see these conflicts not merely as attempts to defend democratic interests but also over the limits of what constitutes the 'political'.

This struggle has important implications: defining what is and is not political determines what is and is not open to debate, and who has a right to have a voice on a given issue. To argue that civil society is not political is to remove NGOs and other CSOs from debates around particular issues, and as a result, potentially to disempower the groups and the communities they claim to represent. Both NGOs and the societies they are seeking to assist need to recognize that in order to promote a broad range of interests they *have* to engage in politics, and to not shy away from issues that are seen as being strictly in the purview of the state. Only in this way can the human security needs of developing communities be identified and addressed.

The three issues around which there has been conflict between the state and NGOs (HR, press freedoms and advocacy) all illustrate the pervasive notion of a separation of roles between civil society and the state. This division of responsibilities has resulted in conflict as the two have attempted to resolve matters that the state sees as falling strictly within the realm of politics.

Understanding conflicts in the human rights sector

The literatures on state–NGO interaction, surveyed in Chapter 3, consistently identify issues of human rights, and freedom of the press, as the source of contestation. Indeed, the scholarly literature on peacebuilding and NGO activity in Cambodia unerringly identifies the promotion of human rights as being a source of conflict with state. Both the academic literature and countless HR groups' reports make mention of the country's dire HR situation during and after the UNTAC period. While NGOs have noted an overall improvement in the status of human rights in Cambodia during the 1990s, there are now numerous reports of slippage.[1]

After the coup in 1997, the government became less accepting of HR organizations, and combined with a drop-off in funding for NGOs, a number of smaller organizations have ceased operation. One NGO representative working on HR issues related, 'most of the HR NGOs are now gone. They disappeared largely after the 1997 coup'.[2] While this cannot be attributed entirely to state interference in HR, NGO representatives were adamant during interviews that it played a direct role. The situation has been reported to have deteriorated further since 2000. The overall environment for HR work was described during an interview with a representative of an election-monitoring NGO as follows:

> The situation for human rights defenders in Cambodia deteriorated markedly in 2003. Human rights advocates, community activists and

> trade union leaders have been among those targeted for their work defending basic human rights. The intimidation they faced included physical and verbal assaults, malicious lawsuits and criminal charges, arrests and detentions. These were symptomatic of a year marked by attacks on civil society and increasing intolerance towards criticism of the Government.
>
> (Interview, election-monitoring LNGO representative, Phnom Penh, 27 October 2003)

When the government has chosen to intervene in NGOs' work in the HR sector, it has done so in a number of ways, including the direct use of force (or the threat of force) against organizations and those individuals connected with them.

Minority groups, discussed in detail in the previous chapter, have been subjected to patterns of discrimination, and women's rights have at best been ignored, and in the case of sex workers, human security is decidedly lacking.[3] Human rights groups and workers have often been subjected to violence, and their work was closely scrutinized and often obstructed by the state. I was not surprised to find, once I began interviewing local and international organizations that were involved in the HR sector, that these patterns continued, though to a lesser degree than in the mid-to-late 1990s. A representative of a large local HR organization asserted that of all the NGO sectors, the one that generally has problems with the government is human rights.[4] To defend themselves against such actions, NGOs established the Cambodian Human Rights Action Committee, an umbrella group of associations, to provide a collective voice (and protection) in pressuring the government on such issues. They also routinely release joint statements about specific HR abuses to blunt the government's response against their accusations.[5]

The history of HR NGOs in Cambodia is relatively short, and the main LNGOs in this sector are able to trace their emergence to the UNTAC era. In a report on the status of Cambodian human rights commissioned by the SIDA, Vijghen writes: 'Human Rights' NGOs are the offspring UNTAC (*sic*)' (2001: 11). The PPA specifically authorized UNTAC to do HR awareness and civic education, and to organize a national election (Downie and Kingsbury 2001). While some NGO sectors were encouraged to grow indirectly (by putting in place an environment amenable to associational growth), this particular group of NGOs was supported directly; human rights was the first sector of NGO activity that was self-consciously and methodically nurtured by UNTAC. The UN and the international donor community contributed to the founding of a number of local HR groups, of which two, founded in 1991, have come to largely dominate the sector: ADHOC and the Cambodian League for the Promotion and Defense of Human Rights (LICADHO). Kek Galabru, President of LICADHO, said that 'without UNTAC we could not have set up our non-governmental organization which is now the biggest in the country'.[6] In addition to these local groups, the most publicly recognizable INGOs, such as Amnesty International, HRW and the ICRC, are also working alongside LNGOs.

The HR sector was promoted due to a belief that liberal human rights are essential to the functioning of any democratic system. In the Second Progress Report on the performance of UNTAC, the UN states: 'Promotion of a better understanding of and respect for human rights and fundamental freedoms is essential in order to create an environment in which free and fair elections may take place' (S/24578, 21 September 1992). As a result of these measures, some observers have credited the HR initiatives as providing the 'fragile foundations of a pluralist society' (Jennar 1994: 147). The expectations, though, go further than the holding of a successful election; the promotion of liberal human rights is expected to transform the very nature of conflict within Cambodia. This clearly echoes the associational literature on the importance of civil society to the effective functioning of democratic government. The promotion of human rights is then one of the cornerstones of establishing a liberal democratic state, and is essential to the fostering of civil society. This is a point Kamaratos has argued; that the protection and implementation of human rights is essential to 'find suitable agents within civil society to multiply and continue this effort, such as non-governmental organizations, co-operatives, association of lawyers, teachers, trade unionists and religious associations' (1995: 493). This highlights a paradox within liberal scholarship on the role of civil society in post-conflict states, where on the one hand civil society is supposed to be apolitical while on the other its transformative role inherently affects the political space of a society.

NGOs, as a component of civil society (and in developing states as what is taken as a measurement of it), are understood to affect politics even while they are supposed to be apolitical. The promotion of human rights by NGOs, as a core component of peacebuilding, must then be understood as falling into this same contradiction: HR organizations are expected to be apolitical actors performing roles that change the politics of a society. However, this is not *seen* as a paradox within liberal thinking where the proper functioning of society, its politics, and the nature of human rights, is *not* taken as political, but rather as an inherent given. In this way NGOs are not then portrayed within liberal scholarship as being political, insofar as they are not inherently engaged in a debate about what is and is not the proper functioning of power.

Local and international HR groups have been at odds with the CPP government from their inception, working against what they see as endemic abuses throughout the 1990s and into the past half-decade. The accusations have been chilling, with an exhaustive list of incidents over the past 15 years. Consider the following statement from ADHOC:

> Between September 1999 and August 2000, ADHOC investigated almost 700 cases of human rights violations. Most of these cases

> concern government employees who torture, injure, kill, rape, illegally detain or otherwise harm a human being. Government officials regularly confiscate or prevent access to a person's personal property, land, farming or fishing supplies. Furthermore, political killings occur during the course of elections in order to prevent individuals from bringing civil or criminal cases to trial.[7]

Not surprisingly, the government, and powerful individuals (all parties have been implicated at times) have not been receptive to this criticism. This has resulted in an ongoing struggle between the government and the HR NGO sector.

The local HR groups have been particularly subject to state intervention. All of the interviewed NGOs' representatives that have engaged in HR advocacy and protection reported that they have had to deal, on occasion, with confrontations with the state.[8] This goes far beyond what HR organizations generally confront, and has included the use of direct violence: physical intimidation, arrests and killings have been reported. State intervention in HR cases has generally followed three patterns (these are not mutually exclusive and one HR NGO may experience all three):

1 the state has sought to treat accusations of HR abuses on an individual basis and to dismiss their relevance;
2 the state has attempted to undermine and silence the HR sector through tactics designed to directly intimidate people working with such organizations; and
3 the state has argued that HR LNGOs are connected with opposition political parties.

In the first instance the state is largely dismissive of claims of HR abuses, often arguing that the incidents were perpetrated by criminals for mundane reasons, such as theft and revenge. In particular, attacks on government opposition members and their supporters have often been explained as having occurred in retaliation for some wrongdoing of the victims of violence, or an unfortunate but random event. NGOs have asserted that in some cases the rich and powerful have forced people into confessing, or have built false cases to 'resolve' the disputes. This serves to deny that an attack is 'politically motivated', and as such would not be an incident of HR abuse. It also may imply that the victim somehow deserved the violence due to some past wrongdoing. However, this tactic is intriguing as it is suffused with a sense that the act, with the result for the victim, is somehow worse if it is perpetrated for reasons to do with the struggle over political power.

This pattern of behaviour often ties into personal power politics. As was stated in Chapter 5, human rights cases that implicate high-ranking members of political parties are the most difficult to address. In such instances it is not unusual for the people directly affected to want to stop prosecution, revealing a fear of the repercussions of pursuing the case due to either direct intimidation, or anticipated outcomes.[9] The elite in Cambodia are able to exercise their own will through the state apparatus, bending the legal system to its own needs, which have occasionally played out in human rights debates. Specific allegations against individuals are often ignored by the state, and on occasion the state has taken action to intimidate civil society groups to prevent accusations of abuse from being brought forward, or court cases from proceeding.

In the second pattern, the government has sought to intimidate NGOs and people working or cooperating with them. This has taken a number of forms, from threatening people who might testify, to threats towards NGOs, through to actual physical attacks on NGOs and communities, including arrests, detentions, physical assaults, robberies and on a few rare occasions, murders.[10] A report by LICADHO states: 'while physical violence towards human rights defenders has decreased over recent years, there has been a shift towards other forms of coercion and intimidation with a veneer of legality'.[11] The most common form of intervention in the work of NGOs is a simple refusal to cooperate with their work. One group running a HR project in Kandal Province related that they were never given permission to work. As the district-level authorities never sent letters of permission for the project, the commune leaders stated that the NGO could not operate.[12] Other groups reported that they would see police stationed in front of their offices, their facilities would be ransacked (but without obvious theft), and that employees would receive anonymous threats.[13]

In part, to understand the government's position on human rights, there is a need to recognize that there are, as with all of Cambodia's politics, differences between the state, provincial, district and commune levels of politics. Several NGOs have pointed out that while the CPP has been, at least publicly, supportive of international norms of HR and democracy, there is less support at the local level.[14] The dynamic that often plays out is one where local authorities have sought to prevent, or limit, the empowerment of local communities, where the micro levels of power are most immediately affected by the promotion of human rights, potentially leading to the destabilization of local power structures. Here, as was discussed, there may be a degree of personal power politics at play as local elites try to avoid a change to the local politics that might erode their authority. One HR LNGO representative working in Battambang stated:

> we had pressure in 1998 on the open forum and democracy programs. We sent a letter to the district chief but he said we couldn't do democracy programs. A democracy only in the national assembly, not in the community.
>
> (Interview, international LNGO representative, Phnom Penh, 8 November 2003)

Another LNGO involved in election monitoring argued that in some regions of the country it is particularly difficult to deliver programmes as the authorities are afraid that people will learn about democratic principles and end up ousting the local representatives.[15] When problems like these are encountered, NGOs often go back to the Ministry of Interior to get the Ministry to pressure those individuals obstructing NGO activities. Intriguingly, the Ministry of Interior has regularly proven willing to support NGOs in such cases, illustrating that the state government is less concerned about the promotion of HR and democracy than some local elites.

So far this story is a typical one, and matches the liberal discourse of a struggle over democratic principles. However, a closer examination of the government's position on the HR sector points to the limitations of liberal perspectives in understanding the nuances of the debate over HR activity in Cambodia. The arguments presented by the government have not been that individual human rights are inappropriate, or that the interests of the community must precede those of individuals. The state's narratives of human rights are that they are of the utmost importance as they help shape the broader societal understandings of the issues, and facilitate the identification of contradictions built into the practices of peacebuilding.

The third dynamic of the state's attempt to restrict the work of HR organizations is a struggle over the roles of civil society. The state has verbally attacked HR NGOs as both being an arm of the opposition parties, and of acting like the opposition. In the words of a representative of one LNGO, '[i]n 1992 the government seemed to see the student groups and NGOs in general as the enemy'.[16] The state has described HR NGOs and IOs as being 'political', and has sought to limit their voices. For example, the government issued numerous public denunciations of the UN Center for Human Rights (UNCHR) in Phnom Penh (including asking the UN to shut the organization in 1995), arguing that it was biased, making unfounded accusations and undermining the state. Khieu Kanhartigh, the chief government spokesman, said: '[s]ome people in the Human Rights Center, they have adopted an anti-government stance. ... They come here and say, "All these guys are bad guys". They have this in mind'.[17] Another LNGO representative working on HR issues related that groups working in this sector are often accused by the government of 'being political'.[18] This is a curious accusation that needs to be un-packed. To use the term 'political' is not to be pejorative of politics itself: after all, the various parties are not decried for this.[19] Therefore it needs to be asked if there is something more going on in such narratives. To get at this requires turning to the second part of the government's attempt to limit the voice of NGOs on human rights by describing them as 'acting like the opposition'. Taken together we find that the accusation is that NGOs are engaged in types of activity that the state feels ought to be beyond their purview.

Interestingly, this was a position that some NGOs also pushed, arguing that many of the HR organizations were simply too quick to criticize the government, were unequal in their attack on a single political party (the CPP), and were clearly pushing a political agenda. Some LNGOs also stated that HR groups were too closely linked with the opposition parties.[20] In one instance, a representative of a research NGO related that HR organizations needed to shoulder some of the blame for the abuses of rights.[21] S/he singled out the style of leadership within the NGOs as being undemocratic as an example of how these groups do not represent the models of human rights they promote. It was further argued that many of the groups over-represent a few cases, painting a picture that is far bleaker than is warranted.[22] Certainly NGOs are predominately run by people with deep connections to either political parties and/or the refugee border camps. These camps were populated by those who opposed the Vietnamese government, and as such the CPP views these people with suspicion, doubting their purported neutrality. This critique is related to the observation that a large number of the first NGOs to be established after 1991 were formed by people who had gained experience working with NGOs in the Cambodian refugee camps in Thailand, in the refugee communities in Western states (for groups considered to be pro-opposition), or conversely within Marxist propaganda camps in Vietnam (for groups considered pro-CPP).[23] As such, state representatives believe that the groups have been populated by individuals who are opposed to the CPP, and that they are closely linked to opposition political parties. But such criticisms of NGOs and civil society are possible only when such groups are expected to be apolitical.

State attempts to limit press freedoms

As with the HR sector, there has been a great deal of attention in peacebuilding policy literature on the necessity of a free press for transforming society, resolving conflict and preventing state abuses of authority. Prior to the arrival of the UN in 1991, the press, as with most of Cambodian society, was tightly controlled by the government. The creation of a free press was one of the first steps taken to establish the conditions for a democratic election. The third progress report on UNTAC states: 'UNTAC has helped to launch a Cambodian Media Association of all Cambodian journalists, which had met twice by mid-December [1992]. Fair access to the media by all political parties during the forthcoming electoral campaign will also be ensured' (S/25154, 25 January 1993, para 70). The role of the UN in facilitating the growth of an indigenous free media has been further described by the ADB:

> The situation changed after the arrival of UNTAC in March 1992. UNTAC drafted a 'Media Charter' that aimed to establish a framework

> for a free press in all areas of the UNTAC operation. The Media Charter, in the absence of a true legal framework, provided an environment in which numerous nonparty, privately owned print media sprang up.
>
> (ADB 2000: 32)

The local press industry flourished during this period, and continued to expand in the mid-to-late 1990s.[24] In discussing NGOs and the media, Chong has argued that groups working in this area have 'proliferated and gained access to public decision-making structures, and the media has become more independent' (Chong 2002: 974). Newspapers, television and radio broadcasts have expanded in both quantity and quality since 1991. However, the initial era of exuberance about a free press has been tempered as the government and political parties have taken actions against the press, attacking individual journalists, various Khmer language press outlets and LNGOs working in this sector. This process has intensified since 2003, with the government having become increasingly critical of the press, and restricted its freedom to publish. As a result, Reporters Without Borders moved Cambodia from seventy-first in the world in its annual ranking of press freedom, down to number 81 in 2003, and by 2007 it had dropped it to one hundred and eighth, reflecting a deterioration of the press' ability to operate free of government control and intimidation.[25]

There was a crackdown on the press following the exit of UNTAC, with the public murder of Nun Chan, the editor of *Samleng Yuveakchun Khmer* (Voice of Khmer Youth). Three Khmer-language newspapers were also shut down, and several editors were reportedly forced into hiding in the fall of 1994.[26] Other organizations, such as the Thai-owned International Broadcasting Corporation (Cambodia), have reportedly agreed to self-censorship after pressure from Cambodia's Ministry of Information.[27] As of 2002, 'local media are rarely professional or independent by international standards. Radio and television are essentially controlled by the state, and there is no functioning press association to promote editorial ethical guidelines'.[28] This points to increased attention by the state on the media, and a growing desire to control the public discourse of politics.

The state's assertion about why it is justified in limiting the voice of the media echoes those made with respect to the HR sector; that the Cambodian press is not neutral, and thus crosses into the purview of political parties. The government perceives any critical press as inherently being supportive of the political opposition, and of being in alignment with the Sam Rainsy Party or FUNCINPEC. The government also argues that the press at times oversteps its role into critiquing the government rather than reporting the news.

Liberal democratic sensibilities value a press that is able to report on whatever it wants. The hope is that in this way the citizenry will be able to have the necessary information to make decisions about who to vote for.

Public statements by government officials, and their actions, reveal a different orientation towards what the role of the press should be, and what ethical behaviour entails. The state's position seems to be that press freedom is acceptable so long as it does not move into the outright critique of government, and particularly of people in positions of power. When the press has crossed this boundary, it has been attacked by the government; this has included direct physical violence, intimidation, legal cases, and in the case of foreign journalists, expulsion from the country:

> Cambodia has banned two French journalists from entering the country following a critical article in the Paris daily LIBERATION [titled 'Paris in the Cambodian Trap'], information ministry spokesman Sien Lapresse said Sunday. It was the first known entry ban on foreign reporters, although Cambodia has been increasingly critical of the media[.]
>
> (*Agence France-Presse* (30 October 1994) 'Government bans entry of two French journalists', Phnom Penh)

From early in the post-UNTAC era, suspicion of, and attempts to limit the voice of the press were not limited to the CPP: opposition parties also supported moves to restrict the press. Prince Norodom Ranariddh stated in September 1994 that foreign journalists who exaggerated the news would be expelled from the country.[29]

This is a pattern that has parallels in the broader Southeast Asian region. In a discussion of civil society in ASEAN, Saravanamuttu has argued that 'the main thrust of the current ASEAN statist leadership is to maintain strong, authoritarian states in the sense of developing the capacity to govern, deliver the goods, and maintaining a tight rein on the instruments of coercion over society' (2001: 93). In this way the supervision and control of the press can be understood as one component of the state's attempt to sustain a particular form of governance. Post-conflict states are also in a situation where their legitimacy is at risk. In such circumstances criticisms of the state are more apt to be treated as security threats. This observation points to the way in which regimes in much of Southeast Asia have been particularly aware of criticisms emerging from within society, and have seen them as threatening the state and the government in power. Press freedom, and NGOs working on media issues, are then of particular concern to the state.

This does not mean that all of the press has been shut down in Cambodia, or that it is all repressed by the state. There is in fact a broad base of media, representing the range of the political spectrum. There are also two English language papers, the *Cambodia Daily* and the *Phnom Penh Post*, which have been able to publish critical stories of Cambodian politics, and the Cambodian government. While both papers have had journalists pressured and threatened, they have been able to continue to print; while unverifiable, the general perception amongst the NGO representatives is that these papers have greater freedom because they work in English and are widely read by the expatriate community. Furthermore, the press outlets that strive to be neutral also did not report significant levels of state interference in their work. Rather it is predominately those Khmer media outlets that take clear editorial stances against the state that run into problems with the government.[30] The state decries stories that might embarrass the government or powerful individuals. This later point was brought up by the Cambodian Centre for Human Rights (CCHR) in a press release in July 2006:

> The Alliance for Freedom of Expression in Cambodia (AFEC) is very worried about the fact that persons from within or close to the Cambodian government are using Article 62 of the UNTAC law on 'disinformation' against journalists who criticized them.... Yesterday, the AFEC has released an international Urgent Alert on the case of the journalist Dam Sithek who was accused by a government lawyer of 'criminal disinformation'. In an article stemming from June 13, 2006, the editor of the newspaper 'Moneakseka' had quoted unidentified members of the ruling CPP party who connected the Deputy Prime Minister Sok An with corruption. He has been summoned by the court to appear on July 12.[31]

This can be interpreted as the actions of government officials who wish to hang on to power, and who do not want to be publicly embarrassed.[32] In this way, the issue of press freedom echoes that of the broader HR sector in that there are patterns of both state attempts to limit the political voice of the press, and of individuals from all parties using the state to protect their own interests. This plays out in particular around the moves to sue the press for defamation.[33] However, while this frequently constitutes part of the dynamic of government interference in the press, it does not account for all of it.

What is of specific interest to this discussion however is that, as with the HR sector, NGOs and press outlets are attacked not only for their critiques of the state, or for embarrassing the country, but also for not being politically neutral.[34] The implication is that if the press were equally critical of the opposition parties as it is of the government that the state could accept critical journalism. The underlying argument is that the role of the press is not to act in a way that would undermine public support of the government, nor should it engage in politics. When taken in combination with other assumptions, this demonstrates a broader pattern where the meaning of politics, and what is political, is in flux. The assaults on the press could be treated primarily as a struggle between authoritarian interests and democratic principles. This is the logic that informed UNTAC's fostering of a domestic free press. This, however, requires looking past and dismissing the arguments that are put forward by those in Cambodia who have tried to limit press freedoms. The arguments that are used to defend the government's actions do matter as they establish the limits of acceptable action by normalizing some forms of activity while simultaneously making others unacceptable. The narratives of the roles of civil society, and the government's assertions about what is and is not appropriate need to be examined in this light. Understanding the government's critiques is essential if we want to address the conditions that restrict the ability of journalists to operate freely.

The core issue for the state (in terms of its public discourse) is that the press is to remain politically neutral. Thus the *act* of engaging in politics is said to be inappropriate for the media, as was the case with the HR sector. NGOs are well aware of this dynamic and groups that had strong media components stressed during interviews that they went out of their way to provide equal airing to the major political parties. Civil society organizations, such as the Women's Media Centre, reported that they did not run into major difficulties with the state, but they have worked to provide balanced political commentary, and to give a fair exposure to different political perspectives.[35] This was seen as an effective strategy to avoid state interference in their projects, and as a means of ensuring the groups' continued capacity to engage in journalism. I was also told in an interview with an NGO involved in professional development of the media, that training journalists was not seen as being problematic by the government, insofar as the state did not intervene in such practices.[36] The situation is then one in which the media is not attacked by the state in terms of general principals about the dangers of a free press, but rather for its engagement in politics.

What is important here, in terms of the immanent critique of peacebuilding, is that the government's way of controlling the media is through narrative practices that are actually embedded within liberalism. Thus fostering a free media, while expected both to promote democratic governance and to uphold human rights, can lead to conflict. Certainly liberalism anticipates this; within this framework the state's objections to a free press arise from concerns that it may erode its capacity to govern without public criticism, and to expose how individuals benefit at the expense of the poor. In short, it is precisely because the media reveals the operations of power that it is resisted. However, liberalism is unable to provide a compelling explanation for why its own narratives are used to undermine the free press. The language of separation between politics and civil society becomes the basis of the state's critique.

Contestation with NGOs over advocacy work

The next area of work that has come under scrutiny, and been criticized by the state, is advocacy. The government's arguments about why it intervenes in NGOs engaged in such activities are similar to those used to explain conflicts over HR and freedom of the press: that some of the work is inappropriate for NGOs because it is the purview of politics. The issue of advocacy provides a window to the assumptions governing NGO activities, how they relate to liberalism, and importantly how they do not reflect an 'objective reality'. Advocacy work is often seen by both the state and, importantly, by many individuals working for NGOs, as crossing the line from policy work and the monitoring of the state, into the realm of politics. In this way advocacy work is even more blatantly a struggle over the very meaning of politics, and what is and is not appropriate activity for NGOs.

Before proceeding, it is necessary to contextualize what is meant by advocacy. It first needs to be distinguished from lobbying efforts, which push particular policies within the government by working behind the scenes, steering clear of eliciting public debates on a given issue. In contrast, advocacy is directly involved in providing a voice to local communities. According to Pact Cambodia, an INGO that is teaching LNGOs how to engage in such activities, it is '[a] series of actions designed to persuade and influence those who hold governmental, political, and economic power so that they will adopt and implement public policy in ways that benefit those with less political power and fewer economic resources' (Mansfield *et al.* 2002: 4). Advocacy work challenges many of the assumptions of the roles of civil society, moving NGOs deliberately into public confrontation with state policies. In some respects, the direct lobbying of various levels of government is a long-running practice of CSOs. This can be seen within the civil society literature, which argues that it has an important role to play in aggregating individuals' interests. These need to be articulated somewhere, and that place is often the state. Certainly we expect to see such activities in established democratic countries, where groups such as Greenpeace, Sierra Defence Fund, etc. regularly push governments to adopt environmentally friendly programmes. In developing countries NGOs have also actively lobbied governments to adopt new legislative positions, or to change existing policies on a broad range of issues. There is an important question, though, about how the government is lobbied, and on whose behalf the NGOs are acting. There are NGOs that lobby the government directly, and usually behind the scenes, on a variety of issues that are seen as benefiting the state as a whole. In contrast, advocacy work is often deliberative in its work as being for a particular community, and generally being against the government or powerful individuals with the capacity to use the powers of the state. However, at the same time, there is something else at play in advocacy programmes that does represent a dramatic shift in the activities of NGOs.

The extent to which advocacy is a new feature in the work of NGOs in Cambodia, let alone to Cambodian society, is made stark when looking at the way the term is translated into Khmer. Petra Peterson, a representative of Forum Syd, a SIDA member organization that funds local development initatives, related during an interview that the meaning of advocacy in Cambodia is particularly contested as it has no inherent equivalent term in the Khmer language.[37] Pact Cambodia, in describing their advocacy programme, wrote:

> A few years ago there was no term in Khmer to describe the concept of advocacy. NGO staff today usually use the phase '*tasumateh*' (to struggle for an idea). However, there is a general consensus that most people do not understand the term clearly and that it has negative connotations at the local level.
>
> (Mansfield *et al.* 2002: 4)

This desire to avoid direct confrontation with the state is common amongst both INGOs and LNGOs, and public struggles with various levels of government are approached with trepidation. Interestingly, the concern about groups being political is shared by the NGO sector and the state. The worry over advocacy is expressed specifically in these terms: NGOs should avoid advocacy as it politicizes both the NGO and the issue it addresses. In part, this is a recognition that maintaining an issue as a technical debate eliminates much of the difficulty in addressing it. However, there is also a broader sense that NGOs should not engage in politics, and that to make an issue political makes it more difficult to address. Once it becomes 'political' then it can no longer be dealt with as a technical matter.

In a further indication of this dynamic, it was related during an interview with an INGO representative that groups that have moved into advocacy have tended to do so around topics that are already the subject of public controversy and thus overlap with issues that were discussed in previous chapters, such as community claims against powerful individuals, and matters pertaining to resource extraction.[38] Engaging in advocacy is then seen as placing an NGO into the middle of struggles between communities and the government, which many CSOs seek to avoid. When it has occurred, the government's reaction has not been positive to such civil society actions. This has on occasion resulted in government attempts to limit the NGOs' activities, and to limit the community's interaction with civil society groups through intimidation and restricting the local government's work with various organizations.

When NGOs in Cambodia talk about becoming involved in advocacy work, they are not usually talking about pushing particular issues, but rather representing the needs of communities to the government. This is a new role that is perceived by the NGOs as being political, and highlights the tension within the writing on civil society and peacebuilding. For an NGO to take up advocacy it needs to begin working on behalf of people; in many ways to move closer to the liberal meaning of civil society. As such, NGOs are supposed to articulate the needs and wants of communities while avoiding politics (the realm of the state). In discussions about advocacy, NGO workers mostly ignored this issue, claiming that while advocacy was an important role of their organizations, they did not see it as a form of politics. Advocacy is then problematic precisely because it highlights the manner in which the roles of CSOs are not inherently apolitical.

What is political?

Peacebuilding is about changing the nature of politics in a state, and about resolving the underlying causes of violent confrontation within and across communities. The creation of civil society in an image familiar to the North is expected to be one of the keystones to holding up a new polity that allows for the peaceful resolution of disputes. Yet, as has been laid out here, while civil society is expected to transform the practice of politics, it is itself separate from politics. At the same time, and paradoxically, civil society is supposed to act as a limit on the state. What the interviews in Cambodia have shown is that there is broad agreement between both the state and organizations that civil society groups should remain apolitical. His Excellency Ek Sam Ol, Deputy Chairman of the Legislative Committee, said that there are 'some groups that don't respect the principle of neutrality, and there are a small number that openly support politics'.[39] That said, there is also clearly a substratum of organizations that are closely affiliated with the political parties, some of which have likely been formed deliberately by them.[40] In addition to parties establishing NGOs of their own, I was told on two occasions that parties have approached NGOs to gain their support, offering money in exchange.[41] However, even these organizations, and the party representatives, have publicly declared a commitment to the apolitical nature of civil society. This illustrates that at the level of official discourse, some of the liberal assumptions of civil society have taken root. In fact, the extolling of an apolitical civil society has not eliminated conflict between civil society and the state, but has resulted in new struggles over whether a group is 'being political' or not, and whether given issues are properly 'political'. Downie and Kingsbury point out that in Cambodia 'without a full understanding of the role of civil society, some government members regarded civil society, especially *non*-governmental organizations, as *anti*-government [italics in original] and therefore as opposition' (Downie and Kingsbury 2001: 57). What these authors miss, though, is that such a view of NGOs is not a rejection of the liberal peace and its associated notions of civil society, but rather emerges from liberal discourse. The civil society literature is premised on a separation of roles and responsibilities, and sees a distinction between what is within the state's purview, and what is legitimately the NGOs'. This division falls down over what is and is not political. NGOs and the state actually agree, for the most part, on this separation. The debates turn on the struggle over defining what is inside and outside of politics.

When asked if groups engaged in politics, the NGOs overwhelmingly said they did not. Some groups reported that they were in fact obliged to avoid politics according to their memoranda of understanding (MOUs) with the Ministry of Interior.[42] Still others stated that 'if they (employees) work for parties they can't work for their group's purpose'.[43] In fact groups decried such activities, arguing that only groups that were directly tied to political parties were 'political'. Groups went out of their way to show that they were apolitical, either avoiding contact with politicians, or ensuring that representatives from all the major parties were invited to their public events. The NGOs thus reproduced the same notion as the state that civil society ought to be apolitical.

CSS, at least as it is deployed here, is engaged in a process of unsettling the assumed logic of security discourses and to move discussions away from technical debates back into the political sphere. The liberal peace and its understanding of civil society does just this, imposing a form of associational behaviour on societies while at the same time striving to limit the ways in which NGOs in turn interact with the state and society, and on which issues they are allowed to have a voice. However, because peacebuilding is an attempt to impose a particular form of societal organization on communities with distinct histories it should not be surprising that the inconsistencies and paradoxes within the North's understanding of civil society should become apparent. This is seen in the language of NGOs and the state in denying the political role of these organizations, while the government and party representatives still actively pursue the support of NGOs, and most groups involved in issues of HR and freedom of the press are clearly understood as being connected to politics even if they vehemently deny such a link.[44]

Arguing that NGOs should not be political has serious ramifications for peacebuilding. In the only instance where this delineation of NGOs' roles was questioned by a representative of an NGO during an interview, the director stated: 'NGOs have schooled people into thinking that things are *not* politics'.[45] This is a problematic position as it rests on the notion that what constitutes the political is already predetermined, and secondly implies that many issues are best resolved by keeping them out of the political realm. Conversely, those things that are political are then beyond the reach of NGOs. While this may well serve the interest of INGOs seeking to avoid confrontation in the societies they are trying to assist, for LNGOs this precludes their participation in crucial debates. This returns us to one of the core arguments CSS makes about security discourses: that narratives, such as peacebuilding, are approached as technical exercises where the goals and aims escape scrutiny because they are taken for granted. The value and nature of civil society are a part of this. In this way the effects of civil society do not need to be examined, as they are already 'known'. Where civil society may come into conflict with the state, the blame is placed either on the particular policy decisions of the group (which then can be addressed) or on a bellicose state that rejects liberal democracy. In the final chapter, the two main contradictions we that have identified within peacebuilding theory and practice are shown to point at the inherent limits of liberal claims of universality. While the struggles between NGOs and the state that have been discussed here are about issues of HR, freedom of the press and advocacy, the terms of the debate are distinct from this. The conflict is around what is politics and what is not, what is properly the purview of civil society, and what is beyond its legitimate mandate.

9 Conclusions

Over the course of researching and writing this book there have been dramatic changes in the patterns of international relations, largely brought about through the Global War on Terror. The war in Afghanistan has now lasted longer than the Second World War, with no evident end in sight. The military components of peace operations have been roundly attacked in scholarly and policy circles, as well as in the North's media. Despite the criticisms of these missions, the idea of peacebuilding has not received the same critical attention, and continues to enjoy considerable popular support, which can be seen by continued calls for peace operations in the Sudan. The manner in which peacebuilding is treated separately from military campaigns is starkly demonstrated by the media responses in the North to the killings of Canadian and British NGO workers in Afghanistan. Their deaths were not portrayed in the same way as those of soldiers from the same countries, and their work did not come under significant scrutiny; their 'humanitarian' missions were lauded within the press. This reflects how the roles of NGOs in these 'ungoverned' spaces are presumed to be a positive force for democratic development, and to represent the potential for the end of conflicts within these states, so while the wars themselves are criticized, the logic of peacebuilding is not. The North's ongoing presence in these states, however, is based on the presumption that a particular form of liberal peacebuilding is both possible and, indeed, necessary. This book has turned a critical lens on the theories and practices of peacebuilding, opting to focus on the policies and practices of civil society re/construction precisely because its goals and means are treated as givens within the policy and academic literatures.

The narratives of peacebuilding are powerful, and have reached a point of general acceptance in the North. Touching us with empathetic calls to help and assist, we are moved to back intervention in the developing world. However, CSS demand a questioning of what makes peacebuilding possible, and what must be assumed in order to accept the viability and validity of peacebuilding practices. The links between the language of Northern intervention, of which peacebuilding is a particular type, and specific forms of power relations have been described in depth by a range of critical scholars, including: Weber (1995); Campbell (1998a); Orford (1999); Whitworth (2004); and Duffield (2005). As these authors have shown, such practices of intervention rely on, and in turn reproduce, images of the South that are racialized and gendered, making possible (and perhaps necessary) the North's intervention.

Peacebuilding has become one of the predominant forms of the North's engagement in the South, and is promoted as a means of alleviating suffering and addressing the sources of conflict for the local communities. However, Foucault's writings demand that critical scholars pay attention precisely to those processes and activities that are presented as 'neutral and independent', to uncover how power is obscured by such practices (Chomsky and Foucault, cited in Flyvbjerg 1998: 223). To challenge the orthodoxy of current peacebuilding theory and practice this analysis has engaged in an immanent critique of peacebuilding, opting to assess its internal logic, claims and practices on its own terms. In so doing, it has concentrated on uncovering the 'contradictions of claim and context' of this form of intervention (Antonio 1981: 338). This has entailed an analysis of the theoretical underpinnings of peacebuilding with an attention to the identification of the sites of potential contradictions within its practice. Because the non-military components of peacebuilding have received considerably less attention within critical academia, this study has opted to target this precise space. This has resulted in a focus on one of the core assumptions of peacebuilding: targeting the centrality of NGOs to the remaking of the South in a democratic model. This faith arises because of the close connection between peacebuilding and the liberal presumptions of peace, and their shared assumptions of the importance of civil society. The manner in which liberalism treats civil society eschews historical context and ignores how its emergence in the Northern context was gradual.

Civil society is broadly understood to be a way of countering the hegemonic and repressive state, and as a space to instil democratic values amongst society. '[C]ivil society can constitute a site for democratization because it can be a place where people choose to live their public lives and solve their joint problems' (Lehning 1988: 241). Within liberal thought it is understood as operating as a space to develop and instil democratic behaviour, as providing a forum within which individuals' wants and needs can be consolidated and mediated in a non-political environment (Rodan 2001). Put another way, it is the place of associational behaviour that teaches people to interact peacefully. It has come to be seen as a crucial component of a functioning democracy (Diamond 1994; Pye 1999). The existence of civil society is understood to be essential for the promotion of democracy, and its size is believed to be a measure for the degree of democratization. As Jørgensen (1996) asserts, the more legitimate a state is, the more room civil society has.

At the same time as liberalism understands civil society as instilling democratic consociational behaviour, it is also seen as providing a check on the powers of the state (Diamond 1994). As Cohen and Arato (1995) argue, because of its roots in the work of Montesqieu and Locke, civil society is widely seen as the source of societal peace, in contrast to the coercive state. From this, liberal associational civil society is expected to counter the worst of the state's abuses, and to constrain the power of the state. In the current neoliberal moment where the role of the state is being diminished in favour of the market, some elements of civil society have contributed to the erosion of the state. This binary opposition between civil society and the state then results in a zero-sum game where the reach and influence of one comes at the expense of the other.

Yet as was laid out in Chapter 2, there is a paradox at the heart of the peacebuilding and civil society literature, which portrays civil associations as both necessary to resolve conflict, but also as being in conflict with the state. This contradiction has been obscured in the North as a gradual accommodation has been achieved where the limits of civil associations and the states have been proscribed. The limits of each undergo constant re-articulation, and there are ongoing debates about the reach and influence of 'special interest groups', and so forth. But these debates take place within a predetermined field of meaning. It is in the course of peacebuilding, where the entire liberal system is being put in place, that the contradictions appear because the historically specific accommodations from the North are not present. These have been identified as moments of conflict between civil society actors and the state.

Peacebuilding and the promotion of civil society through NGOs

In exploring civil society and peacebuilding, one of the first dynamics that becomes apparent is that the international community is not involved in re/constructing the breadth of associational behaviour, but is instead primarily involved in replicating those types of organizations that mirror those found in the North. In particular, the focus has been on the formal organizations that have been involved in the development project. Pouligny (2005) has pointed out that in looking for Northern types of civil society in post-conflict states, it should not be surprising that they cannot be found. As a result of this lack of recognizable domestic civil society, peacebuilding has come to rely extensively on NGOs to both represent and foster its growth, a point noted by David Chandler: 'The main focus of civil society-building has often been local non-governmental organizations (NGOs) as a sphere for articulating needs independently of vested political interests and involving grassroots community "voices" ' (1999: 110). At the same time, the North's sense that Southern states are inept and/or corrupt has further bolstered the place of NGOs in development projects.

NGOs have become partners in peacebuilding, and are also now treated as markers of civil society. The calls to strengthen civil society are then in effect calls to support NGOs in the development state. The presence of NGOs is now (in conjunction with the holding of democratic elections, and the move to market capitalism) one of the main indicators of successful peacebuilding.

Assessing the successes of peacebuilding in Cambodia on its own terms

Examining the impacts of peacebuilding in Cambodia has revealed a complex dynamic with both obvious improvements in the quality of life for the majority of people living in the state, alongside the entrenchment of communitarian politics, the consolidation of the power of elites and the apparent erosion of some personal freedoms. The market has undergone considerable growth with year-on-year expansion of the domestic economy and increasing integration into the global economy, yet the country remains mired in poverty and continues to sit near the bottom of the HDI. The initial peacebuilding mission did end much of the direct military conflict between the major participants in the civil war (with the exception of the KR), and arguably led to the eventual end of the KR's grip on power in the Northwest. The country has also held regular elections, although these have served more to provide guidance than a specific mandate for the governance of the state. Importantly, both the threat and use of violence have become less common in the resolution of conflicts within the state. Just the same, the rule of law remains a distant ideal, HR abuses continue, and there are increasing attempts to control the media and limit public opposition to the government. For all of these reasons there are numerous debates about the legacy of UNTAC, with no consensus on whether it was a success, a failure, or something in-between. Despite these apparent differences, there is remarkable agreement amongst the various analyses about what peacebuilding should strive to produce. These commonalities are obscured by the debates, and become readily apparent only from a critical security perspective. This has allowed the exposure of a number of the assumptions built into liberal peacebuilding, and to explore how peacebuilding has transformed – rather than eliminated – conflict within Cambodia.

Any critical examination of peacebuilding must seek to embed analysis within broader historical contexts in order to develop an appreciation for assumptions that inform its practice. Central to peacebuilding is the 'liberal presumption', the faith in the universal potential for the liberal peace (Call and Cook 2003a; Duffield 2005). Its practice is marked by the imposition of both liberal pluralist governance and a capitalist market, which are understood as being essential to the long-term resolution of conflicts within any given society. This logic was particularly clear in the lead-up to the peacebuilding mission in Cambodia:

> [O]ne of the Paris accord's most striking features was that the international community and the Cambodian factions agreed to a system of liberal democracy as the basis for its constitution. The Agreements specified all the elements necessary for a constitutional democracy: periodic and genuine elections; freedom of assembly and association including that for political parties; due process and equality before the law; and an independent judiciary.
>
> (Doyle and Suntharalinam 1994: 122)

The practice of peacebuilding is thus embedded within the broader context of a liberal democratic and economic hegemony, demanding its extension into the South. As a result, the confrontations between NGOs and the state in peacebuilding should not be seen as arising *in spite* of liberalism, but rather because of its logic.

These narratives construct the world around us in a particular way, which dictates how the North should engage with it. Peacebuilding has imagined the world as having an unrealized democratic possibility where people are both awaiting and desiring (even if they do not recognize it) to be budding democrats. But it goes further than this, envisaging a world structured around states, with internal tensions between the state and society mediated by civil society. Within this, people are inevitably self-maximizing individuals. This has clear implications for the types of development projects that are pursued. If the state is retrograde and is seen as the source of problems, then it only makes sense to look outside of the government for solutions to peace and conflict in society. This effectively translates into programmes that in part eschew the state and focus instead on the local level, particularly in terms of democratization projects.[1] Such moves are not politically neutral with respect to the validity or value of culturally specific forms of social organization, or of locally developed means of conflict resolution. In effect this then means that peacebuilding works against such variety and, in trying to apply a single model of social organization, is working to eliminate difference.

What this research has shown is that the relationship between civil society and the state is much more complex than the one advanced within the peacebuilding literature. Civil society has not been universally a force for stabilization and democratization in Cambodia. Its relationship, both with the broader society it is supposed to represent, and the state, is exceedingly complex, and to understand this one needs an appreciation for the historical dynamics at play in Cambodia. To begin with, civil society has developed in a situation where societal trust had largely eroded over the preceding decades. Furthermore, it emerged from within a particular community that had clear links with political interests that were in opposition to the political party (CPP) that would come to rule Cambodia after the exit of UNTAC. The LNGO leadership traces its roots either to the communist associations or to the NGOs that worked in the refugee camps in Thailand. Any claim that civil society is apolitical is a stretch (even from within a liberal framework). We also find that the interaction between civil society and the state has been decidedly mixed. The country is remarkably open to both INGOs and LNGOs, the majority of which operate with little direct interference from the state. However, to say that the explosive growth of civil society has led to a more peaceful country, and that it is resolving the causes of conflict in Cambodia, is also unsubstantiated. What has been found in this research is that there has been a gradual transformation of the forms of conflict within the state. While there appears to be less direct state violence against individuals and communities, the state and civil society do clash on some issues. The state has come into conflict with civil society in some instances because it is now representing local communities' needs to the state (meaning that the conflict was either there prior to the arrival of NGOs, or that the roots of the particular disputes are related to the broader democratization and capitalization of the state). In other instances the fostering of civil society has itself led to new forms of contestation.

Some forms of conflict that have emerged between the state and civil society associations are consistent with liberalism. The fight over the rights of communities versus those of powerful individuals is to be expected as states move towards democratic liberal economic forms of governance. Therefore, struggles over rights of access are to be expected, with NGOs predictably playing both intermediary roles and working to articulate local concerns. That many NGOs have been reticent to participate in such activities is not in itself a critique of peacebuilding, but does indicate that NGOs funded outside of the communities they are striving to assist may often have interests and demands that mitigate against aggravating the state. The second form of conflict between the state bureaucracies and NGOs over policy agendas is also consistent with liberal global governance, which has pursued a minimal state, and understands governments, particularly in the South, to be less efficient and less representative of local needs than civil society actors.

These two types of state–NGO conflict pose questions for the advocates of liberal peacebuilding about the equation of NGOs with civil society, and of the ways in which fostering an expanded NGO sector can lead to a domestic civil society. However, these issues do not indicate a failure of the liberal approaches to peacebuilding either to describe the nature of state–civil society relations, or to prescribe policies to resolve their sources of conflict. Two other dynamics of conflict were discussed that arise from the limitations of liberal theory. The conflict over identities, and over the meanings of politics, cannot be examined effectively from within the liberal framework as it presumes a particular answer to these questions, and thus occludes these issues.

State–NGO conflict over identity politics

The first of these contradictions is that liberal peacebuilding theory and practice understand the promotion of civil society as a core component of resolving disputes over identity within modern territorial states. Peacebuilding then is not seen as re/writing identity narratives, but rather as minimizing their impact on society, and of putting in place the system of governance, the plural democracy, that is best able to redress and resolve conflicts over identity. If peacebuilding is about the re/imagination of a society, and thus the re/alignment of power, then it must be acknowledged that it is inherently concerned with questions of identity. The practices of the international community, in attempting to reconstitute the state and society in a way that encourages non-violent resolution of politics, and in the strengthening of the state, are about changing the nature of politics in these communities, and altering the way in which people see themselves and their neighbours. This is, as Walker argues, a core insight of CSS literature:

> [T]he process of rethinking security must respond especially to questions about whose security is being assumed and under what conditions. (This is why the complex debates about political identity that have come to be so influential in literatures on, for example, feminism and postcolonialism, cannot be avoided in this context.)
>
> (Walker 1997: 69)

The promotion of civil society rests on a claim about how society should be organized, and how people should interact with one another and the state. In advocating a particular vision of politics and social organization, one centred on the rational individual within a democratic environment, peacebuilding cannot be neutral and is implicated in the identity debates within the country.

NGOs are involved in these processes on two levels. At the simplest level, and the one least challenging to liberal theory, by their engagement or non-engagement with various ethnic, religious, and gender groups (to list the most commonly articulated identity groups) civil society associations can either challenge or support the state's attempts to advance particular narratives of identity and state belonging. When a humanitarian NGO chooses to not be involved with a particular group, it is making a public statement through its inaction of the group's outsider status; while working with groups has effect of legitimizing their presence in the country.

In terms of security, this means that the needs of some portions of society are necessarily obscured, and some voices are muffled or drowned out by the calls of the dominant conception of identity. As Hoogensen and Rottem argue, '[s]ecurity claims cannot be heard from identities that have been enveloped and hidden by the dominant discourse' (2004: 165).

Security discourse on the part of the state then cannot serve all members of society equally, and inevitably represents the interests of some groups over others. In the process, some groups are provided greater legitimacy and rendered as 'normal', while others are pushed aside as marginal or minority with less of a right to expect assistance and protection from the government.

However, the promotion of liberal associational civil society affects identity politics at a more abstract level. By their very existence, civil society associations are propagating a particular form of identity narrative that prioritizes the rational individual who participates in associational life of the state. NGOs, by operating in Cambodia, shape the ways in which people and communities interact, and establish the limits of what constitutes a valid claim against neighbours and the state, and on whose behalf it can be made. This also calls attention to the limitations of much of the critical Left's faith in civil society as a space for the protection and promotion of diversity, as the ways in which these diversities can manifest are severely proscribed by a pre-set liberal pluralist model that argues that it is individuals that should interact with the state.

Conflicts between NGOs and the state over the politics of politics

As Walker has shown, security discourse, and the related language of state sovereignty, delineates 'where politics can occur' (Walker 1990: 14). Following Pouligny (2005), it is clear that this statement does not capture the entirety of the disciplining move. It is not only a matter of dictating 'where' politics can happen, but also more fundamentally what counts as 'politics'. This is one of the fundamental limits of relying on civil society associations as an emancipatory force, as it is inherently implicated in a division of politics and society, and of reinforcing the notion that politics occurs at the level of the state. Pouligny argues:

> The ... limit of the 'civil society' concept, as it is commonly used, is that it conveys the idea of a clear dichotomy between what is supposed to be and what is not supposed to be political. Obviously, even in Western contexts, this distinction is far from being so clearcut, but it tends to be considered in an even more rigid way in places where 'civil society' is presented as an alternative to dysfunctional or even 'failed' state [*sic*].
>
> (Pouligny 2005: 500)

In another critique of the concept, Jaeger (2007), drawing on Foucault's governmentality literature, argues that despite popular refrains that civil society can *politicize* issues that had been viewed as technical matters of regulation, in fact it often works to *depoliticize*. Civil society operates within the broader political system; it is not outside of it. He is building on Lipschutz's (2005) differentiation between distributive and constitutive politics, wherein he sees civil society politicizing distributive issues, but depoliticizing the latter. This in effect ensures the governability of society.

Civil society is not naturally the realm of apolitical associational behaviour, though the types of activities that NGOs engage in may or may not be *seen* as political. More to the point, the 'political nature' of various issues is a result of contestation, meaning it is itself political. Advocating an image of civil society that obscures this point misses how the promotion of NGOs can introduce new axis of conflict, and misses the opportunity to have such organizations participate in discussions around issues deemed 'political' and thus outside of their purview. If civil society and the state are constructed in a way that places them in opposition to one another, in a context where what is and is not in their respective purview is being struggled over, then the perpetuation of civil society in environments of conflict should not be expected to resolve conflict. Rather, it transforms its character, addressing some aspects of conflict, but opening up new dynamics at the same time.

Understanding peacebuilding as *techne*

In addressing the underlying causes of conflict, peacebuilding has sought to turn issues into technical debates in order to ensure that conversations about development are in effect forums of experts (made up predominately of NGOs, foreign contractors, and government representatives), a move they expect to benefit society in the long run. The favouring of NGOs is a core part of this practice as they are deemed to be effective in identifying societal development needs and in turn to implement appropriate projects. These NGOs do often attempt to consult the local stakeholders about particular projects in order to shape their delivery to meet local needs. Such forms of consultation are remarkably constrained, however, with the groups having already decided on the types of activities required and the shape that communities need to take. This moves issues of both development and conflict resolution into the realm of the technical, and effectively beyond politics. In short, peacebuilding tries to resolve conflict, not by normalizing politics, but by putting in place a form of *non-politics*. Politics is the purview of the state. Yet clearly, not everything the state does is seen as being political. The liberal turn has denuded much of its political content. This is, as Foucault has argued, a function of *techne*. This obscures the manner in which what is, and is not, a 'political' issue is itself a subject of debate, and is not inherently settled. In states such as Cambodia, treating these issues as resolved introduces new forms of confrontation at the same time as it may address other causes of violence.

To understand these processes of conflict it is necessary to move past the liberal framework that has dominated thinking about peacebuilding.

The first step that must be taken is to embrace the politics of peacebuilding. This does not mean the debates between the various stakeholders that take place, or the decisions by international actors about whether or not to intervene in a given situation; instead it is an assertion that peacebuilding cannot be approached as a technique to solve internal conflict. This means that we have to recognize that attempts to resolve conflict demands debates about the form the society should take, and that this requires that local society have a voice in such discussions. The literature on civil society is silent about the question of politics; it does not have anything to tell us about its meaning, short of saying that civil society should not be engaged in it. But, as has been shown, there is a politics of what is political, as it determines who can and cannot speak about a given issue. Within security studies we talk about processes of securitization that move issues in an out of the rubric of security discourse. Yet for politics itself, the language at our disposal is quite poor.

Peacebuilding is a political process, in the same way that critiques of peacebuilding are. Unlike the traditional approaches to social science that claim that scientific analysis is possible, CSS assumes that all studies and critiques are inherently political. As a result, approaching the questions that have been broached here requires that the theory be ethically grounded, which provides a means of adjudicating claims and making political decisions about what is observed. By working against dominant discourses on issues like security, the very possibility of politics is opened up, and in the process is shown to require debate. That this is a method that holds out the possibility for alternative voices to be heard cannot be ignored.

A cautionary note for critical scholarship

It is not only liberal approaches to peacebuilding and state reconstruction that actively promote civil society. Critical scholarship has long viewed civil society and social movements as the space for resistance against the state, and for resistance against universalism. This must be questioned, particularly as it pertains to the introduction of civil society in the South. Because civil society is perceived as an alternative to the state, it has also been favoured by a range of social theory, including critical scholarship. In fact, it is actually lauded by many critical voices as a site of struggle against the state, and as such a means of realizing emancipatory goals (Cox 1997). The similarities with liberalism in this regard should be apparent, as they are both (for their own separate reasons) motivated to strengthen civil society at the expense of the state. The irony is that one of the hallmarks of critical scholarship is scepticism of the value of dominant narratives, and a desire to resist movements towards hegemony. Civil society needs to be seen in this light, as being a hegemonic discourse in its own right.

A commitment to CSS demands scepticism of any dominant narrative, and while this is generally applied to a critique of the state and its security practices, we must also apply this to civil society. This means we must not assume that it is the natural space for more inclusive and emancipatory politics. Nor, for that matter, can it be treated as an antidote to the state, as it is inseparable from its own logic. Civil society makes sense only when placed in opposition to the government. But this opposition is itself constrained by the broader discourse it is located within. While civil society can confront the state on some policy issues, and can act as a check and balance on its power, it is not able to challenge it on any more profound basis. Furthermore, favouring civil society over the state does not inherently resolve conflict within societies, but as has been shown, creates new forms at the same time as others are supposedly addressed.

For critical scholarship and praxis, these findings should be seen as a caution against assuming that civil society can be a site of emancipation. It is neither necessarily a site that welcomes or supports diversity of identities, nor a means to resist the universalizing drives. This is not because such communities are unable to take advantage of civil society, but rather that civil society, as it is being advanced, is a part of the broader liberal governance regime. It is implicated in the propagation of particular forms of politics and dictates what issues are open to public debate, and which are not. It further serves to reinforce the sense that some issues are the purview of the state, and others of society.

What questions are raised?

Arising from this study are a number of questions that warrant closer examination. Besides an obvious value in conducting a similar study in other sites of peacebuilding, such as in Timor-Leste, Afghanistan and Iraq, there are related avenues of inquiry that this study has flagged. In conducting an immanent critique of peacebuilding, the focus has been on NGOs as the dominant form of civil society in post-conflict states. Even within the liberal associational literature, such forms of associations represent a narrow slice of what is understood to constitute civil society, albeit a dominant form in many states emerging from periods of civil war. This study has been quite critical of the emancipatory potential of NGOs, but do New Social Movements (NSMs) offer greater opportunities and support more diversity? Additionally, might NSMs provide for a greater local voice in mediating local communities' engagement with liberal governance and economics?

The second area of research that emerges from this analysis is the requirement for a more detailed theorization of civil society within critical scholarship. Can civil society be conceptualized in a way that does not simultaneously reinforce the divide between the public and private, and between social and political matters?

What is to be done?

Peacebuilding theory is presented first and foremost as a guide for action. It is, in this respect, problem-solving theory of the highest order. This book has illustrated the ways in which peacebuilding practices, based on universalized notions of the nature of liberal civil society, have created new dynamics of conflict in Cambodia. This study has set out with a critical intent, to expand the grounds of debate and to identify and commence conversations about the appropriateness of current forms of international intervention. Yet, the problem-solving imperative remains, articulated by the questions posed by Immanuel Kant, 'What ought I do?', and by Lenin, 'What is to be done?'.

If peacebuilding, as it has been put into practice in Cambodia, is problematic and has served to introduce new tropes of conflict instead of resolving the underlying threats to peace and stability, then where does this leave the international community? Does this then imply that the North should not be engaged in peacebuilding in the South, and that we should leave 'them' to their own devices? Although this issue has not been engaged here, the arguments that have been presented must affect decisions about how and when to intervene in the South. This movement, however, from a critical to a problem-solving mode is difficult and requires the abandonment of some of the theoretical principles upon which CSS is built. That said, the pursuit of emancipatory politics serves as a means of movement from the space of critique into advocating for knowledge and policy production.

The first significant point that needs to be made is that peacebuilding cannot be approached as it has been, as a technical issue where the focus is on how its given goals can best be achieved. The scholarly and policy literatures on peacebuilding broadly agree that in attempting to address the sources of conflict, societies must be reconfigured in some manner. It is involved, by necessity, in changing how people interact with one another, how communities interact, and more broadly how these in turn relate with the various levels of government. In contrast with most of the work on peacebuilding, we cannot take for granted either the assumed end-point, or the means of its achievement. Instead of treating all Southern communities as nascent liberal democracies, with all people containing the seeds of its concomitant wants and desires, we need to be aware that such views develop over time, and are subject to their specific historic contexts. It should then be expected that this would emerge in a unique way in each instance, rather than following some perfect Northern model. Directly related to this is that, rather than imposing such a form of politics on a society (such as with the democratic elections in Cambodia), there first needs to be a debate within the given communities about the form of society they wish to pursue. How this might be done is a question that requires further investigation.

The next observation is that peacebuilding must be forthright in its attempts to reconstruct state–societal relations and that it must recognize the political nature of such endeavours. This means that local voices must be included in debates about how to escape cycles of violence. Peacebuilding has assumed both its end-point and the means of its achievement at the expense of local voices. When peacebuilding does solicit local involvement in the development programme, it is after the general framework of peacebuilding has already been decided, thus NGOs' solicitiations of community input into how to best bring a village into the new market excludes the local voices from the most important decisions (it also largely determines the choices available to the community). Providing for a more fulsome voice for local communities is clearly not easily done, but this does not alter the ethical imperative of empowering peoples that are to be affected by peacebuilding.

Related to this point is that peacebuilding needs to reframe its engagement with NGOs, and how they are fostered within the target societies. INGOs are clearly not representative of the local communities they seek to assist. This does not mean that the groups are unable to help peoples in the South, but at the same time the presence of INGOs should not be taken as any indication of the success or failure of peacebuilding. Furthermore, in the design of interventions there needs to be a greater recognition that favouring INGOs for the delivery and implementation of development projects comes at the expense of local government capacity. Next, fostering local NGOs should not be *assumed* to be an effective means of either controlling the state, or of giving voice to local communities. The focus on LNGOs obscures other historic forms of associational behaviour, as well as means of resolving conflict that have developed within the given society's cultural contexts. LNGOs do not, by being brought into being, transcend local politics; rather they merely introduce a new layer of such politics and bring new actors into the disputes. And critically, by its support of NGOs, the international community is favouring the position of NGOs in the state's political disputes. This should not be read as a rejection of LNGOs, or of a return to the old patterns of state-centric development practices. It is a call for greater flexibility in engagement with local communities and a call to pay far greater attention to local forms of conflict resolution. This all means that imposing Northern norms of civil society needs to be undertaken with far more caution, and the implications for particular historic contexts needs to be taken far more seriously than it currently is. The position at present is to assume that any attempt to regulate or control this sector is a form of anti-democratic movement that must be resisted.

Finally, the position that we must end at is that liberal practices of peacebuilding, in seeking to resolve conflicts have, have sought to depoliticize issues and to shift issues into the spheres of technical discussion. Civil society is promoted as a core component of such measures, yet this restricts the limits of the possible, serves to reproduce particular Northern images of what the world should look like, and denies a substantive voice to local peoples in determining how they will move forward as a community. This brings us back to Rancière's writing on critical politics. 'What we must do instead is repoliticize conflicts so that they can be addressed, restore names to the people and give politics back its former visibility in the handling of problems and resources' (2007: 106).

Annex A

List of interviews

Interview, HR and good governance LNGO representative, Phnom Penh, 19 September 2003.

Interview, academic, Phnom Penh, 21 September 2003.

Interview, Pierre Lacerte, Food Security Fund, Canadian Cooperation Office, Phnom Penh, 22 September 2003.

Interview, HR and good governance LNGO representative, Phnom Penh, 29 September 2003.

Interview, education and development LNGO, Phnom Penh, 29 September 2003

Interview, Kristina Mitchell, Health and Nutrition Fund, Canadian Cooperation Office, Phnom Penh, 30 September 2003.

Interview, Michael Barton, Canadian Cooperation Office, Phnom Penh, 30 September 2003.

Interview, Chris Turner, Canada Fund Manager, Canadian Cooperation Office, Phnom Penh, 1 October 2003.

Interview, Cambodian representative, INGO, Phnom Penh, 3 October 2003.

Interview, health INGO representative, Phnom Penh, 8 October 2003.

Interview, research LNGO representative, Phnom Penh, 9 October 2003.

Interview, research LNGO representative, Phnom Penh, 10 October 2003.

Interview, development LNGO representative, Phnom Penh, 10 October 2003.

Interview, capacity-building INGO representative, Phnom Penh, 13 October 2003.

Interview, Cambodian representative, INGO, Phnom Penh, 16 October 2003.

Interview, INGO representative, Phnom Penh, 16 October 2003.

Interview, health LNGO representative, Phnom Penh, 17 October 2003.

Interview, INGO representative, Phnom Penh, 21 October 2003.

Interview, Cambodian representative, INGO, Phnom Penh, 21 October 2003.

Interview, INGO representative, Phnom Penh, 22 October 2003.

Interview, election-monitoring LNGO representative, Phnom Penh, 27 October 2003.

Interview, academic, Phnom Penh, 27 October 2003.

Interview, good governance LNGO representative, Phnom Penh, 28 October 2003.

Interview, international donor organization representative, Phnom Penh, 5 November 2003.

Interview, health INGO representative, Phnom Penh, 5 November 2003.

Interview, education INGO representative, Phnom Penh, 6 November 2003.

Interview, international LNGO representative, Phnom Penh, 8 November 2003.
Interview, Ministry of Health official, Sen Monorom, 12 November 2003.
Interview, health INGO representatives, Sen Monorom, 13 November 2003.
Interview, education INGO representative, Sen Monorom, 13 November 2003.
Interview, gender LNGO representative, Phnom Penh, 15 November 2003.
Interview, international donor representative (Cambodian), Phnom Penh, 17 November 2003.
Interview, youth LNGO representative, Phnom Penh, 17 November 2003.
Interview, gender and media LNGO representative, Phnom Penh, 18 November 2003.
Interview, press LNGO representative, Phnom Penh, 18 November 2003.
Interview, HR and health LNGO representative, Phnom Penh, 19 November 2003.
Interview, HR and good governance LNGO representative, Phnom Penh, 19 November 2003.
Interview, culture and education LNGO representative, Phnom Penh, 19 November 2003.
Interview, environment INGO representatives, Phnom Penh, 19 November 2003.
Interview, youth LNGO representative, Phnom Penh, 19 November 2003.
Interview, micro-credit LNGO representative, Phnom Penh, 20 November 2003.
Interview, gender LNGO representative, Phnom Penh, 20 November 2003.
Interview, health and education LNGO representative, Phnom Penh, 21 November 2003.
Interview, HR and good governance LNGO, Phnom Penh, 24 November,
Interview, Islamic development LNGO representative, Phnom Penh, 25 November 2003.
Interview, fisheries LNGO representative, Battambang, 27 November 2003.
Interview, education LNGO representative, Battambang, 27 November 2003.
Interview, HR and good governance LNGO representative, Battambang, 28 November 2003.
Interview, development LNGO representative, Battambang, 28 November 2003.
Interview, health LNGO representative, Battambang, 28 November 2003.
Interview, HR and good governance LNGO representatives, Battambang, 29 November 2003.
Interview, development LNGO representative, Battambang, 29 November 2003.
Interview, women's education LNGO representative, Battambang, 29 November 2003.
Interview, HR LNGO representative, Phnom Penh, 1 December 2003.
Interview, health and education INGO representative (Cambodian), Phnom Penh, 1 December 2003.
Interview, development INGO representative (Cambodian), Phnom Penh, 2 December 2003.
Interview, NGO umbrella group representative (international), Phnom Penh, 2 December 2003.
Interview, HR LNGO representative, Phnom Penh, 4 December 2003.
Interview, HR NGO umbrella group, Phnom Penh, 4 December 2003.
Interview, HR LNGO director, Phnom Penh, 4 December 2003.
Interview, His Excellency Chea Sophorn, Secretary of State for the Council of Ministers, Phnom Penh, 4 December 2003.
Interview, In The, Ministry of Education, Phnom Penh, 5 December 2003.

Interview, youth LNGO representative, Phnom Penh, 7 December 2003.
Interview, Say Va, Deputy Director of Khmer Literature and Culture Association (ICLCA), Phnom Penh, 7 December 2003.
Interview, Cambodian youth LNGO representative, Phnom Penh, 8 December 2003.
Interview, women's LNGO representative, Phnom Penh, 9 December 2003.
Interview, HR INGO representative, Phnom Penh, 9 December 2003.
Interview, environment LNGO representative, Phnom Penh, 11 December 2003.
Interview, development INGO representative, Phnom Penh, 12 December 2003.
Interview, HR LNGO representative, Phnom Penh, 17 December 2003a.
Interview, HR LNGO representative, Phnom Penh, 17 December 2003b.
Interview, HR IO representative, Phnom Penh, 18 December 2003.
Interview, HR INGO representative, Phnom Penh, 19 December 2003.
Interview, HR IO representative, Phnom Penh, 19 December 2003.
Interview, women's LNGO representative, Phnom Penh, 10 August 2004.
Interview, Islamic development LNGO representative, Phnom Penh, 10 August 2004.
Interview, education INGO representative, Phnom Penh, 10 August 2004.
Interview, research LNGO representative, Phnom Penh, 11 August 2004.
Interview, de-mining INGO representative, Phnom Penh, 11 August 2004.
Interview, HR and gender LNGO representative, Phnom Penh, 12 August 2004.
Interview, environment INGO representative, Phnom Penh, 13 August 2004.
Interview, KKK HR and education LNGO, Phnom Penh, 13 August 2004.
Interview, health LNGO representative, Phnom Penh, 13 August 2004.
Interview, Mrs. Sieng Sorvathana, Director of Early Childhood and Education Department, MoEYS Gender Secretariat, Phnom Penh, 13 August 2004.
Interview, youth LNGO representative, Phnom Penh, 16 August 2004.
Interview, KKK HR LNGO representative, Phnom Penh, 17 August 2004.
Interview, de-mining INGO representative, Phnom Penh, 17 August 2004.
Interview, Vietnamese translator, Phnom Penh, 17 August 2004.
Interview, women's LNGO representative, Phnom Penh, 18 August 2004.
Interview, KKK development LNGO representative, Phnom Penh, 18 August 2004.
Interview, HR LNGO representative, Phnom Penh, 19 August 2004.
Interview, development LNGO representative, Phnom Penh, 19 August 2004.
Interview, youth LNGO representative, Phnom Penh, 19 August 2004.
Interview, Mrs. Hang Lina, Deputy Director General, Ministry of Planning, Phnom Penh, 20 August 2004.
Interview, development INGO representative, Phnom Penh, 20 August 2004.
Interview, education INGO representative, Banlung, 23 August 2004.
Interview, environment and development LNGO representative (international), Banlung, 24 August 2004.
Interview, Tim Sangvat, Provincial Director of Ratanakiri, Education Ministry Office, Banlung, 25 August 2004.
Interview, Mr Kham Khoeun, Governor of Ratanakiri, Governor's Office, Banlung, 25 August 2004.
Interview, health INGO representative, Banlung, Ratanakiri, 26 August 2004.
Interview, His Excellency Ek Sam Ol, Deputy Chairman of the Legislative Committee, Legislature Building, Phnom Penh, 1 September 2004.
Interview, development INGO representative, Phnom Penh, 2 September 2004.
Interview, youth LNGO representative, Phnom Penh, 4 September 2004.
Interview, election-monitoring NGO representative, Phnom Penh, 3 September 2005.

Annex B

Categorization of NGOs interviewed

The categorization of NGOs is a complicated process for a number of reasons. The work of any given organization often does not fit neatly into any single description. For example, the Apsara Arts NGO teaches orphaned and poor urban youth traditional Khmer performance arts. Such an organization is engaged in some forms of education, some forms of cultural promotion, and nominally involved in development as well (as one of the hopes is to provide a livelihood to youth). Next, groups will run multiple projects, varying across time and place. Large organizations may run different types of projects in various locations. Additionally, the projects that are run can change substantially from year to year.

NGOs have been categorized according to the broad type of work that they conduct. The categories, indicated in the table below, are broad by design in order to ensure that a wide spectrum of organizations have been interviewed. The names of the organizations have been removed to ensure anonymity.

Annex B Table

NGO/ donor number	*Interview date*	*INGO/ LNGO*	*Business assistance*	*Human rights*	*Environment*	*Good governance*	*Health*	*Gender*	*Education*	*Development*	*Other*
1	19 September 2003	LNGO		x		x					
2	22 September 2003	Donor									
3	29 September 2003	LNGO		x		x					
4	29 September 2003	LNGO							x	x	
5	30 September 2003	Donor		x		x	x				
6	30 September 2003	Donor			x					x	
7	1 October 2003	Donor			x		x			x	
8	3 October 2003	INGO								x	
9	3 October 2003	INGO					x			x	
10	8 October 2003	INGO					x		x		
11	9 October 2003	LNGO	x	x		x				x	
12	10 October 2003	LNGO		x		x					
13	10 October 2003	LNGO	x								
14	13 October 2003	INGO		x		x				x	
15	16 October 2003	INGO					x	x			
16	16 October 2003	INGO		x	x		x	x	x	x	
17	17 October 2003	LNGO					x				
18	21 October 2003	INGO			x						
19	21 October 2003	INGO		x			x		x	x	
20	22 October 2003	INGO					x		x	x	
21	27 October 2003	LNGO		x		x					
22	28 October 2003	LNGO				x					
23	5 November 2003	Donor		x		x		x		x	
24	5 November 2003	INGO					x				
25	6 November 2003	INGO							x		
26	8 November 2003	LNGO								x	
27	13 November 2003	INGO					x				

28	13 November 2003	INGO							x	x	
29	15 November 2003	LNGO						x			
30	17 November 2003	Donor		x		x		x		x	
30a	17 November 2003	LNGO		x		x			x		
31	18 November 2003	LNGO		x				x			
32	18 November 2003	LNGO		x					x		
33	19 November 2003	LNGO		x			x				
34	19 November 2003	LNGO		x				x			
35	19 November 2003	LNGO									x
36	19 November 2003	INGO			x						
37	19 November 2003	LNGO		x		x	x		x		
38	20 November 2003	LNGO	x								
39	20 November 2003	LNGO		x				x			
40	21 November 2003	LNGO					x		x		
41	24 November 2003	LNGO		x		x					
42	25 November 2003	LNGO							x	x	
43	27 November 2003	LNGO			x					x	
44	27 November 2003	LNGO							x		
45	28 November 2003	LNGO		x		x					
46	28 November 2003	LNGO						x	x		
47	28 November 2003	LNGO					x				
48	29 November 2003	LNGO		x		x					
49	29 November 2003	LNGO						x		x	
50	29 November 2003	LNGO	x					x	x		
51	1 December 2003	LNGO		x			x	x			
52	1 December 2003	INGO/ Donor					x		x		
53	2 December 2003	INGO/ Donor	x		x	x		x		x	
54	2 December 2003	Umbrella	x	x	x	x	x	x	x	x	
55	4 December 2003	Umbrella		x							
56	4 December 2003	LNGO		x		x		x			

continued

Annex B Table continued

NGO/ donor number	*Interview date*	*INGO/ LNGO*	*Business assistance*	*Human rights*	*Environment*	*Good governance*	*Health*	*Gender*	*Education*	*Development*	*Other*
57	7 December 2003	LNGO							x		
58	8 December 2003	LNGO		x		x					
59	9 December 2003	LNGO				x		x	x	x	
60	9 December 2003	INGO/ Donor		x							
61	11 December 2003	LNGO			x						
62	12 December 2003	INGO								x	
63	17 December 2003	LNGO		x		x		x			
64	17 December 2003	LNGO		x		x					
65	18 December 2003	IO		x							
66	19 December 2003	INGO		x						x	
67	19 December 2003	IO		x		x					
68	10 August 2004	LNGO		x				x	x		
69	10 August 2004	LNGO		x						x	
70	10 August 2004	INGO							x		
71	11 August 2004	LNGO							x	x	
72	11 August 2004	LNGO									
73	12 August 2004	LNGO		x				x			
74	13 August 2004	INGO			x						
75	13 August 2004	LNGO			x				x		
76	13 August 2004	LNGO					x				
77	16 August 2004	LNGO	x		x		x		x	x	
78	17 August 2004	LNGO		x							
79	17 August 2004	INGO								x	x
80	17 November 2004	LNGO		x					x		
81	18 August 2004	LNGO		x				x			
82	18 August 2004	LNGO							x		
83	19 August 2004	LNGO		x					x		

84	19 August 2004	LNGO	x						x
85	19 August 2004	LNGO						x	
86	20 August 2004	LNGO			x				
87	20 August 2004	LNGO				x	x		
88	23 August 2004	INGO						x	
89	24 August 2004	LNGO		x					
90	26 August 2004	INGO				x			
91	2 September 2004	INGO	x					x	x

Notes

1 Introduction

1 www.un.org/Depts/dpko/dpko/co_mission/untacbackgr1.html.

2 Critical scholars that have studied peacebuilding in Cambodia include: Lizée 2000; and Whitworth 2004, in contrast the authors applying traditional approaches to peacebuilding in Cambodia include: Akashi 1994; Boua 1993; Brown and Zasloff 1998; Chetty 1993; Chong 2002; Collacott 1996; Downie 2000; Downie and Kingsbury 2001; Doyle and Suntharalinam 1994; Farris 1994; Hughes and Öjendal 2006; Jennar 1994; Moniroth 1995; Peou 1998b; Roberts 2001, 2003; and Um 1994.

3 The terms 'North' and 'South' are used in this study to differentiate between those states and actors (including NGOs) that are situated in the advanced industrialized world that have the ability to dictate the terms of international intervention.

4 Refer to Paris (1997), and Keating and Knight (2004), for an overview of the major debates within both academic and policy literature on peacebuilding.

5 The focus on the holding of an election is also noted as being necessary as it provides a clear benchmark that allows for the withdrawal of UN troops. This was a particularly important point in the early 1990s where states were concerned with being embroiled in long-term military engagements.

6 Of the CSS literature that has examined the role of civil society refer to the work of Duffield (2001, 2007). For studies that have critiqued the actions of NGOs refer to Young (1994) for analysis of how such associations are often fragmented and uncooperative. Numerous researchers have pointed out the links between NGOs and the spread of neoliberal ideals, including Farrington and Bebbington 1993; Robinson 1997; Edwards *et al.* 1995; Zaidi 1999; and Mercer 2002.

7 There are an exhaustive number of studies of peacebuilding that seek to assess the methods of state/society reconstruction and provide recommendations about future operational design. For a sample of academic work done on the subject refer to: Boyce 2002; Donini *et al.* 2003; Keating and Knight 2004; Junne and Verkoren 2004; Paris 2004; Sweetman 2004; Caplan 2005; Jeong 2005; Lederach 2005; and Mazurana *et al.* 2005.

8 Those authors who have worked on this issue, and whose work has formed an important source for this study include: Campbell 1998b; Duffield 2001; Orford 2003; Whitworth 2004; and Pouligny 2005.

9 The post-colonial literature has explored this issue in part, illustrating how present forms of international politics, while masked by discourses of the pursuit of human rights, nevertheless constitute an imposing of a particular political model on states and societies in the South.

10 This is argued in part by Lizée (2000) who critiques the 1995 UN statement that the failures in peacebuilding in Cambodia, Somalia and Bosnia arose due to implementation limitations, rather than a more profound limitation in theories of peacebuilding.

2 Critical analysis of peacebuilding

1 The early UN peace operations, commonly considered to be examples of peacebuilding include: United Nations Observer Mission in El Salvador (ONUSAL) deployed in July 1991; UN/OAS International Civilian Mission in Haiti (MICIVIH), deployed between February 1993 and February 1994; and the United Nations Transitional Authority in Cambodia (UNTAC).

2 The term emancipation is being used in the post-structural sense, which seeks to liberate people's from multiple structures of domination. This is in contrast to the Marxist and post-Marxist literature that focuses on a dominant political/economic structure.

3 There is a very lively debate over the validity of pursuing goals of emancipation, with some scholars falling on the side of more post-structural arguments asserting that talking about emancipation is a continuation of colonial discourses, and that regardless, it is impossible to arrive at a common conception of the good life. At the same time, I remain convinced that it is possible (and necessary) to strive to improve the conditions of the external world, even while arguing that we need to continuously question the dominant narratives of what this world should look like. For a summary of this debate refer to: Stamnes 2004: 162–163.

4 In terms of the critical work on peacekeeping, refer to Whitworth's (2004) study of peacekeeping forces in several case studies including Cambodia. Critical work on peacebuilding includes: Bellamy 2004; Duffield 2001; Fetherston 2000; Pouligny 2005; Pugh 2004; Stamnes 2001; and Schwarz 2005. For critiques of peacebuilding that are constructed around specific case studies refer to Campbell's (1998a) work on Bosnia, and Lizée's (2000) work on Cambodia.

5 Stamnes' particular approach to CSS is rooted more solidly in the work of the Frankfurt school than the more post-structural inspired work. He then applies the method of immanent critique to the study of the UN mission in Macedonia.

6 Overviews of immanent critique are found in: Held 1980; Neufeld 1997; and Heine and Teschke 1996.

7 It should be noted that this is at odds with the Marxist dialectic tradition of immanent critique. For a summary of such positions, refer to: Neufeld 1997; Wyn Jones 1995; and Browne 2008.

8 Patterson and Monroe, drawing on the work of Somers and Gibson (1994), argue that there are four dominant forms of narratives (Patterson and Monroe 1998: 325):

- ontological narratives, which we use to operate as social actors;
- public narratives, which come from institutions or large social organizations;
- conceptual narratives, which are developed by researchers; and
- meta-narratives, within which we are embedded as people.

9 Scwhartz-Shea and Yanow see two possibilities for qualitative research; where on the one hand the observer is 'objective' and external to the observations, on the other, consistent with interpretive methodology, the researcher as 'situated' and 'researchers must, perforce, interpret what they observe' (Scwhartz-Shea and Yanow 2002: 461).

10 Dick (2006) has labelled this style of interviewing as an 'ethnographic interview', as it involves aspects that can be described as both structured and

unstructured, but where there is no attempt to limit the type or scope of the response to questions.

11 While there are a very large number of registered NGOs working in Cambodia, a significant number of them have little or no project delivery. Discussions with NGO workers placed the actual number of active NGOs around 1,000. Even at that point the extent of their activities varied considerably from group to group. My sample of 150 has provided an adequate picture of the issues confronting the range of organizations working in the country.

12 One area that has been excluded is groups working specifically on economic issues. This substantial grouping, while obviously important, presents serious methodological problems.

13 For a comprehensive discussion of the differences between peacekeeping, peacemaking and peacebuilding, as well as the difference between first-, second- and third-generation peace operations, refer to: Griffin (1999). Paris (2004: 14–15) describes only two deviations from this model, that of the Belgian Congo in the early 1960s, and the UN Security Force in western New Guinea between October 1962 and April 1963. For histories of peacebuilding refer to: Goodhand and Hulme 1999; Griffin 1999; Fetherston 2000; Talentino 2002; Paris 2004.

14 This literature is typified by the New Wars thesis that argues that the 1990s have brought about new forms of intra-state conflict that pose a risk to the North, and are distinguished by a lack of civility on the part of combatants. This has been advanced most forcefully by Kaldor (1999), who has also been a strong proponent of global civil society.

15 The difficulty with this typology is that in stressing the military component, peacebuilding itself can be seen as a militarized form of development. As such, peacebuilding can then be perceived as forced reconstruction, out of the control of local authorities.

16 Peacebuilding is said to have been made possible through the demise of the Cold War. The rapprochement between the East and West permitted cooperation between the Great Powers that enabled the promotion of peace in the developing world. The term 'peacebuilding' has been traced back to the work of Galtung (1969); this however does not represent the point of general acceptance of the concept by the policy community (Call and Cook 2003b; Knight 2003).

17 Peacebuilding as a form of intervention only makes sense when we consider states as sovereign entities, and the interference of one state in another's internal business as being warranted in the most serious cases of a break-down of law and order.

18 For an example of how peacebuilding is directly linked to the narratives of the success of the Marshall Plan refer to: www.c-r.org/ccts/ccts13/paralys.htm; Goodhand 2002; and Last 2003.

19 Such arguments are rooted in institutionalism and place faith in the ability to alter the forms of politics through changes to political structures.

20 This is not to belittle the internal dissent, but neither Japan nor Germany was experiencing a civil war.

21 This debate about security versus development also plays out in the human security literature that is divided according to those who advocate a freedom from want (also referred to as the Japanese approach), and those who assert that a condition of security must exist in order to pursue development goals (the Canadian approach). For a typical academic work engaged in the study of peacebuilding policy that engages this issue, refer to Jeong (2005). Doyle and Sambanis (2006) focus on the relationship between war-fighting and peacebuilding.

22 In part this shows that peacebuilding actors are not unitary; they tend to disagree on approaches and goals. As an example, what the US State Department might be trying to achieve through peacebuilding can differ substantially from the vision of Oxfam UK. While they may both advocate a peaceful democratic society, the ways to arrive at this, and what such a society will look like, can be dramatically different.

23 The orientation of Kissinger and Mandelbaum towards peace operations is laid out by Richmond (2005b): online at www.st-andrews.ac.uk/intrel/media/Richmond_understanding_the_liberal_peace.pdf.

24 This is certainly the case with respect to the study of peacebuilding in Cambodia, where the focus has been on errors of judgment by the UN leadership in implementing the PPA, with debates around issues such as whether the KR should have been disarmed, and whether the UN should have taken over the running of the bureaucracy. The validity of the process is not in itself questioned, nor are its goals contested.

25 This study does not delve into the debate about whether peacebuilding is done for self-serving interests in preserving the international system. While international stability may affect state decision-making, it does not alter the way in which the logic of peacebuilding dictates a particular form of intervention.

26 Those who support this position, and thus advocate the integration of states into the global economy, though at a slow and cautious pace include David (1999) and Goodhand (2002). This position can also be seen in the Japanese human security literature, which deliberately links economic development and security. In contrast Richmond (2004a) and Cox (1981) represent voices of dissent on the emancipatory potential of economic liberalization and globalization.

27 These arguments have been advanced both by the neoliberals and Gramscians, though with obviously different normative takes on the dominant economic and social order.

28 This is one of the few areas in which we find a critique of NGOs and peacebuilding. These arguments are based in a particular reading of market capitalism. Pugh (2004) refers to the most explicit articulation of this argument (predominant after 11 September 2001) as the 'New York orthodoxy', where the UN is seen as incapable of achieving these goals. As such, the US and other like-minded states must take the lead in these peace operations.

29 Tom Palmer connects the emergence of civil society to much earlier political developments in cities through Europe in the eleventh century (2002: 49–51).

30 This was a constant theme over the course of the interviews with NGOs in Cambodia. The NGO representatives were quick to point out that they were doing work the government was incapable of doing, and that they were far more able to speak for the people as they were embedded within the communities. This is representative of the sense that the state was disconnected from the needs of its citizens.

31 This book has not engaged with the critical approaches to civil society as represented by Marxist or Gramscian perspectives. Nor has it engaged with the New Social Movements (NSM) literatures that emerged from Neo-Marxist perspectives. These positions, while clearly important, have not directly informed peacebuilding practices.

32 The major studies on the roles of CSOs in developing countries include: Biekart 1998; Riddell *et al.* 1997; Fowler 2000b; Robinson and White 1997.

33 It is important to note that there is no consensus on whether NGOs can be equated to civil society. Carothers has pointed out that according to Gramsci, NGOs are not representative of the totality of civil society: 'NGOs are outweighed by more traditional parts of civil society. Religious organizations,

labour unions, and other groups often have a genuine base in the population and secure domestic sources of funding, features that advocacy groups usually lack, especially the scores of new NGOs in democratizing countries' (Carothers 1999–2000: 20).

34 Rose *et al.* (1997) draw a strict line between voluntaristic organizations, and groups to which membership is mandatory. The latter are seen to have limited usefulness in the production of social capital.

35 Take for example Fisher's book, *Non-Governments: NGOs and the Political Development of the Third World* (Fisher 1998), which contains not a single cautionary note about the potential of NGOs to destabilize states and societies or to contribute to conflict. The entire book operates on the premise that NGOs are able to promote the rights and interests of society in the face of developing states that are either incapable of doing so, or worse, are opposed to democratic ideals.

36 This is not to argue that NGOs were directly involved in the violence, but rather that they provided indirect support to the genocidal forces through decisions about where, and with whom, to work.

4 A brief history of Cambodia and peacebuilding

1 Even though patron–clientalism (*khsae*) remains a core part of Cambodian society, its workings have been transformed. The reciprocal aspect of traditional patterns of this relationship has been largely subsumed by patterns where responsibilities flow upwards without a commensurate obligation towards subordinates.

2 The racist colonial practices have been detailed by Bit 1991, David P. Chandler 1983 and Higham 2001. In his text on the development of nationalism in Southeast Asia, Anderson noted: 'The French made no bones about expressing the view that if the Vietnamese were untrustworthy and grasping, they were nonetheless decisively more energetic and intelligent than the "child-like" Khmer and Lao. Accordingly, they made extensive use of Vietnamese functionaries in Western Indochina' (B. Anderson 1991: 129).

3 A Wat is a Buddhist temple complex generally consisting of a number of buildings including a large central shrine as well as living quarters for monks. These sites are often the focal point of rural communities, and appear to fulfil many of the roles that are linked with liberal associational behaviour.

4 There are two main sects of Theravadda Buddhism in Cambodia: *Mahanikay* (the traditionalists) and *Thommakay*. I. Harris (2005) reviews the development of Buddhism in Cambodia, paying particular attention to the impact of the KR on the religion, and the subsequent entanglement of Buddhism with politics in the late 1990s.

5 The Sangha is often used as an inclusive term to represent both the Buddhist religious orders and their associated laity. In this instance I am referring specifically to the monastic orders.

6 The impact of the American military strategy in Southeast Asia has been laid out by a number of scholars, including Kiernan 1996 and David P. Chandler 1991, 1983. They point to the ways in which the bombings and special forces' incursions into the country served to disrupt rice harvests on a massive scale, leading to substantial internal migration. This led to greater support within rural Cambodia for anti-government parties and forces.

7 The rise of the KR has been described and analysed in depth by David P. Chandler, Kiernan, and Vickery.

8 The nature of the KR regime is hotly contested. Peou (2000) and David P. Chandler (1996) have argued that it was a Stalinist form of government, while Kiernan (1991) has described it as a totalitarian fascist state.

9 The recognition that there was a utopian vision behind the horrors of the KR should not diminish outrage over what was perpetrated in its name. An awareness of the aims of the KR leadership is necessary to understand the atrocities that occurred.
10 Kiernan (1996: 107) relates that between May and September 1975, over 150,000 Vietnamese were forced out of Cambodia into Vietnam.
11 Heder and Vickery have both noted that there were direct military confrontations between DK and Vietnam after April 1975. While there was little conflict between the two countries in 1976, in 1977 there were dramatic escalations of violence as Cambodia began to attack across the Vietnamese border. Vickery (1984: 194), Heder (1979: 18), and Roberts (2001: 10) also draw attention to documentary evidence of cross-border skirmishes beginning as early as May 1975.
12 Roberts argues that there is no evidence that the Vietnamese invasion of Cambodia was driven by a desire to expand its borders or to exert any form of colonial control over its neighbours. In fact, he highlights the role played by KR defectors and Cambodian refugees in both advocating a Vietnamese invasion of Cambodia, and in subsequently leading many of the changes that were to take place.
13 Roberts argues that the discussion of the legitimacy of the Vietnamese invasion is crucial because it delineates the debate about the international response to the actions of Vietnam. Two excellent discussions of the Vietnamese-dominated era in Cambodia are Peou 2000 and Gottesman 2002.
14 According to the Yale University Cambodian Genocide Project, 1.7 million people died between 1975 and 1979, representing 21 per cent of the country's population (www.yale.edu/cgp/).
15 I have not located any references to the amount of support provided by the Soviet Union or Vietnam. It is worth noting that this did extend to the education of many professionals within the state, including engineers, doctors, bureaucrats and military officers. This is crucial as it illustrates that there was a nucleus of a professional bureaucracy in place prior to the commencement of the United Nations missions in 1991.
16 Following convention, the Party of Democratic Kampuchea (PDK) is referred to as the Khmer Rouge (KR) through the remainder of this study to highlight how the leadership of the newly named organization remained largely unchanged.
17 The Sangha, which had played a central part in Khmer life, had been devastated by the KR. According to Kiernan, 'of a total of 2,680 Buddhist monks from eight of Cambodia's 3,000 monasteries surveyed by Chantou Boua, only 70 monks were found to have survived in 1979' (1990: 39). The Heng Samrin government provided a strictly controlled space for the reintroduction of Buddhism. However, the monastic orders, which had to be largely rebuilt, became far more politicized during this time, and were required to be supportive of the new government (I. Harris 2005: 197).
18 This point has been made by most of the observers of the peace process. Yasushi Akashi, for example, argued, 'These agreements were made possible by the end of the confrontation between the United States and the former Soviet Union, reconciliation between China and Vietnam and the consequent disappearance of the need for "proxy war" by the Cambodia factions' (Akashi 1994: 211).
19 It has been argued that while the Cold War left Cambodia in limbo, the end of the Cold War dynamic made a peace process necessary as the external supporters of the conflict were no longer willing to sustain the status quo. Without financial and logistical support the various Cambodian factions were pushed to look for a resolution to the conflict. This coincided with a renewed interest in

the United Nations to resolve intra-state conflict. The negotiations were therefore well timed.

20 The P5 began to dictate some of the terms of the agreement (Brown and Zasloff 1998: 65). This led to the Comprehensive Political Settlement of the Cambodian Conflict (23 October 1991).

21 This resolution also announced the appointment of A. H. S. Ataul Karim, from Bangladesh, as the UNAMIC Chief Liaison Officer, and Brigadier General (BGen) Michel Loridon, from France, as the Senior Military Liaison Officer.

22 The official results of the vote are found in the 'Report of the Secretary-General on the conduct and results of the election in Cambodia', S/25913, 10 June 1993.

23 There is a great deal of excellent analysis of the 1993 elections which details the processes undertaken by UNTAC, the positions of the various parties towards the event, and assessments of the relative merits of the election and the subsequent power-sharing agreement between the two main parties (in contravention of the election result). In particular, refer to the following works: Boua 1993; Akashi 1994; Doyle and Suntharalinam 1994; Farris 1994; Brown and Zasloff 1998; Um 1994; Lizée 2000; Chong 2002.

24 The fact that the election results were in part ignored has been interpreted as both a failure of the peacebuilding process (representing the victory of individuals' particular interests), and conversely as a local solution to a crisis recognizing local context. In fact both positions are accurate; it does represent a failure of liberal democracy, but it likely prevented an immediate slippage back into factional warfare.

25 There was no apparent alternative to this arrangement. The UN was not able to supply the personnel to provide more supervision of the bureaucracy, nor was the CPP willing to cede further control. Despite this area of perceived failure the elections were still held, and CPP was defeated at the ballot box. However, their grip on the ministries provided Hun Sen sufficient political strength to push for a coalition government with Ranariddh.

26 While the mandate of UNTAC ended on 24 September 1993, on 4 November that year the Security Council provided an extension to the mine-clearing, military police and medical programmes until 31 December (S/RES/880 (1993) 4 November 1993).

27 Prince Ranariddh had been warned of the impending coup by senior military leaders and had fled the country, but he failed to notify senior members of his party (Peou 2000: 298–302).

28 For an assessment of the 2002 commune elections refer to Slocomb (2004), who lays out the move towards the strengthening of the commune-level administration in Cambodia in the 1980s.

29 Downie (2000: 43) raises four main arguments about why the elections were not free: that there was no separation between the state and the political parties (particularly the CPP); that the executive and judiciary were not separate; that there was no rule of law or respect for human rights; and that the government did not accept political opposition. Furthermore, while violence was not widespread, there were some events, like a grenade attack on an opposition party rally on 30 March 2007, and the subsequent coup, that still undermined any pretence to a free election.

30 Sam Rainsy, who served as the Finance Minister for FUNCINPEC after the 1993 elections, gained a reputation as an opponent of corruption, and as a free market advocate. However, he was expelled from the party in May 1995, and from the National Assembly in June of that year. He then set out to form the Khmer Nation Party (KNP) in 1995, which was renamed the Sam Rainsy Party in 1998 in response to legal challenges.

31 These statistics were taken from: 'NGO Statement to the 2002 Consultative Group Meeting on Cambodia', Phnom Penh, 19–21 June 2002, and 'NGO Statement to the 2006 Consultative Group Meeting on Cambodia', Phnom Penh, 2–3 March, 2006. More recent statistics are not publicly available.
32 Council for the Development of Cambodia, Development Cooperation Report, 2004 and 2005, February 2006, Phnom Penh www.cdc-crdb.gov.kh/cdc/8cg_meeting/dcr2004–2005/default_eng.htm (accessed 5 April 2010).
33 While an extensive search was conducted for a survey of earnings for the NGO sector in Cambodia, no such data was located. This is exacerbated by a tendency to rely heavily on volunteer labour for many NGO activities, especially in the recipient community. This raises a point worth further study, as the volunteer labour appears to be conducted predominately by women, pointing to the creation of a bifurcation where women's labour is not remunerated.
34 According to the *Declaration on the Rehabilitation and Reconstruction of Cambodia* (23 October 1991) the ICORC is mandated to coordinate development policy of international donors following the 2003 general election.
35 In fact it is argued by Slocomb (2002) that the shift towards a more market-oriented economy began in 1986. However, the drive increased in earnest during the era of peacebuilding.
36 The requirements for Cambodian ascension are found in the WTO document: WT/MIN(03)/18, 11 September 2003.
37 'Cambodia on target to make tourism record', *Thai News Service*, 30 May 2008.
38 ADB Key Indicators; *Dow Jones News Wire*, 'DJ Cambodia's rice yield hit record', 9 April 2007.
39 Ibid.
40 From http://hdrstats.undp.org/en/countries/profiles/KHM.html, 2006 (accessed 28 December 2011).
41 Data taken from the UNDP Human Development Report, /hdrstats.undp.org/countries/data_sheets/cty_ds_KHM.html (accessed 22 July 2008).
42 WB, Cambodia: Rural Sector Note and Business Plan, March 2007.
43 For election data refer to both www.electionguide.org/election.php?ID=1188 (accessed 1 September 2008); and the National Election Committee (NEC), www.necelect.org.kh/English/elecResults.htm (accessed 2 July 2009).

5 State intervention in NGOs for personal gain

1 According to Transparency International, an INGO that tracks perceptions of corruption, Cambodia rated 164 out of 180 states, with a rating of 2.1 out of 10.0, where 5.0 is argued to be a minimally accepted level. The data are available at: http://cpi.transparency.org/cpi2011/results/ (accessed 27 December 2011).
2 I will not be dealing with these differences in depth. This would require more focused research on NGOs working in the resource sector and a detailed examination of the interaction between the various NGOs and the affected communities.
3 Interview, Cambodian HR umbrella group, Phnom Penh, 4 December 2003.
4 For a summary of two instances of conflict between communities (Kanleng Phe and An Chh'aoet) and powerful individuals refer to WPM (2002).
5 While it is outside of the context of the current discussion it is important to note that this conflict over access to fishing lots can be linked to the increasingly capitalist economy under the peace process. The large-scale commercial exploitation of the fisheries has been enabled by the introduction of market capitalism. For an overview of the SOC's fisheries refer to Mak (2000).
6 Interview, fisheries LNGO representative, Battambang, 27 November 2003, also related in WPM (2002).

7 This incident, related in WPM (2002: 21–24), was eventually resolved in the community's favour, but only after substantial direct community action. It is important to note that this matter was resolved without NGO intervention.

8 The NGO Forum has documented cases in Battambang in 2000, Stung Treng in 1999, and Kompong Chhnang in 1995, where the fishing lot owners used the military and police to intimidate local communities.

9 As stated in an interview with an LNGO (interview, fisheries LNGO, Battambang, 27 November 2003).

10 Refer to the NGO Forum website: http://www.ngoforum.org.kh/eng/enpublications.php?docs=eapdoc (accessed 26 December 2011), for a more complete listing of various fisheries incidents.

11 To review the instances of violence surrounding the fisheries refer to NGO Economic, Social and Cultural Rights Monitoring Committee 2002; WPM 2002; NGO Forum reports on: *Fishing Conflict in Battambang*; *Fishing Conflict in Kompong Chhnang*; *Review of Fishery Conflict in Stung Treng*, http://www.ngoforum.org.kh/eng/enpublications.php?docs=eapdoc (accessed 10 June 2006); Mak 2000.

12 These include the use of electrical fishing, fishing with pesticides, drag-netting and dynamiting in fish lots. These all have long-term detrimental effects on fish habitat and are likely to endanger the sustainability of the resource.

13 This was related during interviews with personnel representing a Cambodian NGO umbrella group (interview, 2 December 2003), an LNGO covering fishing issues (interview, 27 November 2003), and a group training LNGOs in how to engage in advocacy work (interview, 30 September 2003).

14 These comments were based on an extensive interview addressing the issue of NGOs and political advocacy. While the issue of fisheries was addressed, the NGO representative stated that land rights were more problematic (interview, capacity-building INGO, Phnom Penh, 13 October 2003).

15 The community has appealed the case in the national court. I asked how the NGO helps in this respect as it is outside of the terms of their MOU. The representative said that this is an example of where they have to work in secret by providing money and expertise.

16 Evidence of this movement by the government came in November 2003 when the Council of Ministers issued a sub-decree that provided 2,000 hectares of waters to subsistence farmers in Kandal province to limit the disputes between communities and larger stock farmers (Van Rouen, 'Fishermen get more waters in Kandal', *Cambodia Daily*, 17 November 2003: 21).

17 *Dow Jones International News*, 'Cambodia faces challenge of dealing with land grabbing', 28 February 2006.

18 Interview, HR and good governance LNGO, Phnom Penh, 29 September 2003. This position was further echoed by international donors in Cambodia. Michael Barton from the Canadian Cooperation Office also noted that land redistribution is a sensitive issue (interview, Michael Barton, Canadian Cooperation Office, Phnom Penh, 30 September 2003).

19 There are Cambodian LNGOs that seek to address this issue by providing legal counsel, such as Legal Aid of Cambodia (www.lac.org.kh), and the Cambodian Defenders Project (www.cdpcambodia.org).

20 Interview, INGO representatives, Phnom Penh, 19 November 2003.

21 Interview, HR LNGO representative, Phnom Penh, 1 December 2003.

22 It has been estimated that in 2004 there were still some four million land mines left in the country, and perhaps as much unexploded ordinance (Sodhy 2004). According to the Cambodian Mine Action Committee (CMAC) land mines and UXOs have killed an average of 800–900 people a year since 2000 (CMAC, *Annual Report: 2005*. Phnom Penh, 2005, accessed online at www.cmac.org.kh/Menu_Progress_Publication_AnnualReport2005.asp).

23 For an overview of de-mining in Cambodia refer to Bottomley (2003), and to the websites of CMAC (www.cmac.org.kh) and the HALO trust (www.halotrust.org/cambodia.html).

24 Related in an interview with a representative of a de-mining organization (interview, INGO representative, Phnom Penh, 17 August 2004). A similar dynamic, where Cambodian soldiers overseeing the de-mining would seize land, was reported (interview, HR and good governance LNGO representative, Battambang, 28 November 2003).

25 For an overview of the politics around the forestry industry refer to Le Billon (2002).

26 Deforestation is an endemic problem in Southeast Asia and is beyond the scope of this research. There has been a great deal of work done on this area by the Cambodian government, the LNGO and INGO sector, and academia.

27 This discussion excludes issues related to non-timber forest products, such as honey and resin, or of the right to use the forest floor of rubber plantations. There are continuing debates about access to these areas, even in forest lots that are owned by private interests.

28 Examples of the Government's public stance against illegal forestry practices were evidenced in 1996 when the Interior Ministry put out the reward for the arrest of illegal loggers operating inside Bokor National Park, Kampot province (Lor Chandara. 'Bounty put on Bokor loggers', in *Cambodia Daily*, 15 January 1996: 9) The closure of the border to the traffic of logs was also reported in the *Bangkok Post*, which specifically referred to the statement by the Cambodian Deputy Finance Minister Sun Chanthol that the borders would remained closed to the timber trade until the state was able to put appropriate forestry management programmes in place ('Logging – UK group finds no signs of log traffic', *Bangkok Post*, 21 January 1997: 2).

29 Quoted by His Excellency Sok An, Senior Minister of Council of Ministers, 23 March 1999.

30 For a discussion of the impact on community forestry planning refer to Hubbard (2002).

31 The logging sector is unique in that all of the major parties, CPP, FUNCINPEC, and until 1996, the KR, benefited directly from the illegal sale of timber (Le Billon 2002).

32 In part logging was an ongoing source of revenue for rebel groups within Cambodia. All sides benefited, with the SOC exporting to Vietnam and the Royalists and KR working with Thai firms to export timber to Thailand. These exports provided essential sources of revenues to the various factions that provided them the financial means to continue their struggles through the 1980s, and in the case of the KR into the mid-1990s.

33 This violence has usually been perpetrated against communities and NGO workers who have tried to reclaim their rights to access to timber resources, and to limit large-scale logging activities. However, as Bottomley (2002) has shown in a study of local resistance to illegal forestry in the highlands of Ratankiri, this has also led to direct action by communities against forestry workers.

34 *Inter Press Service*, 'Cambodia: Donors likely to give loans even as forests fade', Bangkok: 7 July 1996.

35 This concern was noted in numerous interviews with NGOs: interview, HR and good governance LNGO, Phnom Penh, 29 September 2003; interview, Michael Barton, Canadian Cooperation Office, Phnom Penh, 30 September 2003; interview, international LNGO representative, Phnom Penh, 8 November 2003; interview, Khmer development INGO representative, Phnom Penh, 2 December 2003; interview, NGO umbrella group, Phnom Penh, 2 December 2003; interview, international LNGO representative, Banlung, 24 August 2004.

36 Details of this event also provided by an international LNGO worker (interview, Phnom Penh, 8 November 2003), and by a Cambodian HR umbrella group (interview, Phnom Penh, 4 December 2003).

37 This dynamic, where NGOs are reticent to confront the government directly, was discussed with respect to the fisheries issues (interview, capacity-building INGO representative, Phnom Penh, 13 October 2003; interview, Cambodian HR NGO umbrella group, Phnom Penh, 4 December 2003).

38 Where there have been deviations from this norm the groups have been working closely with particular communities prior to the forestry issue becoming a source of significant friction with the government. An example here is the group Non-Timber Forest Products, operating in Ratanakiri, which because of their close work with groups in the Som Thom Commune was approached regularly by community leaders to help address problems with both the government and forestry companies (McCaul 2000).

39 Interview, capacity-building INGO representative, Phnom Penh, 13 October 2003.

40 There have been instances of individuals being told they should leave the country, but this has usually happened through personal intimidation, and has not been done in the public manner from the central government that has defined the Global Witness case.

41 For a listing of the press releases issued by Global Witness refer to their website: www.globalwitness.org/press_releases/pressreleases.php?type=cambodia.

42 LICADHO (June 2006: 18).

43 US Department of State, Press Statement, 'Cambodia's termination of forest monitoring by Global Witness', 25 April 2003.

44 These numbers come from the Cambodian Women's Development Association, quoted in Equality Now submission to the United Nations Human Rights Council (UNHRC) (July 1999). For an overview of the representation of the sex trade in Cambodia refer to Sandy (2007).

45 Interview, HR and gender LNGO representative, Phnom Penh, 12 August 2004.

46 Equality Now reports that there are reports of 'government corruption and a common perception that police and military officials facilitate trafficking in women and girls' (Equality Now, July 1999: 1).

47 There is no universal agreement on how to address sex work in Cambodia. While most NGO workers argued that they pursued a complete elimination of the sector, a minority argue that to do so would not end sexual exploitation, and that criminalization would further endanger sex workers' lives.

48 Interview, children's rights NGO representative, Phnom Penh, 19 August 2004.

49 Indeed, many of these groups reported a formal process whereby Ministry employees were seconded to the NGO, where the group would augment their salaries. This capacity building enabled the NGOs to maintain good networks with the ministries. However, the misnomer of the term 'capacity building' must be highlighted; these are employees that are paid by the government who do the work of the NGO, not the Ministry. This kind of secondment, while increasing what the NGOs can achieve, does nothing to build state capacity, even though the state pays for it. Additionally, whenever I asked how long these bureaucrats worked for the NGO before returning to the government with their new-found capacity, I was told no one had returned from the groups I interviewed.

6 Bureaucratic intervention in NGO activities

1 The big exception here is the medical sector, where a number of NGOs argued that the government has been gaining technical and managerial expertise.

Though even here it was stated that the Ministry is constrained by a severe shortage of resources.

2 Mercer (2002) provides a good critical overview of the ways in which neoliberalism is related to the expansion of NGOs as the lead of civil society.

3 This is problematic as it focuses attention predominately on the central government and largely occludes the other strata of governance in Cambodia. The provincial, district and commune governments are passed over and ignored. This misrepresents the nature of politics in Cambodia where, as one moves further from Phnom Penh, the local governments are able to exert greater control over development in their circles of influence. However as a result of this, there is a lack of coordination between local and central levels of government. This is has been argued by both Hughes (2003), and Öjendal and Sedara (2006).

4 Some authors have argued that Northern development practices have worked to extend hegemony over the South. Refer to the work of Alvares 1992; Escobar 1992; Rahnema 1992; Esteva 1992; Brigg 2002.

5 Based on a study of NGO work in Guatemala, Abom found that Northern NGOs generally had poor relations with grassroots and community organizations (Abom 2004: 349). This further challenges the assumption that social capital can be effectively built through INGO involvement in development. What Abom does argue is that these types of groups can be very effective in service delivery and poverty reduction.

6 Interview, research LNGO representative, Phnom Penh, 11 August 2004; interview, HR and gender LNGO representative, Phnom Penh, 12 August 2004; interview, international donor organization representative, Phnom Penh, 5 November 2003; interview, LNGO representative, Phnom Penh, 17 December 2003b; interview, youth LNGO representative, Phnom Penh, 17 November 2003; interview, micro-credit LNGO representative, Phnom Penh, 20 November 2003.

7 One individual related that when the average pay of a ministry worker is around US$50 per month, which he asserted was well below a living wage, that people sought additional revenues through corruption, secondary employment and payment from patrons (interview, good governance LNGO representative, Phnom Penh, 28 October 2003).

8 Current data on aid disbursements, from both states and NGOs, can be found at the CDC website: www.cdc-crdb.gov.kh/ (accessed 26 December 2011).

9 Unfortunately the donor agendas are often set overseas and speak more to the interests of the donor and the community in which it is embedded than the particular needs of the target society. The NGOs in Cambodia expressed some concern over this dynamic, arguing that the donors were not well placed to recognize local needs. In turn, and ironically, some donors lamented that NGOs would chase donor funding and move away from some issue areas on which they would like to see work carried out.

10 Toepler and Salomon (2003) undertook an empirical study exploring how NGOs' roles in Eastern Europe have grown while state capacity to deliver social services has declined.

11 Loevinsohn and Harding (2005: 680) published research results that claim that '[t]he current weight of evidence suggests that contracting with non-governmental entities will provide better results than government provision of the same services'.

12 Interview, Kristina Mitchell, Health and Nutrition Office, Canadian Cooperation Office, Phnom Penh, 30 September 2003.

13 On numerous occasions I dealt with Cambodians who had received professional education in the Soviet bloc. They had risen to senior position in NGOs

and government. This demonstrates that there was not a complete absence of any professional cadre within the state prior to the arrival of the United Nations in 1991.

14 Interview, INGO representative (Cambodian), Phnom Penh, 2 December 2003.
15 Interview, international LNGO representative, Phnom Penh, 8 November 2003.
16 This data comes from the Council for the Development of Cambodia (CDC) 'First Cambodia Development Cooperation Forum' report.
17 Interview, His Excellency Ek Sam Ol, Deputy Chairman of the Legislative Committee, Phnom Penh, 1 September 2004; interview, NGO umbrella group representative, Phnom Penh, 2 December 2003; interview, gender LNGO representative, Phnom Penh, 15 November 2003; interview, good governance LNGO representative, Phnom Penh, 28 October 2003.
18 Interview, gender LNGO representative, Phnom Penh, 15 November 2003.
19 Interview, Pierre Lacerte, Canadian Cooperation Office, Food Secuity Fund, Phnom Penh, 22 September 2003.
20 In discussing Canadian funding of LNGOs in Cambodia, Pierre Lacerte of the Canadian Cooperation Office stated that groups working in the health sector would change their mandates to follow the funding streams. This has resulted in a large number of groups working on HIV/AIDS, while making it difficult for the Canadian government to find partners who are willing to work on malarial prevention, maternal health and nutrition projects (interview, Pierre Lacerte, Canadian Cooperation Office, Phnom Penh, 22 September 2003).
21 This is obviously a generalization and there were a few instances when it did not hold, such as with the groups that represented the KKK.
22 Interview, good governance LNGO representative, Phnom Penh, 28 October 2003.
23 According to a report on the state of NGOs in Cambodia, '[t]he Cambodian government has become increasingly aware of the positive role and reputation of NGOs. Cambodian NGOs represent an effective, reliable and functioning form of support for micro public sector in Cambodia (Khus 2000: 33).
24 Interview, INGO Cambodian representative, Phnom Penh, 3 October 2003.
25 Puplampu and Tettey (2000: 257) relate how Kenya and Uganda both set up offices to coordinate NGO activity.
26 'Cambodia sets measures to control foreign NGOs', *Kyodo News International*, 6 December 1999. When I conducted interviews with NGOs there were no groups that expressed concern with this measure.
27 Interview, gender LNGO representative, Phnom Penh, 15 November 2003.
28 Serey and Gretchen Peters, 'NGO fears unfounded, Interior says', *Cambodia Daily*, 8(19), 9 July 1996: 1, 6.
29 Joe Cochrane, 'Hun Sen pledges to shelve NGO bill', *South China Morning Post*, 16 July 1999. Pin Sisovann, 'Sar Kheng pledges better NGO cooperation', *Cambodian Daily*, 2 April 2001: 14.
30 For an unofficial translation of the 2000 version of the draft law to deal with Associations and NGOs refer to Annex No. 2 in Khus (2000).
31 Interview, Bunleng Men, Phnom Penh, 28 October 2003.
32 While most of the NGO representatives that discussed the proposed NGO law believed that it was slowly moving forward, at least one individual argued that Hun Sen does not want or see a need for such legislation (interview, Cambodian youth LNGO representative, Phnom Penh, 8 December 2003).
33 Interview, His Excellency Ek Sam Ol, Deputy Chairman of the Legislative Committee, Phnom Penh, 1 September 2004.
34 Some INGO representatives have expressed some concern that the law may

result in a decline in civil society, and force many groups that currently lack stable funding to close their doors (interview, international donor organization representative, Phnom Penh, 5 November 2003).

35 Interview, gender LNGO representative, Phnom Penh, 15 November 2003. Soeung Veasna, 'Cambodia shouldn't limit work of NGOs', *Cambodia Daily*, 7 October 1998: 13.

36 Craig Guthrie (14 November 2008), 'The end of an NGO era in Cambodia', *Asia Times Online*, www.atimes.com/atimes/Southeast_Asia/JK14Ae02.html (accessed 15 November 2011).

37 ARHC, www.ahrchk.net/ua/mainfile.php/2006/1788/; LICADHO (Cambodian HR NGO), Briefing Paper, September 2006, www.licadho.org/reports.php?perm=88.

38 Interview, international LNGO worker, Phnom Penh, 8 November 2003.

39 Interview, Chris Turner, Canada Fund Manager, Canadian Cooperation Office, Phnom Penh, 1 October 2003.

40 For an overview of the role of NGOs in the medical sector in developing countries refer to the work of Green and Matthias (1995).

41 This is not to say that Cambodia enjoys a modern health care system; medical care continues to be an enduring concern in the state. Anyone with the available funds is recommended to head to Bangkok for medical treatment for any but the simplest of medical services. Thai hospitals along the border with Cambodia have seen an increase of Khmer peoples crossing the border to seek medical attention because their local clinics lacked funding and/or staff ('Thai–Cambodian relations – Khmer cross border for health care', *Bangkok Post*, 8 May 2001).

42 Interview, INGO representative (individual has worked with several groups in Cambodia), Phnom Penh, 20 November 2003.

43 Interview, LNGO representative, Phnom Penh, 19 August 2004.

44 Interview, health INGO representative, Phnom Penh, 8 October 2003. An article in the *Cambodia Daily* argued that the MoH has not been effective in accessing the national health budget, spending only 6.9 per cent of the funds in the first six months of the 2003 fiscal year. 'This very low budget access has resulted in making it impossible for health facilities at all levels to deliver appropriate health services to the people' (*Cambodia Daily*, 26(5), 21 July 2003: 15).

45 The Disability Action Committee (DAC) asked the Ministry of Interior for permission to work in 12 provinces. The government has never asked them to change their work.

46 This process has been noted by the *Business News Review*: 'The government health service in the Memot has been put under the management of the Australian Save the Children's Fund.... the Asian Development Bank has provided US$1.9 million for operating the service for four years. This is the first district health to be handed over for private management to ease the burden on the government's limited resources' (*Business News Review* (Cambodia), Chamber World Network, 10 May 1999).

47 Pierre Lacerte, working with the Canadian Cooperation Office, stated that the Ministry of Health would reject groups that don't work through the Ministry. Groups that apply that do not have linkages with the Ministry will be told by the fund coordinator to seek out these connections. He said that this makes life more difficult for NGOs and they often do not like this interference (interview, Pierre Lacerte, Food Security Fund, Canadian Cooperation Office, 22 September 2003).

48 www.medicam-cambodia.org/aboutus.asp.

49 Ibid.

50 Proposals must be approved by the Project Appraisal Committee (PAC), which is chaired by the Cambodia Ministry of Health, and has MEDiCAM and CIDA representation (Government of Canada, Health and Nutrition Initiatives Fund, Cambodia, *Annual Report 2002*. Phnom Penh 2002: 6).
51 Interview, Chris Turner, Canada Fund Manager, Canadian Cooperation Office, Phnom Penh, 1 October 2003.
52 Interview, Pierre Lacerte, Food Securities Fund, Canadian Cooperation Office, Phnom Penh, 22 September 2003.
53 Groups such as World Education, ICC and Care International all stated that they maintained a close working relationship with the MoEYS.
54 Interview, education INGO representative, Phnom Penh, 10 August 2004.
55 Note that this does not indicate what constitutes education spending. The data for 2002 are further complicated by the fact the CDC began reporting funding for 'human resources development' rather than education, and as such likely contain more than just core education disbursements.
56 Interview, education INGO representative, Phnom Penh, 10 August 2004.
57 For a link to the NEP, refer to: www.nepcambodia.org (accessed 27 December 2011).
58 Interview, education INGO representative, Phnom Penh, 10 August 2004.
59 Interview, Sieng Sorvathana, Director of Early Childhood and Education Department and Permanent Secretary of MoEYS Gender Secretariat, Phnom Penh, 13 August 2004.
60 Interview, Tim Sangvat, Provincial Director of Ratanakiri, Education Ministry Office, Banlung, 25 August 2004.

7 Intervention on identity issues

1 The actress has denied making the statements: 'Cambodia crisis – credibility ruined, says analyst' in *Bangkok Post*, 31 January 2003.
2 The category of 'youth' is a flexible one that relies on local cultural context. Rather than putting in a specific age range, 'youth' is defined here as that age range that is seen as being able to act independently of their parents, and of having the potential of being politically engaged, without yet being seen by society as having become an adult. A general rule of thumb places the age groups that are commonly found in senior levels of primary education through a post-secondary education as being within the category of 'youth'.
3 This is recognized in Cambodia's education programmes which aim at socializing the Khmer youth. The role of education in this regard has been discussed at length in the literature on nationalism. While there are considerable points of contention amongst the range of authors on nationalism, they all agree on the role of public education in fostering and perpetuating nationalist ideals. This is true of Nairn 1977; A. D. Smith 1981; Gellner 1983; B. Anderson 1991; and Hobsbawm 1990.
4 This continued after UNTAC as the KR would reach out directly to students to pursue their political agendas, such as inciting anti-Vietnamese hatred (FIBS-EAS-94–176, from Radio of the Provisional Government of National Union and National Salvation of Cambodia, 10 September 1994).
5 For example, on one end of the spectrum is the Students Movement for Democracy, considered supportive of the Sam Rainsy Party, and FUNICINPEC, and on the other is the Pagoda Boys Association which is argued to be an arm of the CPP.
6 Interview, capacity-building INGO worker, Phnom Penh, 13 October 2003.
7 Interview, youth LNGO deputy director, Phnom Penh, 7 December 2003.
8 This is not to say that all of the groups that are established by youth are motivated

by a genuine desire to help the broader community. However, I was never presented with any evidence that the propensity for selfish motivations was any more prevalent amongst youth-led organizations than those established and led by adults. Furthermore, this ignores that it is entirely possible to have both personal motivations and still hold altruistic goals at the same time.

9 Interview, capacity-building INGO representative, Phnom Penh, 13 October 2003.

10 The march itself consisted of nearly 500 volunteers, almost exclusively Cambodians. There were perhaps six or seven Westerners present. The march was organized into 12 groups, each led by a chief volunteer. The march itself has a strange atmosphere, the volunteers, mostly young university students and members of different youth groups, such as Youth for Peace, looked decidedly uncomfortable marching publicly. Attempts to get the march to conduct organized chants were unproductive and quickly died out. Some of the organizers continued doggedly yelling into megaphones and managed to elicit shouts in return. Throughout the march I was struck by the reactions the march received from onlookers. People everywhere stopped and paid rapt attention to the proceedings, crowding windows and the pavement to see what was occurring. However, I never once saw any attempt by the viewers to interact with the marchers. A few waved back when waved at by marchers, but this did not feel like any show of support for the march's cause or the people themselves.

11 Within such arrangements relationships between the youth are mediated by adults.

12 Interview, youth LNGO representative, Phnom Penh, 4 September 2004; interview, youth LNGO deputy director, Phnom Penh, 7 December 2003; interview, youth LNGO representative, Phnom Penh, 8 December 2003; interview, youth LNGO representative, Phnom Penh, 19 November 2003; interview, good goveranance LNGO representative, Phnom Penh, 28 October 2003.

13 There are no available statistics indicating the amount of money political parties provide to youth organizations. However, representatives of youth organizations, who all claimed to be seeking a degree of independence from the party system, said the available funding was substantial and provided groups the ability to run programmes, sustain regular social events and to ensure that the NGOs' youth leadership would be under the influence of party elites.

14 When asked about the Pagoda Boys, people were adamant that they did not constitute an NGO, period. One individual stated that the Pagoda boys, as with many student NGOs, gather information for parties and then work to quash dissent. Furthermore, the extent of their resources was also flagged as an indication of their close relationship with political parties (such as the CPP support of the Pagoda Boys). The Prime Minister may give indirect funding to these groups by providing funds to pagodas.

15 Interview, good governance LNGO representative, Phnom Penh, 28 October 2003.

16 There has been a significant explosion of private 'universities' in Cambodia, with new schools emerging every year. These are predominately business enterprises and offer programmes, such as MBAs to young Cambodians eager to find lucrative jobs. However, these programmes are generally of questionable quality and are preparing a great number of students for a limited number of jobs.

17 The Director of the University is a CPP member, and the Prime Minister appoints all the Department Heads. As a consequence it was reported that only CPP connected student groups are allowed to operate on the state university campuses (interview, education INGO representative, Phnom Penh, 6 November 2003).

18 The UN Security Council resolution 1325 (31 October 2000) called for the incorporation of considerations of gender in to peace operations. This reflects recognition of the ways in which conflict impacts on the lives of men and women differently. Refer to: UNDP, *Gender Approaches in Conflict and Post-Conflict Situation*, 2001. www.undp.org/gender/docs/gendermanualfinalBCPR.pdf; and CIDA, *Gender Equality and Peace building: An Operational Framework*, Ottawa, 2001. www.acdicida.gc.ca/cida_ind.nsf/d86cbc87319a898c8525677e0072d6f8/38e406811791e81485256990004f1c1e?OpenDocument#51.

19 Juan Gasparini, 'Cambodia: UN troop presence linked to growing prostitution trade', in *Inter Press Service Global Information Network*, 8 November 2003.

20 The report on prostitution from Human Rights Task Force on Cambodia was reported in: Johanna Son, 'Cambodian Women: Prostitution worsens following peace', in *Inter Press Service*, 28 March 1997.

21 For a comprehensive report on gender issues in Cambodia refer to: UNIFEM, WB, ADB, UNDP and DfID/UK, *A Fair Share for Women: Cambodia Gender Assessment*, Phnom Penh (2004): UNIFEM, WB, ADB, UNDP, DfID/UK, ISBN:1-932827-00-5.

22 In January 2003, the draft Bill was approved by the Council of Ministers and sent to the National Assembly. Chheng Chan, 'Cambodia – call for gender issue coordination – new Minister sets guideline', in *Business News Review*, 14 December 1998. Michelle Vachon, 'NGO input on domestic violence sought', *Cambodia Daily*, 26 April 2001: 9.

23 Yukiko Ochi, 'Cambodian women face long road ahead, but changes seen', in *Japan Economic Newswire*, 27 February 1999.

24 'Cambodian PM calls for society change toward gender equality', *Xinhua News Agency*, 7 March 2005.

25 Interview, international donor representative (Cambodian), Phnom Penh, 17 November 2003; interview, gender LNGO representative, Phnom Penh, 20 November 2003.

26 'Cambodian women facing rising tide of violence and impunity: NGOs', in *Agence France-Presse*, 4 October 1999.

27 Mu Sochua, Cambodian Minister for Women's and Veteran's Affairs, quoted in Yukiko Ochi, 'Cambodian women face long road ahead, but changes seen', in *Japan Economic Newswire*, 27 February 1999.

28 The US government has commended the Cambodian government for the efforts it has taken to attack human trafficking, as reported in the State Department's 2006 Trafficking in Persons Report (Puy Kea, 'U.S. praises Cambodia for improvement in anti-human trafficking', in *Kyodo News*, 6 June 2006).

29 The classification of the sex trade in Cambodia encompasses a range of activities where women are expected to provide some form of sexual service as a part of their employment. This ranges from the primary sex trade of prostitution, through to the secondary sex trade that encompasses 'beer-girls' and textile workers. When discussing trafficked women, the literature is referring to women forced into prostitution.

30 One study argues that 80 per cent of the women in the Cambodian sex trade who have been trafficked are from Vietnam. Porter Barron, 'Sex-worker poll lowers nationwide estimates', *Cambodia Daily*, 3 November 2003: 1–2.

31 This has been particularly evident around child prostitution, with government initiatives going back to 1993. The government's position on the trafficking of children has generally been positive, they have shown a willingness to arrest foreigners who engage in paedophilia, and have worked with the NGO community to free children, including Vietnamese. For example, 'Four Vietnamese girls aged from nine to 13 were rescued from a brothel just north of Phnom Penh … in a police raid coordinated with an anti-child sex group' (*Agence*

France-Presse, 'Child prostitutes rescued from capital's largest red-light district', 20 August 1996). Refer also to: Bronwyn Sloan, 'Cambodia – madness in their method: The government is cracking down on foreign pedophiles', in *Far Eastern Economic Review*, 25 March 2004. However, when dealing with Vietnamese adults, the government's policies reflect the broader anti-Vietnamese sentiment. The charging of women with 'illegal immigration' reflects a view that the women were not trafficked, but are rather engaging in prostitution out of their desire, reinforces racial stereotypes of the Vietnamese women of being overly sexualized ('Cambodian police arrest 14 women trafficked into brothels', *Agence France-Presse*, 8 July 2002).

32 Interview, INGO representative, Phnom Penh, 3 October 2003.

33 Gender mainstreaming has been reduced at the policy level to equate to women's rights and empowerment.

34 For example, issues of gender factor into a multitude of NGO projects, and UN-led gender mainstreaming has led to movements to incorporate women into NGO projects as recipients and participants. The observation of a lack of coordinated NGO efforts around women's issues was also raised during an interview with one international donor representative who identified this as a shortcoming in Cambodia's civil society (interview, international donor organization representative, Phnom Penh, 5 November 2003).

35 Ibid.

36 This is in part a function of how donors construct their programmes. Addressing women and/or gender issues is seen as an important part of most successful NGO applications for funding.

37 This is not meant to imply that NGOs should avoid using volunteer staff. The point is that groups have to be more reflective about the implications of relying heavily on women in such positions.

38 Hughes sees the *dhammayietra* as defending a space for civil society participation, even while it undercuts Western norms of politics. '[T]he faith placed by mystics in the utility of individual conscience as a check upon power, and the lack of attention to more public measures of accountability. The reliance upon conscience as a check upon abuse of power is a distinctly non-liberal strategy. Yet equally, the march annually reaffirms a right of non-governmental collective action, supported by the power of the Buddhist narrative in rural Cambodia' (Hughes 2001: 57). For a further discussion of the *dhammayietra*, refer to the work of Poethig (2002).

39 Interview, research LNGO representative, Phnom Penh, 9 October 2003.

40 The LNGO representative asserted that the state, meaning in this case the CPP, rehabilitated religion not for religious purposes but because it would serve political goals. He then argued that Wats served political agendas (interview, research LNGO representative, Phnom Penh, 9 October 2003).

41 Interview, Sieng Sorvathana, MoEYS Gender Secretariat, Phnom Penh, 13 August 2004.

42 The UNRISD report from September 1993 that highlighted this issue singles out Christian groups as being of particular concern.

43 Interview, Sieng Sorvathana, MoEYS Gender Secretariat, Phnom Penh, 13 August 2004.

44 Interview, health INGO representative, Phnom Penh, 8 October 2003.

45 He did add that the size of these institutions matters; many of the mosques and churches were very small, many with fewer than 20 active participants.

46 This information was provided by an academic researcher engaged with the Cham community, and by an NGO working with the Islamic community.

47 The US government is paying particular attention to the Muslim community in Cambodia, funding a range of projects to instil 'democratic' principles and a

respect for the rule of law amongst its population. Additionally, the American embassy in Phnom Penh has become a fortress. This reflects the fear of a potential terrorist attack within the country against the American government. The Cambodian government found Hambali guilty in absentia of plotting a bomb attack in Phnom Penh (BBC News, 'Cambodian court convicts Hambali', 29 December 2004).

48 'Cambodia deports 11 Thais for alleged involvement with terror network', in *BBC Monitoring Asia Pacific*, 31 May 2003.

49 The project's aim was to target the Islamic community for eye surgery (interview, health INGO representative, Phnom Penh, 5 November 2003).

50 Interview, health INGO representative, Phnom Penh, 8 October 2003; interview, development INGO representatives, Sen Monorom, 13 November 2003.

51 Interview, development INGO representatives, Sen Monorom, 13 November 2003.

52 Interview, capacity-building INGO representative, Phnom Penh, 13 October 2003.

53 Interview, HR and good governance LNGO representative, Phnom Penh, 19 September 2003.

54 Ibid.

55 Seth Mydans, 'Vietnamese in Cambodia unnerved by upheaval', in *New York Times*, 3 August 1997: 4.

56 In one example Prince Norodom Ranariddh was attacked by the Provisional Government of National Union and National Salvation of Cambodia, a media voice for the KR, for selling Cambodian land to four million Vietnamese in Cambodia. This was a gross exaggeration of the numbers of Vietnamese in the country (FBIS-EAS-94–179, 10 September 1994).

57 There is not a single organization listed in the CCC directories of international or local NGOs that indicates a focus on Vietnamese within either their title or project descriptions.

58 For the state's estimates refer to: Pen Dareth, 'National policy for indigenous peoples in Cambodia', in ICC, *Report of Proceedings of Bilingual Education Seminar*, ICC: Phnom Penh, December 2002: 7. Seth Mydans, 'Vietnamese in Cambodia unnerved by upheaval', in *New York Times*, 3 August 1997: 4.

59 Groups have not been identified to avoid problems that may arise from such programmes.

60 Interview, international LNGO representative, Phnom Penh, 8 November 2003.

61 Interview, human rights and good governance LNGO representative, Phnom Penh, 19 November 2003.

62 Interview, HR and gender LNGO representative, Phnom Penh, 12 August 2004. This also ignores the fact that women working in brothels are often instructed by their pimps on what to say to government and NGO representatives.

63 Interview, Say Va, Deputy Director of Khmer Literature and Culture Association (ICLCA), Phnom Penh, 7 December 2003.

64 Interview, INGO representative, Phnom Penh, 3 October 2003; interview, good governance LNGO representative, Phnom Penh, 28 October 2003; interview, youth LNGO representative, Phnom Penh, 19 November 2003; interview, NGO umbrella group representative, Phnom Penh, 2 December 2003.

65 Interview, His Excellency Chea Sophorn, Secretary of State for the Council of Ministers, Phnom Penh, 4 December 2003.

66 Interview, LNGO representative, Phnom Penh, 13 November 2003.

67 This was laid out explicitly by a female researcher who had conducted numerous interviews within the mosques. She said that the current international environment, with the war on terror, made it highly unlikely that a white male Westerner would be able to get an interview with any religious leaders.

68 It is also unclear to what extent the US Government is driving this fear. Certainly they have provided substantial funds to border monitoring and passport control. They have supported the introduction of modern computer tracking at the main airports in Phnom Penh and Siem Reap.
69 Until early 2001, the single dirt road in to the province Mondulkiri was impassable during the monsoon season.
70 In July 2002, the English/Khmer language newspaper, *Cambodia Daily*, published a story reporting that Vietnamese policemen were engaged in clearing land inside the Cambodian border and forcing Cambodian farmers off adjacent land. The story cited how a local provincial deputy governor, Moung Poy, had complained to the central government of the activities: Thet Sambath, 'Officials: VN police violating Ratanakiri', *Cambodia Daily*, 5 July 2002: 13.
71 The plight of the Montagnard refugees, a term that has been used to refer to all of the highland peoples, but in this case refers more specifically to the Jarai people, is complicated. The history of the Montagnards involves the role of Christian missionaries amongst some groups, support during the Vietnamese war by American military forces, and a vocal minority of the Montagnard diaspora in the United States that has pushed for an independent state in the highlands. The refugees currently claim systematic abuse by the Vietnamese government, and have been fleeing into Cambodia to seek asylum.
72 Matt Reed and Thet Sambath, 'Rights Group: Montagnards forcibly deported', *Cambodia Daily*, 21 May 2001: 1, 2.
73 Yun Samean and Daniel Ten Kate, 'PM threatens to use army on Montagnards', *Cambodia Daily*, 7 July 2004: 1.
74 Interview, LNGO representative (non-Cambodian), Banlung, 24 August 2004.
75 Phann Ana and Daniel Ten Kate, 'NGOs must get gov't OK to leave Ratanakiri', *Cambodia Daily*, 11 June 2004: 1.
76 Ibid.
77 The two journalists and two HR workers were detained by Cambodian authorities for helping a group of Montagnard refugees (Phann Ana and Daniel Ten Kate, 'Montagnards arrive; 2 journalists detained', in *Cambodia Daily*, 27 July 2004: 1, 13). While it is unclear what level of government ordered the crackdown on journalists, reporters travelling by car were prohibited from visiting several districts in Ratanakiri in early August 2004 (Kevin Doyle and Phann Ana, 'Reporters covering Montagnards restricted', *Cambodia Daily*, 9 August 2004: 1, 17).
78 Daniel Ten Kate and Phann Ana, 'UN is accused of smuggling Montagnards', *Cambodian Daily*, 23 April 2004: 16.
79 Kevin Doyle and Phann Ana, 'UN to seek out Montagnards near border', *Cambodia Daily*, 13 August 2004: 1, 16.
80 Daniel Ten Kate, 'UN envoy: Montagnards deported "recently"', *Cambodia Daily*, 6–7 December 2003: 1.
81 The destruction of the camp in Mondulkiri (the camp in Ratanakiri was not burned down but rather left to locals to dismantle for their own use) should be interpreted as a signal to the potential refugees that there was no longer a safe site for them to go to in Cambodia, and to the international HR community that no more interference in the issue would be allowed. The event itself is documented in: David Kihara, 'Final Montagnards leave UNHCR camps', *Cambodia Daily*, 17 April 2002: 8.
82 The Jesuits were contracted by the government to represent refugee claimants to assist in adjudicating who met the UN criteria for a refugee.
83 Interview, development INGO representative, Phnom Penh, 12 December 2003; interview, HR IO representative, Phnom Penh, 18 December 2003; interview, LNGO representative, Banlung, 24 August 2004.

84 Interview, development INGO representative, Phnom Penh, 12 December 2003.

85 Interview, LNGO representative, Banlung, 24 August 2004.

86 Non-formal education programmes are generally state-approved and entail a curriculum that is outside of the 'formal education system', providing lessons on a wide range of life skills including health, nutrition, hygiene and farming.

87 Many of the highland cultures lack indigenous forms of writing; their languages have oral traditions.

88 The ICC commenced their work informally in 2001, and officially in 2002.

89 The Vietnamese had developed a script for the Phnong language based on the Roman alphabet; the writing system has been adopted by some Phnong communities living in Vietnam.

90 The core non-formal education programmes in Ratanakiri are run by CARE and ICC. CARE works primarily with children's education, while the ICC targets adults.

91 The Governor identifies as being Khmer and is a member of the ruling CPP. His comments were related by a project leader of an INGO (interview, INGO representative, Sen Monorom, 13 November 2003).

92 The scholarly New Social Movements (NSM) literature has illustrated how crucial issues of identity politics are for many civil society movements across the globe (Melucci 1989; Boggs 1986; Mooers and Sears 1992). These movements are seen as being new as they are not about economic rights or about struggles for full rights of citizenship and the ability to make claims against the state accordingly. Additionally, the organization takes place outside of traditional party structures.

93 Behnke has asked similar questions with respect to how Bosnia has been framed and how its identity has been manipulated, noting particularly how 'Islamicization' has been represented as a disease (Behnke 1998). This shows how particular forms of identity are made into security threats to the state and to the dominant representation of the state's identity.

8 The non-politics around the meaning of politics

1 The HRW report for 2002 indicates that there has been progress in some sectors of human rights, while erosion in others. Refer to www.hrw.org/wr2k2/asia3.html. For scholarly reports of human rights in Cambodia refer to: Eng 1998; Downie and Kingsbury 2001; Hughes 2007.

2 Interview, HR and good governance LNGO worker, Phnom Penh, 19 September 2003.

3 UNTAC Human Rights Director, Dennis McNamara told the press that he was disappointed in the government's responses to HR abuses of the Vietnamese (Brian Hansford, 'Upholding human rights after UNTAC', *Bangkok Post*, 17 August 1993).

4 Interview, HR and good governance LNGO representatives, Battambang, 29 November 2003.

5 Both LICADHO and ADHOC maintain websites that publish their most recent reports and provide overviews of their perceptions of the HR situation in Cambodia: www.licadho.org; and www.adhoc-chra.org.

6 By the end of UNTAC's mandate LICADHO had 115 representatives working in HR education in all 21 provinces (Brian Hansford, 'Upholding human rights after UNTAC', *Bangkok Post*, 17 August 1993: 2).

7 From the ADHOC website: www.bigpond.com.kh/users/adhoc/about_adhoc/about_adhoc.htm (accessed 20 June 2007).

8 Interview, HR and good governance LNGO representative, Phnom Penh, 19

September 2003; interview HR and good governance LNGO representative, Phnom Penh, 29 September 2003; interview, international LNGO representative, Phnom Penh, 8 November 2003; interview, HR and health LNGO representative, Phnom Penh, 19 November 2003; interview, youth LNGO representative, Phnom Penh, 19 November 2003; interview, gender LNGO representative, Phnom Penh, 20 November 2003; interview, HR and good governance LNGO representative, Battambang, 28 November 2003; interview, HR and good governance LNGO representatives, Battambang, 29 November 2003; interview, HR LNGO representative, Phnom Penh, 1 December 2003; interview, HR NGO umbrella group, Phnom Penh, 4 December 2003; interview, HR LNGO director, Phnom Penh, 4 December 2003; interview, HR IO representative, Phnom Penh, 19 December 2003; interview, development research LNGO representative, Phnom Penh, 11 August 2004; Twice interviewees indicated that the only resistance they had was local officials refusing to allow their groups to operate.

9 For a detailed report of the issue of legal immunity for the powerful in Cambodia refer to 'Impunity in Cambodia: A report by ADHOC, LICADHO, and Human Rights Watch', published on the UNHCR website: www.unhcr.org/home/RSDCOI/3ae6a8520.html (accessed 20 July 2007).

10 This observation has been made in NGO documents, and was also related to me in numerous interviews, including: interview, HR and good governance LNGO representative, Battambang, 28 November 2003; interview HR LNGO representative, Phnom Penh, 1 December 2003; interview, HR LNGO representative, Phnom Penh, 4 December 2003; interview, HR LNGO representative, 17 December 2003a.

11 LICADHO (2005) 'Threats to human rights defenders in Cambodia', Phnom Penh: LICADHO.

12 Interview, research LNGO representative, Phnom Penh, 11 August 2004.

13 Interview, health LNGO representative, Battambang, 28 November 2003; interview, HR and good governance LNGO representatives, Battambang, 29 November 2003; interview, HR LNGO representative, Phnom Penh, 1 December 2003; interview, HR LNGO representative, Phnom Penh, 4 December 2003.

14 Roberts argues that the killing of opposition members by the CPP is best explained by focusing on the grassroots level, rather than looking at the leadership of Prime Minister Hun Sen. '[C]ompetition, and the numerous political killings of Opposition party agents and activists, is not something carefully orchestrated by Prime Ministerial direction. It is far better explained by local resistance to challenges to positions that have long empowered and rewarded numerous loyal members of the CPP at grass roots level.' (Roberts 2003: 255).

15 Interview, election-monitoring LNGO representative, Phnom Penh, 27 October 2003.

16 Interview, youth LNGO representative, Phnom Penh, 19 November 2003.

17 Reported in: Kay Johnson, 'Human Rights Center takes government flak', *Cambodia Daily*, Phnom Penh, 22 September 1998: 1.

18 Interview, HR and good governance LNGO representative, Battambang, 28 November 2003.

19 This is not to say that the dominant political party today, the CPP, does not attack the opposition political parties. Rather that the basis of the criticisms levelled against opposition parties is distinct from those disagreements with NGOs.

20 Interview, HR and good governance LNGO worker, Phnom Penh, 19 September 2003; interview, LNGO director (non-Cambodian), Phnom Penh, 10 August 2004; interview, research LNGO representative, Phnom Penh, 11 August 2004.

21 Interview, good governance LNGO representative, Phnom Penh, 28 October 2003.
22 Interview, research LNGO representative, Phnom Penh, 9 October 2003.
23 The main HR groups are considered by the Government to be pro-opposition, while groups that grew out of communist party groups, such as the Teachers' Association, are generally considered to be pro-CPP.
24 For an overview of the status of Cambodia's media refer to Neumann (2002) (see note 28 below).
25 This data is taken from: www.rsf.org/rubrique.php3?id_rubrique=639.
26 Barton Biggs (12 September 1994) 'More repercussions to newspaper editor killing', *Cambodia Daily*.
27 Lor Chandara (22–23 September 1994) 'Broadcaster decides to impose self-censorship', *Cambodia Daily*, Phnom Penh.
28 A. Lin Neumann (22 June 2002) 'Cambodia's newspapers emerge from a repressive era', *Nieman Reports*, 56(2).
29 'Ranarridh issues warning to unruly press', *Cambodia Daily*, Phnom Penh, 7 September 1994: 6.
30 For example, Mam Sonando, owner of Beehive Radio, was arrested on 11 October 2005 and charged with defamation. This followed an interview where he talked about whether Cambodia had ceded land to Vietnam. This move was decried by Reporters Without Borders ('Media watchdog condemns arrest of Cambodia radio manager', *Agence France-Presse*, 11 November 2005.)
31 CCHR press release (11 July 2006), 'AFEC very concerned about the use of Article 62 of the UNTAC law for silencing journalists who criticize powerful politicians', Phnom Penh. Online at www.cchr-cambodia.org/display.php?action=showarticle&art_id=137&needback=1 (accessed 24 August 2006).
32 Reporters without Borders issued a statement that 'Prime Minister Hun Sen has no right to invoke national security in order to imprison journalists and NGO activists, and it is increasingly clear that the authorities are ready to sacrifice press freedom in order to hold on to power and avoid all criticism' ('EU calls for release of jailed Cambodian activists', *Agence France-Presse*, 11 November 2005). The threat to the press has been further noted by Downie and Kingsbury (2001).
33 For example, Sam Rainsy's move to sue the English language daily, *Cambodian Daily*, for slander: Mea Nop (1 November 1994) 'Sam Rainsy to sue newspaper for defamation', FBIS-EAS-94–211.
34 However, I was told by a number of groups that the government has not taken action against pro-CPP outlets.
35 'Cambodia – First NGO radio set to take off – Focus on women, youth', *Business News Review*, 8 February 1999. This point was also made during an interview with an LNGO working on media issues: interview, gender and media LNGO representative, Phnom Penh, 18 November 2003.
36 Interview, press LNGO representative, Phnom Penh, 18 November 2003.
37 Interview, Petra Peterson, Forum Syd, Phnom Penh, 5 November 2003.
38 Interview, INGO representative, Phnom Penh, 30 September 2003.
39 Interview, His Excellency Ek Sam Ol, Deputy Chairman of the Legislative Committee, Phnom Penh, 1 September 2004.
40 The second note of caution is that there are groups that are definitely wings of political parties. A number of NGOs focusing on cultural issues are supportive of FUNCIPEC, and others, like Women For Prosperity (WFP) are strong CPP supporters (interview, capacity-building INGO representative, 13 October 2003). Pouligny (2005) has discussed how individuals in the post-conflict states often move freely between the political and civil society sectors.
41 In the case of one women's rights NGO, the group stated they were approached

by the Sam Rainsy Party who wanted to fund them (the group declined this offer wishing to remain neutral) (interview, women's rights NGO, Phnom Penh, 18 August 2004). In a second case a youth group stated they were approached by FUNCINPEC (interview, youth LNGO representative, Phnom Penh, 7 December 2003).

42 Interview, health INGO representative, Phnom Penh, 8 October 2003.

43 Interview, youth LNGO representative, Phnom Penh, 7 December 2003.

44 Although HR and democracy NGOs try to avoid the impression that they side with political parties, sometimes opposition politicians join at rallies or manifestations organized by election observer coalitions to offer support. However, this does not constitute a relationship. Similarly no relationship exists with labour unions for fear of being drawn into a political struggle (Vijghen 2001: 48).

45 Interview, LNGO director (non-Cambodian), Phnom Penh, 10 August 2004

9 Conclusions

1 Lehning (1998) follows Putnam (1993) in arguing that democracy cannot be built from the top down.

Bibliography

ADB (2000) *Cambodia: Enhancing Governance for Sustainable Development*, Manila: Asian Development Bank.

ADB (June 2002) *Peoples: Ethnic Minorities and Poverty Reduction*, Manila: Asian Development Bank.

ADB (2005) 'Grant assistance to the Kingdom of Cambodia for improving the access of poor floating communities on the Tonle Sap to social infrastructure and livelihood activities', JFPR: CAM 38602.

AHRC (16 June 2006) 'Cambodia: Government set to curb rights and activities of NGOs' (UA-192-2006): Asia Human Rights Commission. Online at www.humanrights.asia/news/urgent-appeals/UA-192-2006.

Abiew, F. K. and Keating, T. (1999a) 'NGOs and UN peacekeeping operations: Strange bedfellows', *International Peacekeeping*, 6(2): 89–111.

Abiew, F. K. and Keating, T. (1999b) 'Outside agents and the politics of peacebuilding and reconciliation', *International Journal*, 55(1): 80–106.

Abom, B. (2004) 'Social capital, NGOs, and development: A Guatemalan case study', *Development in Practice*, 14(3): 342–353.

Acharya, A. (1994) 'Cambodia, the United Nations and the problems of peace', *Pacific Review*, 7(3): 297–308.

Acharya, A., Frolic, B. and Stubbs, R. (2001) *Democracy, Human Rights, and Civil Society in South East Asia*, Toronto: Joint Centre for Asia Pacific Studies.

Acharya, A., Lizée, P. and Peou, S. (eds) (1991) *Cambodia – The 1989 Paris Peace Conference: Background Analysis and Documents*, Toronto: Centre for International and Strategic Studies.

Ackermann, A. (2003) 'The idea and practice of conflict prevention', *Journal of Peace Research*, 40(3): 339–347.

Aggestam, K. (2003) 'Conflict prevention: Old wine in new bottles?', *International Peacekeeping*, 10(1): 12–23.

Akashi, H., Yamada, T., Huot, E., Kanal, K. and Sugimoto, T. (2004), 'User fees at a public hospital in Cambodia: Effects on hospital performance and provider attitudes', *Social Science and Medicine*, 58(3): 553–564.

Akashi, Y. (1994) 'The challenge of peacekeeping in Cambodia', *International* Peacekeeping, 1(2): 204–215.

Alagappa, M. (1994) *Democratic Transition in Asia: The Role of the International Community*, Honolulu: East–West Centre.

Alagappa, M. (2004) *Civil Society and Political Change in Asia: Expanding and Contracting Democratic Space*, Stanford, CA: Stanford University Press.

Alvares, C. A. (1992) *Science, Development and Violence: the Revolt Against Modernity*, Oxford: Oxford University Press.

Anderson, B. (1991) *Imagined Communities: Reflections on the Origin and Spread of Nationalism*, London: Verso.

Anderson, M. (1999) *Do No Harm: How Aid Can Support Peace – or War*, London: Lynne Rienner.

Annan, K. A. (1999) 'Preventing war and disaster: A growing global challenge', 1999 Annual Report on the Works of the Organization (A/54/1), New York: United Nations.

Antonio, R. J. (1981) 'Immanent critique as the core of critical theory: Its origins and developments in Hegel, Marx and contemporary thought', *British Journal of Sociology*, 32(3): 330–345.

Arendt, H. (1970) *On Violence*, London: Allen Lane.

Arendt, H. (1973) *The Origins of Totalitarianism*, 5th edn, New York: Harcourt Brace Jovanovich.

Ashley, R. (1986) 'The poverty of neorealism', in R. Keohane (ed.) *Neorealism and its Critics*, New York: Columbia University Press.

Atack, I. (1999) 'Four criteria of development NGO legitimacy', *World Development*, 27(5): 855–864.

Ball, N. and Halevy, T. (1996) *Making Peace Work: The Role of the International Development Community*, Washington, DC: Overseas Development Council.

Barber, M. and Bowie, C. (2008) 'How international NGOs could do less harm and more good', *Development in Practice*, 18(6): 748–754.

Barnes, C. (2006) *Agents for Change: Civil society roles in preventing war and building peace*, Den Haag: European Centre for Conflict Prevention.

Bebbington, A. (1997) 'New states, new NGOs? Crises and transitions among rural development NGOs in the Andean region', *World Development*, 25(11): 1755–1765.

Bebbington. A., Carrasco, H., Peralbo, L., Ramon, G., Trujillo, J. and Torres, V. (1993) 'Fragile lands, fragile organizations: Indian organizations and the politics of sustainability in Ecuador', *Transactions of the Institute of British Geographers*, 18: 179–196.

Behnke, Andreas (1998), 'The enemy inside. The Western involvement with Bosnia and the problem of securing identities', *Alternatives*, 23(3): 375–395.

Bell, C. and O'Rourke, C. (2007) 'The people's peace? Peace agreements, civil society, and participatory democracy', *International Political Science Review*, 28(3): 293–324.

Bellamy, A. (2004) 'The "next stage" in peace operations theory?', *International Peacekeeping*, 11(1): 17–38.

Bellamy, A. J., Williams, P. and Griffin, S. (2005) 'Understanding peacekeeping', *International Peacekeeping*, 12(4): 633–638.

Bertram, E. (1995) 'Reinventing governments: The promise and perils of United Nations peace building', *Journal of Conflict Resolution*, 39(3): 387–418.

Bevir, M. and Rhodes, R. (2003) *Interpreting British Governance*, London: Routledge.

Bevir, M. and Rhodes, R. (2006) 'Defending interpretation', *European Political Science*, 5(1): 69–83.

Biekart, K. (1998) *The Politics of Civil Society Building: European Private Aid Agencies and Democratic Transitions in Central America*, Utrecht: International Books/Transnational Institute.

Bit, S. (1991) *The Warrior Heritage: A Psychological Perspective of Cambodian Trauma*, California: El Cerrito.

Boggs, C. (1986) *Social Movements and Political Power*, Philadelphia: Temple University Press.

Bottomley, R. (2002) 'Contested forests: An analysis of the Highlander response to logging, Ratanakiri Province, Northeast Cambodia', *Critical Asian Studies*, 34(4): 587–606.

Bottomley, R. (2003) 'Balancing risk: Village de-mining in Cambodia', *Third World Quarterly*, 24(5): 823–838.

Boua, C. (1993) 'Development aid and democracy in Cambodia', in B. Kiernan (ed.) *Genocide and Democracy in Cambodia: The Khmer Rouge, the United Nations and the International Community*, New Haven, CT: Yale University Southeast Asian Studies.

Boulding, E. (2000) 'A new chance for human peaceableness?', Peace and Conflict: Journal of Peace Psychology, 6(3): 193–215.

Boutros-Ghali, B. (17 June 1992) *An Agenda for Peace: Preventative Diplomacy, Peacemaking and Peace-keeping*. New York: Department of Public Information, United Nations.

Boutros-Ghali, B. and UN (1995) *The United Nations and Cambodia, 1991–1995*, New York: United Nations, Department of Public Information.

Boyce, J. K. (2002) 'Aid conditionality as a tool for peacebuilding: Opportunities and constraints', *Development and Change*, 33(5): 1025–1048.

Bratton, M. (2003) 'Briefing: Islam, democracy and public opinion in Africa', *African Affairs*, 102: 493–501.

Brigg, M. (2002) 'Post-development, Foucault and the colonisation metaphor', *Third World Quarterly*, 23(3): 421–436.

Brannan, T. (2003). 'From antipolitics to anti-politics: What became of east European civil society', Working Paper, 41, London: London School of Economics and Political Science.

Brown, F. Z. and Timberman, D. G. (1998) *Cambodia and the International Community: The Quest For Peace, Development, and Democracy*, Singapore: Institute of Southeast Asian Studies.

Brown, K. (2006) 'War economies and post-conflict peacebuilding: Identifying a weak link', *Journal of Peacebuilding and Development*, 3(1): 6–19.

Brown, M. and Zasloff, J. J. (1998) *Cambodia Confounds the Peacemakers, 1979–1998*, Ithaca, NY: Cornell University Press.

Browne, C. (2008) 'The end of immanent critique?', *European Journal of Social Theory*, 11(1): 5–24.

Buckland, J. (1998) 'Social capital and sustainability of NGO intermediated development projects in Bangladesh', *Community Development Journal*, 33(3): 236–248.

Buiter, W. (2005) 'Country ownership: A term whose time has gone', in S. Koeberle, H. Bedoya, P Silarsky and G. Verheyen (eds) *Conditionality Revisited: Concepts, Experiences, and Lessons*, Washington, DC: World Bank.

Burton, J. and Dukes, F. (eds) (1990) *Conflict: Practices in Management and Resolution*. London: Macmillan.

Butler, M. (2009) *International Conflict Management*, London: Routledge.

CCC (2011) *Directory of Cambodian NGOs: 2010–2011*, Phnom Penh: Cooperation Committee for Cambodia.

CDRI (2008) *Annual Development Review 2007–2008*, Phnom Penh: CDRI.

CICP (1995) *Cambodia in ASEAN*, Phnom Penh: Cambodian Institute for Cooperation and Peace.

Call, C. and Barnett, M. (1999) 'Looking for a few good cops: Peacekeeping, peacebuilding and CIVPOL', *International Peacekeeping*, 6(4): 43–68.

Call, C. T. and Cook, S. E. (2003a) 'Introduction: postconflict peacebuilding and democratization', *Global Governance*, 9(2): 135–139.

Call, C. T. and Cook, S. E. (2003b) 'On democratization and peacebuilding', *Global Governance*, 9(2): 233–246.

Campbell, D. (1998a) *National Deconstruction: Violence, Identity, and Justice in Bosnia*, Minneapolis, MN: University of Minneapolis Press.

Campbell, D. (1998b) *Writing Security: United States Foreign Policy and the Politics of Identity*, rev. edn, Manchester: Manchester University Press.

Candio, P. and Bleiker, R. (2001) 'Peacebuilding in East Timor', *Pacific Review*, 14(1): 63–84.

Caplan, R. (2005) *International Governance of War-Torn Territories: Rule and Reconstruction*, New York: Oxford University Press.

Carment, D. and Schnabel, A. (eds) (2003) *Conflict Prevention: Path to Peace or Grand Illusion?*, New York: United Nations University Press.

Carroll, T. (1992) *Intermediary NGOs: The Supporting Link in Grassroots Development*, West Hartford, CT: Kumerian Press.

Carothers, T. (1999–2000) 'Civil society: think again', *Foreign Policy* (winter): 18–29.

Castells, M. (1997) *The Power of Identity*, Oxford: Blackwell.

Chanboreth, E. and Hach, S. (2008) 'Aid effectiveness in Cambodia', Wolfensohn Center for Development Working Paper, 7.

Chandler, D. (1999) 'The limits of peacebuilding: International regulation and civil society development in Bosnia', *International Peacekeeping*, 6(1): 109–125.

Chandler, D. P. (1983) *A History of Cambodia*, Boulder, CO: Westview Press.

Chandler, D. P. (1991) *The Land and People of Cambodia*, New York: Harper Collins.

Chandler, D. P. (1992a) *Brother Number One: A Political Biography of Pol Pot*, Oxford: Westview Press.

Chandler, D. P. (1992b) *The Tragedy of Cambodian History: Politics, War, and Revolution since 1945*, New Haven, CT: Yale University Press.

Chandler, D. P. (1993) 'Democratisation in Cambodia – here today and gone tomorrow?', *Asian Studies Review*, 17(1): 28–32.

Chandler, D. P. (1996) *Facing the Cambodian Past: Selected Essays, 1971–1994*, Chiang Mai: Silkworm Books.

Chandler, D. P. (1999) *Voices from S-21: Terror and History in Pol Pot's Secret Prison*, Berkeley, CA: University of California Press.

Chandler, D. P. (2000) *A History of Cambodia*, 3rd edn, Boulder, CO: Westview Press.

Chazan, N. (1992) 'Africa's democratic challenge', *World Policy Journal*, 9(2): 279–307.

Chetty, L. (1993) 'The Cambodian peace process: Problems and prospects', *Asian Thought and Society*, 18(52): 30–43.

Chong, D. P. L. (2002) 'UNTAC in Cambodia: A new model for humanitarian aid in failed states?', *Development and Change*, 33(5): 957–978.

Clapham, C. (1998) 'Rwanda: The perils of peacemaking', *Journal of Peace Research*, 35(2): 193–210.

Clarke, G. (1998a) *The Politics of NGOs in Southeast Asia: Participation and Protest in the Philippines*, London: Routledge.
Clarke, G. (1998b) 'Non-governmental organizations (NGOs) and politics in the developing world', *Political Studies*, (46): 36–52.
Clarke, G. (2001) 'From ethnocide to ethnodevelopment? Ethnic minorities and indigenous peoples in Southeast Asia', *Third World Quarterly*, 22(3).
Cohen, J. L. and Arato, A. (1995) *Civil Society and Political Theory*, 3rd edn, Cambridge, MA: MIT Press.
Collacott, M. (1996) 'Review: [untitled]', *Pacific Affairs*, 69(3): 447–449.
Cousens, E. (2001) 'Introduction', in E. Cousens, C. Kumar and K. Wermester (eds) *Peacebuilding as Politics*, London: Lynne Rienner.
Cousens, E. and Kumar, C. (2001) *Peacebuilding as Politics: Cultivating Peace in Fragile Societies*, Boulder: Lynne Rienner.
Cox, R. W. (1981) 'Social forces, states and world orders: Beyond international relations theory', *Millennium: Journal of International Studies*, 10(2): 126–155.
Cox, R. W. (1986) 'Social forces, states and world orders: Beyond international relations theory', in R. O. Keohane (ed.) *NeoRealism and Its Critics*, New York: Columbia University Press.
Cox, R. W. (1997) 'An alternative approach to multilateralism for the twenty-first century', *Global Governance*, 3(1): 103–116.
Curtis, G. (1994) 'Transition to what? Cambodia, UNTAC and the peace process', in P. Utting (ed.) *Between Hope and Insecurity: The Social Consequences of the Cambodian Peace Process*, Geneva: UNRISD.
Curtis, G. (1998) *Cambodia Reborn?: The Transition to Democracy and Development*, Washington, DC: Brookings Institution Press.
Cutter, A. (2005) 'Peace building: A literature review', *Development in Practice*, 15(6): 778–784.
Dahl, R. A. (1961) *Who Governs? Democracy and Power in an American City*, Yale: Yale University Press.
David, C. P. (1999) 'Does peacebuilding build peace? Liberal (mis)steps in the peace process', *Security Dialogue*, 30(1): 25–41.
Deac, W. (1997) *Road to the Killing Fields: the Cambodian War of 1970–1975*, College Station: Texas A&M University Press.
de Larrinaga, M. and Sjolander, C. T. (1998) '(Re)presenting landmines from protector to enemy: The discursive framing of a new multilateralism', in M. Cameron, R. Lawson and B. Tomlin (eds) *To Walk Without Fear: The Global Movement to Ban Landmines*, Toronto, ON: Oxford University Press.
Diamond, L. (1994) 'Rethinking civil society: Towards democratic consolidation', *Journal of Democracy*, 4(1): 3–15.
Dick, H. (2006) 'What to do with "I don't know": Elicitation in ethnographic and survey interviews', *Qualitative Sociology*, 29(1): 87–102.
Dicklich, S. (1998) *The Elusive Promise of NGOs in Africa: Lessons from Uganda*, Basingstoke: Macmillan.
Donini, A., Niland, N. and Wermester, K. (2004) *Nation-Building Unraveled?: Aid, Peace and Justice in Afghanistan*, Bloomfield, CT: Kumarian.
Doty, R. L. (1993) 'The bounds of "race" in international relations', *Millennium: Journal of International Studies*, 22(3): 443–461.
Doty, R. L. (1996) *Imperial Encounters: The Politics of Representation in North–South Relations*, Minneapolis, MN: University of Minnesota Press.

Downie, S. (2000) 'Cambodia's 1998 election: Understanding why it was not a "miracle on the Mekong"', *Australian Journal of International Affairs*, 54(1): 43–62.

Downie, S. and Kingsbury, D. (2001) 'Political development and the re-emergence of civil society in Cambodia', *Contemporary Southeast Asia*, 23(1): 43–64.

Doyle, M. W. (1995) *UN Peacekeeping in Cambodia: UNTAC's Civil Mandate*, London: Lynne Rienner.

Doyle, M. W. and Sambanis, N. (2006) *Making War and Building Peace: United Nations Peace Operations*, Princeton, NJ: Princeton University Press.

Doyle, M. W. and Suntharalingam, N. (1994) 'The UN in Cambodia: Lessons for complex peacekeeping', *International Peacekeeping*, 1(2): 117–147.

Duffield, M. (2005) 'Social reconstruction: The reuniting of aid and politics', *Development*, 48(1): 16–24.

Duffield, M. (2009) 'Liberal interventionism and fragile states: Linked by design?', in M. Duffield and V. Hewitt (eds) *Empire, Development and Colonialism: The Past in the Present*, Oxford: James Currey, pp. 116–129.

Duffield, M. R. (1997) 'NGO relief in war zones: Towards an analysis of the new aid paradigm', *Third World Quarterly*, 18(3): 564–571.

Duffield, M. R. (2001) *Global Governance and the New Wars: The Merging of Development and Security*, London: Zed.

Duffield, M. R. (2002) 'Social reconstruction and the radicalization of development: aid as a relation of global liberal governance', *Development and Change*, 33(5): 1049–1071.

Duffield, M. R. (2007) *Development, Security and Unending War: Governing the World of Peoples*, Cambridge, UK: Polity Press.

Dunne, T. (1997) 'Colonial encounters in international relations: Reading Wight, writing Australia', *Australian Journal of International Affairs*, 51(3): 309–323.

Edwards, M. (1993) '"Does the doormat influence the boot?": Critical thoughts on UK NGOs and international advocacy', *Development in Practice*, 3(3): 163–175.

Edwards, M. and Hulme, D. (1996) 'Too close for comfort: NGOs, the state and donors', *World Development*, 24(6): 961–973.

Edwards, M., Hulme, D. and Save the Children Fund (1992) *Making a Difference: NGOs and Development in a Changing World*, London: Earthscan.

Edwards, M., Hulme, D. and Save the Children Fund (1995) *Non-Governmental Organisations: Performance and Accountability Beyond the Magic Bullet*, London: Earthscan.

Eng, P. (1998) 'Cambodian democracy: In a bleak landscape, strong signs of hope', *Washington Quarterly*, 21(3): 71–91.

Escobar A. (1992) 'Reflections on development: Grassroots approaches and alternative politics in the third world', *Futures*, (June): 411–435.

Esteva, G. (1992) 'Development', in W. Sachs (ed.) *The Development Dictionary: A Guide to Knowledge as Power*, London: Zed.

Farrington, J. and Bebbington, A. (1993) *Reluctant Partners? Non-Governmental Organisations, the State, and Sustainable Agricultural Development*. London: Routledge.

Farris, K. (1994) 'UN peacekeeping in Cambodia: On balance, a success', *Parameters*, 24(1): 38–50.

Feldman, S. (1997) 'NGOs and civil society: (Un)stated contradictions', *Annals*, AAPSS, 554: 46–67.

Ferguson, J. (1994) *The Anti-politics Machine: 'Development', depoliticization and bureaucratic power in Lesotho*, Cambridge: Cambridge University Press.

Fetherston, A. (2000) 'Peacekeeping, conflict resolution and peacebuilding: A reconsideration of theoretical frameworks', *International Peacekeeping*, 7(1): 190–218.

Finlayson, A. (2007) 'From beliefs to arguments: Interpretive methodology and rhetorical analysis', *British Journal of Politics and International Relations*, 9(4): 545–563.

Fischer, M. (ed.) (2006) *Peacebuilding and Civil Society in Bosnia-Herzegovina – Ten Years after Dayton*, Münster and London: Lit-Verlag.

Fisher, J. (1998) *Non-Governments: NGOs and the Political Development of the Third World*, West Hartford, CT: Kumarian Press.

Flyvbjerg, B. (1998) 'Habermas and Foucault: Thinkers for civil society?', *British Journal of Sociology*, 49(2): 210–233.

Fowler, A. (1996) 'Strengthening civil society in transition economies – from concept to strategy: Mapping an exit in a maze of mirrors', in A. Clayton (ed.) *NGOs, Civil Society and the State: Building Democracy in Transitional Societies*, Oxford: INTERAC.

Fowler, A. (1997) *Non-Governmental Organisations Performance and Accountability: Beyond the Magic Bullet*, London: Earthscan.

Fowler, A. (2000a) *NGOs, Civil Society and Social Development: Changing the rules of the game*, Geneva: UNRISD.

Fowler, A. (2000b) 'NGO futures: Beyond aid: NGDO values and the fourth position', *Third World Quarterly*, 21(4): 589–603.

Frangonikolopoulos, C. (2005) 'Non-governmental organisations and humanitarian action: The need for a viable change of praxis and ethos', *Global Society*, 19(1): 49–72.

Frantz, T. R. (1987) 'The role of NGOs in the strengthening of civil society', *World Development*, 15(1): 121–127.

Galtung, J. (1969) 'Violence, peace, and peace research', *Journal of Peace Research*, 6(3): 167–192.

Galtung, J. (1996) *Peace by Peaceful Means: Peace and Conflict, Development and Civilization*, London: Sage.

Garrison, J. (2000) *From Confrontation to Collaboration: Civil Society–Government–World Bank Relations in Brazil*, Washington, DC: World Bank.

Gellner, E. (1983) *Nations and Nationalism*, Oxford: Blackwell.

Global Witness (2002, July) *Deforestation Without Limits: How the Cambodian Government Failed to Tackle the Untouchables*, London: Global Witness Ltd.

Goodhand, J. (2002) 'Aiding violence or building peace? The role of international aid in Afghanistan', *Third World Quarterly*, 23(5): 837–859.

Goodhand, J. and Hulme, D. (1999) 'From wars to complex political emergencies: Understanding conflict and peace-building in the new world disorder', *Third World Quarterly*, 20(1): 13–26.

Goodhand, J. and Lewer, N. (1999) 'Sri Lanka: NGOs and peace-building in complex political emergencies', *Third World Quarterly*, 20(1): 68–87.

Gordenker, L. and Weiss, T. G. (1995b) 'NGO participation in the international policy process', *Third World Quarterly*, 16(3): 543–555.

Gottesman, E. R. (2002) 'Cambodia after the Khmer Rouge: Inside the Politics of Nation Building', New Haven, CT: Yale University Press.

Green, A. and Matthias, A. (1995) 'Where do NGOs fit in? Developing a policy framework for the health sector', *Development in Practice*, 5(4): 313–323.

Green, M. (2000) 'Participatory development and the appropriation of agency in southern Tanzania', *Critique of Anthropology*, 20(1): 67–89.

Griffin, M. (1999) 'Retrenchment, reform and regionalization: Trends in UN peace support operations', *International Peacekeeping*, 6(1): 1–31.

HRW (23 December 2011) 'Cambodia: Revise or abandon draft NGO law', *Human Rights Watch*, www.hrw.org/news/2011/12/23/cambodia-revise-or-abandon-draft-ngo-law. Accessed 27 December 2011.

Hall, J. (ed.) '(1995) *Civil Society: Theory, History, Comparison*, Cambridge: Polity Press.

Hall, R. (2001) 'Applying the self/other nexus in international relations', *International Studies Review*, 3(1): 101–111.

Harris, G. (1999) 'Peacebuilding and reconstruction after war in developing countries', *Journal of Interdisciplinary Economics*, 10(2): 107–122.

Harris, I. C. (2005) *Cambodian Buddhism: history and practice*, Honolulu: University of Hawaii Press.

Harvey, D. (2003) *The New Imperialism*, Oxford: Oxford University Press.

Hay, C. (2002) *Political Analysis: A Critical Introduction*. Houndmills: Palgrave.

Heathershaw, J. (2008) 'Unpacking the liberal peace: The dividing and merging of peacebuilding discourse', *Millennium: Journal of International Relations*, 35(3): 597–621.

Heder, S. (1979) 'Kampuchea's armed struggle: The origins of an independent revolution', *Bulletin of Concerned Asian Scholars*, 11(1): 2–23.

Heder, S. and Ledgerwood, J. (1996) *Propaganda, Politics, and Violence in Cambodia: Democratic Transition Under United Nations Peace-keeping*, London: M.E. Sharpe.

Heder, S. R. (2004) *Cambodian Communism and the Vietnamese Model: Imitation and Independence, 1930–1975*, Bangkok: White Lotus Press.

Hedman, E. (2001) 'Contesting state and civil society: Southeast Asian trajectories', *Modern Asian Studies*, 35(4): 921–951.

Heine, C. and Teschke, B. (1996) 'Sleeping Beauty and the dialectical awakening: On the potential of dialectic for international relations', *Millennium: Journal of International Studies*, 25(2): 399–424.

Hekman, S. (2000) 'Beyond identity: Feminism, identity and identity politics', in *Feminist Theory*, 1(3): 289–308.

Held, D. (1980) *Introduction to Critical Theory: Horkheimer to Habermas*, Cambridge: Polity Press.

Heurlin, C. (2010) 'Governing civil society: The political logic of NGO–state relations under dictatorship', *Voluntas*, 21: 220–239.

Higham, C. (2001) *The Civilization of Angkor*, Berkeley: University of California Press.

Hobsbawm, E. J. (1990). *Nations and Nationalism since 1780: Programme, Myth, Reality*, Cambridge, UK: Cambridge University Press.

Hojman, D. (1993) 'Non-governmental organisations (NGOs) and the Chilean transition to democracy', *European Review of Latin American and Caribbean Studies*, 54(1): 7–24.

Hoogensen, G. and Rottem, S. (2004) 'Gender identity and the subject of security', *Security Dialogue*, 35(2): 155–172.

Hubbard, C. (2002) *Seeing the Community for the Trees: Assessing Locally-Developed Sustainability Indicators for the Angkor Community Forest Project*, Vancouver: Simon Fraser University, School of Resource and Environmental Management.

Hughes, C. (2001) 'Mystics and militants: Democratic reform in Cambodia', *International Politics*, 38(1): 47–64.

Hughes, C. (2002a) 'Parties, protest and pluralism in Cambodia', *Democratization*, 9(3): 165–186.

Hughes, C. (2002b) *The Political Economy of Cambodia's Transition, 1991–2001*, Richmond, VA: Curzon.

Hughes, C. (2002c) 'International intervention and the people's will: The demoralization of democracy in Cambodia', *Critical Asian Studies*, 34(4): 539–562.

Hughes, C. (2003) *The Political Economy of the Cambodian Transition*, Richmond, VA: Curzon.

Hughes, C. (2007) 'Transnational networks, international organizations and political participation in *Cambodia: Human rights, labour rights and common rights'*, *Democratization*, 14(5): 834–852.

Hughes, C. and Öjendal, J. (2006) 'Reassessing tradition in times of political change: Post-war Cambodia reconsidered', *Journal of Southeast Asian Studies*, 37(3): 415–420.

Hulme, D. (2008) 'Reflections on NGOs and development: The elephant, the dinosaur, several tigers but no owl', in A. Bebbington, S. Hickey and D. Mitlin (eds) *Can NGOs Make a Difference?*: The challenge of development alternatives, London: Zed Books.

Hulme, D. and Edwards, M. (1997) *NGOs, States and Donors: Too Close for Comfort?*, Basingstoke: Macmillan in Association with Save the Children.

Hun Sen (29 June 2004) Cambodia New Vision, Issue 6. Online at www.cnv.org.kh/cnv_html_pdf/cnv_77_june_04.pdf.

Hyden, G. (1997) 'Civil society, social capital, and development: Dissection of a complex discourse', *Studies in Comparative International Development*, 32(1): 3–30.

ICC (December 2002) *Report of Proceedings of Bilingual Education Seminar – Ratanakiri Province*, Phnom Penh: International Cooperation Cambodia.

International Crisis Group (10 September 1998), 'Cambodia's elections turn sour', *Asia Report*, no. 3.

Jaeger, H. (2007) '"Global civil society" and the political depoliticization of global governance', *International Political Sociology*, 1(3): 257–277.

Jenkins, R. (2002) 'Mistaking "governance" for "politics": Foreign aid, democracy and the construction of civil society', in S. Kaviraj and S. Khilnani (eds) *Civil Society: History and Possibilities*. Delhi: Foundation Books.

Jennar, R. M. (1994) 'UNTAC: "International triumph" in Cambodia?', *Security Dialogue*, 25(2): 145–156.

Jeong, H. W. (2005) *Peacebuilding in PostConflict Societies: Strategy and Process*, Boulder, CO: Lynne Reinner.

Johnson, C. and Forsyth, T. (2002) 'In the eyes of the state: Negotiating a "rights-based approach" to forest conservation in Thailand', *World Development*, 30(9): 1591–1605.

Jørgensen, L. (1996) 'Strengthening civil society', in A. Clayton (ed.) *NGOs, Civil Society and the State: Building Democracy in Transistional Societies*, Oxford: INTERAC.

Junne, G. and Verkoren, W. (eds) (2004) *Postconflict Development: Meeting New Challenges*, London: Lynne Rienner.

Kaldor, M. (1999) *New and Old Wars: Organized Violence in a Global Era*, Cambridge: Polity Press.

Kaldor, M. (2000) 'The implications of the "battle in Seattle"', *Millennium: Journal of International Studies*, 29(1): 105–114.

Kamm, H. (1998) *Cambodia: Report from a Stricken Land*, New York: Arcade Publishing.

Kao, K. H. and CICP (1999a) *Cambodia and Southeast Asia*. Phnom Penh: Cambodian Institute for Cooperation and Peace.

Kao, K. H. and CICP (1999b) *Cambodia's Prospective Membership in ASEAN: Opportunities, Challenges and Prospects*, Phnom Penh: Cambodian Institute for Cooperation and Peace.

Kao, K. H., Samraing, K. and CICP (1999c) *Grassroots Democracy in Cambodia: Opportunities, Challenges and Prospects*, Phnom Penh: Cambodian Institute for Cooperation and Peace.

Kao, K. H., Kaplan, J. A. and CICP (1998a) *Cambodia's Future in ASEAN: Dynamo or Dynamite?*, Phnom Penh: Cambodian Institute for Cooperation and Peace.

Kao, K. H., von Hofmann, N. and CICP (1998b) *National Elections: Cambodia's Experiences and Expectations*, Phnom Penh: Cambodian Institute for Cooperation and Peace.

Kamaratos, A. (1995) 'Building peace, democracy and human rights: International civilian missions at the end of the millennium', *International Peacekeeping*, 2(4): 483–509.

Keating, T. F. and Knight, W. A. (2004) *Building Sustainable Peace*, Edmonton, AB: University of Alberta Press.

Khus, T. (2000) *Country study: Non-governmental organizations in Cambodia*. Phnom Penh: SILAKA.

Kiernan, B. (1985) *How Pol Pot Came to Power*, London: Verso.

Kiernan, B. (1990) 'The genocide in Cambodia, 1975–79', *Bulletin of Concerned Asian Scholars*, 22(2): 35–40.

Kiernan, B. (1996) *The Pol Pot Regime: Race, Power, and Genocide in Cambodia under the Khmer Rouge, 1975–79*, New Haven, CT: Yale University Press.

Kiernan, B., Shui, Y., Roberts, D., Hughes, C., Billon, P. L. and Bottomley, R. (2002) 'Conflict and change in Cambodia', *Critical Asian Studies*, 34(4): 483–606.

Kilby, P. (2005) 'The voice of marginalised women in controlling small scale development projects: Some lessons from India', International Conference on Engaging Communities, United Nations and Queensland Government. Online at http://www.engagingcommunities2005.org/abstracts/Kilby-Patrick-final.pdf: 1.

Kilcullen, D. (2009) 'The accidental guerrilla: Fighting small wars in the midst of a big one', in D. Kilcullen (ed.) *Critical War Studies*, London: Hurst.

Kilcullen, D. (2010) *Counterinsurgency*, London: Hurst.

Knapman, G. (2006) 'Liberal dreams: Materialism and evolutionary civil society in the projection of nation in Southeast Asia', *Asian Ethnicity*, 7(1): 19–36.

Knight, W. A. (2003) 'Evaluating recent trends in peacebuilding research', *International Relations of the Asia Pacific*, 3(2): 241–264.

Kothari, S. (1996) 'Rising from the margins: The awakening of civil society in the Third World', *Development*, (3): 11–19.

Krause, K. (1998) 'Critical theory and security studies: the research programme of "Critical Security Studies"', *Cooperation and Conflict*, 33(3): 298–333.

Krause, K. and Jütersonke, O. (2005) 'Peace, security and development in post-conflict environments', *Security Dialogue*, 36(4): 447–462.

Kymlicka, W. (1989) *Liberalism, Community and Culture*, Oxford: Clarendon Press.

Laclau, E. (1990) *New Reflections on the Revolution of our Time*, London: Verso.

Laclau, E. (2006) 'Ideology and post-Marxism', *Journal of Political Ideologies*, 11(2): 103–114.

Laclau, E. and Mouffe, C. (1985) *Hegemony and Socialist Strategy: Towards a Radical Democratic Politics*, London: Verso.

Lambrou, Y. (1997) 'The changing role of NGOs in rural Chile after democracy', *Bulletin of Latin American Research* 16: 107–116.

Last, D. (2003) 'From peacekeeping to peacebuilding', *OJPCR: The Online Journal of Peace and Conflict Resolution*, 5(1): 1–8.

Le Billon, P. (2002) 'Logging in muddy waters: The politics of forest exploitation in Cambodia', *Critical Asian Studies*, 34(4): 563–586.

Lederach, J. (1997) *Building Peace: Sustainable Reconciliation in Divided Societies*, Washington, DC: United States Institute for Peace.

Lederach, J. (2005) *The Moral Imagination: The Art and Soul of Building Peace*, New York: Oxford University Press.

Ledgerwood, J. and Un, K. (2003) 'Global concepts and local meaning: Human rights and Buddhism in Cambodia', *Journal of Human Rights*, 2(4): 531–549.

Lehning, P. (1998) 'Towards a multicultural civil society: The role of social capital and democratic citizenship', *Government and Opposition*, 32(2): 221–242.

Levinson, J. (2002) 'An examination of the Community Fisheries Sub-Decree in Cambodia: Changes and developments during the drafting process', Bangkok: NACA-STREAM.

LICADHO (June 2006) 'Attacks and threats against human rights defenders in Cambodia', Phnom Penh: LICADHO.

Lipschutz, R. (2005) 'Global civil society and global governmentality. Resistance, reform or resignation?', in G. Baker and D. Chandler (eds) *Global Civil Society: Contested Futures*, London: Routledge.

Lizée, P. (1997) 'Cambodia in 1996: Of tigers, crocodiles, and doves', *Asian Survey*, 37(1): 65–71.

Lizée, P. (2000) 'Civil society and regional security: Tensions and potentials in post-crisis Southeast Asia', *Contemporary Southeast Asia*, 22(3): 551–570.

Lizée, P. (2002) 'Human security in Vietnam, Laos, and Cambodia', *Contemporary Southeast Asia*, 24(3): 509–527.

Loevinsohn, B. and Harding, A. (2005) 'Buying results? Contracting for health service delivery in developing countries', *Lancet*, (366): 676–681.

Lund, M. (2002) 'Preventing violent interstate conflicts: Learning lessons from experience', in van Tongeren, van de Veen and Verhoeven (eds) *Searching for Peace in Europe and Eurasia: An Overview of Conflict Prevention and Peacebuilding Activities*, Boulder, CO: Lynne Rienner, 99–119.

MacLean, S. J. (1998) 'Contributions from civil society to building peace and democracy', in A. L. Griffiths (ed.) *Building Peace and Democracy in Post-Conflict State*, Halifax, NS: Dalhousie University.

Mak, Sithirith (2000) *Vulnerability of Fisheries in Cambodia*, Phnom Penh: NGO Forum.

Makoba, W. (2002) 'Nongovernmental organizations (NGOs) and Third World development: An alternative approach to development', Journal of Third World Studies, 19(1): 53–63.

Mandelbaum, M. (1994) 'The reluctance to intervene', *Foreign Policy*, 95: 3–18.

Mansfield, C., MacLeod, K., Greenleaf, M. and Alexander, P. (2002) *Advocacy*

Handbook: A Practical Guide to Increasing Democracy in Cambodia, Phnom Penh: Pact Cambodia.

Marchetti, R. and Tocci, N. (2009) 'Conflict society: Understanding the role of civil society in conflict', *Global Change, Peace and Security*, 21(2): 201–217.

McCargo, D. (2005) 'Cambodia: Getting away with authoritarianism?', *Journal of Democracy*, 16(4): 98–112.

McCaul, J. (2000) 'Som Thom commune community based natural resource management project: An example of successful mediation between local communities and provincial government', Asia-Pacific Community Forestry Newsletter, 13(2): 21–28.

McSweeney, B. (1998) 'Durkheim and the Copenhagen School: A response to Buzan and Wæver', *Review of International Studies*, 24(1): 137–140.

Melucci, A. (1989) *Nomads of the Present: Social Movements and Individual Needs in Contemporary Society*, Philadelphia, PA: Temple University Press.

Mercer, C. (2002) 'NGOs, civil society and democratization: A critical review of the literature', *Progress in Development Studies*, 2(1): 5–22.

Mertus, J. and Sajjad, T. (2005) 'When civil society promotion fails state-building: The inevitable fault-lines in post-conflict reconstruction', in O. P. Richmond and H. F. Carey (eds) *Subcontracting Peace*, Aldershot: Ashgate.

Ministry of Health, Cambodia (2008) *Health Strategic Plan for Cambodia 2008–2015*, Phnom Penh: Royal Government of Cambodia.

Möller, K. (1998) 'Cambodia and Burma: The ASEAN way ends here', *Asian Survey*, 38(12): 1087–1104.

Moniroth, A. P. (1995) *Democracy in Cambodia: Theories and Realities*, Phnom Penh: Cambodian Institute for Cooperation and Peace.

Mooers, C. and Sears, A. (1992) 'The "new social movements" and the withering away of state theory', in W. Carroll (ed) *Organizing Dissent: Contemporary Social Movements in Theory and Practice*, Toronto: Garamond.

Moser-Puangsuwan, Y. (1995) 'U.N. peacekeeping in Cambodia: Whose needs were met?', *Pacifica Review*, 7(2): 103–127.

Munck, R. (1999) 'Deconstructing development discourses: Of impasses, alternatives and politics' in R. Munck and D. O'Hearn (eds) *Critical Development Theory: Contributions to a New Paradigm*, London: Zed Books.

Mysliwiec, E. (1988) *Punishing the Poor: The International Isolation of Kampuchea*, Oxford: Oxfam.

NGO Economic, Social and Cultural Rights Committee (2002) Cambodia NGO Parallel Report Under International Covenation Economic, Social and Cultural Rights, Phnom Penh: NGO Economic, Social and Cultural Rights Monitoring Committee.

NGO Forum (2000) *Fishing Conflict in Battambang*, Phnom Penh: NGO Forum.

NGO Forum (2011) *Statistical Analysis of Land Disputes in Cambodia, 2010*, Phnom Penh: NGO Forum.

Nairn, T. (1997) *Faces of Nationalism: Janus Revisited*, London: Verso.

National Democratic Institute (1998) Preliminary Statement of the Joint NDI/IRI Delegation to the July 26, 1998 Elections in Cambodia. Online at www.ndi.org/node/12679.

Narayan, D. (1999) *Bonds and Bridges: Social Capital and Poverty*, Washington, DC: World Bank.

Neufeld, M. (1997) 'The "dialectical awakening" in international relations: For and against', *Millennium: Journal of International Studies*, 26(2): 449–454.

Neumann, I. (1999) *Uses of the Other: 'The East' in European Identity Formation*, Manchester: Manchester University Press.
Nonan-Ferrell, C. (2004) 'The state, civil society and revolutions: Building political legitimacy in twentieth century Latin America', *Latin American Research Review*, 39(3): 294–304.
O'Brien, C. (1998). Religion, nationalism and a civil society. Online at www.nhc.rtp.nc.us/publications/civilsoc/obrien.htm (accessed 28 May 2012).
Öjendal, J. (1996) 'Democracy lost? The fate of the U.N.-implanted democracy in Cambodia', *Contemporary Southeast Asia*, 18(2): 193–218.
Öjendal, J. and Antlov, H. (1998) 'Asian values and its political consequences: Is Cambodia the first domino?', *Pacific Review*, 11(4): 525–540.
Öjendal, J. and Sedara, K. (2006) 'Korob, Kaud, Klach: In search of agency in rural Cambodia', *Journal of Southeast Asian Studies*, 37(3): 507–526.
Okin, S. M. (1989) *Justice, Gender and the Family*, Chicago, IL: Basic Books.
Orford, A. (1999) 'Muscular humanitarianism: Reading the narratives of the new interventionism', *European Journal of International Law*, 10(4): 679–711.
Orford, A. (2003) *Reading Humanitarian Intervention: Human rights and the use of force in international law*, Cambridge: Cambridge University Press.
Orjuela, C. (2003) 'Building peace in Sri Lanka: A role for civil society?', *Journal of Peace Research*, 40(2): 195–212.
Owen, J. M. (1994) 'How liberalism produces democratic peace', *International Security*, 19(2): 89–101.
Palmer, T. (2002) 'Classical liberalism and civil society: Definitions, history, and relations', in N. Rosenblum and R. Post (eds) *Civil Society and Government*, Princeton: Princeton University Press.
Paris, R. (1997) 'Peacebuilding and the limits of liberal internationalism', *International Security*, 22(2): 54–89.
Paris, R. (2002) 'International peacebuilding and the "mission civilisatrice"', *Review of International Studies*, 28(4): 637–656.
Paris, R. (2004) *At War's End: Building Peace after Civil Conflict*, Cambridge, UK: Cambridge University Press.
Parks, T. (2008) 'The rise and fall of donor funding for advocacy NGOs: Understanding the impact', *Development in Practice*, 18(2): 213–22.
Pateman, C. (1988) *The Sexual Contract*, Stanford: Stanford University Press.
Patrick, Ian (2001) 'East Timor emerging from conflict: The role of local NGOs and international assistance', *Disasters*, 25(1): 48–66.
Patterson, M. and Monroe, K. (1998) 'Narrative in political science', *Annual Review of Political Science*, 1(1): 315–331.
Pearson, G. and Salter, M. (1999) 'Getting public law back into a critical condition: the rule of law as a source for immanent critique', *Social and Legal Studies*, 8(4): 483–508.
Peou, S. (1998a) 'Cambodia in 1997: Back to square one?', *Asian Survey*, 38(1): 69–74.
Peou, S. (1998b) 'The Cambodian elections of 1998 and beyond: Democracy in the making?', Contemporary Southeast Asia, 20(2): 279–289.
Peou, S. (2000) *Intervention and Change in Cambodia: Towards democracy?*. Singapore: Silkworm Books.
Poethig, K. (2002) 'Movable peace: Engaging the transnational in Cambodia's Dhammayietra', *Journal for the Scientific Study of Religion*, 41(1): 19–28.

Polsby, N. W. (1963) *Community Power and Political Theory*, London: Yale University Press.

Portes, A. (1998) 'Social capital: Its origins and applications in modern sociology', *Annual Review of Sociology*, 24(1): 1–24.

Pouligny, B. A. (2000) 'Promoting democratic institutions in post-conflict societies: Giving diversity a chance', *International Peacekeeping*, 7(3): 17–35.

Pouligny, B. A. (2005) 'Civil society and post-conflict peacebuilding: Ambiguities of international programmes aimed at building "new" societies', *Security Dialogue*, 36(4): 495–510.

Pradhan, U. and Roy, I. (2006) 'Pluralism and civil society partnerships: Perspectives from Nepal and Uttar Pradesh', *Contemporary South Asia*, 15(1): 55–74.

Pugh, M. (2004) 'Peacekeeping and critical theory', *International Peacekeeping*, 11(1): 39–58.

Puplampu, K. (2003) 'State–NGO relations and agricultural sector development', in W. Tettey, K. Puplampu and B. Berman (eds), *Critical Perspectives on Politics and Socio-Economic Development in Ghana*. Leiden: Koninklijke Brill, pp. 135–152.

Puplampu, K. P. and Tettey, W. J. (2000) 'State–NGO relations in an era of globalisation: The implications for agricultural development in Africa', *Review of African Political Economy*, 27(84): 251–272.

Putnam, R. (1993) *Making Democracy Work: Civic Traditions in Modern Italy*. Princeton: Princeton University Press.

Putnam, R. D. (1995) 'Bowling alone: America's declining social capital', *Journal of Democracy*, 6(1): 65–78.

Putnam, R. D. (1995) 'Tuning in, tuning out: The strange disappearance of social capital in America', *PS: Political Science and Politics*, 28(4): 664–683.

Pye, L. (1999) 'Civility, social capital and civil society: Three powerful concepts for explaining Asia', *Journal of Interdisciplinary History*, 29(4): 763–782.

RGC (2000) Draft Discussion Paper, Phnom Penh: Royal Government of Cambodia.

Rahnema, M. (1992) 'Poverty', in W. Sachs (ed.) *The Development Dictionary: A Guide to Knowledge as Power*, London: Zed.

Ramsbotham, O. (2000) 'Reflections on UN post-settlement peacebuilding', *International Peacekeeping*, 7(1): 169–189.

Ramsbotham, O., Woodhouse, T. and Miall, H. (2005) *Contemporary Conflict Resolution*, 2nd edn, Cambridge: Polity.

Rancière, J. (2007) *On the Shores of Politics*, London: Verso.

Rawls, J. (1971) *A Theory of Justice*, Boston, MA: Harvard University.

Rawls, J. (1993) *Political Liberalism*. New York: Columbia University Press.

Razack, S. (2004) *Dark Threats and White Knights: The Somalia Affair, Peacekeeping, and the New Imperialism*. Toronto: University of Toronto Press.

Richmond, O. P. (2004a) 'The globalization of responses to conflict and the peacebuilding consensus', *Cooperation and Conflict*, 39(2): 129–150.

Richmond, O. P. (2004b) 'UN Peacebuilding operations and the dilemma of the peacebuilding consensus', *International Peacekeeping*, 11(1): 83–101.

Richmond, O. P. (2005a) 'The dilemmas of subcontracting the liberal peace', in O. Richmond and H. Carey (eds) *Subcontracting Peace*. Aldershot, UK: Ashgate.

Richmond, O. P. (2005b) *The Transformation of Peace*, New York: Palgrave Macmillan.

Richmond, O. P. (2008) *Peace in International Relations*, London: Routledge.

Richmond, O. P. (2009) 'A post-liberal peace: Eirenism and the everyday', *Review of International Studies*, 35(4): 557–580.

Richmond, O. and Franks, J. (2008) 'Liberal peacebuilding in Timor Leste: "The Emperor's new clothes"?', *International Peacekeeping*, 15(2): 185–200.

Richmond, O. P. and Franks, J. (2007) 'Liberal hubris? Virtual peace in Cambodia', *Security Dialogue*, 38(1): 27–48.

Riddell, R. and Robinson, M. (1995) *Non-Governmental Organizations and Rural Poverty Alleviation*, Oxford, UK: Oxford University Press.

Riddell, R., Kruse, S.-K., Kyllonen, T., Ojanpera, S. and Vielajus, J.-L. (1997) *Searching for Impact and Methods: NGO Evaluation Synthesis Study for OECD/DAC.* Helsinki: Ministry of Foreign Affairs.

Rieff, D. (1999). 'The false dawn of civil society', *The Nation*, 22 February, 11–16.

Roberts, D. (2001) *Political Transition in Cambodia 1991–1999*, Cornwall, UK: Curzon Press.

Roberts, D. (2003) 'From "communism" to "democracy" in Cambodia: A decade of transition and beyond', *Communist and Post-Communist Studies*, 36(2): 245–258.

Robinson, M. (1997) 'Privatising the voluntary sector: NGOs as public service contractors?', in D. Hulme and M. Edwards (eds) NGOs, *States and Donors: Too Close for Comfort?*, London: Macmillan, 59–78.

Robinson, M. and White, G. (1997) *The Role of Civic Organizations in the Provision of Social Services: Towards Synergy*, Helsinki: World Institute for Development Economics Research.

Rodan, G. (1997) 'Civil society and other political possibilities in Southeast Asia', *Journal of Contemporary Asia*, 27(2): 156–178.

Rodan, G. (2001) 'The prospects for civil society and political space', in A. Acharya, B. Frolic and R. Stubbs (eds) *Democracy, Human Rights, and Civil Society in Southeast Asia*, Toronto, ON: Joint Centre for Asia Pacific Studies.

Rose, R., Mishler, W. and Haerpfer, C. (1997) 'Social capital in civic and stressful societies', *Studies in Comparative International Development*, 32(3): 85–111.

Ross, M. H. and Rothman, J. (1999) *Theory and Practice in Ethnic Conflict Management: Theorising Success and Failure*, London: Macmillan.

Roy, I. (31 August 2002) 'Community, organization and representation: Implications for development', *Economic and Political Weekly*, 37(35): 3591–3595.

Roy, I. (2008) 'Civil society and good governance: (Re-) conceptualizing the interface', *World Development*, 36(4): 677–705.

Roy, O. (2005) 'The predicament of "civil society" in Central Asia and the "Greater Middle East"', *International Affairs*, 81(5): 1001–1012.

Rubin, H. J. and Rubin, I. S. (1995) *Qualitative Interviewing: The Art of Hearing Data*, Thousand Oaks, CA: Sage.

Russett, B. M. (1993) *Grasping the Democratic Peace: Principles for a Post-Cold War World*, Princeton, NJ: Princeton University Press.

SIDA (2005) SIDA Country Report 2004, Cambodia. SIDA4726en.

Sandy, L. (2007) 'Just choices: Representations of choice and coercion in sex work in Cambodia', *The Australian Journal of Anthropology*, 18(2): 194–206.

Saravanamuttu, J. (2001) 'Emergent civil societies in ASEAN: Antinomies of discourse and practice', in A. Acharya, B. Frolic and R. Stubbs (eds) *Democracy, Human Rights, and Civil Society in Southeast Asia*, Toronto, ON: Joint Centre for Asia Pacific Studies.

Schwartz-Shea, P. and Yanow, D. (2002) '"Reading" "Methods" "Texts": how research methods texts construct political science', *Political Research Quarterly*, 55(2): 457–486.

Schwarz, R. (2005) 'Post-conflict peacebuilding: The challenges of security, welfare and representation', *Security Dialogue*, 36(4): 429–446.

Seligman, A. B. (1992) *The Idea of Civil Society*, New York: Free Press.

Shapiro, M. J. and Der Derian, J. (1989) *International/Intertextual Relations: Postmodern Readings of World Politic*, Lexington, MA: Lexington Books.

Siaroff, A. (1999) 'Premature democracies, the promotion of development and political–cultural factors', *Third World Quarterly*, 20(2): 405–419.

Silliman, G. and Noble, L. (1998) 'Citizen movements and Philippine democracy', in Silliman, G. and Noble, L. (eds) *Organizing for Democracy: NGOs, civil society and the Philippine state*, Honolulu: University of Hawaii Press.

Slocomb, M. (2002) 'Forestry policy and practices of the People's Republic of Kampuchea, 1979–1989', *Asian Survey*, 42(5): 772–793.

Slocomb, M. (2003) *The People's Republic of Kampuchea, 1979–1989: The Revolution after Pol Pot*, Chiang Mai: Silkworm Books.

Slocomb, M. (2006) 'The nature and role of ideology in the modern Cambodian state', *Journal of Southeast Asian Studies*, 37(3): 375–395.

Smith, A. D. (1981) *The Ethnic Revival*, Cambridge, UK: Cambridge University Press.

Smits, K. (2003) 'Liberalism's identity problem', *Polity*, 35(3): 347–367.

Sodhy, P. (2004) 'Modernization and Cambodia', *Journal of Third World Studies*, 21(1): 153–174.

Somers, M. R. and Gibson, G. D. (1994) 'Reclaiming the epistemological "other": Narrative and the social constitution of identity', in C. Calhoun (ed.) *Social Theory and the Politics of Identity*, Oxford: Blackwell.

St John, R. (1995) 'The political economy of the Royal Government of Cambodia', *Contemporary Southeast Asia*, 17(3): 265–281.

Stamnes, E. (2004) 'Critical security studies and the United Nations preventive deployment in Macedonia', *International Peacekeeping*, 11(1): 161–181.

Stepan, A. (1966) 'Political development theory: The Latin American experience', *Journal of International Affairs*, 20(2): 223–234.

Stiles, K. W. (1998) 'Civil society empowerment and multilateral donors: International institutions and new international norms', *Global Governance*, 4(2): 199–216.

Storey, A. (1997) 'The non-neutral humanitarianism: NGOs and the Rwanda crisis', *Development in Practice*, 7(4): 384–394.

Sweetman, C. (ed) (2004) *Gender, Peacebuilding, and Reconstruction*, Oxford: Oxfam GB.

Talentino, A. (2002) 'Intervention as nation-building: Illusion or possibility?', *Security Dialogue*, 33(1): 27–43.

Talentino, A. (2003) 'Evaluating success and failure: Conflict prevention in Cambodia and Bosnia', in D. Carment and A. Schnabel (eds) *Conflict Prevention: Path to Peace or Grand Illusion?*, New York: United Nations University Press.

Thayer, C. (2009) 'Vietnam and the challenge of political civil society', *Contemporary Southeast Asia*, 31(1): 1–27.

Thayer, N. (1991) 'Cambodia – Misperceptions and peace', *Washington Quarterly*, 14(2): 179–191.

Toepler, S. and Salomon, L. (2003) 'NGO development in central and eastern Europe: an Empirical Overview', *East European Quarterly*, 37(3): 365–378.

Truman, D. (1962) *The Governmental Process*, New York: Alfred A. Knopf.

UN (1995) *The United Nations and Cambodia: 1991–1995*, New York: United Nations.
UNDP (1994, November) *Development Cooperation for Cambodia: 1992/1993 Report.*
UNRISD (1993, September) *Rebuilding Wartorn Societies: Report of the Workshops on the Challenge of Rebuilding Wartorn Societies and the Social Consequences of the Peace Process in Cambodia*, Geneva: UNRISD.
UNTAC (25 February 1993a) NGO Statement for the Donors' *Review Meeting*: 1.
UNTAC (1993b) *The United Nations in Cambodia: A Vote for Peace*, New York: United Nations Transitional Authority in Cambodia.
Ulvila, M. and Hossain, F. (2002) 'Development NGOs and political participation of the poor in Bangladesh and Nepal', *Voluntas*, 13(2): 149–63.
Um, K. (1994) 'Cambodia in 1993: Year Zero plus one', *Asian Survey*, 34(1): 72–81.
Um, K. (1995) 'Cambodia in 1994: The year of transition', *Asian Survey*, 35(1): 76–85.
United Nations Division for Public Administration and Development Management (2004) *Reconstructing Governance and Public Administration for Peaceful, sustainable Development*, New York: UN
United States General Accounting Office (2002, June) *Cambodia: Governance Reform Progressing, but Key Efforts are Lagging*, Washington, DC: USGAO. GAO-02–569, 2002.
Van Rooy, A. (1998) 'Civil society and democratization: Wishful thinking?', in A. L. Griffiths (ed.) *Building Peace and Democracy in Post-Conflict Societies*, Halifax, NS: Centre for Foreign Policy Studies.
Vickery, M. (1984) *Cambodia 1975–1982*, Hemel Hempstead: Allen & Unwin, in association with South End Press.
Vickery, M. (1986) *Kampuchea: Politics, Economics and Society*, London: Pinter.
Vijghen, J. (2001), *Cambodian Human Rights and Democracy Organizations: Understanding NGOs.* Phnom Penh: Experts for Community Research.
WB (1999) *Sub-Saharan Africa: From Crisis to Sustainable Growth.* Washington, DC: World Bank.
WPM (2002) *Community Responses to Threats of Violence: Case Studies from Cambodia*, Phnom Penh: Women Peace Makers.
Wallace, T. (2004) 'NGO dilemmas: Trojan horses for global neo-liberalism?' in L. Panitch and C. Leys (eds) *The New Imperial Challenge*, London: Merlin.
Walker, R. B. J. (1990) 'Security, sovereignty, and the challenge of world politics', *Alternatives*, 15(1): 3–27.
Walker, R. B. J. (1993) *Inside/Outside: International Relations as Political Theory*, Cambridge, UK: Cambridge University Press.
Walker, R. B. J. (1997) 'The subject of security', in K. Krause and M. C. Williams (eds) *Critical Security Studies: Concepts and Cases*, Minneapolis, MN: University of Minnesota Press.
Walzer, M. (1991) 'The idea of civil society', *Dissent*, 293.
Wenman, M. A. (2003) 'What is politics? The approach of radical pluralism', *Politics*, 23(1): 57–65.
Whitworth, S. (2004) *Men, Militarism, and UN Peacekeeping: A gendered analysis*, London: Lynne Rienner.
Wyn Jones, R. (1995) '"Message in a bottle"? Theory and praxis in critical security studies', *Contemporary Security Policy*, 16(3): 299–319.
Young, C. (1994), 'In search of civil society', in J. Harbeson, D. Rothchild, D. and

N. Chazan (eds), *Civil Society and the State in Africa.* London: Lynne Reinner, 33–50.

Zaidi, S. (1999) 'NGO failure and the need to bring back the state', *Journal of International Development,* 11(2): 259–271.

Zalewski, M. and Enloe, C. (1995) 'Questions about identity in international relations', in K. Booth and S. Smith (eds) *International Relations Theory Today,* New York: Polity Press.

Zaum, D. (2009) 'International non-governmental organisations and civil wars', *Civil Wars,* 11(1): 22–38.

Zizek, S. (1997) *The Abyss of Freedom,* Ann Arbor, MI: University of Michigan Press.

Zizek, S. (1999) *The Ticklish Subject: The Absent Centre of Political Ontology,* London: Verso.

UN Documents

Report of the Secretary-General on Cambodia (S/23613 and Add.1) (n.d.)

UN General Assembly (28 October 1982) 'The situation in Kampuchea', UN GA A/RES/37/6, New York: United Nations General Assembly.

UN Secretary General (1993) Report of the Secretary-General on the conduct and results of the elections in Cambodia (S/25913).

UN Secretary General Report, 14 November 1991, S/23218.

UN Secretary-General Report, 21 September 1992, S/24578.

UN Secretary-General Report, 25 January 1993, S/25154.

UN Security Council Resolution (20 September 1990) Resolution 668 (1990) S/RES/668 (1990).

UN Security Council (30 September 1991) 'Report of the Secretary-General on Cambodia', S/23097 and S/23097/Add.1.

UN Security Council (1991) Resolution 717 (1991) Adopted by the Security Council at its 3,014th meeting, on 16 October 1991, S/RES/717.

UN Security Council (4 November 1993) Resolution 880 (1993) (S/RES/880).

UN Resolution 745 (28 February 1992).

Index

Page numbers in *italics* denote tables.

Made in the USA
Las Vegas, NV
01 November 2024

f102dd1a-550f-44cf-81ca-0c694c3066fcR01